FILELFO IN MILAN

FILELFO IN MILAN

*

WRITINGS 1451–1477

Diana Robin

PRINCETON UNIVERSITY PRESS

PRINCETON, NEW JERSEY

PA
8520
'F5
Z85
1991

LIBRARY OF CONGRESS CATALOGING-IN-PUBLICATION DATA

ROBIN, DIANA MAURY.

FILELFO IN MILAN : WRITINGS 1451–1477 / BY DIANA ROBIN.

P.   CM.

INCLUDES BIBLIOGRAPHICAL REFERENCES AND INDEX.

ISBN 0-691-03185-1 (CL)

1. FILELFO, FRANCESCO, 1398–1481. 2. LATIN POETRY, MEDIEVAL AND
MODERN—ITALY—HISTORY AND CRITICISM. 3. AUTHORS, LATIN (MEDIEVAL
AND MODERN)—ITALY—CORRESPONDENCE. 4. MILAN (ITALY)—COURT AND
COURTIERS—CORRESPONDENCE. 5. MILAN (ITALY)—INTELLECTUAL LIFE.
6. HUMANISTS—ITALY—CORRESPONDENCE. 7. RENAISSANCE—ITALY—MILAN.
I. TITLE.

PA8520.F5Z85   1991   001.3′092—DC20   91-6546   CIP

THIS BOOK HAS BEEN COMPOSED IN LINOTRON GALLIARD
PRINCETON UNIVERSITY PRESS BOOKS ARE PRINTED ON ACID-FREE PAPER,
AND MEET THE GUIDELINES FOR PERMANENCE AND DURABILITY OF THE
COMMITTEE ON PRODUCTION GUIDELINES FOR BOOK LONGEVITY OF THE
COUNCIL ON LIBRARY RESOURCES

PRINTED IN THE UNITED STATES OF AMERICA BY PRINCETON UNIVERSITY PRESS,
PRINCETON, NEW JERSEY

3   5   7   9   10   8   6   4   2

For my mother, Helen Kurtz, and
my children, Anne and
Robin Benning

CONTENTS

FIGURES

ACKNOWLEDGMENTS

I WOULD LIKE to express my appreciation and thanks to the friends, colleagues, and institutions whose support enabled me to write this book. Sponsoring four summer research trips to Italy, the Research Allocations Committee of the University of New Mexico provided me with seed money to initiate the project. An Andrew W. Mellon Fellowship for study in the Vatican Film Archive at St. Louis first whetted my interest in the collections of humanist manuscripts I would later study in Rome. My residence as an Exxon Education Foundation Fellow at the Newberry Library in Chicago in 1985 was a turning point for me; there I met the late Eric Cochrane, Paul Gehl, Dale Kent, John Marino, Tom Mayer, Cynthia Truant, Albert Ascoli, and Florence Sandler, from whom I would learn so much. By the time I had written drafts for some of the chapters in this book, I was ready to benefit from the Andrew W. Mellon Post-Doctoral Fellowship I received in 1987 to spend the coming year at the American Academy in Rome. Indeed, without my studies—and unexpected discoveries—in the libraries and archives of Rome, Milan, and Florence, and minus the many conversations and consultations I enjoyed that year in the Vatican Library bar with Martha Baldwin, Concetta Bianca, the late John D'Amico, Katherine Gill, Ken Gouwens, Greg Gouderian, and Ingrid Rowland, this book would have been a much poorer work. I also wish to thank the staffs of the Italian libraries and archives, who were as helpful to me as it is possible to imagine: at the Vatican Library, with special gratitude to the prefect Father Leonard Boyle; at the State Archives in Milan, the Trivulzian and Ambrosian Libraries in that city; and at the Laurentian and Riccardian Libraries, and also the National Library in Florence. At the University of New Mexico my thanks go also to Dorothy Wonsmos and her staff at Interlibrary Loan.

To Dale Kent, without whose guidance and encouragement this book would not have reached fruition, I owe the greatest debt. In addition, I am very much beholden to a few generous friends and colleagues who read parts of the manuscript in its various stages: Margaret King, Paul Gehl, Anthony Grafton, Jack Holtsmark, Roger Hornsby, Ira Jaffe, Craig Kallendorf, Natasha Kolchevska, Patricia Labalme, Tom Mayer, John Monfasani, Betty Rose Nagle, and Tina Nielson. And finally, I would like to thank Joanna Hitchcock and Lauren Oppenheim at Princeton University Press for their elegant transformation of a manuscript as awkward as mine—booby-trapped both with the idiosyncratic orthographies of a number of Renaissance Latin writers and with humanist Greek—into the volume you now see.

ABBREVIATIONS

Adam, *F. Filelfo*	Rudolf Georg Adam, "Francesco Filelfo at the Court of Milan: A Contribution to the Study of Humanism in Northern Italy (1439–1481)" (Ph.D. dissertation, Oxford University, 1974)
ASF	Archivio di Stato, Florence
ASI	*Archivio storico italiano*
ASL	*Archivio storico lombardo*
ASM	Archivio di Stato, Milan
Benadduci, ed., *Atti*	Giovanni Benadduci, ed., *Atti e memorie della R. Deputazione di Storia Patria per le province delle Marche*, vol. 5 (Ancona, 1901)
Calderini, *Ricerche*	Aristide Calderini, "Ricerche intorno alla biblioteca e alla cultura greca di Francesco Filelfo," in *Studi Italiani di Filologia Classica* 20 (1913)
DBI	*Dizionario biografico degli italiani* (Rome, 1960–)
De morali disciplina	Francesco Robertello, ed., *Francisci Philelphi de morali disciplina libri quinque* (Venice, 1552)
Filelfo, *Epistolae*	*Epistolarum familiarium libri XXXVII* (Venice, 1502)
Filelfo nel V Cent.	*Francesco Filelfo nel V Centenario della morte. Atti del XVII convegno di studi macerateni* (Padua, 1986)
Legrand, *Lettres*	Emile Legrand, ed., *Cent-dix lettres grecques de François Philelphe* (Paris, 1892)
RIS[1]	L. A. Muratori, ed., *Rerum italicarum scriptores*, 25 vols. (Milan, 1723–1751)
RIS[2]	L. A. Muratori, ed., *Rerum italicarum scriptores*, 34 vols. (Bologna, 1900–1935)
Rosmini, *Vita*	Carlo de' Rosmini, *Vita di Francesco Filelfo da Tolentino*, 3 vols. (Milan, 1808)
Traversari, *Epistolae*	Ambrogio Traversari, *Aliorumque ad ipsum, et ad alios de eodem Ambrosio latinae epistolae*, ed. L. Mehus, 2 vols. (Florence, 1759)
Trivulzianus	Codex Trivulzianus 873, *Francisci Philelfi epistolarum familiarium libri XLVIII* (Milan, ca. 1481–1488)

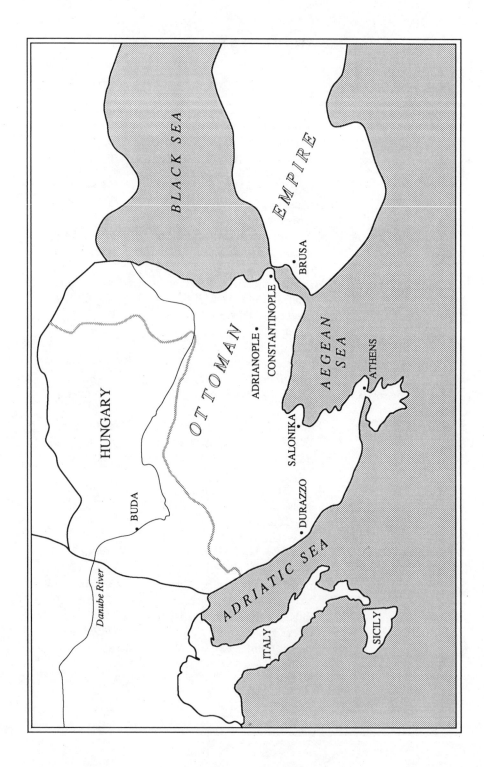

BLACK SEA

EMPIRE

BRUSA

CONSTANTINOPLE

ADRIANOPLE

OTTOMAN

AEGEAN
SEA

HUNGARY

SALONIKA

ATHENS

BUDA

DURAZZO

ADRIATIC SEA

Danube River

ITALY

SICILY

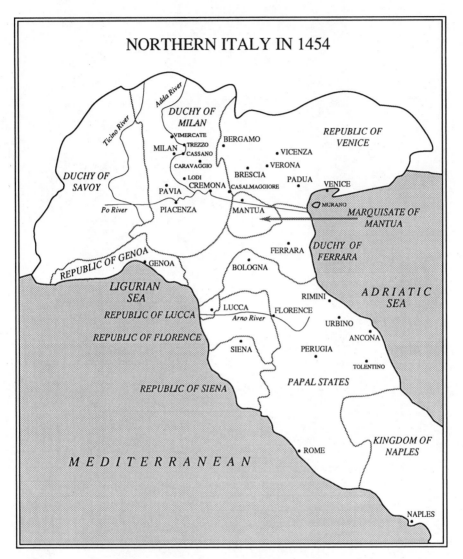

NORTHERN ITALY IN 1454

DUCHY OF MILAN

Adda River

Ticino River

VIMERCATE

MILAN

TREZZO

CASSANO

CARAVAGGIO

BERGAMO

REPUBLIC OF VENICE

VICENZA

VERONA

BRESCIA

LODI

CREMONA

CASALMAGGIORE

PADUA

VENICE

DUCHY OF SAVOY

PAVIA

Po River

PIACENZA

MANTUA

MURANO

MARQUISATE OF MANTUA

FERRARA

DUCHY OF FERRARA

REPUBLIC OF GENOA

GENOA

BOLOGNA

LIGURIAN SEA

ADRIATIC SEA

RIMINI

LUCCA

FLORENCE

REPUBLIC OF LUCCA

Arno River

URBINO

REPUBLIC OF FLORENCE

ANCONA

SIENA

PERUGIA

TOLENTINO

REPUBLIC OF SIENA

PAPAL STATES

KINGDOM OF NAPLES

M E D I T E R R A N E A N

ROME

NAPLES

The Duchy of Milan and the Republic of Venice in the Mid-Fifteenth Century.

FILELFO IN MILAN

INTRODUCTION

FRANCESCO FILELFO came, in an age of aristocratic ideals, from the bottom of the social ladder.[1] He was born in the provincial Italian town of Tolentino in 1398, of parents so unassuming he never thought to speak of them in his autobiographical letters. Yet the flamboyant Filelfo—who took pleasure in advertising himself as the "bard with three testicles"—rose to a position of power and influence almost unheard of in the fifteenth century for a man of his background.[2] As a young man, he had studied abroad for several years, in Constantinople; when he returned to Italy, he moved from one university to another, drawing crowds in Bologna, Florence, and other cities, who thronged to hear him lecture on Greek philosophy and poetry. But at the age of forty, he settled in Milan, where for most of the rest of his long life he occupied the posts of professor at the university of Pavia and poet-in-residence at the courts of the Visconti and Sforza dukes.

Historians have long tended to denigrate the intellectuals who were attached to the great signorial courts in early modern Italy as mere tools—rhetoricians and public-relations men—of the princes whose policies they represented, whose brutality they rationalized, and whose images they softened.[3] Nor has Filelfo escaped such charges. Indeed, scholars, both in the last century and in our own time, have singled him out as an example of the flagrant sycophancy that existed in the Quattrocento courts, perhaps because he was at once so famous and at the same time so notoriously indigent.[4] Filelfo has generally been described as the quintessential Renaissance court writer, whose body and mind were for sale. My purpose is to overturn, through my discussion of Filelfo's writings and their publication in this book—most of them for the first time since the Renaissance—the prevailing assumptions about his work.

[1] Carlo de' Rosmini, *Vita di Francesco Filelfo da Tolentino*, 3 vols. (Milan, 1808) is still the only authoritative, published biography of Filelfo. Rudolf Georg Adam's 1974 Oxford dissertation, "Filelfo at the Court of Milan: A Contribution to the Study of Humanism in Northern Italy (1439–1481)," is not available in print as of this writing.

[2] Filelfo used the Greek word Τριόρχης ("triple-testicled," exceptionally potent sexually) to advertise his unique literary and personal powers; see also his epigram in which he calls himself "vates tribus testibus," published in Rosmini, *Vita*, 1.113.

[3] Lauro Martines' chapter, "Humanism: A Program for the Ruling Classes," pp. 191–214, in his influential study, *Power and Imagination* (New York, 1979), encapsulates the prevailing view of the humanist courtiers.

[4] See Eugenio Garin, "L'età Sforzesca dal 1450 al 1500," in *Storia di Milano* (Milan, 1953–1966), 7.541–97, who among Filelfo's modern detractors has been the most widely quoted and paraphrased.

Filelfo was no lackey. Nor, on the other hand, was he a rebel. Unlike the fourteenth-century radical, Cola da Rienzo, he never advocated the overthrow of a government—he was more likely to assign blame for the political decay he saw in Florence, Rome, and Milan to the human condition than to the failure of this or that regime. It is true enough that in the Renaissance courts intellectuals and artists were retained with the expectation that their works would represent both their prince's magnificence and their own obeisance. But to see the relations between prince and subject, patron and client, solely in the polarities of dominance and submission, lordship and servility, and majesty and abasement is to deal in surfaces and refracted images of a misleading sort. In human relationships, as Michel Foucault has so persuasively suggested, power may meet with submission, but it always engenders resistance. Power, in his paradigm, is everywhere present in the social body. Starting with such a model of society, we should not be surprised to find that hostility and mockery often accompany, or are hidden in, what appears to be an attitude of homage or a gesture of humility in a courtier's salute to his prince.[5] Filelfo's writings neither openly oppose nor uniformly praise the programs, ideas, and attitudes of the powerful men who were his sole means of support. What his works reveal, rather, are strategies and tactics for resistance to the policies and actions of his patrons. Among such tactics are his penchant for couching his observations of his patrons' actions in ironies, for portraying in the most convincing manner the claims and viewpoints of his patrons' enemies, and for inserting into his victory paeans and triumphal commissions lists of attendant miseries. Thus, in his encomiastic and dedicatory writings, often the masks of collaborator and resister are curiously superimposed, the apparition of the one glinting confusingly through the fabric of the other.

In many ways, Filelfo was indeed typical of the humanists of his era—those fifteenth-century intellectuals, that is, whose aim it was to revive the long-banished art and thought of the ancient Greco-Roman world. Like Leon Battista Alberti and Antonio Beccadelli, as a very young man he sat at the feet of the great Gasparino Barzizza at the university of Padua, and later, like them, he moved from city to city, finally settling in a court where a powerful padrone would protect him. What was unusual about Filelfo was his long apprenticeship in Constantinople, in an age when few Italians traveled so far east, and the effect that his Greek studies would have on

[5] On the mechanisms and articulations of power and resistance in the paternalistic relationship, I owe much to the work of E. P. Thompson and Eugene D. Genovese, as well as to that of Michel Foucault. See E. P. Thompson, "Eighteenth-century English Society: Class Struggle without Class?" in *Social History* 3 (1978): 133–66; Eugene D. Genovese, *Roll, Jordan, Roll: The World the Slaves Made* (New York, 1947; reprint 1976); Michel Foucault, *The History of Sexuality*, trans. R. Hurley (New York, 1980), esp. 1.94–96; and idem, *Discipline and Punish*, trans. A. Sheridan (New York, 1979), esp. 135–69 and 231–308.

both his own intellectual development and the generations of scholars who followed him. His poems, personal letters, and dialogues were in fact so widely circulated and imitated in his lifetime that his collected works offer a representative picture of fifteenth-century humanistic culture.

The issue of humanistic patronage provides an important impetus for this study.[6] The five major works of Filelfo's treated in this book address eminent patrons of the arts not in just one city, but in Venice, Milan, Paris, Rome, and Florence. Thus, considered together, Filelfo's works offer an unusual view of patronage in the Renaissance and, moreover, one seen through the eyes of a client. While none of Filelfo's larger works, with the exception of the satires, was undertaken until he was in his fifties, all of them are in a sense autobiographical. We must beware, however, of Filelfo's distortions of himself and his world. Not only was he always sorting through the debris of his experience in search of materials that would fit the complex persona he was molding and burnishing for himself—and we should keep in mind that in his writings there is no one, private, inner self that awaits revelation, there are only layers of personae.[7] But he took care to omit from his autobiographical letters key events in his life that he perceived as dishonorable or disgraceful. Among these were his near arrest and deportation from Florence in 1431, the circumstances that actually attended Filippo Masi Bruno's alleged attempt on his life in 1433, and Francesco Sforza's jailing of him in 1464.

Chapter 1 considers Filelfo's letterbook, the *Epistolae familiares* (1451–1477), a collection of Latin letters many of which were fictitious, addressed to friends and patrons in the manner of Cicero's and Petrarch's Latin *Epistolae*.[8] This chapter focuses on Books 1–3 of Filelfo's *Epistolae* letters as characteristic of the published letterbook as a whole. These letters

[6] On Renaissance patronage I am chiefly indebted (throughout my book) to Dale Kent's recent papers (1988–1990) and to her forthcoming book on charity; see also Francis William Kent and Patricia Simons, eds., *Patronage, Art and Society in Renaissance Italy* (Oxford, 1987), esp. Ronald Weissman, "Taking Patronage Seriously: Mediterranean Values and Renaissance Society," pp. 25–45; on Florentine patronage see also R. Weissman, *Ritual Brotherhood in Renaissance Florence* (New York, 1982); D. Kent, *The Rise of the Medici* (Oxford, 1978); and F. W. Kent, *Household and Lineage in Renaissance Florence: The Family Life of the Rucellai* (Princeton, 1977). On patronage in modern societies and patronage theory see S. N. Eisenstadt and L. Roniger, *Patrons, Clients, and Friends: Interpersonal Relations and the Structure of Trust in Society* (Cambridge, 1984); Ernest Gellner and J. Waterbury, *Patrons and Clients in Mediterranean Societies* (London, 1977); and Sharon Kettering, *Patrons, Brokers, and Clients in Seventeenth-Century France* (Oxford, 1986).

[7] My thinking about Filelfo's writings has been very much influenced by the controversies about the self among the theorists of autobiography: James Olney, *Metaphors of Self: The Meaning of Autobiography* (Princeton, 1972); and Paul John Eakin, *Fictions in Autobiography: Studies in the Art of Self-Invention* (Princeton, 1985); and Paul de Man, "Autobiography as De-facement," in *Modern Language Notes* 94 (1979): 919–30.

[8] On Filelfo's several redactions of the *Epistolae* see Appendix A, Note on the Editions.

deal with the early years of Filelfo's career, beginning with his arrival in Venice in 1427 and continuing through his troubled years as a professor in Bologna, Florence, and Siena. Most of the letters from this early period were either composed or reconstructed after 1451, when he decided to publish his correspondence. Here Filelfo portrays himself as a questing figure, in search of happiness, meaningful work, and security for himself and his family. Time and time again he finds himself in conflict with the most powerful of his patrons, men well known to his contemporaries: the Venetian statesman Leonardo Giustiniani, the self-made lord of Milan Francesco Sforza, the influential Florentine priest and Hellenist Ambrogio Traversari, and Cosimo de' Medici. The climactic moment in the first three books of the *Epistolae* is Filelfo's narrative of the attempt made on his life by a swordsman hired by the Medici, which left a prominent scar on the right side of his face. More significantly, however, the assault left him with a psychological scar that would shade his relationships with subsequent patrons with a certain bitterness.

Filelfo's letterbook is virtually a manual of literary clientage. A writer such as Filelfo, who was neither a priest nor a man of property, was dependent on private patronage and the relationships he built up over time with the powerful and wealthy. Yet by maintaining relationships with several patrons at a time and fostering those friendships over the years, he was able to gain more autonomy for himself than he would have done, had he remained the client of a single patron.[9] With Cicero as his exemplar, his letters are models of the euphemisms of the aristocratic patronage of republican Rome, where a writer's relationship to his employer was called an *amicitia* (friendship) and wages for a commission were delicately alluded to as *benivolentia* or *humanitas* (goodwill, kindness). The letters in the *Epistolae* are ordered so as to form an autobiographical novel containing a series of plots and subplots, structured for suspense. Most of the letters are brief, sometimes gossipy bulletins to his *amici*; but interspersed among these are a number of longer, more formal epistolary essays in which Filelfo showcases his classical learning. Among these essays are letters of advice to princes and popes, and learned philological or philosophical treatises.

Chapter 2 considers Filelfo's next major work, the *Sforziad* (*Sphortias*). Filelfo seems to have begun work on the *Sforziad* in 1453, two years after Francesco Sforza's investiture as duke of Milan. Although he may have completed the final version of the first tetralogy of the *Sforziad* in 1453–1454, he continued to work sporadically on the later books of the poem (Books 5–11) until 1473. The *Sforziad* is an epic poem indebted to both Vergil's *Aeneid* and Petrarch's *Africa*. It tells in Latin epic meters the story

---

[9] See Sharon Kettering, *Patrons, Brokers, and Clients*, on the common practice in early modern France of what she aptly calls "clientele-hopping" or "patron-leapfrogging."

of Francesco Sforza's rise to power against a background of shifting political alliances in Milan and Venice after the death of Filelfo's patron Duke
Filippo Maria Visconti in 1447. Chapter 2 focuses on Book 3 of the *Sforziad*, Filelfo's account of the siege and sack of Piacenza in November 1447.
During the sack of the city, according to contemporary chroniclers, Sforza
allowed his soldiers to strip bare and burn the city and its surrounding
farmlands, while they continued to abuse and torture the townspeople for
several months after the siege. Book 3 is of particular interest since it presents a courtier-poet's critical view of his patron Sforza's role in the town's
sack. It also presents an unvarnished picture of the workings of patronage
at the state level. Piacenza is depicted here as the victim of the territorial
aspirations of two patron states, Venice and Milan, each of them vying to
"protect" Piacenza and enlist the city in its clientage. At the climax of Book
3, Filelfo presents a moving account of the rape of the Piacenzan women
and girls by Sforza's men. In a choral ode that recalls Euripides' *Trojan
Women*, Filelfo allows the women collectively to tell their own story. In
Filelfo's sympathetic portrayal of the Piacenzan women, an analogy is implicitly suggested between the women's fate and the violence perpetrated
on Filelfo's person by his former patron Cosimo de' Medici in 1433. Book
3 was clearly meant to be the centerpiece of the first tetralogy in the *Sforziad*: Books 1–4, which were probably completed in 1453–1454 during
the heyday of Sforza's signory. The *Sforziad* has always been assumed to be
a panegyric of the duke, despite the fact that by Filelfo's time there was
already a long tradition among the humanists of hostility toward the condottieri. Filelfo originally dedicated the poem to Sforza, who became duke
of Milan and Filelfo's protector in 1451. In any case, it is clear that Filelfo
aimed this learned poem at patrons far more sophisticated than Sforza,
among whom were the marquis of Mantua and the duke of Urbino.

Chapter 3 treats Filelfo's *Odae*, a lyric work of fifty Latin odes in Horatian meters probably completed in 1456 for presentation to King Charles
VII of France. By 1455, a year after the Peace of Lodi was signed, Filelfo
began to lose hope that he would ever be properly appreciated by Francesco Sforza. Sforza's regime was firmly entrenched by this time, and Filelfo had published a number of encomiastic works about the duke's ac-
complishments. Still, the duke kept him in poverty, insisting on his
presence at court yet seldom paying him his contracted wages. It is clear
from the eighteen published letters he wrote in 1455 to the chancellor of
France, Guillaume Jouvenel des Ursins and Charles's personal physician
Thomas de Coron that Filelfo wrote his antirepublican, promonarchist
Odae specifically for the French king in hopes of obtaining an offer of employment at the Valois court.

The *Odae* present images of a little-understood episode in Italian history, the brief emergence of a popular republic in Milan in 1447–1450, a

time when signorial regimes were the rule in Italy. Modeled on Horace's *Odes* and *Epodes*, the *Odae* are topical, comic, and perhaps the most original of all Filelfo's works. Certainly the lyric work contains his most violent and forceful poetry. Books 1–3 contain ruthlessly satirical portraits of the chief officers of the so-called Ambrosian Republic. The popular leaders of the republic came in for Filelfo's worst criticism, since above all he feared rule by the uneducated "plebs" whom he—like most of the humanists—considered a danger to the survival of learning and humane government. Filelfo paints the excesses of the republic—the corruption, extortion, confiscation of the lands of the gentry, the summary executions of citizens, and finally the famine and plague—with broad brush strokes, veering always toward the cartoon. And the dominant image in the odes is always hunger: the hunger of his own family and the hunger of the poor and hapless. Famine is the emblem of the failed state, of the city unable to provide either material or spiritual sustenance for its citizens, and of the dearth of charity among men. Filelfo makes it clear in the odes that famine comes from no natural disaster, but rather from human failing. Although he is unrelenting in his vilification of the republican governors, Filelfo refuses to praise Francesco Sforza unequivocally. Instead he draws the duke in terms now grandiose, now diminished and jejune. Sforza was after all unable to protect the Milanese from either the famine or the plague that resulted in thirty thousand deaths the year the war ended. In this chapter, I discuss Filelfo's odes in the context of representations of the Milanese wars of succession by his contemporaries Cristoforo da Soldo, Giovanni Simonetta, and Pier Candido Decembrio. Perhaps the finest of all Filelfo's autobiographical writings is *Odes* 4.5, the story of his family's journey to Cremona by mule-train and boat at the height of the Milanese plague of 1451.

Chapter 4 considers Filelfo's major Greek opus, the *Psychagogia*, a work of forty-four odes in Sapphic and elegiac meters in classical Greek. While imitations of the great Latin authors were de rigueur among the fifteenth-century poets, Filelfo was the first writer to produce a large-scale work in ancient Greek. He was, moreover, one of the few Quattrocento writers ever to publish in that recherché tongue. Only Poliziano would try his hand at a comparable collection of Greek poems. Filelfo had seen his most productive years in the 1450s, under the protection of Francesco Sforza. By the end of the decade he had published several volumes of his autobiographical *Epistolae*, his *Sphortias*, his *Satyrae*, and his lyric *Odae*, and yet he was still not earning enough to feed his family. Nor, despite vigorous efforts, was he able to secure a better offer either in Italy or with King Charles VII's entourage in France. Moreover, when King Ferrante requested Milan's assistance in expelling the French from Naples, Sforza simply cancelled the stipends of his courtiers, and Filelfo's economic position grew more desperate than ever. Filelfo was soon to be equally disappointed

INTRODUCTION · 9

in the patronage of a former student of his, the Latin poet Enea Silvio Piccolomini, who became Pope Pius II in 1458. Even though there was suddenly a glut of Greek scholars looking for academic positions in Italy after the fall of Constantinople, Filelfo still believed that with a substantial work in Greek to his credit he would be more marketable than ever. While some of the dedicatees of the poems in the *Psychagogia* numbered among the most powerful prelates and princes in Italy, also among Filelfo's addressees were a number of Greek refugees whom he had known in Constantinople. Though the Greek poems lack the authority and color of Filelfo's Latin verse, they and their audiences still testify to an astonishing level of learning and sophistication in the northern Italian courts of the fifteenth century. The poems in the *Psychagogia* are also of interest since, in typically Filelfian fashion, they contain swipes at the very men Filelfo sought to retain as his protectors—Francesco Sforza, whom he insults by refusing to dedicate more than a very short poem to him, and his ex-pupil Pope Pius, whom he would later castigate for his greater interest in exporting Christianity to Greece than in fostering Greek culture in Italy.

Six years after his investiture, Pius II died in Ancona, as he was preparing to set sail for Greece to fight the Turks. In the ensuing years, Filelfo never altogether relinquished his hope of obtaining a place in the papal court. During the period of desperate hardship that followed Francesco Sforza's death in 1466, Filelfo continued to devote himself to finishing the *Sforziad*, to a biography of the duke of Urbino, and above all to his autobiographical letters. But not for another decade, with the accession of Sixtus IV to the papal throne, would Filelfo receive an invitation to Rome. The bait Filelfo held out this time was a philosophical work, the *De morali disciplina*. This new work, he intimated to friends, would address the current dispute in Rome over the compatibility of Plato and Aristotle with Christian theology. Although Filelfo was well into his seventies when he began writing the *De morali disciplina*—and this was his first major philosophical essay— he still wanted his *amici* to know that even in distant Milan he was writing about the same ontological and ethical problems that Bessarion and Ficino were pondering in Rome and Florence.

Chapter 5, the last in the book, looks at the *De morali disciplina*, the book Filelfo regarded as his crowning achievement. Dedicating the work to Lorenzo de' Medici, he carried a partly finished draft of the *De disciplina* to his new post as professor of moral philosophy in Rome, where he planned to complete the work. It is noteworthy that while the *De disciplina* proposes a synthesis of the metaphysical and ontological teachings of Plato and Aristotle, and was surely written expressly with the pope and the Roman intelligentsia in mind, Filelfo largely ignores Christian theology in the work. Indeed Filelfo's image of God is Platonic and abstract rather than Christian and personal.

And so in this final chapter in his life, faced with the indifference of Sforza's heir Galeazzo, and feeling that his only hope lay if not in Florence then in Rome, Filelfo characteristically took a defiant stance toward his patron—this time Pope Sixtus IV. In the end he quarreled with the pope, but only, it was said, over money. After teaching at the Roman Studio for what amounted to little more than a few months during the two years he was under contract to the pope, in 1476 he again took the road north to Milan.

· · · · ·

In 1481, Lorenzo de' Medici offered Filelfo the Chair of Greek at the Florentine Studio. On 31 July of that year, though, two weeks after his arrival in Florence, the eighty-three-year-old Filelfo died. According to one sixteenth-century historian, Filelfo was so poor at the time of his death, that the meager furnishings in the rooms he had rented, and even his cooking utensils, had to be sold to cover the cost of his burial. His biographer Rosmini, however, objected that the story was false; his patron Lorenzo, he wrote, had taken care of Filelfo's funeral himself.[10]

[10] Rosmini, *Vita*, 2.271.

ONE

THE SCAR

B Y HIS OWN testimony, Filelfo was already in his fifty-third year when he began to toy with the idea of publishing his epistolary autobiography.[1] He had not wanted to publish his private correspondence earlier, but his public was beginning to hound him for it—this was his claim at any rate.[2] In February 1451 he had first approached his friend Niccolò Ceba, asking him to return the letters he had sent Ceba, so that he could include them in his forthcoming *Epistolae familiares*.[3] He was still finding it difficult to think about undertaking a major project that year, though the civil war in Milan was over and the Milanese had at last received Francesco Sforza as their duke and padrone.

In the summer and fall of 1451 the plague visited Milan with an unprecedented virulence, and for the next year and a half Filelfo spent months at a time on the road.[4] At first he and his family took refuge in the smaller towns along the Po where the disease had not yet spread.[5] Later, when the danger of contagion waned, he shuttled back and forth on his own between Lodi, Pavia, Calvisio, or wherever the duke was encamped with his

[1] See Filelfo, *Epistolae*, to Niccolò Ceba (16 February 1451), fol. 62v, for Filelfo's first mention of the publication of his letters.

[2] Ibid., to Ludovico Petroni (15 June 1464), fol. 153v: "Nam cum plaerosque bonos viros, nescio quo pacto, nostrae delectare epistolae coeperint, ob idque ab me non petant solum, sed contendant, sed importunius rogent, ut eas undique collectas in codicem unum redigam, sum veluti coactus eorum curiositate potius uti quam diligentia mea." Georg Voigt, in *Die Wiederbelebung des classischen Althertums*, 3 vols. (Berlin, 1888–1897), 2.432, notes that the same topos of being "forced" by one's fans to publish private letters is used by Antonio Beccadelli in his introduction to his collected letters.

[3] Ibid., fol. 62v: ". . . abs te petieram quascunque antea ad te dedissem epistolas aliis aliisque temporibus, eas ire ad me curares, quo redigerentur in codicem." *Redigo*, which literally means to reduce or return to another state, is the technical term for editing, revision, and redaction.

[4] Guiliana Albini, *Guerra, fame, peste. crisi di mortalita e sistema sanitario nella Lombardia tardo medioevale* (Bologna, 1982), pp. 117–25: the chroniclers say variously that thirty thousand, sixty thousand, and eighty thousand died of the bubonic plague in 1451. See also ASM, Cart. int. Sforz.: here are the first "bollettini" from the Officio di Sanita, listing the number who died each day of plague; the first of these date from 27 September 1451.

[5] The story of the Filelfo's family's flight from Milan in September 1451 is told in his *Odes* 4.5; and Filelfo, *Epistolae*, to Giammaria Filelfo (14 September 1451), fols. 66v–67.

troops. On occasion he took the road to Ferrara where he visited his old friends at the Este court.[6]

Filelfo made no mention of his letterbook again until May 1453, when he promised Giacomo da Camerino that he would mail him a draft of the first ten books of his *Epistolae* sometime that year.[7] He routinely promised quantities of work he could not deliver, and his promise to Camerino was no exception. One year later, when Alberto Parisi asked him for a copy of the first part of his letterbook—namely, the letters from the late 1420s and 1430s—he put his friend off.[8] If Parisi could send him the opening phrases of whatever old letters of his he could manage to locate, Filelfo suggested, he might then be able to reconstruct some of the letters from that period of his life. Otherwise, he could not fulfill his friend's request—"for most of those letters are missing, as far as I know," he wrote.[9]

When Filelfo returned from his travels through the plague-torn cities of Lombardy at the close of 1452, he was in a reflective mood. In the space of twenty years, he had lost two cherished wives, the mothers of his children. He had seen civil wars all but destroy Bologna, Florence, and most recently Milan, and he had lived amid pestilence and famine. These recurrences of violence and disease seemed to him the inevitable consequences of nature. In describing the trajectory of his life in his epistolary memoirs, Filelfo returned always to the same images. His themes were Augustan, gilded with reminiscences from Horace and Vergil. He was an exile—a fugitive from the misfortunes of other lands, and his journey through the glittering cities and courts of Quattrocento Italy was a voyage by sea. Whenever the water looked its most tranquil, he knew then that a squall— civil war, sedition, or perhaps plague—was on its way. Soon there would be gale winds, towering waves, and for him, the voyager, shipwreck— *naufragium*.

Thus, Filelfo located his first book of letters appropriately in Venice, that most shiplike of cities, in the plague year of 1427:

> For you press me [he wrote his friend Daniele Vitturi], and with such an abun-
> dance of affection, not to agree to remain in Venice during so searing an epi-

[6] Adam, *F. Filelfo*, pp. 29–30.

[7] Filelfo, *Epistolae*, to Iacopo da Camerino (7 May 1453), fol. 77v: ". . . Epistolarum libros decem hoc anno aedere institui; has tu omnium primus habiturus es usurusque pro arbitrio tuo."

[8] Ibid., to Alberto Parisi (26 March 1454), fol. 152: ". . . De epistolis autem meis quod scribis, idcirco nonnulli priores libri non iverunt ad te, quod illos nondum aedi voluerim, ob eam causam quod plaeraeque epistolae quas alias Florentiae, alias Senae, alias Bononiae [i.e., the letters from 1428 to 1438, the period he taught at Florence, Siena, and Bologna] scripsissem nondum in codicem sunt redactae . . . *Desunt enim mihi quamplurimae*. Itaque rem mihi gratam efficies, si initia earum epistolarum quas tibi esse dicis ad me propediem dederis, ut intelligam sintne istae ex illarum numero quas dixi deesse mihi" (my emphasis).

[9] Ibid.

demic of plague, but to depart for Padua, or wherever else I can come to a decision about my life under safer circumstances. If I were to say I am totally without fear, I would be lying.[10]

Petrarch, whose largely fictitious Latin epistolario was certainly a model for Filelfo's own work, had begun his first book of letters in much the same spirit, with an epistle written the year the great plague came to Italy from Asia:[11]

Time, as they say [wrote Petrarch], has slipped through our fingers; our former hopes are buried with our friends. The year 1348 left us alone and helpless; it did not deprive us of things that can be restored by the Indian or Caspian or Carpathian Sea. It subjected us to irreparable losses. Whatever death wrought is now an incurable wound.[12]

The futility of hope, the pain of betrayal, and with it the impossibility of trust in anything in this life, were also to be important themes in Filelfo's letters. But his letterbook resembled Petrarch's *Epistolae familiares* in more ways than this one. Like Petrarch's letters, Filelfo's were for the most part addressed either to his patrons or to other writers and scholars who were clients of his patrons. Thus, his letters yield, among other things, a series of tableaux of Renaissance patronage, seen from the viewpoint of a client.

Views of Patronage: From Science to Satire

Patronage was by no means a new phenomenon in the Renaissance. While Gene Brucker saw the immediate roots of the system in the agrarian feudalism of medieval Europe, Richard Saller's study of the ideology of pa-

---

[10] Ibid., fol. 1v: "Non enim sine magna quadam amoris vi me hortaris, ut in tantis pestilentiae ignibus Venetiis esse nolim, sed vel Patavium concedam, vel alio ubi tutius vitae meae consultum sit. Si dixero me esse omnino expertem metus, plane mentiar."

[11] On the fictitiousness of the letters in Petrarch's published epistolario (his *Familiares*), see Giuseppe Billanovich, "Petrarca letterato, 1. Lo scrittoio del Petrarca," in *Storia e letteratura* 16 (Rome, 1947): 3–55; Ernest H. Wilkins, *Life of Petrarch* (Chicago, 1961), pp. 87–88; see also Aldo Bernardo, *Artistic Procedures Followed by Petrarch in Making the Collection of the "Familiares"* (Ph.D. diss., Harvard University, 1949; partially reprinted in *Speculum* 33 [1958]). See also idem, *Rerum familiarium libri I–VIII* (Albany, 1975), pp. xxv ff.; and idem, *Francesco Petrarca. Letters on Familiar Matters. Rerum familiarium libri IX–XVI* (Baltimore, 1982), xviii ff. On the tradition of literary, fictional letters and letterbooks from the middle ages onward, see J. Leclerq, "Le genre epistolaire au moyen age," in *Revue du moyen age latin* 2 (1946): 63–70; Eugenio Garin, ed. *Prosatori latini del Quattrocento* (Milan, 1952), pp. xi–xiii; Gianvito Resta, *L'epistolario del Panormita* (Messina, 1954), pp. 3–12; and Ronald Witt, "Medieval 'Ars Dictaminis' and the Beginnings of Humanism: A New Construction of the Problem," in *Renaissance Quarterly* 35 (1982): 1–35.

[12] Bernardo, *Francesco Petrarca: Rerum familiarium libri. I–VIII*, p. 3.

tronage in imperial Rome pointed to still earlier models for the system as a phenomenon of urban culture in the Mediterranean.[13] Anthropologists such as Ernest Gellner, S. N. Eisenstadt, and L. Roniger, moreover, have seen a common amalgam of core traits as characteristic of client-patron relations in both modern and traditional societies the world over.[14] Ronald Weissman, Dale Kent, and F. W. Kent have recently suggested that the work of these anthropologists on the social phenomenon of patronage might provide a useful conceptual framework for Renaissance historians.[15] The core traits in patron-client relations were seen as these: the inequality of its partners in terms of power and resources; the long-term nature of the patronage bond; its distinctive ideological and ethical basis as opposed to a legal one; and the diffuse and multistranded nature of its exchanges—the patron, that is, might furnish not only gifts and protection to his clients but also brokerage, influence, access to networks of friends, and the like.[16]

Some anthropologists, however, emphasized the more dysfunctional aspects of the patronage relationship. Eisenstadt and Roniger noted that dissonance was inevitably created when an ethos of intellectual egalitarianism was superimposed on an economic relationship that was inherently hierarchical, as was the case in the dominant-dependent dyad in patronage.[17] If one were to disregard this dissonance, one might assume with some social scientists that patronage would tend to reinforce stability in societies.[18]

[13] Gene Brucker, "The Structure of Patrician Society in Renaissance Florence," in *Colloquium* 1 (1964): 8–11; Richard P. Saller, *Personal Patronage Under the Early Empire* (Cambridge, 1982). On patronage in ancient Rome, see also P. A. Brunt, " 'Amicitia' in the Late Roman Republic," in *The Crisis of the Roman Republic: Studies in Political and Social History*, ed. R. Seager (Cambridge, 1969), pp. 197–218.

[14] Among the anthropologists who studied modern Mediterranean societies, see Ernest Gellner and J. Waterbury, *Patrons and Clients in Mediterranean Societies* (London, 1977); J. Pitt-Rivers, *The People of the Sierra* (London, 1954); F. G. Bailey, ed., *Gifts and Poison: the Politics of Reputation* (Oxford, 1971); and J. G. Peristiany, ed., *Honour and Shame: the Values of Mediterranean Society* (Chicago, 1966). For an overview of patronage throughout the world, see S. N. Eisenstadt and L. Roniger, *Patrons, Clients, and Friends: Interpersonal Relations and the Structure of Trust in Society* (Cambridge, 1984). For bibliography on patronage, see Eisenstadt and Roniger, "Patron-Client Relations as a Model of Structuring Social Exchange," in *Comparative Studies in Society and History* 22 (1980): 43–48.

[15] See Francis William Kent and Patricia Simons, eds., *Patronage, Art and Society in Renaissance Italy* (Oxford, 1987): see esp. Ronald Weissman, "Taking Patronage Seriously: Mediterranean Values and Renaissance Society," pp. 25–45; on Florentine patronage, see also R. Weissman, *Ritual Brotherood in Renaissance Florence* (New York, 1982); Dale V. Kent, *The Rise of the Medici* (Oxford, 1978); F. W. Kent, *Household and Lineage in Renaissance Florence: the Family Life of the Capponi, Ginori, and Rucellai* (Princeton, 1977); D. V. and F. W. Kent, "Two Vignettes of Florentine Society in the Fifteenth Century," in *Rinascimento* 23 (1983): 237–60; see also Anthony Molho, "Cosimo de' Medici: *Pater Patriae* or *Padrino*?" in *Stanford Italian Review* 1 (1979): 5–33.

[16] Weissman, "Taking Patronage Seriously," pp. 25–26.

[17] Eisenstadt, *Patrons, Clients, and Friends*, pp. 48–49.

[18] Saller, *Personal Patronage*, 37–39. Most studies of Renaissance patronage tend to be pa-

But as soon as one looked more closely at the contradictions underlying the relationship, the solidarity between the two partners appeared tenuous indeed. Though the partners might profess a shared ethos or a unity of purpose around that ethos, because of the inherent inequalities in the relationship, that ethos was bound to be interpreted differently by the client and patron, giving rise to varying degrees of ambivalence. Second, in patron-client relations voluntary services and mutual obligations were peculiarly, yet characteristically, coupled with an ever-present potential for coercion and abuse. If we consider the system from the vantage point of its contradictions and paradoxes, then, we cannot help but see in patronage the seeds not for cohesion and stability but for the violence and conflict that characterized life in the great cities of Renaissance Italy.

Sharon Kettering's recent study of clientage in seventeenth-century France demonstrates that in case after case the contradictions inherent in the patron-client nexus made instability and conflict an inevitable condition of the relationship.[19] What often led to anger and violence in a relationship, as she saw it, was the illusion of the immutability of its partners. Because the *fides* relationship was based on mutually professed interests, it invariably ended amid charges of hypocrisy and betrayal when those interests changed:

> Client relationships began as a slow, stately dance in which the opening step was a carefully plotted move to attract a patron's attention. They ended in frenzy of emotion, with cries of disloyalty and ingratitude mingled with charges of betrayal. A patron considered himself betrayed if a client accepted the favors and the patronage he offered and then did not obey him, provide the services he expected, or defend his interests. A client considered himself betrayed if his loyalty and services went unrewarded by a patron, or if his interests were neglected for a long period of time.[20]

Filelfo's letters to his numerous patrons manifest, generally, the same kinds of phenomena that modern scholars have seen in the *fides* relationships they studied. The fact that fifteenth-century clients and patrons, as we shall see in the letters, more often than not perceived the *fides* relationship and its obligations very differently from one another led to the inevitable misunderstandings, tension, resentment, and disillusionment that characterized Renaissance *amicitia*. On the other hand, it is precisely Filel-

---

tron-centered: cf. Peter Burke, *Culture and Society in Renaissance Italy* (New York, 1972); Werner L. Gundsersheimer, "Patronage in the Renaissance: an Exploratory Approach," in G. F. Lytle and S. Orgel, eds., *Patronage in the Renaissance* (Princeton, 1981), pp. 3–23. For a more client-oriented study, see Sharon Kettering, *Patrons, Brokers, and Clients in Seventeenth-Century France* (Oxford, 1986).

[19] Kettering, *Patrons, Brokers, and Clients.*
[20] Ibid., p. 186.

fo's representation of this volatility, this emotional lability in his relationships, that gives the letters their intensity and charge.

Often Filelfo is at pains to show that no ethical code is more fraught
with hypocrisy than his patron's concept of *amicitia*. At other times he
plays the role of the dutiful client, espousing the terms of *amicitia*, as he
found them codified in Cicero and Seneca.[21] Cicero, who made his way to
the upper echelons of Roman society through a series of strategic friendships, had idealized the patronage relationship (*amicitia*) as a symbiotic
bonding of kindred spirits, but one that tended fortunately to result in
economic gain for those who engaged in it. Indeed, in the same breath that
Cicero eulogized friendship he found it necessary to defend himself against
the charge that his intellectual and spiritual alliances were perhaps venal:

> For nothing gives more pleasure than the return of goodwill and the inter-
> change of zealous service [between kindred souls] (14.49) . . . And again, it
> seems to me at any rate that those who falsely asssume expediency to be the
> basis of friendship take from friendship's chain its loveliest link. For it is not
> so much the material gain procured through a friend as it is his love, and his
> love alone that gives us delight; and that advantage which we derive from him
> becomes a pleasure only when his service is inspired by ardent zeal. (*De amic.*
> 14.51)[22]

Filelfo satirizes and sabotages the ideals of patronage on a number of
planes in his writings—that of the state's relationship with its client cities
in the *Sforziad*, in city politics in the *Odes*, and on the most intimate level,
in his *Epistolae*. In his correspondence with Leonardo Giustiniani, Cosimo
de' Medici, and Francesco Sforza, he lays bare the hollowness of those assumptions he seems once to have trusted. Though he may appear weak and
ineffectual to his unsuspecting benefactors, he will show in the *Epistolae*
that he has learned to take the upper hand—to play David to his patron's
Goliath. Like Nietzsche's man of *ressentiment* he is one who "loves hiding
places, secret paths and back doors, . . . [who] understands how to keep

---

[21] See Saller, *Personal Patronage*, pp. 7–39 for an extensive discussion of the vocabulary of
patronage in Cicero and Seneca.

[22] Cicero, *De Senectute, De Amicitia, De Divinatione*, trans. W. A. Falconer (London, reprint
1971), pp. 161–63: "Nihil est enim [inter animos similes] remuneratione benevolentiae, nihil
vicissitudine studiorum officiorumque iucundius. . . . Atque etiam mihi quidem videntur, qui
utilitatis causa fingunt amicitias, amabilissimum nodum amicitiae tollere. Non enim tam utilitas parta per amicum quam amici amor ipse delectat, tumque illud fit, quod ab amico est
profectum . . ." (*De amic.* 14.48–51). Cf. Cicero, *Letters To his Friends*, tr. W. Glynn Williams,
3 vols. (London, 1927; reprint 1965), vol. 1, p. 18 (to Lentulus Spinther): "Tametsi mihi
nihil fuit optatius, quam ut primum abs te ipso, deinde a ceteris omnibus quam gratissimus
erga te esse cognoscerer, tamen afficior summo dolore, eiusmodi tempora post tuam profec-
tionem consecuta esse, ut et meam et ceterorum erga te fidem et benevolentiam absens expe-
rirer . . ."

silent, how not to forget, how to wait, how to be provisionally self-depre-
cating and humble."[23]

Violence, Honor, and Suppression in the *Epistolae*

Filelfo took care to excise from his *Epistolae* the more coercive, exploita-
tive, and violent aspects of his relationships with his patrons. If he ever
experienced a loss of *dignitas*, or physical abuse at the hands of his patrons,
he suppressed it in his published letters. Twice in his life, in 1431 in Florence and some thirty years later in Milan, Filelfo's patrons issued warrants
for his arrest and imprisonment because they did not like what he wrote
about them.[24] Yet no traces of these brushes with the law—and with public
dishonor—are to be found in either the Trivulzian manuscript or the
printed editions of his *Epistolae*.

Filelfo's letter to Enea Silvio Piccolomini, in which he lavishly frames
what is perhaps the most flambuoyant moment in the *Epistolae*, provides
us with a paradigm of his constant preoccupation with the process of re-
constituting himself, muting whatever violence he suffered and masking
his humiliation. On 18 May 1433, as he made his way to deliver his morning lectures in Florence, he was almost murdered—this was his claim—by
an armed assassin.[25] His assailant, Filelfo later testified, was a paid assassin,
responsible ultimately to Cosimo de' Medici himself, the man whose patronage had brought Filelfo to Florence four years before.

By the spring of 1433 Filelfo's outspoken criticism of the party in power,
the Medici, and his advocacy of the opposition party had brought his relations with the Medici to a point of no return. It is also a matter of record
that on the morning of 18 May 1433 Filelfo was physically attacked and
that his assailant was an employee of persons close to Cosimo.[26] Doubt

---

[23] Michel Foucault, "Preface," in G. Deleuze and F. Guattari, *Anti-Oedipus*, trans. R. Hurley, M. Seem, and H. R. Lane (Minneapolis, 1988), xii–xiii.

[24] Both these incidents are treated at length later in chap. 1. On the decree calling for Filelfo's arrest on 10 March 1431, see Angelo Fabroni, *Magni Cosmi Medicei vita* (Pisa, 1789),
2.69; and Rosmini, *Vita*, 1.43; on the College of Cardinals' demand that Filelfo be incarcerated for his defamation of the pope, see Rosmini, *Vita*, 2.139–40; cf. also a letter expressing
indignation over Filelfo's sacrileges by Cardinal Iacopo Piccolomini Ammanati, *Epistolae et
commentarii* (1608), p. 29.

[25] Filelfo, *Epistolae*, to Enea Silvio Piccolomini, fols. 17–18. For the complete text of this
letter, see Appendix A.

[26] The relevant documents on the case, the *Atti* from the Florentine office of the *Podestà*,
have been published in Giuseppe Zippel, *Il Filelfo a Firenze (1429–1434)* (Rome, 1899) [re-
printed in Gianni Zippel, ed., *Storia e cultura del Rinascimento italiano* (Padua, 1979), 215–
53]. According to the *Atti*, Lorenzo de' Medici came forward to pay the fine of Filelfo's
assailant, Girolamo Brocchardi (*Storia*, pp. 238–39).

remains, however, as to whether in 1433 there was actually a plot to *assassinate* Filelfo. The fifteenth-century Florentine bookseller and biographer Vespasiano makes no reference to the incident in his *vita* of Filelfo. Indeed, Filelfo's only explicit reference in the *Epistolae* to the 18 May assault occurs not in Book 2, where all the letters for the Florence years (1429–1434) are contained, but in a letter he wrote to Enea Silvio Piccolomini, dated 28 March 1439—six years after the event. Filelfo's two modern biographers, Carlo Rosmini and R. G. Adam, have simply accepted as fact Filelfo's story of the alleged attempt on his life, and subsequent historians have followed suit.[27] Nonetheless, at the end of the last century Giuseppe Zippel published two documents that at least cast suspicion on the account of the events in question given in the letter to Piccolomini.[28] One of these was an unedited letter Filelfo himself wrote to Tommaso de Bizzocchi, secretary at the Malatesta court in Rimini, one month after the alleged assassin's attack.[29] The other, from the *Atti del tribunale del Podestà* of Florence for the year 1433, contains the official record of the mayor's proceedings against the defendant in the case, Girolamo Brocchardi di Imola, rector of the Florentine Studio.[30] To see how Filelfo represented events—embellishing some facts, suppressing others altogether—depending on his particular purposes, we have only to compare the three sources we have on the attack. The first, the *Atti del Podestà*, contains the following charges leveled against Brocchardi in court, to which he confessed under torture,

> that in the present year and month immediately prior, May, of the said year, the said Messer Girolamo [Brocchardi] willfully and with forethought, caused the crime of the conscious, guileful, zealous, and premeditated commission and perpetration of the here below described *cutting and wounding*, and ordered Filippo Masi Bruni da Imola . . . to *cut and wound* the said Francesco Cecchi, also known as Filelfo of Tolentino of Ancona in the Marches, with whatever sort of *cut or wound*—namely on lord Francesco's face itself and elsewhere as well—*so long as he did not kill him*. This Filippo in executing and fulfilling the order issued by Messer Girolamo consciously, guilefully, zealously and with premeditation, cut the said lord Francesco causing the greatest flow of blood [from the wound], from which cutting there followed a [disfigurement] of lord Francesco's face because of the prominent cicatrice or mark [left by the wound]; and in this manner, by cutting the said lord Francesco, Filippo executed and consigned for execution the said commission.[31] (my emphases)

[27] Rosmini, *Vita*, 1.64–66; Adam, *F. Filelfo*, p. 124.
[28] Zippel, *Storia*, pp. 244–50.
[29] Ibid., pp. 244–46.
[30] Ibid., pp. 248–50.
[31] ASF, *Podestà* 4469, *Liber sententiarum*: "Quod de hoc anno presenti et de proxime pre-

Girolamo Brocchardi's hostility toward Filelfo had its own peculiar history. As rector of the Studio and a Medici partisan, he had not only openly opposed Filelfo's tenure since 1431 but had also exposed him to continual harrassment at the university.[32] The key clause, however, in Brocchardi's testimony was "dummodo eum non occideret": the hoodlum he hired was under strict orders to cut and wound Filelfo in any way he liked—"so long as he did not kill him." Also of crucial importance here are the threefold repetition of the instructions "to cut and wound" and Brocchardi's highly specific directive to Filippo to cut Filelfo's *face*. We should also take note of the emphasis placed in the testimony on the cicatrix Filelfo sustained from the assault. This last part of the report, concerning the scarring of Filelfo's face, makes it clear that the assault—a kind of ritual branding in effect—constituted a profound affront to his honor.

A letter Filelfo wrote a month after the incident to Tommaso de' Bizzocchi in Rimini, which he did not publish in the *Epistolae*, presents a picture of the assault different from the one in the official record of the *Podestà*. First of all, Filelfo characterizes his assailant as a "sicarius" ("assassin"), a word not found in the *Podestà* report. Second, Filelfo's letter makes it clear that his assailant's purpose was to kill him ("caput mihi letali vulnere ferire voluisset"), and that, savage as it was, the man's cutting of his face was merely accidental. Third, he makes the point that a lucky blow on his part saved him from sure death:

> With the sword that he had kept hidden under his clothing now drawn, he extended it to stab me, its point aimed at my breast. And then the dastardly assassin's hopes would have been dashed—since suddenly, though I was unarmed and barely even clothed, I knocked him back against the nearest wall with my right hand. But with a second parry, although he would have liked to strike me on the head, wounding me mortally there, his blow landed on my face—beyond the hopes of the cowardly thief, but still with such a perilous and terrifying thrust that it resulted not only in cutting deep but also in almost

terito mense May dicti anni dictus Magister Geronimus, animo et intentione, infrascriptum malefitium commictendi et perpetrandi, scienter, dolose, studiose et appensate fecit *percuti et vulnerari*, et mandavit Philippo Masi Bruni . . . ut *percuteret et vulnaret* dictum dominum Franciscum Cechi, alias vocatum Filelfo de Tolentino, provintie Marchie anconitane, quacumque *percussione seu vulnere*, videlicet tam in facie ipsius domini Franscisci quam alibi, *dummodo eum non occideret*. Qui Filippus . . . percussit dictum dominum Franciscum cum maxima sanguinis effusione, ex qua percussione sequit[u]r vituperatio [*vituperatio* makes no sense; perhaps the text should have read *turpitudo*] faciei dicti domini Francisci per apparentem cichatricem vel signum; et dictum mandatum dictus Philippus ita, percutiendo dictum dominum Franciscum, executus fuit et executioni mandavit." Gianni Zippel, the editor of the 1979 reprint of Giuseppe Zippel's article, notes that this particular document was irreparably damaged in the flood of 1966 in Florence (p. 248).

[32] See Filelfo's own letters about the harrassment he was experiencing on a daily basis in Rosmini, *Vita*, 1.138.

amputating my entire right cheek and nose. Indeed, when he had done the deed, he turned and fled suddenly.[33]

What we need to be aware of in this version of the attack is its purpose. In seeking protection from the Malatesta, Filelfo sought to elicit pity for himself. And so while he underlined the utter defenselessness of his position —he was "inermis ac pene nudus"—on the one hand, he exaggerated the severity of his injuries on the other.

Six years later Filelfo wrote a completely new version of the assault, which he addressed to Enea Silvio Piccolomini (later Pope Pius II) and designed so that it could be included in the published *Epistolae*. In rewriting the story, he had still another aim in mind. Both Enea and Cosimo were men he had hoped would be his most generous patrons. Since Filelfo's vicious lampoons of Cosimo in his satires were no doubt well known to Piccolomini by 1439, this letter seems at least to carry the implicit warning to Enea that if his own ethics should ever resemble Cosimo's he could easily become a victim of Filelfo's damaging satires himself.

In Filelfo's letter to Piccolomini, the roles of assailant and victim are nearly reversed. Here Filelfo portrays himself as a plucky little David who, armed only with his fists, emerges victorious over a sword-brandishing Goliath. In contrast to his unedited letter to Bizzocchi, here Filelfo takes control of the situation from the first. Here it is he who lunges at his alleged assassin "with tremendous force" ("magna vi"), landing the first punch squarely on his opponent's chest. With this one powerful blow, he is able to throw his would-be assassin so far off balance that he, not Filelfo, is made to look the fool. The assassin is left slashing at the air, while, except for a nick on the face, Filelfo emerges David-like at the battle's end, completely unscathed—"omni illaesum vulnere."

After suddenly drawing out the fairly long sword he had hidden under his clothes, he thrust its point straight toward my breast, and would have run me clean through, had I not set upon him with tremendous force there and then— dealing him a blow to the chest with my right hand. Thus his blow, falling astray of the place where it was aimed, struck me in the left arm—leaving me free of all injury. For his blow was a paltry thing since, after he was knocked backward by my blow, he was somewhat out of range. At that point, with his

[33] Zippel, *Storia*, 244–46: "Districto gladio quem sub vestibus tenebat tectum, directo in pectus mucrone, percutere nos porrexit. Que ubi sceleratissimum sicarium fefellisset spes; nam illum subito manu dextera, ut eram inermis ac pene [ne] nudus, reieci ad proximum parietem; secundo ictu, cum caput mihi letali vulnere ferire voluisset, descendit ictus preter ignavissimi spem latronis in faciem, cum ac formabili ac periculosissima percussione, adeo ut et nasum ac dexteram genam cum penitus tum prope totam absciderit. Quo quidem perpetrato facinore repente in fugam vertitur . . ."

sword upraised again to strike me on the head with its blade, he cut me in the face.[34]

In comparison to his rambling letter to Bizzocchi, Filelfo's letter to Piccolomini is a polished essay, obviously written for publication. It has a tight seven-part structure, consisting of a formal prologue and epilogue that frame five internal sections, in which purely narrative sections alternate with political commentary on those narratives. While this carefully crafted epistolary essay and the purely "factual" account of the assault in the *Podestà atti* represent the opposite poles in the types of reportage we have for the period, we can no more rely uncritically on the *Podestà* report than we can on Filelfo's testimony.

What else was at stake in Filelfo's careful retailoring in the *Epistolae* of his story of the alleged assassination attempt? If Filelfo had reported that his former patrons at the Studio had meant not to kill but only to humiliate him by leaving on his person a visible mark of their power over him, he would have virtually admitted that he had been dishonored—that he had indeed lost face, in this case literally as well as metaphorically. It was of great importance to Filelfo to suppress in the Piccolomini letter (which clearly contained the account of the attack he wanted made public) any reference to what had been the central piece of evidence in the Brocchardi *Podestà* trial: his scar. To disseminate an image of himself, however, as the triumphant survivor of a struggle with an armed assassin who represented the most powerful clan in Europe was to emerge from the incident not a pitiful victim but a hero.

Taking Filelfo's refiguration, after 1451, of the events of his life and of his agonistic relations with his patrons in his letter to Piccolomini as my guiding paradigm, I will focus in this chapter on the theme of patronage in his epistolary autobiography. The letters in the *Epistolae familiares* fall into three broad categories: those addressed to patrons and colleagues in the academic world; those advising princely patrons in the world of politics and war; and finally the showpieces on purely literary or philosophical topics addressed to colleagues—but circulated as bait to attract new patrons, commissions, and invitations to lecture. To show how Filelfo arranged his letters so that, like a novelist, he could develop and interweave a series of story lines, I have confined myself in the discussion that follows to Books 1–3 (the letters for the years 1427–1440), taking the 1502 Venice edition

[34] Filelfo, *Epistolae*, to Piccolomini, fols. 17–18: "Qui educto repente longiore gladio, qui toga tegebatur, cuspidem mihi direxit in pectus. Transfodissetque me omnino, nisi dextera manu facto pugno in eius pectus illico magna vi irruissem. Itaque a proposito loco ictus ille abberans in sinistrum bracchium me percussit omni illaesum vulnere. Elanguerat enim ictus, quoniam ille a me reiectus pugno paululum esset amotus. Qui rursus sublato gladio, quo me acie feriret in caput, in faciem me percussit."

of the *Epistolae* as my text, since it is the most complete and accessible of all the early printed editions.[35]

Three Relationships: Images of Clientage

Filelfo's letters addressed to Leonardo Giustiniani, Giovanni Aurispa, and Ambrogio Traversari reveal the development over time of his relationships with three very different men, each of whom did much to advance the new studies of Greek literature in Italy. The patrician Giustiniani, whose aim— so Filelfo thought—was to establish a new school of classical learning under Filelfo's aegis in Venice, played the role of Filelfo's first patron in academia. The Sicilian Aurispa, who was an itinerant professor on the university circuit, played the roles of both mentor and colleague to Filelfo. Traversari, an ordained priest and a widely recognized authority on both classical and patristic texts, worked to undermine Filelfo's position in the academy.

Giustiniani: Aristocrat and Book Thief

Leonardo Giustiniani came from a family whose lineage and wealth were legendary, even among the elite of the Venetian patriciate.[36] He met the seventeen-year-old Filelfo at Padua, where he was already teaching classes for his professor, the renowned Gasparino Barzizza. In 1420, Giustiniani secured a place for Filelfo with the Venetian embassy in Constantinople. Filelfo was expected to further his Greek studies there, buy as many codices of ancient Greek works as he could, and then return to Venice to teach after one or two years.

Seven years later, Giustiniani enticed Filelfo to leave Constantinople, promising him five hundred ducats a year if he came back to teach in Venice—so Filelfo claimed.[37] But when his ship pulled into the harbor in October 1427, Filelfo found the city ravaged by the plague, and all but deserted by the nobility. His patrons and potential students—Francesco

[35] On the redactions of the *Epistolae*, see Appendix A.

[36] Patricia H. Labalme, *Bernardo Giustiniani: A Venetian of the Quattrocento* (Rome, 1969); and Berthold Fenigstein, *Leonardo Giustiniani (1383?–1446): Venetianischer Staatsmann, Humanist und Vulgardichter* (Halle, 1909). See also Giovanni degli Agostini, *Notizie istorico-critiche intorno la vita e opere degli scrittori viniziani*, 2 vols. (Venice, 1752–1754); and Giorgio Castellani, "Documenti veneziani inediti relativi a Francesco e Mario Filelfo," *ASI* 17 (1896): 364–70.

[37] Traversari, *Epistolae*, Filelfo to Traversari, bk. 24, letter 36 (31 August 1428), cols. 1013–14.

Barbaro, Daniele Vitturi, Marco Lippomani, Gabriele Moro, Federico Cornelio, Pietro Tommasi, and Andrea Giuliani, and most probably Giustiniani's own son Bernardo as well—all had abandoned the city.[38] Only Leonardo Giustiniani remained nearby, at his country house on the island of Murano, across the lagoon from San Marco.

The opening letter in the *Epistolae* is addressed to Giustiniani. The first in a cycle of fifteen letters to his Venetian patron, this letter provides the program for the rest of the book. For it encapsulates, in Eisenstadt's terms, the fundamental paradox of the *fides* relationship: the contradiction between the ethical solidarity of the patron and client and their unequal economic positions.[39] Theirs had been a bond founded on a common moral and intellectual outlook, Filelfo reminds Giustiniani with a kind of nostalgia—and it is worth noting that the first half of the letter is all in the past tense. Chief among these values were loyalty, moral support, advice, generosity and its counterpart, gratitude; the exchange of a broad array of goods, advantages, and services; and finally the freely given service and sense of mutual obligation. Alluding over and over to the length of their relationship with such phrases as "nothing more hallowed by time," "for a very long time now," "I cannot ever forget," "long-standing kindnesses," and "everlasting service," Filelfo seems almost to mourn already the loss of a friendship that is now only a memory, and at the same time to rebuke Giustiniani for his absence.

> Because I have held nothing more hallowed by time among my possessions than your goodwill (*benivolentia*), nothing more sacred than your loyalty (*fide*), you can easily understand, Leonardo Giustiniani, that it was because of you that I abandoned both Constantinople—the new Rome that pleased me so much—and also the Emperor John Paleologus himself, who certainly was deserving of (*meritum*) the best possible service from me. For not only did the highest hope (*spes*)—which you held out to me in your so frequent and generous (*liberalissimis*) letters—cause me to obey you (*obsequerer*), but you yourself did so, since I had long known, and was well aware, that I was very much loved (*carissimum*) by you. Nor is there anything I should prefer more than that I should not only be thought most grateful (*gratissimum*), but that I should also be so. For while liberality (*liberalitas*) is occasionally the mark of a man of property (*opulenti*), gratitude (*gratitudo*) is always that of the just and virtuous man. Therefore, when I set sail from Constantinople at noonday on the twenty-seventh of August, seven years and five months after I first embarked for Greece, I returned to you, surely led to do so by your advice (*con-*

---

[38] Labalme, *Bernardo Giustiniani*, p. 43, speculates that since Cristoforo left Venice for Padua in 1425, Bernardo may have followed him there. According to Agostini, *Notizie*, 1.305, Bernardo received his doctorate from Padua.

[39] Eisenstadt, *Patrons, Clients, and Friends*, pp. 48–49.

silio), and because I wished to repay, to the best of my ability, the debt of gratitude I owe (*debeo gratiam*) both to you and the rest of the nobles. For I could never either forget the most beautiful favors (*beneficia*) you have done me in the past, nor could I fail to value properly those worthy offices (*digna*), by virtue of which I am bound (*obstrictus*) to you in everlasting service (*perpetua observantia*).[40]

The first paragraph of the letter glistens with the Ciceronian euphemisms of patronage.[41] The realities of survival in the world are suppressed as obscenities—thoughts about labor, wages, contracts, and the like must never cross the minds of men of letters. Also taboo among Renaissance intellectuals were the terms *patronus* and *cliens*, since they made the social inferiority of the client-writer too explicit. Such images had already been banned by Cicero, Seneca, Tacitus, and Pliny for the same reason.[42] No matter who paid whom, relationships among men of letters were between *amici*—"friends." Still, the truth about this friendship, its utter asymmetry, comes out in the final paragraph. While Filelfo waits with his family in grim lodgings in a city now crowded with funeral trains, Giustiniani sits on his island—godlike and aloof amid his *objets d'art*.

If only this horrible, ravenous, and virulent pestilence, under whose weight I see the city bitterly toiling, would not impede my thoughts. For I cannot but fear arrows of this sort . . . and so I see no reason why I should have to live amid so much peril. Thus, I should be much obliged if you would inform me as to what plan you think I should follow. For I see that nearly the entire citizenry has gone far away from the city, all except you, who sit among those glass vases of yours on Murano, as though you were protected from Apollo's shafts by the shield of Vulcan. Vale.[43]

[40] Filelfo, *Epistolae* (10 October 1427), fol. 1: "Quod nihil apud me duxerim antiquius benivolentia, tua nihil sanctius tua fide, facile vel ex hoc potes existimare, Leonarde Iustiniane, quod et Constantinopolin novam Romam mihi iucundissimam, et regem ipsum Iannem Paleologum de me quam optime certe meritum tua causa reliquerim. Non enim me movit spes amplissima, quam tuis tam crebris, tamque liberalissimis litteris mihi ostendisti, ut tibi obsequerer, sed ipse tu, cui [me] carissimum esse iampridem multumque cognoram. Nec est quicquam quod malim quam et haberi me et esse gratissimum. Nam liberalitas opulenti est nonnunquam; at gratitudo iusti semper et boni viri. Cum igitur ad sextum Kalendas Septembres solvissem ex urbe Constantinopoli, hoc die circiter meridiem post annum septimum ac menses quinque posteaquam hinc primum navigaram in Thraciam, ad vos redii ductus sane consilio tuo, cupiensque et tibi et caeteris patriciis viris referre eam quam debeo gratiam pro virili mea. Nam pristina vestra illa erga me et pulcherrima beneficia neque oblivisci unquam possim, nec minus digna censere, quibus sim obstrictus perpetua observantia."

[41] See nn. 21 and 22 on Cicero: Filelfo found the appropriate vocabulary on which to pattern his own patronage letters in Cicero's *Epistolae ad familiares* and his *De amicitia*.

[42] Saller, *Personal Patronage*, pp. 8–9, points out that the terms *patronus* and *cliens* were never used by the major post-Augustan prose writers, and only rarely by Cicero.

[43] Filelfo, *Epistolae*, to Giustiniani, cont., fol. 1: "Utinam saeviens haec atque perhorrenda

The next fourteen letters to Giustiniani, which Filelfo threaded through the first three books of the epistolario, show a changing dynamic between the two men. Time, during Filelfo's four-month sojourn in Venice, seemed to stand still. Day after day, he recorded the dwindling of his hopes, his patron's inaction and broken promises, his usurpation of Filelfo's property, his empty expressions of concern, and his vacant words of encouragement.

It was in these early letters that Filelfo introduced a theme he would bring up time and time again in his epistolario—that of his lost books.[44] Before he left Greece, Filelfo forwarded to Giustiniani several boxes containing clothing and a sizeable cache of rare codices of ancient Greek texts. As soon as he arrived in Venice, he asked for the return of his book boxes, but Giustiniani demurred. Since no letters of Giustiniani's about the books have survived, we have only Filelfo's word as to his patron's reasons for keeping the books. According to Filelfo's letters, Giustiniani was defensive and evasive. He apologized that he was unable to return the books because someone had died of the plague in the room where they were stored: now they were contaminated and would have to remain in quarantine.[45] Later when Filelfo had moved away to Bologna, Giustiniani explained that there was no point in sending Filelfo's books to him there when he would soon require them for the important new position he was to be offered in Venice.[46] And so on. Giustiniani's excuses were endless—or so Filelfo claimed.

Whatever the exchange between the two men may in fact have been, Filelfo's letters about his lost books illustrate the very different meanings that he and his patron attached to their relationship, and, moreover, to the *fides* relationship in general. It is probably true that each man felt betrayed by the other. While Filelfo considered the rare books he had bought in Greece his own property to do with as he saw fit, Giustiniani clearly thought of these books as his property: it was, after all, through his pa-

---

pestilentiae vis, qua urbem video acerbissime laborare, non impediat cogitationes meas. Non enim possum non metuere huiusmodi sagittas . . . Quo fit, ut quid me agere oporteat in tanta pernicie, non intelligam. Itaque mihi gratissimum sis facturus, si per te certior factus fuero quid mihi consilii capiundum censeas. Video enim universam propemodum civitatem ab urbe eminus abesse praeter unum te, qui Murani inter vitrea ista vasa, quasi clypeo tectus Vulcani ictus Apollinis, contemnas. Vale."

[44] The list of books Filelfo brought back from Constantinople is contained in part in Remigio Sabbadini, *Le scoperte dei codici latini e grechi ne' secoli xiv e xv* (Florence, 1905), 1.48; the whole list is given in Traversari, *Epistolae*, bk. 24, letter 32. For Filelfo's seven published letters to Giustiniani about his books, see Filelfo, *Epistolae* (17, 18, and 24 December 1427), fol. 2; (22 April 1428), fol. 4v; (1 June 1428), fol. 5; (9 April 1429), fol. 9; (15 July 1437), fol. 14. He had also sent books to two other Venetian patrons for safekeeping, Francesco Barbaro and Marco Lippomani: see *Epistolae*, to Lippomani (15 October 1427), fol. 1v; and to Barbaro (15 February 1428), fol. 4.

[45] Ibid., to Giustiniani (18 December 1427), fol. 2.

[46] Ibid. (1 June 1428), fol. 5v.

tronage that Filelfo had been able to go to Constantinople in the first place.[47]

Filelfo's struggle to recover his books from Giustiniani, carried on over a twenty-year period, exemplified the paradoxical nature of his relations with his patrons. Books were complex symbols in Quattrocento Italy. They were, before the age of printing, a rare and expensive commodity. Yet they were the common coin among friends in Filelfo's Ciceronian world of *amicitia*, and their exchange served, in the ethos of the humanists, as the great leveler of men. No matter how rich or poor, all men of letters belonged to one brotherhood. In this brotherhood, the sharing or hoarding of books became emblematic of men's conduct toward one another, and of their attitudes toward property and wealth. However, in a society in which property, wealth, personal adornment, and at least a veneer of learning were also the outward symbols of one's status, one's social identity—one's honor in Quattrocento terms—books were important signifiers. For a scholar without property, such as Filelfo, books were the chief symbols of identity. Thus, the story of his lost books has very much to do with the theme of honor in the letters.

Honor is perhaps the central theme in Filelfo's relationships with his *amici*. Cicero, as we noted earlier, perceived the *fides* relationship as conferring not only honor but also utility on its partners (*honestas et utilitas*). But the emphasis in republican Rome, as in the aristocratic culture of the Renaissance, was on honor; utility was strictly of secondary value. According to Filelfo, Giustiniani had sent him a letter arguing that, on the twin premises of honor and utility, it was his duty to remain in Venice. Filelfo took this occasion to mock the meaninglessness of Giustiniani's use of the code:

> I see that during this intolerably dangerous time I've paid full and total homage to the principle of honor, to such an extent that now more honor is owed to me than I owe to honor. The only consideration left is that of utility—and of this I know there has been none whatever since the day I returned to you from Greece to this day.[48]

The problem with the concept of honor, as Filelfo demonstrated in a sequel to this letter, was that, so often, it was just a word. After the death of one of his own slaves in February 1428, he decided to set sail for Bolo-

[47] For the conflicting views on Giustiniani's conduct in the matter of Filelfo's books, see Fenigstein, *Leonardo Giustiniani*, pp. 50–56; Calderini, *Ricerche*, 224–25; Labalme, *Bernardo Giustiniani*, pp. 36 and 42. On Giustiniani's possible commissioning of Filelfo to purchase books, see Agostini, *Notizie*, 1.141.

[48] Filelfo, *Epistolae*, to Giustiniani (24 December 1427), fol. 2: "Ego me honestati ita video satisfecisse in tanta periculorum ac tam intolerabili magnitudine, ut plus mihi honestas iam debeat quam ego honestati. Reliqua ratio est utilitatis, quam in hanc diem scio mihi fuisse nullam, posteaquam ex graecia ad vos redii."

gna in spite of his patron's advice to the contrary.[49] His next letter to Giustiniani on the subject of honor was sent from the safe distance of that city, where he had met Giovanni Corbizzi, a member of a prominent Florentine family in the wool trade, who offered to act as Filelfo's emissary in the matter of his books.[50] When Giustiniani again refused to allow Corbizzi to carry the books back to Bologna, Filelfo retaliated with the chilliest of his letters to date. Using six different derivatives of the Latin word *honor* in the space of the shortest of letters, he pounded away at Giustiniani's use of the code until he had made utter nonsense of it, mocking at the same time his protestations of affection (*caritas*). In order to convey the tone of this letter, in which politeness and insolence, deference and contempt, are confusingly interwoven, we need to look carefully at the whole text of the letter:

> Giovanni Corbicci has told me that you embrace me with best wishes and that you spoke of me not only amicably but honorably (*honorifice*). He also added that you would see to it that in the very near future I would be able to reside at either Venice or Padua in the most honorable (*honestissime*) of all circumstances, and therefore it was not necessary for you to give my books to him, since I would soon be there with you in the most honorific (*honorificentissime*) situation imaginable. Now there's nothing I count on with greater certainty than your goodwill. Therefore it should come as no surprise that you always speak and think of me amicably and honorably (*honorifice*). I am grateful to you for taking the trouble publicly and privately to see that everyone knows that you esteem me very highly. However, concerning the matter of my return to you, there is no point in your troubling yourself. For my position at Bologna is such that I could not honorably (*honeste*) leave here. Surely by now you are familiar enough with my nature to know that I consider honor (*honor*) more important than utility.[51]

[49] Ibid., to Giustiniani (11 February 1428); to Barbaro (12 February 1428); and to Barbaro (15 February 1428), all on fol. 4.

[50] Lauro Martines, *The Social World of the Florentine Humanists: 1390–1460* (Princeton, 1963), pp. 320 and 370, lists Jacopo di Niccolò Corbizzi and Giovanni di Filippo Corbizzi as members of an ancient Florentine family of merchants in the wool trade.

[51] Filelfo, *Epistolae*, to Giustiniani (1 June 1428), fol. 5v: "Narravit mihi Ioannes Corbitius quanta me benivolentia complecteris, et quam de me non modo amice sed etiam *honorifice* es locutus, Addiditque te propediem effecturum, ut vel Venetiis vel Patavii quam *honestissime* esse possem, quare non esse opus ut libros sibi meos ad me dares, cum apud vos sim quam *honorificentissime* futurus. Benivolentia tua mihi certius nihil est. Itaque mirandum non est, si de me semper amice atque *honorifice* et sentis et loqueris. Tibique habeo gratiam, quod das operam et privatim et publice, ut omnes intelligant me tibi esse carissimum. De me autem ad vos reditu nihil est hoc tempore quod labores. Ea enim mihi apud Bononienses conditio est ut hinc *honeste* abire non liceat. Nosti tu sane iampridem meum ingenium quam pluris facio quod *honestum* est quam quod utile . . ." The emphases are mine. I have corrected the Latin

Filelfo did not write Giustiniani again for a full year, according to the *Epistolae*, and then it was only to tell him he would be moving on to Florence—and to remind him to take good care of his books.[52] Lecturing at the university of Bologna had proved far less safe than waiting out the plague in Venice. Not long after his arrival there, he had found himself caught in the midst of a civil war. In February 1429 he wrote Leonardo Bruni, then the chancellor of the Florentine republic, that torture, mutilation, and executions of ordinary citizens were now daily occurrences in Bologna's marketplaces.

> I am beset by the worst anxieties; nor do I know what plan I should adopt— unless you think I perhaps like the daily sight of swords and savagery, where some are hung by the neck with nooses, some are mutilated, others are drawn and quartered, stabbed or otherwise slain. No need to write more. Everything is wet with the blood of men.[53]

Now, writing on the eve of his departure for Florence, in April 1429, he had to worry that his situation would be equally precarious at the Studio, though he made no mention to Giustiniani of any qualms he might have harbored. A costly war with Milan from 1424 to 1428 had all but drained dry the Florentine treasury, and now only a year later, Florentine troops had marched on Lucca, where they would be embroiled in another four years of war.[54]

By 1430 the Luccan war was already going badly for Florence. At home, the issues of the war and its conduct were becoming the focus of a widening division among the Florentines themselves. The principal factions were the Medici, who at the time leaned toward tightening Florence's alliance with Venice as a bulwark against Milanese expansionism, and the Albizzi who, regarding Venice with suspicion, wished to reach an early settlement with Milan on Lucca.[55] Filelfo's worsening relations with Giustiniani and his increasingly tenuous position at the Florentine Studio reflected this division. As the war ran its course Filelfo became more and more closely identified with the Albizzi party. Indeed, the letters Filelfo included in his *epistolario* from this period reflect an effort on his part to tighten his earlier

---

text from Trivulzianus, since the printed editions have garbled the text here: Venice 1502 reads *sit* instead of *sim*; the 1473 Venice edition reads *darem* for *dares*.

[52] Filelfo, *Epistolae*, to Giustiniani (9 April 1429), fol. 9.

[53] Ibid., to Leonardo Bruni (15 February 1429), fols. 8–8v.

[54] On the Luccan war, see Lawrence W. Belle, *A Renaissance Patrician: Palla di Nofri Strozzi, 1372–1462* (Ph.D. dissertation, University of Rochester, 1971), pp. 279–87; Belle suggests that military expenditures alone may have cost Florence over 3,500,000 florins during the 1424–1428 war with Milan (p. 274); see also A. Pellegrini, "Tre anni di guerra le reppubliche di Firenze e di Lucca (1430–1433)," in *Studi e documenti di storia e diritto* 19, pt. 1 (1898).

[55] On the factionalism occasioned by the war, see Belle, *A Renaissance Patrician*; and D. Kent, *The Rise of the Medici*, pp. 256–88.

ties with certain influential friends at the Milanese court, such as Visconti's ambassador Niccolò Arcimboldi and Antonio Beccadelli, then the court poet at the Visconti court.[56]

In the meantime, by the spring of 1431 it appeared that Giustiniani's patronage of Filelfo was turning into a violent settling of accounts. As we shall see later, almost as soon as Filelfo arrived at the university in Florence, his relationships with certain members of the university community were precarious. Among these was the influential scholar and general of the Camaldulensian Order, Ambrogio Traversari, who during this period maintained almost constant contact with Giustiniani. Filelfo's alienation from Giustiniani, and perhaps from other members of the Venetian patriciate such as Francesco Barbaro and Marco Lippomani, reached a climactic point in March 1431. On the tenth of that month, the Florentines issued a decree ordering Filelfo's expulsion from their city and his incarceration in Rome for a three-year period for "having spoken slanderously and recklessly" of their ally and friend, the Venetian republic.[57] The decree was subsequently revoked, but in October of the same year the directors of the Studio removed Filelfo from his university chair, replacing him with Carlo Marsuppini, a man who was among those closest to Cosimo de' Medici at the time. Though Filelfo was able to resecure his appointment at the university at the end of 1431, the stage was set nonetheless for the humiliation he would suffer two years later when he walked into the Borgo S. Jacopo Oltarno one morning, on his way to the university.[58]

The mortifying order for Filelfo's deportation from Florence in March 1431 is nowhere mentioned in his published letters, and his subsequent dismissal from the Studio he simply recast in the *Epistolae* as no more than an abortive attempt on the regents' part to cancel the entire humanities program at the university due to the mounting costs of the Luccan war.[59] But, as we noted before, any event in his life that seemed to diminish the image he sought to project of himself as the super-professor, the poet and counselor to kings, he either represented in a light more flattering to himself or simply deleted from his *Epistolae*.

Filelfo's last letters to Giustiniani, purportedly written after his departure from Florence in 1434, take a more amicable tone toward his former

[56] Filelfo, *Epistolae*, to Arcimboldi, fols. 10–10v; to Beccadelli, fol. 10v; see also ibid., to Cardinal Niccolò Albergati, fols. 10v–11, soliciting his assistance to obtain a post at the Visconti court.

[57] The decree and a second decree revoking the first one are published in Fabroni, *Cosmi Medicei vita*, 2.69; see also Rosmini, *Vita*, 2.43.

[58] Rosmini, *Vita*, 1.54ff.

[59] Filelfo, *Epistolae*, to Cosimo de' Medici (1 May 1433), fols. 12–12v, tells the story of Filelfo's brave and ultimately successful championing of the humanities at the Studio, in the face of almost universal opposition from the Medici party.

patron—with one notable exception dated 15 July 1437. One wonders why Filelfo, at this late date, inserted such a virulently bitter letter, rebuking his patron once again about his books.[60] His reopening of this old wound after seven years of silence on the point seems so strange that we must assume he included it to add fiber to his own self-portrait. Certainly he positioned this incongruous letter strategically, at the close of his volume of letters from Florence (Book 2), to demonstrate that in his dealings with his patrons it was he who would ultimately call the shots. The letter was also a sad reminder, however, that in his relations with Giustiniani and men like him, he was unlikely to experience anything more than a series of disappointments.

> I do not know by what right you so immure yourself, that contrary to every law of friendship and polite society you fail to restore my books and clothing to me. For it had once been the mark of your justness—you who *call* yourself "the just one"—that whatever I left with you and entrusted to your word you restored to me for the sake of your own honor and righteousness. Therefore I beseech and warn you not to cheat me any longer with empty hope, not to cause me further pain, and not to force me to forget our longtime friendship. Vale.[61]

Aurispa: Gypsy Scholar and Antimodel

The Sicilian Giovanni Aurispa, born in Noto in 1376, played the role of antimodel, colleague, confidante, and foil for Filelfo in the letterbook.[62]

---

[60] The letter reviving the book dispute is in ibid., to Giustiniani (15 July 1437), fol. 14; the amicable letters to Giustiniani surrounding it are (9 January 1431), fol. 10; (31 January 1435), fol. 13; (15 October 1438), fols. 16v–17; (1 May 1440), fol. 21v. Prior to these letters, Trivulzianus, fol. 33, contains an additional letter to Giustiniani, dated 1 January 1435, which is not contained in the printed editions. Certainly it is the most unflattering commentary on the methods and personality of Cosimo de' Medici among the letters. Here Filelfo represents Cosimo as corrupt, unjust, and completely insincere; according to the picture that Filelfo paints here, Cosimo is no better than a common thief. Since the printed edition was being prepared in the early 1470s, when Lorenzo had become Filelfo's chief patron, it makes sense that the humanist would naturally be careful to edit out of the letterbook anything too offensive to the Medici.

[61] Filelfo, *Epistolae*: "Nescio quo tandem iure te adeo offirmaris, ut contra omne vel amiciciae vel humanitatis ius meos libros ac vestis non restituas. Tuae enim iusticiae fuerat—qui te Iustinianum cognomines—ut quae apud te deposueram tuaeque fidei commendaram, mihi pro tua fide tuaque innocentia restitueres. Quare te et hortor et moneo ne me diutius vana spe ludas, ne iniuria me afficias, ne me veteris amiciciae nostrae oblivisci cogas. Vale."

[62] Remigio Sabbadini, *Carteggio di Giovanni Aurispa* (Rome, 1931). Aurispa was a member of the papal court in Rome from 1419 to 1421; at the end of 1421 he made a second trip to the Orient, and in 1423 he returned to Constantinople. He taught at Florence in 1425–1427;

He, too, had come to the more prosperous cities of the north, without friends or patrons, to seek employment as a teacher and a scholar. Aurispa had also been in Constantinople in the early 1420s, though he was the first of the two men to assemble a sizeable library of Greek books in that city, using his books as Filelfo would later do to attract job offers when he returned to Italy. In 1425, he had preceded Filelfo in one of the few academic positions that had, in those years, an air of glamour about it—the Chair of Greek at the Florentine Studio. With Aurispa's arrival at the Este court in Ferrara in 1427 and Filelfo's move to Bologna the following year, the two men continued to lead look-alike careers.

The Greek-speaking gypsy scholar trod the same path as Filelfo, yet was everything Filelfo was not. In Filelfo's hands, Aurispa is a cartoon of a man—a Sicilian sophist as ready to sell his manuscripts as his learning. Burckhardt's classic description of the humanists comes to mind:

> They were a crowd of the most miscellaneous sort wearing one face today and another tomorrow; but they clearly felt . . . they formed a wholly new element in society. The *clerici vagantes* of the twelfth century . . . may be perhaps taken as their forerunners—[they led] the same unstable existence.[63]

Filelfo's cycle of twelve letters to Aurispa in Books 1–3 forms a counterpoint to the Giustiniani letter cycle. Nothing could be more different in tone from the letters to his one-time patron than these to his colleague. Gone in the Aurispa letters is the vocabulary of patronage, and with it the stiff, formal invocations of friendship, honor, and loyalty. Instead, the Aurispa letters convey an easy familiarity, a rib-prodding teasing, and a sense of complicity natural to two men engaged in the same business.

Filelfo and Aurispa had kept in touch with one another since their meeting at the court of John Paleologus in Constantinople in the early 1420s.[64] When Filelfo left Venice in February 1428 on his way to Bologna, he made a point of stopping at the Este court in Ferrara to visit his old friend. As soon as he arrived in Bologna, Aurispa was the first to be regaled with the details of his warm reception. An "enormous" crowd had turned out to meet him, and the papal envoy, Cardinal Ludovico Alamanni, had entertained him lavishly. On top of everything else, he was looking forward to being paid what he considered a decent salary.[65]

In May of that year, Filelfo again turned first to Aurispa, to confide the

---

at Ferrara in 1428–1435, in Bologna in 1436, at Ferrara again in 1438–1439, and at Florence in 1443. He died in 1459.

[63] Jacob Burckhardt, *The Civilization of the Renaissance in Italy*, 2 vols. (Reprint. New York, 1958), 1.211.

[64] Filelfo, *Epistolae*, to Aurispa (23 December 1427), fol. 3.

[65] Ibid., to Aurispa (23 February 1428), fol. 4.

news that rumblings of civil war were in the air in Bologna.[66] At the end of summer, Filelfo reported that the palace of Cardinal Ludovico Alamanni had been sacked and street fighting had broken out in the city. He would have to go on the move again. "Everything is fraught with storms and stormwinds here, nor is there room for serenity or peace of mind amid the tides of discord and sedition," he told his friend.[67]

The second of two prefatory letters to Book 2, dated 31 July 1429, came to Aurispa from Florence.[68] Aurispa, who three years earlier had been forced from his chair at the Studio, and who had commented bitterly that "the place was full of fools and the envious," must have smiled at his friend's first impressions of the city.[69] Filelfo's long and glowing letter praising the Florentines and their city presaged, however, the beginning of the same cycle of hope and disillusionment, and the same disintegration of civic harmony that Filelfo had witnessed in Bologna. He boasted, if uneasily, about his high salary and the crowds that thronged to hear him lecture on Greek literature, and the court paid him by Florence's two most prominent citizens, Cosimo de' Medici and Palla Strozzi. It was clear from the first, though, that rival factions were already dividing the city and the university into two warring camps. Although he would later formulate the conflicts that he noted between the members of the two major factions, the Albizzi and the Medici, in political terms, he perceived them in this first letter purely as personal animosities.[70] Carlo Marsuppini, Niccolò Niccoli, and the monk Traversari had tried to elicit his aid against Leonardo Bruni, then chancellor of the city, whose learning and integrity they obviously envied. Right from the first, he had taken the role of a partisan, he confessed. He would defend the chancellor, he told Aurispa, from all such slings.

Two years later, on 13 December 1432, Filelfo wrote Aurispa a letter from Florence, recalling his experiences during his last months in Bologna.[71] The great city of Florence was being rent asunder by factions, he wrote, and as in a sea storm, it seemed to swell and rock with the rage of its citizens.[72] Many years later, Filelfo would again resort to the Vergilian

[66] Ibid., to Aurispa (27 May 1428), fol. 5: "Nam nescio quid monstri inter hos inter se cives latere audio."

[67] Ibid., to Aurispa (15 September 1428), fol. 7.

[68] Ibid. (31 July 1429), fols. 9–9v. This letter is part of bk. 1 in Trivulzianus, fols. 14v–15; it is clear that Filelfo placed it in bk. 2 in the revised edition of the letterbook because he wanted to use it as a programmatic letter for the themes and events in this book.

[69] The full text of this letter (dated February 1426), from which I have quoted here, is in Sabbadini, *Carteggio*, p. 41.

[70] A more sophisticated view of Florentine politics can be seen, for example, in Filelfo, *Epistolae*, to Niccolò Albergati, Cardinal of Bologna (22 September 1432), fols. 10v–11.

[71] Ibid., to Aurispa (13 December 1432), fol. 11.

[72] Ibid.: "Universa haec civitas factionibus tumet."

imagery of the voyage in his letters to Aurispa from Milan. "The whole atmosphere is turbulent," he would write after the death of his patron, Duke Filippo Maria Visconti, in 1447.[73] "I sail amid the Syrtes, and I must be very much afraid during the journey lest I be drowned or perish in the shipwreck," he told Aurispa, confiding his worst fears to his old friend.[74]

As in Filelfo's correspondence with Giustiniani, books and their exchange served here as an emblem for the reciprocity involved in both friendship and learning itself. In a series of four letters, Filelfo built up a characterization of Aurispa as a money-grubbing bookseller, engaged solely in marketing and profit making rather than reading and literature—in "mercatura, non lectura."[75] Though wealth in the fifteenth century was, as Lauro Martines has shown, a decisive factor in the conferring of honor and status, at the same time it had to be obtained "honorably." To amass money either too quickly, or by means of excessive profit making, was considered dishonorable.[76]

Previous writers have all commented that Filelfo was more generous with his books than Aurispa, and that the Sicilian was really a bookdealer rather than a teacher or scholar. But these conclusions lean too much on Filelfo's representations of Aurispa. The point that needs to be made here is that in depicting him in this one-dimensional manner, Filelfo used Aurispa for his own purposes. In the adaptation of a tradition as old as Plato's denigration of the Sophists, Filelfo was careful to etch in these letters a new image for himself as an aristocrat and a philosopher—he was a scholar who exemplified the principle of honor while he scorned that of utility. In any case, the tone throughout these letters is anything but serious, and depends upon the casting of punning, laconic insults modeled on the epigrams of Martial.

In a series of letters he wrote to Aurispa during what was perhaps the first carefree period he had ever experienced, under the protection of the duke of Milan in the 1440s, Filelfo polished his Martialian abuse. He painted his correspondence with his Sicilian friend as a battle of wits in which he strove not only to prove his own magnanimity, and thus his honor and gentility, but also to show himself the cleverer rhetorician of the two. In the first of these letters Filelfo wrote, "You are always asking for

---

[73] Ibid., to Aurispa (1 September 1447), fol. 40v: "Omnia sunt turbulenta . . ."

[74] Ibid., to Aurispa (25 July 1449), fol. 43v: "In Syrtibus navigo . . . et inter navigandum ne obruar ac peream naufragio, plurimum est metuendum." See also the letter that Filelfo wrote to Aurispa shortly before the Ambrosian republic fell: ibid. (15 October 1449), fol. 46: "Tota haec civitas fluctuat. Nec reliquum est quod expectetur praeter ultimum naufragium." ("This whole state pitches and rolls. Nothing else can be awaited except the final shipwreck.")

[75] Ibid., to Aurispa (15 December 1439), fol. 20v; (9 July 1440), fol. 22; (12 June 1441), fol. 32; (23 August 1448), fol. 41v.

[76] Martines, *The Social World*, pp. 18 and 26–27.

something, but you seldom reciprocate."[77] In a sequel to this letter, he continued the game. "You," he began, "are totally occupied with selling books; I'd prefer it were with reading. If you were, you'd do a lot more for yourself and the Muses. For what good is it to buy and sell books—but never read them?"[78]

The brief note on the book theme that Filelfo sent Aurispa on 12 June 1441—in the heyday of his residence at the Visconti court—perhaps represented, with its easy rhyming, tight paradox, and sound play, the perfection of his epigrammatic style. But Filelfo's moralizing—on the reciprocity and generosity of the "good client" versus the hypocrisy of the bad—was drearily the same: "No one is quicker on the take than you—or slower on the other end. You make a great fuss over my generosity: you pontificate on this virtue in a lecture—and rightly. But why don't you practice what you seem to love so much?"[79]

Traversari: Monk and Saboteur

A rough give-and-take marked the friendships of over thirty years' standing that Filelfo sustained with both Giustiniani and Aurispa. His letters to both men indicate that fallings out and misunderstandings arose from time to time, but in the end there was always a rapprochement. Filelfo's relationship with Ambrogio Traversari, on the other hand, was proof that friendship and patronage could just as easily turn into bitter and lasting enmity. In the mythology of Quattrocento Florence, Ambrogio Traversari and Francesco Filelfo were two characters as unlike one another as one could imagine: the virgin and the whore. Vespasiano had remarked of Traversari, "Everybody held him to be a virgin, through his having gone into this monastery pure and undefiled at an early age, and having lived

---

[77] Filelfo, *Epistolae*, to Aurispa (15 December 1439), fol. 20v.: "Tu semper aliquid petis. Inservis autem raro . . . Ibit enim codex ille ad te mutuo non dono. Quam ob rem facito, ut ex commodo tuo, nihil mihi tandem incommodes."

[78] Ibid., to Aurispa (9 July 1440), fol. 22: "Totus es in librorum mercatura, sed in lectura mallem. Quod si faceres, longe melius et tibi et Musis consultum esset. Quid enim prodest libros quottidie, nunc emere, nunc vendere, legere vero nunquam."

[79] Ibid., to Aurispa (12 June 1441), fol. 32: "Nemo te uno accipiendo facilior: te rursus nemo difficilior dando. Tu me liberalitatis plurimum laudas. Et hanc virtutem extollis oratione ac recte tu quidem. Caeterum quam ipse virtutem tanti facere videris, cur eam minus amplecteris? . . ." My translations of the letters to Aurispa are freer than elsewhere, in the interest of capturing some of the terseness and sound effects in the Latin. Filelfo wrote what was obviously a variation on this prose epigram some years later. Ibid. (23 August 1448), fol. 41v: "Te uno mi Aurispa nemo est in accipiendo liberalior, in dando autem nemo rursus avarior. Quare ne prodigus possim a quoquam iudicari, quod a me petis ad te non ibit." This is the reading of Trivulzianus, fol. 83. Venice 1502 reads "ne possim pro iure iudicari," which makes no sense. Other incunable editions have the correct reading.

forty years in this cloister."[80] As for Filelfo, who would one day jokingly refer to himself as "the poet with three testicles," a story about his having had an affair with his professor's wife in Constantinople was already circulating in Florence long before his arrival.[81]

Traversari himself seems to have been the author of the story of Filelfo's adultery, at least in Florence. As early as 1424, he gossiped to Niccolò Niccoli that Guarino had seemed stung to hear that the latter's eminent teacher's (Manuel Chrysoloras's) sister-in-law's "virtue had been up for sale," and that "she had preferred an adulterer [Filelfo]" to her own husband.[82] Thus, it was a strange trick of fate that, when Palla Strozzi, Cosimo, and Niccoli made up their minds that Filelfo was the man they needed at the Studio, it fell to Traversari, and to Leonardo Bruni too—since they were the most eminent Florentine scholars in Filelfo's field—to initiate the correspondence with Filelfo, and to begin the business of negotiating the terms of his employment.[83]

Traversari, who was close to fifty when the thirty-one-year-old Filelfo arrived in Florence, could not help but envy the younger man's fluency in Greek, his personal charisma, and his ease before a crowd. The monk, by comparison, had once become so rattled, according to Vespasiano, that he broke down in the middle of his speech in an assembly at the Council of Basel.[84] At all events, the monk would play no small role in driving a wedge between Cosimo de' Medici and Filelfo that would lead to his nearly lifelong exile from the Arno city.

When Filelfo left Venice he had risked permanently alienating his benefactor Leonardo Giustiniani. Once he was in Florence, he strained further whatever ties still bound him to his former patron by continuing to air his resentment over Giustiniani's refusal to return his books.[85] Meanwhile

---

[80] Vespasiano, *Renaissance Princes, Popes, and Prelates*, trans. W. George and E. Waters with an intro. by M. Gilmore (New York, 1963).

[81] Filelfo claimed he was *triorchēs*, triple-testicled, exceptionally sexually active; see also in Rosmini, *Vita*, 1.113, an unedited epigram from Filelfo's *De iocis et Seriis*, in which Filelfo calls himself "vates tribus testibus."

[82] Traversari, *Epistolae*, bk. 8, letter 9: "Nuper a Guarino accepi literas, quibus vehementer in fortunam invehitur, quod filiam clarissimi vir Ioannis Chrysolorae is acceperit exterus . . . , quaeriturque substomachans uxorem Chrysolorae venalem pudicitiam, moechumque antea habuisse quam socerum." Guarino's alleged letter about the affair has not survived (if it ever existed), nor do we have any contemporary testimony on its existence. Rosmini, *Vita*, 1.17 n. 1 and G. Tiraboschi, *Storia della lettera italiana*, 4 vols. (Milan, 1772–), p. 1005, both questioned the authenticity of the letter. Poggio's Fourth Invective against Filelfo does repeat Traversari's story of the adultery: see the text in E. Walser, *Poggius Florentinus: Leben und Werke* (Leipzig, 1914); but Poggio's invectives against Filelfo are notoriously fictitious, and he is clearly using Traversari for his source material in this case.

[83] Belle, *A Renaissance Patrician*, p. 165.

[84] Vespasiano, *Princes, Popes, and Prelates*, p. 209.

[85] See Traversari, *Epistolae*, to Giustiniani (August 1429), bk. 6, letter 28: Traversari in fact informed Giustiniani immediately of Filelfo's grumblings to him about the book dispute.

Traversari, a man who posed as Filelfo's friend and broker, was busy doing everything he could to damage Filelfo's image in the eyes of his Venetian friends, Giustiniani and Francesco Barbaro, and no doubt with Cosimo and his circle as well.[86]

Filelfo had delivered his opening lecture at the Studio to a packed house. The report that Traversari sent to Giustiniani by courier about the event in May 1429 was innocuous enough, though it called to mind Guarino's complaint about the coolness toward outsiders that he experienced among the Florentine literati: "No one gives praise except with blunted and slighting phrases . . . If they know you praise someone they do not like, they grumble, make faces, and as if the praise given to others would take away one's own praise, they resent those who receive praise, and carp at those who give it."[87]

"I was not able to attend his lecture myself," Traversari wrote of Filelfo's debut, "so I cannot give you a first-hand report. He did draw a crowd; but the verdict on him among the learned varied."[88] Traversari's next letter to Giustiniani, however, left little doubt that he would do whatever he could to chip away at the younger man's reputation. "Filelfo's got something about him—quite a lot really," the monk remarked, "of the Greeks' levity, and this combined with vanity. . . . He makes great claims for himself. But among those who are actually acquainted with the merchandise he has to sell, as are you—and all too well—he would serve himself better if he spoke more sparingly about himself."[89]

And as to the "merchandise" he deprecatingly alluded to, Traversari made it clear to Giustiniani that there was not much there either. Filelfo— so he claimed—had hounded him in his cell at Santa Maria degli Angeli because he could not translate certain passages from Greek to Latin without the monk's help.[90] So urgent in fact was Filelfo's need for his help, according to Traversari, that he even offered to pay the monk for his tutoring—with a book. But worse still, once again Filelfo's indecorous conduct had offended him. No matter how firm Traversari tried to be, the younger man's "rudeness" (*improbitas*) always seemed to win out over the monk's gentility and good breeding.[91]

---

[86] See Traversari, *Epistolae*, bk. 6, letters 28–41. The monk's copious correspondence with Giustiniani and Barbaro during this period reveals his calculated defamation of Filelfo; we may be sure that whatever he was writing to his Venetian friends he was *saying* to Cosimo, Niccoli, and company.

[87] Remigio Sabbadini, *Vita di Guarino Veronese* (Turin, 1964), 1.18.

[88] Traversari, *Epistolae*, to Giustiniani (May 1429), bk. 6, letter 34.

[89] Ibid., letter 26: ". . . Nonnihil, immo vero plurimum habet Graecae levitatis, et vanitatis admixtum . . . Magna de se pollicetur. Sed apud eos, qui (ut ipse quoque verissime sentis) huiusce merces probe callent, melius consuleret sibi, si parcius de se loqueretur . . ."

[90] Ibid. (14 October 1430), letter 30.

[91] Ibid.

But Filelfo was just as capable of dissembling. While he made an out-ward show of respect and gratitude to the monk's face, he sniped at him in most of the letters he wrote Aurispa after he arrived in Florence, though some of these gossipy asides—which were usually in Greek—were ulti-mately excised from the printed editions of the *Epistolae*. Even before he arrived in Florence, Filelfo ridiculed a letter Traversari had written him in Greek, telling Aurispa that his usage was completely "un-Greek."[92] Once he was in Florence, he complained to Aurispa that the monk criticized people behind their backs in a way that was "not the mark of a good man."[93]

For the most part, however, Filelfo took care to suppress in his pub-lished letters the respectful, and sometimes even servile, letters he had writ-ten to the monk during the courtship phase of their relationship before his arrival in Florence.[94] Indeed, the letters to Traversari that Filelfo selected to include in the *Epistolae* ranged in tone from distant to hostile—with one exception. Filelfo's letter of 20 June 1428 differed from all his later letters to the monk, because of his extreme modesty in this instance, his obvious respect, and even warmth toward the man:

> Because you pursue me sight unseen, with such kindness that you seem already not only to esteem me, but even to love me, I am singularly thankful to you. For you are a kind and gentle person by nature. The praises you give me, however, I ascribe to your kindness and goodness. For I am really not a man of whom you should think so highly. Thus I have every reason to believe that you are an exceptionally good person, since you say I have the qualities of a man who is very erudite, very eloquent, and wise—a man of the very sort I discern you as being, judging from both your letters. May God grant your wish, that at some time or other we may be able to meet face-to-face and that we may be able to enjoy a most delightful conversation . . .[95]

After this letter the tide changed, for Filelfo made no attempt to address Traversari in public until January 1433. But already in 1429, we should recall, Filelfo's letters to Aurispa had indicated that he had been suspicious, even at the outset, of the monk's show of friendship toward him.[96] Late in 1430, when the bubonic plague struck Florence again, Cosimo fled to Ve-rona accompanied by Traversari's close friends Niccolò Niccoli and Carlo Marsuppini. When Cosimo and his entourage returned to the city in March of 1431, at the height of the Luccan war, certain of the Medici *amici* moved to have Filelfo dismissed from his teaching post at the university

[92] Filelfo, *Epistolae*, to Aurispa (8 April 1428), fol. 4v.
[93] Ibid., to Aurispa (31 July 1429), fols. 9–9v.
[94] Traversari, *Epistolae* (June 1428–May 1429), bk. 24, letters 30–41, cols. 1008–17.
[95] Filelfo, *Epistolae*, to Traversari (28 June 1428), fol. 5v.
[96] Ibid., to Aurispa (31 July 1429), fols. 9–9v.

and deported from Florence—two events that, as we noted before, Filelfo suppressed in the *Epistolae*.[97] Though Filelfo managed to get himself reinstated two months later, after 1431 he became increasingly alienated from the Medici faction.

It was soon after Cosimo and his friends returned from Verona that Traversari launched the bitterest of his attacks to date against Filelfo in a letter to Francesco Barbaro. The letter was sent to Barbaro as a response to a speech that Filelfo had made ridiculing the monk's friend and mentor Niccolò Niccoli.[98] Traversari's extravagantly rhetorical exposition in this letter of Niccoli's virtues and Filelfo's faults, his florid use of antithetical epithets for the two men, and his abundant use of superlatives all set this work apart from his usual spare reportage and place the letter firmly within the tradition of the invective. Thus Filelfo's disgraceful abuse, his penchant for discord, and his maniacal lunacy serve rhetorically in the passage I quote here, as a foil for Niccoli's constant righteousness, extraordinary kindness, great enthusiasm, and selfless concern for others—to the point "almost of slavishness." Could this be the same Niccoli whose abrasive manner, it has generally been agreed, hastened the departure from Florence of Filelfo's three predecessors at the Studio—Chrysoloras, Guarino, and Aurispa?

> For Niccolò never behaved toward Francesco, that I can recall, with anything but the utmost kindness, the greatest enthusiasm, and unassuming concern, with the result that his manner seemed almost to border on slavishness . . . Yes, Francesco is inclined to hunt up all of the most trivial occasions and causes which might possibly provide breeding grounds for discord . . .
>
> Filelfo vomited up an invective against Niccolò . . . which is indeed the most foul, impudent, and bitter of all the speeches I have ever read . . . His oration, I wrote him, would bring the worst ignominy upon himself, and it would arouse the indignation of all good men for whom Niccolò's life has always been a model of righteousness and chastity from boyhood on. . . .
>
> Such disgusting, disgraceful abuse would not be acceptable to decent men even if it were aimed at a scoundrel or some parasitical do-nothing. So, I continued to beg, plead, and implore Filelfo not to hound, not to wound a man who had been an irreproachable friend, and whom he knew to be the most excellent of men. Well, what I actually accomplished with these pleas with which I strove to dispel the madness of that lunatic was as follows . . .[99]

---

[97] Fabroni, *Vita Cosmi Medicei*, 2.69; Rosmini, *Vita*, 1.43; Belle, *A Renaissance Patrician*, p. 167; Vespasiano, *Princes, Popes, and Prelates*, p. 408, remarks that it was Filelfo's known partisanship that caused him to be expelled from Florence in 1434.

[98] Charles L. Stinger, *Humanism and the Church Fathers: Ambrogio Traversari (1386–1439) and Christian Antiquity in the Italian Renaissance* (Albany, 1977), has documented Traversari's longstanding loyalty to Niccoli.

[99] Traversari, *Epistolae*, to Barbaro (undated), letter 21, bk. 6: "Quum [Nicolaus] enim

Nor was Filelfo unaware, as factional tension continued to mount in 1431 and 1432 in the city, that Traversari's cell at the convent of S. Maria degli Angeli had become the regular meeting place for a group of scholars, including Gianozzo Manetti, Marsuppini, Niccoli, and both Lorenzo and Cosimo de' Medici, who ardently opposed Filelfo's tenure at the university.[100] In fact, Filelfo's letters after his reinstatement in 1432 make it clear that, between the daily taunts he suffered and the more serious worry he had about his physical safety, his position at the Studio had become increasingly untenable.[101] His letter to Traversari of 20 January 1433, the first since his thoroughly deferential one in 1428, reflected the radical change that his relationship with his former patron and colleague had undergone. The letter began with the statement, heavy with irony, that while he had always found the monk's letters "much to his liking," he was far more delighted with this letter than he had ever been, since this one "shows me with perfect clarity of whom I need to beware." It was in this letter that Filelfo drew up the battle lines between himself and Traversari's friends. "Although I am hurt by the injury done me," he wrote, "I will not strike back at anyone, and I will remember that I am a man."[102]

Filelfo's letter of 4 May 1433 to Traversari, coming after a three-month silence, was nonetheless the sequel to his January letter. Traversari, still acting as Cosimo's broker, had relayed Cosimo's message that Filelfo should neither fear nor be on the lookout for any evil.[103] In view of the 18 May stabbing of Filelfo, for which he would always in some measure hold

nihil ante illum [Franciscum], quod ego reminisci possum, manarit, praeter indicia summae benevolentiae, summum studium, observationemque adeo submissam, ut servituti fere propinqua videretur. . . . [Franciscus] causas omnes, immo occasiones omnes, levissimas licet, aucupari studiose nisus est, quae discordiae possent esse seminaria . . . Evomuitque orationem in illum [Nicolaum] . . . omnium, quas unquam legerim, teterrimam, impudentissimam, atque acerbissimam . . . Rescripsi . . . admonens illum [Philelphum] . . . ista oratio summum sibi dedecus, indignationemque bonorum omnium pareret, quibus nota vita Nicolai est, hactenus iam tunc a pueritia pudicissime acta semper, atque honestissime . . . Non placere sobriis auribus maledicta tam foeda, tam turpia, ne si in scurram aliquem, et circumforaneum nebulonem iaciantur; ceteraque in hunc modum, orans, obsecrans, obtestans, ut dolori, quem summum esse non ignoraret, parceret, amicum integerrimum istis iaculis non insectaretur. Quid autem istis adhortationibus, quibus furibundi insaniam excantare nitebar perfecerim, audi . . ."

[100] Belle, *A Renaissance Patrician*, p. 167.

[101] Filelfo, *Epistolae*, to Cardinal Niccolò Albergati, fols. 10v–11; to Tommaso da Sarzana, fol. 11; and see also the unedited letters in Trivulzianus to Antonio Petrucci, Manetti, Palla Strozzi, and Giustiniani in Rosmini, *Vita*, 2.135–39.

[102] Filelfo, *Epistolae*, to Traversari (20 January 1433), fol. 11: "Litterae mihi tuae semper gratissimae fuerunt, et in praesentia quam antea longe gratiores. Indicant enim dilucide ab quibus mihi cavendum sit. Verum utar equidem more meo ut et nemini noceam et, lacessitus iniuria, me virum esse meminerim. Vale."

[103] Ibid., to Traversari (4 May 1433), fols. 12v–13: "Mihi non modo non esse formidandum mali quicquam ne cavendum quidem."

Cosimo responsible, every sentence of this letter must be read ironically.[104] Certainly, he wrote, "nothing should be more trustworthy in my eyes than Cosimo's word." "Why then," he asked, in a remark designed to be unsettling, "does Cosimo's brother Lorenzo avert his face whenever he passes me—and why when I greet him does he say nothing at all in return?"[105]

After 1433 the letterbook contains no further letters to Traversari until 1 October 1437. A great deal had happened since 1433. On 18 May of that year Filelfo had been stabbed in the face on his way to the Studio, in Florence. There had been a coup d'état in September of that year, and Cosimo was expelled from the city, only to be recalled with his party the following year. Numerous alleged anti-Mediceans had been forced to flee the city, and Filelfo had retreated to Siena. In May 1436, Filelfo's tranquility was again threatened when he learned that the same man who had attacked him in Florence had followed him to Siena.[106] Following a tip from Filelfo, the Sienese police apprehended the suspect before he found Filelfo, and he was convicted by the Sienese Podestà of having plotted to kill Filelfo. Again Filelfo accused Cosimo of instigating the attack, but this time no evidence was found linking the alleged assassin to the Medici.[107] It was in this context that Filelfo had received a letter sometime in 1437 from Traversari who, once again acting as Cosimo's agent and broker, wrote to explore the possibility of a reconciliation. For Cosimo things may have gone far enough, but for Filelfo it had become a matter of his honor. He wrote back saying that Traversari could tell Cosimo that the assassin Filippo had already shown him enough of his master's "goodwill," and that regardless of Cosimo's wish to convey his greetings with swords and poison, he, Filelfo, would retaliate with only a pen and his wits.[108]

But here again he was not quite telling the truth. Despairing of seeing justice done by legitimate means, Filelfo had, in the fall of 1436, joined with a group of Florentine exiles in Siena to hire an assassin to kill Cosimo, Carlo Marsuppini, and Girolamo Brocchardi. Almost as soon as the assas-

---

[104] The description of the 18 May 1433 stabbing (which Filelfo referred to as an assassination attempt) is in Filelfo, *Epistolae*, to Piccolomini (28 March 1939), fols. 17–17v.

[105] Ibid., to Traversari (4 May 1433), fol. 13: "Verum miror quid Laurentius Cosmi frater, quotiens in me incidit, semper obliquat faciem, salutatusque a me, respondet omnino nihil. Sed quoniam Cosmi fide debet mihi certius esse nihil. . . ."

[106] The story of the second alleged assassination attempt is also told in ibid., to Piccolomini (28 March 1439), fols. 17–17v; in Rosmini, *Vita*, 2.81–86; and in L. Feo Corso, "Il Filelfo in Siena," in *Bollettino di storia patria* 47 (1940): 181–209 and 292–316; the article includes transcriptions of the court proceedings (pp. 300–306).

[107] Filelfo, *Epistolae*, to Piccolomini, fol. 17v.

[108] Ibid., to Traversari (1 October 1437), fol. 14v: ". . . Istius in me benivolentiam, Philippus sicarius declarat. Itaque de reconcilianda gratia mihi posthac verbum nullum facito. Sicis ipse venenisque utatur. Ego autem ingenio et calamo." (1502 ed.: scis; Trivulzianus: sicis.)

sin set foot in Florence, however, he was arrested, and the plot was thus foiled.[109]

Filelfo's last letter to Traversari in the *Epistolae*, supposedly mailed from Siena on 14 December 1437, formally brought both the correspondence and the friendship between the two men to a close. As in many a relationship between patron and client of the period, Filelfo's feelings toward Traversari had in these five letters spanned the gamut of emotions, from the first letter, in which the young man, buoyed by hope, respectfully courted the monk, to this note in which he closes the door on all future overtures from this former friend. Although what first strikes us here is Filelfo's repudiation of one of the most powerful men in Italy, it is also clear that invective of this sort provided Filelfo with the opportunity to display what had become a stock weapon in his epistolary arsenal—the unilateral dismissal of an enemy: "I shall respond briefly to your rather prolix letter. I have no wish for Cosimo de' Medici's friendship; his feuds I find contemptible. For there is nothing more ruinous than the false goodwill of a hostile heart; moreover, I have so stoutly fortified myself with the arms of prudence, that I shall fear no treachery."[110]

Eleven letters from Filelfo to Traversari dating from the first year of their correspondence, which were published in the monk's letterbook but never appeared in Filelfo's, however, illumine a different side of the relationship altogether.[111] In these letters nothing is more striking than Filelfo's posture of diffidence; nothing is more patent than his deference to Traversari, particularly about his work: "Look how much I have trusted in your regard for me [he wrote Traversari]: I have not been afraid to send you my inept pieces to read. I'm sending you the enclosed orations which I gave as public lectures over the past few days, if they should even be called orations, and not just idle nonsense."[112]

Shortly before he received the official invitation to teach at the Studio

---

[109] Fabroni, *Cosmi vita*, 2.111; Rosmini, *Vita*, 1.85. Filelfo suppresses his participation in the plot in his letterbook.

[110] Filelfo, *Epistolae*, to Traversari (11 December 1437), fol. 14v: "Paucis respondebo tuae prolixiori epistolae. Ego amiciciam Cosmi Medicis nolo, inimicicias contemno. Nam et infensi animi simulata benivolentia nihil est perniciosius et ego ita prudentiae armis munivi me, ut nullas insidias pertimescam. Vale."

[111] Traversari, *Epistolae* (June 1428–May 1429), bk. 24, letters 30–41, cols. 1008–17.

[112] Traversari, *Epistolae* (10 September 1428), bk. 24, letter 37, col. 1014: "Vide quanti facio amorem tuum, ut nec ineptias meas ad te dare sim veritus. Mitto hasce orationes, si orationes quidem, et non nugae dicendae sunt, quas superioribus diebus publice habuissem." In view of Filelfo's sarcastic comments about the crudeness of Traversari's Greek in his letter to Aurispa dated 8 April 1428 (fol. 4v), we should be cautious about taking these letters at face value. On the other hand, in view of the possibility that most of the letters were composed years after the dates given in the epistolario, the letter to Aurispa may be just another one of Filelfo's reconstructions of the past, to make himself appear more perceptive, less naive.

from Leonardo Bruni, chancellor of Florence, Filelfo wrote Traversari a strange letter, full of the images we usually associate with the erotic poems of Catullus and Ovid—an unrequited yearning to touch and to see the beloved (Traversari, in this case), a sensation of interior burning, a feeling of pain in the beloved's absence, and a longing for death as the only release from the agony of love.[113] In any case, it is worth noting that there is nothing similar in tone to this letter in Filelfo's *Epistolae*:

> What do you think I desire, my Ambrogio? Day and night I burn to see, to converse with, and to embrace you. Sometimes I imagine Florence, often the Monastery of the Angels, and constantly I imagine you, Ambrogio, and place you before my eyes. And when I have embraced and addressed you and am awaiting the alternating rounds of a conversation, I am left feeling sad and bereft in the midst of speaking; but even this brings me such a respite from pain and bitterness that I would prefer to die rather than to be deprived of such a pleasure. From this you can very easily guess my thoughts.[114] (17 August 1428)

Thus in his own published letters Filelfo made sure to correct the impression that certain of his letters might have left of servility or adulation in his relations with Traversari. By eliminating all such letters, Filelfo made it clear that he felt no need to defer to anyone. He was ready to play either role, dominant or submissive, in his *fides* relationships—now gratefully receiving gifts and bounty from his friends, now meting out punishments as he saw fit. But in the court of his *Epistolae*, he would be the ultimate arbiter of right.

Filelfo's Philosopher-Kings

Filelfo's attempts to influence the policies of such Renaissance princes as Cosimo de' Medici, Francesco Sforza, Alfonso of Naples, Federigo da Montefeltro, and Pope Paul II are mirrored both in his published letters and in the many dedicatory poems he addressed to them. These letters and poems, and his own lifelong preoccupation with the philosophers, suggest that Filelfo took seriously Plato's famous injunction to kings and their

---

[113] It may be that this sort of eroticism is also found in certain Neoplatonic texts; the seeds for such imagery can certainly be seen in Plato's *Phaedrus*.

[114] Traversari, *Epistolae* (17 August 1428), bk. 24, letter 35, cols. 1012–13: "Quid autem me cupere, mi Ambrosi, putas? Dies noctesque eo sum in ardore visendi, colloquendi, complectendi tui. Nonnumquam Florentiam mihi, persaepe Angelorum Monasterium, Ambrosium vero semper et fingo et ante oculos pono, quem ubi complexus suavissime, adloquutusque sum, sermonis vices opperiens et tristis et solus medio in sermone relinquor. Quae quidem res tantum mihi damnum moeroris et amaritudinis adfert, ut emori quam tanta voluptate privari maluerim. Potes ex his facillime coniectare animi nostri sententiam . . ."

counselors in the *Republic*.[115] And if Filelfo's princes had no time to study philosophy, or even history, he would distill the wisdom of the ancients for them. As the respected court poet first of Filippo Maria Visconti and later of Francesco Sforza, he had come to believe in his role as *vates*, though he saw nothing of the prophet in himself except his knowledge of the past, that repository of wisdom that should enable any man to know something of the future. As such, he sought to counsel his princely patrons in a prudent, compassionate, and clement course of action. Though he too lived in an age of violence, Filelfo could not have agreed with Machiavelli that chief among the tools of the successful prince were fear and coercion. "Only the just man, who is not feared but loved and esteemed by the people, is the good ruler," he wrote Sforza in 1438, when the duke was laying siege to the smaller cities in the Marches.[116]

Although Filelfo was well aware of his duty to serve the policies of his princely patrons, he still felt the need to articulate a higher allegiance, one that transcended personal interest, when he acted in his role as counselor. The long epistolary essays he addressed to Cosimo de' Medici and Francesco Sforza, during the particularly turbulent years 1433–1438, exemplify Filelfo's characteristic literary strategy of framing rather severe criticisms of his patrons within a structure of praise. Thus, each of these hortatory letters adheres to a set format, containing some or all of the following themes: praise of the leader's character; an apology for offering advice to one so wise and experienced; a definition of virtuous as opposed to evil conduct; criticism of the prince's conduct and motives; an exhortation to consider the mandates of reason, wisdom, and prudence; a roster of classical exempla; and, finally, an expansion upon and a reiteration of his initial praise of the prince's character. Both letters represent Filelfo's attempt to deal in a rational manner with the phenomena of war and urban violence.

Intimations of Civil War in Florence

The date of Filelfo's long hortatory letter to Cosimo de' Medici is strategic: 1 May 1433, about two weeks before the alleged attempt on Filelfo's life, for which he would hold Cosimo responsible, and about four months before Cosimo's expulsion from Florence by the Albizzi faction. The theme of the letter is, moreover, friendship—*amicitia*, that "most pleasing bond of kind goodwill," as Filelfo calls it in the letter's opening sentence—and

---

[115] *Republic* 473 d–e. .

[116] Filelfo, *Epistolae*, to Francesco Sforza (8 October 1438), fols. 16–17. A Latin text of this letter with numbered passages is provided in Appendix A.

its betrayal.[117] *Amicitia* was the chain, as we learned in the letters to Giustiniani, that not only bound together the community of civilized men, but
also made possible the cultivation of the arts, letters, and learning among
men. Thus, the loosening, the undoing of that chain, becomes analogous
to the coming-apart of the city-state itself. The implication here is that
Cosimo's breaking-off of his once strong and caring bond with Filelfo will
be metonymic for, and predictive of, the dissolution of Florentine society,
in the coups d'état of 1433 and 1434.

While much space is given over to deprecatory remarks about Carlo
Marsuppini and Niccolò Niccoli, who in 1433 were the men closest to
Cosimo, the most interesting part of the letter contains an account of how
Filelfo single-handedly carried the day by rescuing the liberal arts at the
Studio. In two impromptu speeches he delivered in the senate, Filelfo was
able to rally sufficient support among the senators to keep the courses in
philosophy and literature at the university from being cancelled due to the
mounting cost of the Luccan war. At the same time, Filelfo pointed out to
Cosimo that it had been "his men" who backed the reduction of faculty
salaries and the elimination of liberal arts courses from the curriculum.
Nonetheless, Filelfo never impugned Cosimo himself. As in Niccolò Uz-
zano's defense of Cosimo in Machiavelli's *History*, Filelfo faulted Cosimo
in this letter not for any vices of his own but only for having the wrong
sorts of friends.[118]

Throughout the letter there is a moving back and forth between private
and public concerns, and at the same time a linking of those two spheres:
that of personal feuds among the *literati*, and that of the more public conflict between the Cosmian and anti-Cosmian (pro-Filelfo) factions over the
allocation of funds at the Studio. At the end of his long and detailed story
of his struggle to save the humanities at the university, Filelfo remarked
prophetically, "But as to their threats [against me] of swords and death, I
cannot by any means be led to believe that you would allow anyone to dare
to engineer such a crime, such a deed, relying on your support."[119] Thus
Filelfo's ironic warning regarding the violence soon to be perpetrated
against his person by Medici *amici* hints at the same time at the violence
that would be mounted against the state by the Medici in 1434.

Reiterating once again, at the letter's close, the same expressions of *car-*

[117] Ibid., to Cosimo (1 May 1433), fols. 12–12v: "Impium illud esse hominum genus arbitror, Cosme medices, quorum artibus atque dolis labefactatur ac solvitur iucundissimum
humanae benivolentiae et amiciciae vinculum," is its Ciceronian incipit. Cf. Cicero's "amabi-
lissum nodum amicitiae" in *De amicitia* 14.51; see n. 22.

[118] Niccolò Machiavelli, *History of Florence and of the Affairs of Italy*, with an intro. by
F. Gilbert (Reprint. New York, 1960), pp. 191–92.

[119] Filelfo, *Epistolae*, fol. 12v: "Quod ferrum autem cruoremque minentur, nulla ratione
adduci possum ut credam te passurum ut quisque, potentia tua fraetus, tantum scelus, tantum
facinus audeat machinari."

itas for Cosimo that he avowed at its beginning, he seizes now the moment to set in high relief the core trait he has been burnishing for himself throughout the *Epistolae*—his independence. In this he distinguishes himself from other courtiers of Cosimo's—namely, Marsuppini and Niccoli. Unlike these men, he takes pride in his autonomy—for herein lies his integrity and his honor. "Shame," he concludes, "has not allowed me to be a parasite in life. Nor have I ever learned to flatter, to adulate, or to be a yes-man."[120]

Rumors of Atrocities at Tolentino

In October 1438, Filippo Maria Visconti's condottiere, Francesco Sforza, besieged Filelfo's birthplace, Tolentino, and entered the small town by force. Persistent reports of atrocities committed against the townspeople by Sforza's men soon reached Filelfo in Siena. His letter to Sforza, published in the *Epistolae* under the dateline 8 October 1438, was his response to Sforza's execution of the siege.[121]

Filelfo begins his hortatory letter to Sforza, following the praise-reproach-praise formula we observed in his letter to Cosimo. He speaks first of Sforza's intellect and character: he has been much impressed with Sforza's probity, the magnitude of his mind, and his goodwill. But this praise is immediately followed by a recital of the disturbing news he has received about Sforza's siege of his hometown, Tolentino. Sforza, he hears, has mounted a massive attack against the defenseless town. Moreover, his soldiers have already laid waste the countryside and burned the crops around the city proper, while at present they occupy the town itself, threatening the citizens not only with captivity and slavery, but with every sort of moral and physical abuse ("omnem contumeliam caedemque")—euphemisms for the more violent images of rape, torture, and mass murder.[122]

As Filelfo moves further into his oration, his stance toward Sforza appears to grow increasingly confrontational, until we realize that his censure is expressed in purely hypothetical terms. Filelfo is careful not to condemn Sforza for what he actually has done; he wonders only how, in theory, such a virtuous mind as Sforza's could commit an act so abhorrent, evil, foul, and savage ("abhorreat, verum etiam iniquum sit et tetrum et immane"). The use of the subjunctive to express the hypothetical is key here. Even so, although Filelfo's rhetorical question assumes an answer that would vin-

---

[120] Ibid., to Cosimo (1 May 1433), fol. 12v: "Pudor vitae parasitum me esse non sinit. Non blandiri, non adulari, non assentari unquam didici."

[121] Ibid., to Sforza (8 October 1438), fols. 16–17.

[122] Cf., in chap. 2, Filelfo's use of the phrase *omnem contumeliam caedemque* to refer specifically to the rape of women, the mass murder, and senseless destruction of houses and churches, which he details in his account of Sforza's sack of Piacenza in *Sforziad* bk. 3.

dicate Sforza, the very posing of such a question nonetheless raises doubts about his character:

> For how can it be that your so great and extraordinary virtue would dare to perpetuate and labor at anything that not only would be inconsistent with a great and lofty mind, but that would at the same time be evil, foul, and savage? Would you threaten those with derision and death who would defend their lives, liberty, and fatherland with brave and unvanquished hearts?[123]

Using Cyrus, Alexander, and Julius Caesar as his models, Filelfo argues against the justice of taking vengeance in war. Starting from the premise of enlightened self-interest he suggests that the prince will maintain his power over client cities far better by diplomacy and economic aid ("arte atque beneficentia") than by threats and brute force. Instead, Filelfo urges Sforza to emulate Philip of Macedon, Alexander, and Scipio Africanus Maior, who were the greatest generals of antiquity precisely because they showed clemency, lenience, and charity (*mansuetudo, facilitas, beneficentia*) in their dealings with the peoples they conquered. Thus, his advice as to how to become a great ruler could not be more different from Machiavelli's:

> For do you prefer to be feared perhaps rather than loved? It is best seen that hatred naturally follows in the footsteps of fear. But you can never be esteemed and loved unless you demonstrate that you are truly just and beneficent. Indeed, the just and beneficent man is neither one who either harms others intentionally nor is he one who either neglects or is unwilling to impose a policy of moderation concerning matters for which he is responsible.[124]

The good prince, Filelfo continues, must restrain his anger, casting away every emotion that stands in the way of reason and deliberation. For the man who cannot rule himself surely cannot rule others; moreover, the greatest victory of all is self-mastery. The rule Filelfo exhorts Sforza to follow is that of the Spartan Aristo, Socrates, and Christ: to be good to your friends, and to make friends of your enemies.

Filelfo's final argument rests on the immortality of the soul (*animus*), which he contrasts to the fragility and transitory nature of the body and worldly things. "Reason," he writes, "not desire, must always be obeyed. For, reason, above all else, demonstrates how superior we are to the rest of the earth's creatures."

Filelfo takes special care in the concluding section of the letter to assure Sforza that all he has said was well intended and expressed as much out of loyalty to him as to his native city. He reiterates that he has a "singularly high regard for Sforza" and that he is "wonderfully pleased" with his en-

---

[123] See Appendix A, letter to Sforza [6].
[124] See ibid. [11].

comium of the general. The last sentence in the letter, however, must be read as a pure piece of irony meant for the ears of anyone but Sforza: "I do entreat you in all sincerity not to allow these praises to be sullied by any stain whatever—I speak not of dishonor but rather of the mere *suspicion* of such a stain."[125] It is important to realize again the disparity between the fictive datelines in the *Epistolae* and the dates at which Filelfo probably edited, and in many cases composed anew, his letters for publication. While Filelfo might in fact have sent a version of the published letter to Sforza in 1438, certainly he substantially revised the letter (which appears as a formal encomium in the *Epistolae*) well after 1451 when he began to prepare his correspondence for publication. Thus the irony of Filelfo's final admonition must be taken into account, since he surely gave the letter its final polishing not only after the siege of Tolentino, but after perhaps the most notorious of all Sforza's actions against a civilian population: the sack of Piacenza in 1447.

Filelfo's "Scholarly Articles"

Fully one-sixth of the letters in the first book of the *Epistolae* are essays of varying lengths on philosophical, literary, or linguistic questions. Beyond Book 1 the percentage of letters dealing solely with intellectual topics drops sharply. Filelfo's scholarly letters grapple with issues of current interest among the humanists and were designed to be published independently of the letterbook—as display pieces, complete in themselves. Because of its programmatic nature and its function as an advertisement for the rest of the epistolary, Book 1 necessarily has more than its fair share of such essays. As we have seen from the chatty style of Filelfo's letters to Aurispa and his more stilted letters to Sforza and Cosimo, Filelfo's habit was to choose his subject matter and tone to suit his addressee. Likewise, in the case of his pedagogic letters Filelfo singled out certain friends to whom he wrote exclusively about matters of intellectual interest, among whom were Bartolomeo Francanzani, Niccolò Fava, and Ciriaco d'Ancona.

Pleasure and Celibacy

Bartolomeo Francanzani was a monk at the monastery of San Giorgio Maggiore, across the lagoon from Venice. He had been a friend of Filelfo's

---

[125] Ibid. [19]: "Nam et amo te unice et delector mirifice tuis laudibus, quas nequaquam—non dicam infamiae—sed ne suspitionis quidem labe pollui patiare, summis precibus abs te peto."

in his student days at the university of Padua. Three of Filelfo's philosophical letters in Book 1 are addressed to him. Revealing his scholastic roots in the first of these letters, a discourse *De voluptate*, Filelfo attempts to demonstrate that the teachings of Aristotle and Epicurus are not incompatible with those of the Church Fathers.[126]

In this letter, like the chief interlocutor in Valla's *De voluptate*, Filelfo follows Epicurus and Aristotle in defining true pleasure as the pleasure of the mind.[127] The greatest of the philosophers, writes Filelfo, have maintained that men ought especially to seek a threefold life: that of contemplation, action, and fruition. The activities that pertain to fruition are those that lead to pleasure. While there are both intellectual and physical pleasures, true pleasure—and Christian pleasure—is that which comes from serenity of the mind. In this pleasure, Filelfo continues, following Epicurus we arrive at what the Greeks called *alypia*, "freedom from pain." It is ridiculous, Filelfo maintains, to understand pleasure, which is no different from what the Greeks called *hedone*, solely as a physical sensation. Rather, pleasure belongs to both the body and the mind: it can be either good or evil, or honorable or shameful, depending on whether it partakes of reason. Aristotle numbered pleasure among the goods of the mind, together with prudence and virtue. And when Epicurus said that pleasure was the greatest good, he meant pleasure of the mind, not of the body. Moreover, writes Filelfo, this kind of pleasure is very much to be sought after, since in it knowledge of the truth is conjoined with honorable action. Truth itself, since it is situated in those things that are unchanging and eternal, can be nothing else than the one immortal God. But since we can only apprehend this truth through practicing the moral virtues in our lives, it is important, Filelfo emphasizes, to be aware that there is a hierarchy among the moral virtues. At the pinnacle of this hierarchy stands *sapientia* (wisdom), personified as the "queen" of all the virtues; next in line, but subject to the rule of *sapientia* is *prudentia* (prudence), which in turn reigns supreme over the moral virtues:

> Indeed, I think that our actions should be in such close harmony with the knowledge of the truth, that we would know that all of our actions should be

---

[126] Filelfo, *Epistolae*, to Francanzani (1 August 1428), fol. 6. For letter text, see Appendix A.

[127] On the highest pleasure defined as that of the mind, see Lorenzo Valla, *De voluptate* (Basel, 1519), bk. 3; Aristotle, *Nicomachean Ethics* 7.13.1153b and 10.7–8; *Cicero, Tusculan Disputations* 5.33, 38; *De finibus* 5.38; *De officiis* 3.12; 117. *De finibus* 1 and *De officiis* 3 contain much about Epicurus's view of pleasure as primarily freedom from pain. In a subsequent letter to Francanzani (19 December 1428), Filelfo faults Cicero for his denunciation of Epicurus's view of pleasure as the good in *De finibus* 2.24–26ff. and *Tusculan Disputations* 5.26–31; but he is also aware that Cicero in *De senectute* 47–50 (and elsewhere) draws a distinction between the pleasures of the body, which may be base, and those of the mind, which are greater and more enduring, because they lead us to virtue.

judged in terms of their relation to the rule of Wisdom. For like some queen or empress who is content in herself, after she has rid herself of all cares concerning nugatory and fleeting matters, Wisdom alone is the one who, so that she may direct herself toward the light of that one supreme and everlasting good and so that she may fix her gaze on it unguarded, places Prudence in charge over all the rest of the moral virtues, and she (as though she were their provider) assigns tasks to each individual virtue according to its own particular duties. Therefore we ought to subordinate all the moral virtues to Prudence. Prudence is the virtue that belongs to reason; but Wisdom, which belongs totally to the intellect, rules over Prudence. Whoever lives in this way, yet refuses to admit that he partakes of the highest pleasure and that he is clearly happy and blessed, should in my opinion be thought not only silly, but foolish and insane.[128]

Filelfo ends the letter by congratulating Francanzani because he is the embodiment of the kind of intellectual and moral *voluptas* (pleasure) about which he has been speaking. In Francanzani contemplation and virtuous action are perfectly conjoined. For "it would be the greatest pleasure for you," writes Filelfo, "if you were to induce all those who prefer to be men (and not beasts) to partake of your goodness."[129]

Filelfo's second letter to Bartolomeo is a discourse on celibacy.[130] The treatise raises this question: Is celibacy preferable to marriage? At the close of the letter Filelfo mentions that when he and Francanzani were young students at Padua he, too, had considered taking religious orders. But here Filelfo, in his role as a married man, is writing his celibate friend a letter in praise of celibacy. The letter is a playful one, and it begins with a mock-serious conceit. Certainly, writes Filelfo, virginity cannot be considered a virtue in the Aristotelian sense, because it is not a mean between extremes. After making this point, Filelfo embarks upon a prolix sophistical argument on the perfection of odd numbers and the imperfection of even, hence the superiority of celibacy (oneness) over marriage (a pair). Filelfo's case *pro caelibatu* is a convoluted discourse on the significance of number, which parodies certain passages concerning number in the *Republic*, the *Greater Hippias*, and the *Epinomis* of Plato,[131] though Filelfo is here at odds with Plato's injunctions against celibacy in the *Laws*.[132] His final argument against the goodness of even numbers, and in favor of that of odd numbers (one and three, in particular) is Aristotelian: the numbers one and three are superior to even numbers because they lack nothing for their own ful-

128 Filelfo, *Epistolae* (9 December 1428), fols. 7–7v.

129 Filelfo's third letter contains a continuation of his *De voluptate: Epistolae* (31 December 1428), fol. 8.

130 *Epistolae*, to Francanzani (9 December 1428), fols. 7–7v.

131 Cf. *Republic* 8.546b; *Hippias Major* 301e and 303b; *Epinomis* 990c.

132 *Laws* 4.721d; and 6.774a.

fillment.[133] Here Filelfo is well aware that his argument is so sophistical that it cannot be taken seriously, for he already anticipates—he adds archly—"being charged with having wished to appear overly clever in a simple issue, as a young man is wont to do."[134] Thus the letter to Francanzani is clearly a very light-hearted exercise in the humanist art of arguing both sides of a question (*in utramque partem*), particularly since at the conclusion of his essay he reveals his contentment with his own lot—however much he may praise the value of celibacy:

> And indeed the human race increases and multiplies, and the earth is replenished by matrimony. But the choir of angels, as it were, is increased by the good of celibacy and virginity. And so, my Francanzani, I cannot fail to congratulate you, who have preferred the military and virginal cloak of Christ to the conjugal, peaceful, secular toga, who think that every human blaze of glory should not even be compared with the smallest ash from the shimmering fire of celestial glory in its splendor. Indeed, you have donned, my dearest Bartolomeo, the vestment of Christ, which belongs to the one and the odd number . . . And so, as you are content with your lot, so am I with mine: thus you may show favor to me among the gods, and I to you among men. For in this way all things are shared among friends, and each of us pursues glory, both in heaven and on earth. But you should be judged also much the happier of the two of us because you will be famous for a heroic virtue; for on my side I would be satisfied if I were praised for marriage among men![135]

Aristotle's Definitions of the Good

Niccolò Fava, a Venetian patrician whom Filelfo addressed as "physican and philosopher," was the recipient of two of Filelfo's philosophical letters. Both letters concern the translation and interpretation of Aristotle's *Nicomachean Ethics*.

[133] Aristotle, *Metaphysics* 5.16.1021b.

[134] Filelfo, *Epistolae*, to Francanzani (9 December 1428), fol. 7: "Ac ne in re perspicua videri voluisse ut iuvenis argutior insimuler . . ."

[135] Ibid., fol. 7–7v: "Et matrimonio quidem crescit ac multiplicatur hominum genus terraque repletur. Virginitatis autem et caelibatus bono chorus quasi quidam angelicus augetur, caelumque repletur. Itaque tibi, mi Francanzane, non possum non gratulari, qui militare Christi et virginale sagulum coniugali ociosaeque togae saeculi praetulisti, qui humanum omnem fulgorem ne minima quidem coruscationis scintilla cum splendore caelestis gloriae conferendum existimaris. Indiusti te inquam, Bartholomaee mi, dilectissimime Christi veste et ea quidem veste quae unius est imparisque numeri . . . Itaque ut tua tu, ita ego mea sorte contentus sum, quo ipse mihi faveas apud superos, ego autem apud homines tibi. Hoc enim pacto cum omnia amicis communia sint, et caeli uterque et terrae gloriam consequemur. Sed tu eo es foelicior iudicandus, quod virtute quadam heroica clarus eris. Nam ego satis sim habiturus, si coniugii lauder apud homines."

In the first of these letters Filelfo answers Fava's question about the exact wording of the text in *Ethics* 1.1094a.[136] Fava, who has only a Latin translation of the work, wants to know whether the Greek actually says that the "highest good" (*summum bonum*) is what all things seek. Filelfo answers that, first of all, there is no compound term (*copulativum verbum*) in Greek that is equivalent to *summum bonum*. Morever, he writes, the word *summum* is neither found in the introduction to the *Ethics*, nor would it be necessary: since Aristotle defines the good as that which all things seek, there is no need to add the superfluous adjective *summum*. Filelfo then explains Aristotle's distinction between happiness (*felicitas*), the one good that is sought for its own sake, and all other goods, which are sought for the sake of something else. Synonymous with the good (*bonum*) is the end (*finis*), toward which all our activities are directed: the good and the end are convertibles (*bonum enim et finis, ut nosti, convertuntur*). These activities of ours are not all of the same sort, but fall into two diverse classes: the active life and the contemplative one (*vita activa; vita contemplativa*). Moreover, action itself—or that which Aristotle called *energeia*—is twofold (*actio est duplex*): interior and exterior. The Latins, adds Filelfo, also call this *energeia operatio* or *agilitas*. The relationship between interior and exterior *actio* is best demonstrated by an analogy: it is like the relation of the general to his military campaigns (*veluti dux ad res gerendas*). This is so, since all action is the consequence of choice (*electio*). And finally, having gone through the many categories of the good, Aristotle teaches us that the ultimate good and arbiter of all things is the one who is the first and last mover of all things in the cosmos (*qui sit agibilium omnium finis*). At the conclusion of his letter to Fava, Filelfo complains that if those who study philosophy were to become versed in the defining of things, they would not misunderstand Aristotle.[137] In the sequel to this letter Filelfo does little more than repeat to Fava what he has already said about the good and the end, and about Aristotle's concept of the highest good. But, as though he were adding a footnote to his earlier letter, Filelfo takes this opportunity to point out to Fava that in the *Magna Moralia* Aristotle goes even further in assigning to pleasure (*voluptas*) a positive value as "the good which all things seek."[138]

In these two letters to Fava, a philosopher by profession, Filelfo demonstrates that the study of philology would have to precede philosophy,

---

[136] Ibid., to Niccolò Fava (14 May 1428), fol. 5.

[137] Ibid., fol. 5: "Quod si definiendi peritiam tenerent, nunquam in tanto versarentur errore."

[138] Ibid., to Fava (9 August 1428), fol. 6v: "Hanc autem propriam esse ac veram Aristotelis sententiam patet alio loco, cum in secundo *Magnorum aethicorum* libro, de voluptate loquens, quam ipsam bonum esse vult, ita scriptum reliquit ad verbum: 'Propterea videretur videlicet voluptas esse bonum, quod hanc omnia appetunt.' "

and that there could in fact be no knowledge of ancient philosophy without its being established on a firm philological foundation.[139] Though Aristotle's works had long been accessible to Westerners in the translations of Averroes and Avicenna, Filelfo shows here that the Italians' knowledge of him was only superficial since they had no firsthand knowledge of the Greek texts. A mastery of Greek grammar, syntax, and vocabulary would prove to be more important in the study of the ancient philosophers than dialectics and vague notions of the ideas of Plato, Aristotle, and the Stoics. Again the important point to take into account is not that this exchange necessarily occurred in 1428 when Filelfo was in Bologna teaching these texts, but that here is yet another persona into which Filelfo easily slips— this time for the purpose of enhancing his reputation as an indispensable interpretor of ancient thought. The key word here is *definiendum*—and Filelfo's impugning of the Italians for their lack of "skill" (*peritia*) at translation and definition.

After the Council of Florence in 1438, Filelfo's letters, particularly those to the Byzantine philosophers Gemistos Pletho and George Scholarios, reflect a renewed interest in both the ontological and ethical doctrines of Plato and Aristotle—but these were areas he was to explore more fully some thirty years later in the *De morali disciplina*. Both the philosophical letters and the *De morali disciplina* make manifest Filelfo's lifelong concern with the relationships among the names of things (*verba*), their referents (*res*), and being (*ens*). In a letter to Guarnerio Castellio, an attorney and senator at the Milanese court, Filelfo had addressed himself to similar questions.[140] Being (*essentia* in Latin; the Greek, *ousia*), Filelfo had explained to Castellio, ought to be understood as threefold, consisting of matter (*materia*, the Greek *hyle*), power (*potentia*, the Greek *dynamis*), and form (*eidos*).

Vergil's Mirror of Virtue

The humanists from Petrarch onward were interested in forming new allegorical interpretations of the *Aeneid*. Although the humanists' readings of Vergil owed much to the commentaries of Servius, Fulgentius, and Ber-

---

[139] Filelfo at least casts Fava in that role, addressing each of his letters to his friend "Nicolo Fabae, philosopho ac medico."

[140] Ibid., to Castellio (14 June 1439), fol. 18v.: "Essentia, quam et *ousian* Graeci et Latinorum eruditissimi substantiam nominant, tribus modis accipiendam existimo. Nam et materiam et formam et quod ex utraque constat 'substantiam' dicimus. Horum autem trium, materia quidem quam *hylen* Graeci dicunt; est potentia, quae a Graecis vocatur *dynamis*; forma vero, quod *eidos* Graece nominatur, est perfectio, quae ab Aristotele dicta est novo nomine *entelexeia*."

nardus of Sylvester, still they would offer much that was new. Filelfo in his letter to Ciriaco d'Ancona responds to his friend's wish for a repudiation of the commentaries of the medieval schoolmen and a new interpretation of Vergil's epic.[141] Ciriaco had told Filelfo that he in no way could accept the dictum of the medieval *magistri* that Vergil's intention was simply "to imitate Homer and praise Augustus." Filelfo does not disagree with the *magistri*. But he sees Vergil's aims as epideictic and allegorical more than parochial and panegyrical: the fictional character—the *figura* of Aeneas— is not an idealized portrait of Augustus, but rather a pattern (*forma*) for Augustus to model himself on. In a passage in which he recapitulates the same ideas he had expressed in his letter to Francanzani on moral virtue, he explains that Vergil created in Aeneas a *figura* of virtue and wisdom:

> For wisdom seems to me to be the one virtue in particular in which we surpass all other animals. For what animal on earth considers the truth which is in heaven? Wisdom alone is that which seeks and recognizes the truth. For prudence, in imitating wisdom the way art imitates nature, indeed seeks after truth, but not of the gods and the divine, but of humans and earthly things. For what else does the contemplation of those things that bring man either material advantages or disadvantages provide than to enable us to discern the true from the false amid this temporal and momentary flux of things—so that we may follow one thing and spurn another? In civic life, then, prudence alone is the master over all the rest of the moral virtues. Prudence alone moderates and rules these. But prudence is but a broken and weak thing—a quality without strength—unless it abides by and is obedient to wisdom alone, as though to a prince or queen. Therefore, those who take prudence (which is called thus from "seeing ahead") as the mediating virtue between the moral and intellectual virtues and those who believe that prudence is the model virtue for the attainment of civic happiness (since it is the source and form for all the civic virtues) surely must be thought to have believed that this prudence was in no way different from truth. Therefore, when Vergil proposed that Aeneas— "man," as it were—should be sung by him, he meant man as the wise and

---

[141] Ibid., to Ciriaco d'Ancona (18 December 1427), fols. 2–2v: "Petis a me ut tibi declarem quae Publii Virgilii Maronis sententia fuerit in scribenda *Aeneide*. Nam communem illam opinionem quam ludi magistri afferunt voluisse Virgilium et imitari Homerum et laudare Augustum nequaquam tibi admodum probari. . . . Quod Virgilius uno *Aenidos* carmine melisigenis Homeri *Iliada Ulysseam*que imitatus, laudans Aenean Augustum quoque laudarit, nequaquam inficior. Sed divinum eius ingenium altius suspexisse nescius certe non sum, quippe qui humanam conditionem contemplative activeque describens, eo cogitatus omnis consiliaque direxerit, ut qua via summum bonum in hac vita parari posset in unius Aeneae sapientia virtuteque ostenderet . . ." The entire text of this letter has been recently published in a new critical edition by V. R. Giustiniani, "Il Filelfo, L'interpretazione allegorica di Virgilio e la tripartizione platonica dell'anima," in *Umanesimo e Rinascimento. Studi offerti a P. O. Kristeller* (Florence, 1980), 33–44.

prudent one. Indeed, these virtues both—sapientia and prudentia—belong to the intellect, or one belongs to the intellect and the other to reason. For reason alone belongs to the temporal kingdom; whereas the intellect belongs to the eternal one: the latter is wholly concerned with contemplation, the former with deliberation. . . . It is our nature then to understand first and then to act. Thus in the first six books of the *Aeneid* contemplation and deliberation occupy the foremost places. In the second six books, however, action is the object of praise. . . . Although there is much about the duty of justice and piety, still fortitude is the virtue that flourishes first and foremost. And just as the beginning of infancy commences first at birth, so death is the end of human life. And so, Vergil writes elegantly at the close of the poem: "And with a gasp his soul life fled indignant to the shades." For Turnus, who had made himself guilty of cowardice and injustice, dies with his name buried in eternal darkness. But Aeneas, a man just and brave, is made to shine more and more every day—almost as though he were a divinity—because of his everlasting glory.[142]

Filelfo follows Servius and Fulgentius in reading the first six books of the *Aeneid* as an allegory of the six stages in every man's journey toward the good: birth, infancy, boyhood, puberty, young adulthood, and maturity. But he also sees this human quest for the highest good as unattainable in this world. We see not how Aeneas has already arrived at the *summum bonum*, but rather the path by which he might approach it (*qua via sum-*

---

[142] Filelfo, *Epistolae*, fols. 2v–3: "Nam sapientia ea mihi virtus sola videri solet, qua caeteris animantibus egregie antecellimus. Quod enim animal in terris eam considerat veritatem quae in caelo est? Hanc sola sapientia est, quae et inquirit et novit. Prudentia enim sapientiam ita, ut ars naturam imitata, veritatem quidem inquirit, sed non rerum superiorum atque divinarum, sed inferiorum et humanarum. Nam consultatio eorum, quae sint homini emolumenta detrimentave allatura, quid aliud efficit quam ut verum a falso in hac temporali et momentanea mutabilitate decernamus, hoc scilicet sequentes, illud autem aspernantes? In vita igitur civili prudentia sola est, quae moralibus cunctis virtutibus dominatur, easque sola et moderatur et regit. At prudentia fracta est et debilis nullorumque nervorum, nisi manet ab una sapientia, ad eamque, tanquam ad principem reginamque referatur. Quare qui prudentiam (a providendo dictam) mediam posuerunt inter moralis intellectualisque virtutes, eamque iccirco perfectam voluerunt esse virtutem in civili foelicitate, quoniam virtutum civilium omnium principium sit et forma, hi nihil sensisse a veritate alienum existimandi sunt. Cum ergo proponit Virgilius Aenean a se canendum ut virum; hoc est ut sapientem eundemque prudentem. Quem quidem virtutes aut intellectus sunt ambae; aut intellectus altera, et rationis altera. Nam ratio temporalium est; intellectus autem aeternorum; ita ut haec tota in contemplando sit posita, illa autem in consultando . . . Natura enim sit ut antea intelligamus, deinde agamus. Itaque in primis sex *Aeneidos* libris contemplatio maxime et consultatio locum habet. In secundis autem libris sex actionis est laus. . . . Quanquam multa de iusticiae, multa de pietatis munere apparent, fortitudinis tamen laus in primis floret. Et quemadmodum initium sumptum est a primo infantiae ortu, ita aetatis humanae finis est mors. Itaque non inepte ultimo loco subdidit: 'Vitaque cum gemitu fugit indignata sub umbras.' Turnus enim qui se iusticiae fecerat ignaviaeque obnoxium in obscuritate nominis moritur sempiterna. Aeneas vero vir iustus et fortis, quasi numen indies magis atque magis diuturnitate gloriae illustratur."

mum bonum parari posset). And at the end of the poem Filelfo sees Aeneas not as a divinity, but "like" one (*quasi numen*). Unlike a God, Aeneas has not attained truth in Filelfo's eyes, but is a traveler moving toward truth. Aeneas does not himself possess immortality at the end of the poem, but rather his image "grows brighter day after day in the long perpetuation of his glory."

The letter to Ciriaco is also illuminating because of the relationship of its subject matter to the other letters that surround it in Book 1. It nests amid a group of letters written in the winter of 1427, in which Filelfo ventilates to Giustiniani and other Venetians his disgust with their failure to fulfill what he considered their obligations as his patrons. In this letter Filelfo seems to recognize in the epic poem that Vergil addressed to Augustus a lesson applicable to his own pursuit of a situation that was gratifying, yet lucrative enough that he could support his family. Like Vergil, Filelfo here weighs the relative merits of certain temporal ends, such as wealth and fame, against the pursuit of virtue. "You are asking neither for just a little favor nor for a short essay hastily thrown together," he comments to Ciriaco, "especially from me who neither enjoys peace of mind at the present time, nor lives free from anxiety—not because of any injury, but first due to the virulence of the plague which forces me to stay cooped up here in Venice as if we were under siege, and second, because I am wasting my time here without any benefit coming out of it—deceived by those to whom such conduct is least becoming."[143]

The incompatibility of wealth and virtue grew to be a major theme in all Filelfo's writings. His warning to his pupil Sassolo da Prato nearly a decade and a half later would show that this early disappointment with private patronage, first in Venice and later in Florence, would linger unabated throughout his life. As he saw the world, the distance between an Aeneas and a Giustiniani was more likely going to be unbridgeable than not.

> I would like you to point out to me one fellow in this day and age, from all those who surpass others—be it in the realm of power, wealth, or good looks—who is a good man. It shames me to say something which I've noticed is almost invariably all too true. And still I will say it. Not only is a man of great wealth not a good man, but he is proud and arrogant.[144]

[143] Ibid., fol. 2v: "Non mediocrem profecto rem petis neque brevis orationis opus a me praesertim, qui hoc tempore ociosus non sum et angor animi non iniuria, tum ob hanc pestilentiae acerbitatem, qua me Venetiis obsessum intueor, tum quia hic inutiliter tempus tero ab his delusus, a quibus minime conveniebat."

[144] Ibid., to Sassolo da Prato (1 April 1440), fol. 21v: "Velim mihi aliquem ex his virum bonum ostendas hoc tempore qui vel formae praestantia caeteros antecellunt, vel divitiis sunt, et potentia aliis civibus superiores. Pudet me dicere, quod verissimum esse in omnibus fere animadverti. Et dicam tamen. Non modo vir opibus abundans non est bonus, sed et superbus et contumeliosus."

TWO

RAPE

IN MAY 1453 the Turks sacked Constantinople, the city the humanists regarded as the last bastion of Greco-Roman culture, nostalgically calling it *nova Roma*.[1] In Italy that year, continuing wars between the great territorial states threatened to destroy everything those cities sought to defend. In the first four years of his signory, Duke Francecso Sforza spent what little was left in Milan's treasury after the civil war, fighting the Venetians. In the early fifties, a great number of the duke's creditors, from his armorers and military architects to the professors at the university in Pavia, began to send notices to the duke's treasurers concerning his debts to them, often warning that they would not continue to serve him without reimbursement.[2] Filelfo, on paper the highest-paid of the professors at Pavia, had to haggle with the duke's stewards to get so much as a trickle of his salary.[3] The duke himself was not at court—he was encamped at Melzo, Trezzo, Cassano, or elsewhere, waiting to engage the Venetians in the next battle.[4]

[1] See Filelfo, *Epistolae*, to Giustiniani (10 October 1427), fol. 1, for his use of the expression "new Rome," signifying Constantinople. Even after the city's sack, Filelfo, who managed to secure the release of his former mother-in-law from a Turkish prison in the ancient city, maintained his close ties with friends and family who remained behind Turkish lines. See also L. Gualdo Rosa, "Il Filelfo e i Turchi," in *Annali della Facolta di lettere e filosofia. Universita di Napoli* 11 (1964–1968): 109–65. The fall of Constantinople stimulated an outpouring of writings from the Italian humanists; on this literature see Robert Black, *Benedetto Accolti and the Florentine Renaissance* (Cambridge, 1985), pp. 226–27n; see also Giovanni Aurispa's prediction that the sack would bring about peace talks between the Italian cities: Aurispa, *Carteggio*, ed. R. Sabbadini (Rome, 1931–1939), p. 133.

[2] For these requests for payment for services rendered, see ASM, Sforzesco Carteggio (hereafter SC), 659–64, September 1452–March 1454.

[3] See ASM, Autografi 127, 3, Series I, 3; and ASM, Archivio da registri di missive ducali 4, fol. 123v. A letter dated 6 April 1451 and signed by Cicco Simonetta assigns a salary of 632 florins per annum to Filelfo for his chair at the university of Pavia, and an additional 200 florins over and above that amount is assigned to him from the ducal treasury. See Adam, *F. Filelfo*, Appendix 28, p. 379; see ibid., pp. 380–81 for two additional letters of Cicco's, dated 25 June and 2 July 1451, ordering Sforza's treasury officers to pay Filelfo 100 of his as-yet unpaid salary; see ibid., pp. 63–64 and 230: the jurist Catone da Sacco drew a salary of 500 ducats per annum.

[4] On the territorial chess game that Sforza and the Venetians played for (and in) the Lombard towns in 1451–1453, see G. Giulini, *Memorie spettanti alla storia, al governo ed alla descrizione della citta e campagna di Milano ne' secoli bassi* (Milan, 1857; reprint Milan, 1975), 6.495ff.

By the fourth year of Sforza's signory, Filelfo had for fourteen years been playing a leading role in the cultural affairs of Milan—as court poet, orator, and professor of rhetoric at the university. And yet he had little to show for those years. Life had been peaceful, but he was drifting. During the five years he taught at Siena before he came to the Milanese court in 1439, he had published a dialogue and some translations from the Greek, and had circulated some of his satires among friends.[5] Otherwise, his work was not well known outside Milan. And so, while it was not clear whether he could continue to support his family in Milan, he was not yet ready to move, either.

In a sense, he felt as gouged by Sforza as he had been by Filippo Masi Bruni's sword in Florence twenty years earlier.[6] In any case, he thought he could still make another move, though it would take some longer-range planning than it had then. He would give his anti-Medici *Satires* a final polishing so that he could present them as a gift to King Alfonso, whose court in Naples he had been invited to visit that summer.[7] There was also the epistolary memoir he told friends he was putting together. Meanwhile, he would hurry to finish the work he considered the first major book of his career, a Latin epic poem, entitled *Sphortias*, on the military conquests of his patron, the condottiere Francesco Sforza.[8]

The Renaissance Cult of War and the *Sforziad*

The culture and cult of war was a powerful current in the Quattrocento.[9] The signori of many of the most brilliant centers of artistic and literary

[5] See Rosmini, *Vita*, 1.56–59, 79, and 87–88: Fiìelfo wrote his first creative works in Siena, his *Satyrae* and the *Commentationum Florentinarum de Exilio*. During his years in Florence and Siena, Filelfo made Latin translations of Lysias's *On the Murder of Eratosthenes* and *Funeral Oration*; Xenophon's *Agesilaus*, *The Constitution of Sparta*; Plutarch's *Lives of Licurgus and Numa, and Galba and Otho* and the *Apothegms*.

[6] On the alleged assassination attempt, see chap. 1, pp. 17–21. Filelfo left copious evidence of the resentment he felt toward Sforza. See Filelfo's letter to the Marquis Ludovico Gonzaga (Trivulzianus [17 February 1477], fol. 556), in which he comments that Sforza had been "an ignoramus when it came to literature of any sophistication and the arts," adding sarcastically that Sforza's "patronage" had helped ruin him financially: "Et fuit sane Franciscus Sphortia [Filelfo wrote] . . . litteraturae urbanioris et Musarum ignarus . . . Quantum is quoque egestati meae profuerit, norunt omnes." See also Filelfo's anti-Sforza epigrams in Adam, *F. Filelfo*, p. 43.

[7] See Filelfo, *Epistolae*, to Niccolò Arcimboldi (25 July 1453), fols. 79–79v.

[8] Filelfo first announced his undertaking of the epic poem to his Venetian friend, Pietro Tommasi: *Epistolae* (14 June 1451), fol. 65; his next reports on his progress on the *Sforziad* went to Ludovico Gonzaga and Sigismundo Malatesta: see ibid. (22 June 1453), fol. 78v and (10 March 1453), fol. 76, respectively. On Tommasi, see Margaret L. King, *Venetian Humanism in an Age of Patrician Dominance* (Princeton, 1986), pp. 58–59 and 424–35.

[9] Michael Mallett, *Mercenaries and Their Masters: Warfare in Renaissance Italy* (London, 1974); Jacob Burckhardt, "War as a Work of Art," in *The Civilization of the Renaissance in*

activity were condottieri or military men. Military tournaments and pageants, where thousands of soldiers displayed their skills in full battle dress, remained extremely popular in Italian cities throughout the century. Almost all the great architects of the period had been involved with the design of fortresses or other military projects at some point in their careers. Depictions of battle scenes and city sieges and sacks were the frequent subjects of paintings, frescoes, and manuscript illuminations. Military treatises, too, were in demand as never before.[10] Moreover, the great humanist educators of the period, Vittorino da Feltre and Guarino da Verona insisted on the vigorous training of the body as well as the mind, on the martial as well as the peaceful arts.[11]

The dynastic epic, with its military themes, was just another manifestation of the aristocratic concerns of the age. Petrarch had written a Latin epic poem, which he dedicated to King Robert of Naples, about the military career of Scipio Africanus.[12] Filelfo borrowed freely from both Vergil and Petrarch in writing his *Sforziad*. The poem, like so many of his other adaptations of ancient authors, soon became a model for the revival of dynastic epic in Italy. After it circulated, Tito Vespasiano Strozzi wrote a *Borsias* about Borso d'Este, Basinio Basini wrote an epic poem for Sigismondo Malatesta, Porcellio Pandoni composed such a work for Federigo da Montefeltro, and Naldi wrote a *Volterrais* for Lorenzo de' Medici.

The *Sforziad* as Propaganda for Sforza's Wars?

Although Filelfo made Sforza the undisputed hero of his *Sforziad*, the duke was the last person for whom Filelfo actually tailored the work. Sforza's not having matriculated at one of the prestigious new schools for the sons

---

Italy, with an intro. by B. Nelson and C. Trinkhaus (New York, 1958), pp. 115–19. But on the antiwar, anticondottieri tradition of the humanists, see also C. C. Bayley, *War and Society in Renaissance Florence: the "De militia" of Leonardo Bruni* (Toronto, 1961); see Petrarca, *Rerum familliarum libri I–VIII*, ed. and trans. A. S. Bernardo (Albany, 1975), pp. 122–25; Coluccio Salutati, *Epistolario*, ed. F. Novato, 4 vols. (Rome, 1891–1911), 1.194; Bayley also cites D. Boninsegni, *Storia della citta di Firenze, 1410–1460* (Florence, 1637); F. Biondo, *Roma Triumphans* (Basel, 1513); L. B. Alberti, *Momus seu de principe*, ed. G. Martini (Bologna, 1942).

[10] On military treatises see Mallett, *Mercenaries*, pp. 171, 176–77, 215, 218, 224; and C. C. Bayley, *War and Society*.

[11] Anthony Grafton and Lisa Jardine, *From Humanism to the Humanities: Education and the Liberal Arts in Fifteenth- and Sixteenth-Century Europe* (London, 1986); W. H. Woodward, *Vittorino da Feltre and Other Humanist Educators* (Cambridge, 1905).

[12] Petrarch, *Africa*, trans. T. G. Bergin and A.S. Wilson (New Haven, 1977); T. G. Bergin, *Petrarch* (New York, 1970), pp. 101–15.

of the rich, and his indifference to Latin literature, made him something of an anomaly among the leading condottiere-princes of his age.[13] The signori of Mantua, Urbino, and Ferrara had attended one or another of the great humanist schools of the period. Ludovico Gonzaga and Federigo Montefeltro studied under Vittorino da Feltre, and Leonello and Borso d'Este with Guarino da Verona. Alfonso the Magnanimous of Naples, next to Sforza the most successful of the Quattrocento administrators of war, retained a number of distinguished humanists at his court for varying lengths of time, among whom were Antonio Beccadelli, Lorenzo Valla, Bartholomeo Facio, Giannozzo Manetti, and Giovanni Pontano.[14] According to the Florentine bookseller and biographer Vespasiano da Bisticci, who was only a generation younger than these men, Sforza differed in this respect even from his own brother Alessandro, the lord of Pesaro, who not only sought the company of men of learning but had amassed a great library of classical and religious books in his castle.[15]

And so, when Filelfo began to send out the first books of his epic poem, Francesco Sforza was not part of his target audience. In the years 1453– 1456, however, a number of other prominent condottiere-princes received advertisements for the poem from him—Ludovico Gonzaga of Mantua, Sigismondo Malatesta of Rimini, Federigo Montefeltro of Urbino, Borso d'Este of Ferrara, and Alfonso of Naples among them.[16] The samples from the poem that he sent to friends might have included the description of a bloody battle, scenes of soldiers pillaging a captured city, the mounting of a carefully calibrated siege, or the erotic encounter between a married woman and one of the book's heroes.[17] When Filelfo stopped at the courts of the Gonzaga, the Malatesta, and the Montefeltro on his way to spend

[13] See n. 11.

[14] Jerry H. Bentley, *Politics and Culture in Renaissance Naples* (Princeton, 1987), pp. 84– 137.

[15] Vespasiano, *Renaissance Princes, Popes, and Prelates* (New York, 1963), pp. 114–17. On Sforza, see E. Rubieri, *Francesco Primo Sforza*, 2 vols. (Florence, 1879); C. Cipolla, *Storia delle signorie italiane dal 1313 al 1530* (Milan, 1881); C. M. Ady, *A History of Milan under the Sforza* (London, 1907); F. Cusin, "L'impero e la successione degli Sforza ai Visconti," in *ASL*, n.s., 1 (1936): 4–116. On his relations with Cosimo de' Medici, see F. Sacchi, "Cosimo de' Medici e Firenze nell' acquisto di Milano allo Sforza," in *Rivista di scienze storiche* 2 (1905): 340–46; E. Jordan, "Florence et la succession lombarde (1447–1450)," in *École Française de Rome. Mélanges d'archeologie et d'histoire* 9 (1889): 93–119.

[16] Filelfo's announcements about the *Sforziad* are in his *Epistolae*, to L. Gonzaga (22 June 1453), fol. 78v; to S. Malatesta (10 March 1453), fol. 76; to F. Montefeltro (1 August 1467), fol. 193; to Borso's secretary, Ludovico Caselli (8 June 1455), fol. 89; and to Alfonso's secretary, Antonio Beccadelli (16 June 1456), fol. 95.

[17] The story of the adulterous love affair between a certain Lyda and Carlo Gonzaga, in *Sforziad* 4, has essentially the same plot as Enea Silvio Piccolomini's very popular novella of the period, the *De duobus amantibus*. The nineteenth-century critics were especially disapproving of Filelfo's language and imagery in *Sforziad* 4.

the month of August at King Alfonso's castle near Naples in 1453, he surely gave readings from his epic poem. His message to his prospective patrons was clear: if they liked what they heard, he was ready to work for them on commission.[18] During the years 1453–1473, Filelfo kept install- ments of the *Sforziad* circulating among friends in Florence, Venice, Bolo- gna, and Rome, sending copies of the work to Pope Pius II, Piero de' Medici, Lorenzo de' Medici, and Nicodemo Tranchedini, Sforza's ambas- sador to Florence.[19]

In spite of the poem's wide circulation during Filelfo's lifetime, no printed edition of the *Sforziad* was ever issued. This circumstance and the misconceptions about the poem, which were first disseminated by Filelfo's nineteenth-century critics, have made the *Sforziad* the least understood of Filelfo's works. Among these first critics, only Carlo Rosmini appears to have known the work well.[20] In Rosmini's judgment, the *Sforziad* was by far the most ambitious of Filelfo's poetic works; nonetheless, he saw its primary purpose as encomiastic.[21] He provided brief synopses for eight of the nine extant books of the *Sforziad*, but said nothing in particular about the poem's style.[22] The nineteenth-century critics Burckhardt, Voigt, and Symonds, seem to have derived their opinions of the poem from Rosmini, since they added nothing of their own to his description of the poem. The chief fault that these critics found with the work was that it lacked the purity and transcendence they thought poetry should have. First, they were disturbed by what they considered the corruption of the poetic idiom by political concerns. Second, these contemporaries of Marx and Malthus

[18] Federigo Montefeltro eventually commissioned a *vita* from Filelfo, which Giovanni Zan- noni thinks he began ca. 1473–1474. For Zannoni's text of Filelfo's *Vita di Federico d'Urbino* [= Vat. Urb. 1022], see Benadduci, ed., *Atti*, pp. 265–393.

[19] Filelfo sent copies to Tranchedini in Florence, Sforza's envoy in that city: see Filelfo, *Epistolae* (19 August 1455), fol. 90, in which he asks Tranchedini whether Carlo Gonzaga has received a copy of the poem; ibid., to Cosimo's son, Piero de' Medici (20 May 1460), fol. 116. See also Rosmini, *Vita*, 2.322, to Lorenzo de' Medici (11 August 1472). Copies were sent to his son Xenophon in Rome to be distributed "to his friends": see his *Epistolae*, to his son (8 October 1452), fol. 72v; to Giacomo Ammanati-Piccolomini, Cardinal of Pavia (13 April 1473), fol. 258; and to Pope Pius II (13 January 1460), fol. 110. In Bologna, samples went to Alberto Zancario and Alberto Parisi: see *Epistolae* (20 February 1453), fol. 74v; and (October 31 1464), fols. 162ff.

[20] Rosmini, *Vita*, 2.156–76.

[21] Rosmini, ibid., wrote that the *Sforziad* was "quella [opera] che . . . mostra l'elevatezza della sua mente e l'estension del sua ingegno"; its aim was simply "di onerare le gloriose geste del Duca di Milano Francesco Sforza."

[22] Filelfo planned a work of twenty-four books; he completed only nine books and the opening lines to bks. 10 and 11. Since Rosmini's time it had generally been assumed that only bks. 1–8 of the *Sforziad* were extant. But G. Giri, "Il codice autografo della Sforziade di Francesco Filelfo," in Benadduci, ed., *Atti*, pp. 420–57 reports discovering a lost autograph manuscript containing bk. 9 and fragments that appear to be the prologues of bks. 10 and 11 in the Biblioteca Casanatense, cod. 415 (C III.9).

deplored the idea that a poet might solicit, require, or even desire money. And finally, they objected that, in the service of the profit motive, the poet had found it useful to lie. Burckhardt dismissed Filelfo as "the ready eulogist of any master who paid him," and grouped the *Sforziad* together with other Renaissance epic poems, characterizing the genre as contemporary history "in a panegyrical style."[23] Voigt charged that the poem was nothing more than a chronicle with epic trappings, and complained that Filelfo had most unfortunately got into the business of selling glory.[24] Symonds, who appears to have paraphrased Voigt, called the poem a "versified chronicle, encumbered with foolish mythological machinery, and loaded with fulsome flatteries."[25] For the most part, scholars in our own era have simply accepted the nineteenth-century critics' assertions about the *Sforziad*, often even embellishing them as though they were their own observations.[26]

As Lauro Martines has shown, from the standpoint of the prince, who paid his courtier poets to represent him favorably to the world, humanism was indeed a program for the ruling classes.[27] On the other hand, the poet himself might construe his task quite differently, particularly the more independent writers such as Aurispa, Valla, and Filelfo.[28] Filelfo, who by the late 1430s had gained a measure of independence by distributing his favors among a number of patrons in different cities, had every reason to create a portrait of Francesco Sforza that was not idealized, much less sycophantic.[29] Even so, Filelfo's patterning of his *Sforziad* after Vergil's *Aeneid* placed his portrait of Sforza within a genre that was at least traditionally considered to be panegyrical.[30] The *Aeneid* was a workable model for the

---

[23] Burckhardt, *Civilization*, pp. 55 and 264.

[24] Georg Voigt, *De Wiederbelebung des classischen Althertums*, 2 vols. (Berlin, 1888–1897), 2.408.

[25] John Addington Symonds, *The Revival of Learning: The Renaissance in Italy*, 2d ed., 3 vols. (New York, 1888), 2.284.

[26] Cf. Eugenio Garin, *Storia di Milano*, 16 vols. (Milan, 1953–1963), 6.555; W. L. Grant, *Neo-Latin Literature and the Pastoral* (Chapel Hill, 1965), p. 45; Adam, *F. Filelfo*, p. 45. But see the more favorable assessments of A. Novara, "Un poema latino del quattrocento: *La Sforziade* di Francesco Filelfo," in *Rivista ligure si scienze, lettere, ad arti* 28 (1906): 3–27, and Guglielmo Bottari, "La 'Sphortias,' " in *Filelfo nel V Cent.* (Padua, 1986), pp. 459–93.

[27] Martines, *Power and Imagination: City-States in Renaissance Italy* (New York, 1979), pp. 191–217, has written the most persuasive assessment to date on the role the humanists played as image-makers in the Quattrocento courts.

[28] The studies of Eugene Genovese, *Roll, Jordan, Roll: The World the Slaves Made* (New York, 1972) and E. P. Thompson, "Eighteenth-century English Society: Class Struggle without Class?" in *Social History* 3 (1978), 133–66, have now made it axiomatic that members of different social ranks (slave/master; gentry/poor tenants; wealthy patron/destitute client) can embrace the same ideology (paternalism), yet interpret it very differently.

[29] For an overview of the range of Filelfo's circle of patrons see the addressees in his *Epistolae*, bks. 1–3.

[30] On the *Aeneid* as a panegyric, see Filelfo in *Epistolae*, to Ciriaco d'Ancona (18 December 1427), fols. 2–3. On the critical tradition of the *Aeneid* from Servius to the Renaissance see

representation of the legitimacy of the duke's claims to the throne, his military campaigns, and his expansionist policies. Analogies could easily be drawn between Vergil's hero and Sforza. Like Aeneas, Sforza had come as a foreigner and a warrior of some renown to the kingdom he would eventually rule. Moreover, as in the case of Aeneas and the Latins, the local inhabitants' acceptance of his rule rested on two pre-conditions: his defeat of a powerful neighboring people and his marriage to the sovereign's daughter. And, like the Trojan hero, Sforza would found a dynasty and an empire of sorts.

Accordingly, a plot-summary of Filelfo's *Sforziad* reveals that it resembles the *Aeneid* at least on a superficial level. Book 1 begins after the death of Duke Filippo Maria Visconti, with the wars of succession underway. Just as Juno and Venus plant the seeds of conflict between the Rutulians and the Trojans in *Aeneid* Book 9, so the gods foment strife between Milan and Venice in the *Sforziad*, so that Sforza may play out his preordained role as the conqueror and pacifier of Lombardy. Book 2 describes a number of Milan's client cities welcoming Sforza with open arms, perhaps recalling Evander's welcoming of Aeneas at Pallanteum, and Latinus's in Latium. While Milan's tribute-paying cities, which at first revolted after the duke's death, soon return to the fold, Piacenza alone refuses to return to the protection of its former patron city. Book 3, sympathetic to the plight of the Piacenzan people and filled with resonances from Vergil's narrative of the fall of Troy in *Aeneid* Book 2, tells the story of Sforza's siege and sack of Piacenza. Book 4, like *Aeneid* Book 4, contains the only love story in the poem. But here Aeneas's conflicting desires are sorted out and manifested in two separate characters. Sforza is the rational, loyal, *pius* Aeneas, while Sforza's chief lieutenant Carlo Gonzaga is the irrational, sexualized Aeneas, who falls in love with a married Piacenzan woman. Drawing on Vergil's portrait of the female warrior Camilla in *Aeneid* Book 11, Book 5 depicts Sforza's wife, Bianca's command over the Cremonese army, and her victory over the Venetians. Book 6 is more like *Iliad* Book 20 than *Aeneid* Book 10: Jupiter sends Mars and Minerva down to assist Sforza against Pluto and Neptune, who have joined the Venetian cause. Books 7 and 8 describe the athletic games held in the Milanese and Florentine camps. Book 9, of which we have only a fragment, tells of the Milanese revolt against Sforza after the Peace of Rivoltella in October 1448.[31]

D. C. Allen, *Mysteriously Meant: The Rediscovery of Pagan Symbolism and Allegorical Interpretation in the Renaissance* (Baltimore, 1970); Michael Murrin, *The Allegorical Epic: Essays in Its Rise and Decline* (Chicago, 1969); and Craig Kallendorf, *Early Humanistic Moral Criticism of Vergil's "Aeneid" in Italy and Great Britain* (Ph.D. dissertation, University of North Carolina, 1982). See also idem, "Cristofori Landino's *Aeneid* and the Humanist Critical Tradition," in *Renaissance Quarterly* 36 (1983): 519–46.

[31] The nine extant books of the *Sforziad*, however, cover only little more than a year: from August 1447 to the end of 1448. Cf. plot-summary in Rosmini, *Vita*, 2.156–76.

The centerpiece of the *Sforziad*'s first four books, composed as a tetralogy in the years 1453–1455, is the narrative in Book 3 of the notorious sack of Piacenza conducted by Sforza in 1447.[32] As we will see in the discussion that follows, there is a marked difference in the representation of the siege and sack of the town, between the anti-Milanese accounts by Ripalta and da Soldo on the one hand and the pro-Milanese, pro-Sforza dispatches by Simonetta and Decembrio on the other. The Milanese writers Simonetta and Decembrio downplayed the violence of the sack and all but suppressed the sexual abuse of the Piacenzan women during and after the sack. But Ripalta, da Soldo, and Filelfo deplored above all else the abductions of the townswomen and girls by Sforza's men, treating the rapes as a kind of emblem for Milan's unlawful and violent penetration of its former client city.

I have selected *Sforziad* Book 3, "The Sack of Piacenza," as the subject for more extensive critical commentary in this chapter,[33] not only because of the unusual historical interest of its subject matter, but also because in it, the themes of clientage and patronage, so important in all Filelfo's work, come to the forefront—this time in a different and more violent guise.[34]

The Violence of Patronage at the City-State Level

The patron-client relationship, as we saw earlier, could easily degenerate from one in which reciprocity and mutuality were the ascendant values, to one where getting even was all that counted.[35] Perhaps the most violent face of fifteenth-century clientage could be seen in the alliances between

[32] For fifteenth-century accounts of the sack, see Antonio di Ripalta, *Annales Placentini*, ed. Muratori, *RIS*[1], 20 (Milan, 1781), pp. 893–96; Giovanni Simonetta, *Rerum gestarum Francisci Sfortiae commentarii*, ed. G. Soranzo, *RIS*[2], 21.2 (Bologna, 1934–1959), pp. 202–12; Soranzo, p. xxxiii, dates the composition of the *Commentarii* to 1470–1479; Cristoforo da Soldo, *La Cronaca*, ed. G. Brizzolara, *RIS*[2], 21.3 (Bologna, 1938), pp. 76–77; Pier Candido Decembrio, *Vita Francisci Sfortiae quarti Mediolanensium ducis*, ed. G. Carducci, V. Fiorino, P. Fedele, *RIS*[2], 20.1 (Bologna, 1919). For modern commentaries on the sack and its political context, see Cipolla, *Storia della signorie*, p. 431; S. Romanin, *Storia documentata di Venezia*, 10 vols. (Venice, 1853–1861; reprint 1912–1925), 4.215f.; Rubieri, *Francesco Primo*, pp. 69–77; C. M. Ady, *A History of Milan*, 42; F. Cognasso, *Storia di Milano* (Milan, 1955), 6.411–13.

[33] A complete text of *Sforziad* 3 is provided in Appendix B.

[34] On the violence of patronage, see chap. 1, pp. 17–21.

[35] On the patronage relationship, see Ronald Weissman, "Taking Patronage Seriously: Mediterranean Values and Renaissance Society," pp. 25–46, in *Patronage, Art and Society in Renaissance Italy*, ed. F. W. Kent and P. Simons (Oxford, 1987); E. Gellner and J. Waterbury, eds., *Patrons and Clients in Mediterranean Societies* (London, 1977); S. N. Eisenstadt and L. Roniger, eds., *Patrons, Clients and Friends: Interpersonal Relations and the Structure of Trust in Society* (Cambridge, 1984).

the great territorial states of the period and the smaller cities in their orbits. Cities like Milan and Venice counted on the tributary taxes paid by smaller neighboring municipalities to finance their own domestic and foreign operations. In return, they promised protection to the smaller states against outside aggression. If a tribute-paying city was loyal to its patron city, it could count on protection. If not, retribution might be exacted. The town might be cruelly sacked, its countryside laid waste, its women raped, its monuments and houses razed, and its inhabitants' belongings pillaged and carried away by the invading army. Some client cities and towns were never successfully protected by their patron states, but served simply as battlegrounds for the competition among the patron states.[36] As Michael Mallett has pointed out, the patron city tried always, and for the most part successfully, not to go too far in punishing a delinquent client city. The commanders of the besieging armies usually issued warnings to the townspeople under siege that if they surrendered quickly, their town would either be spared the sack, or the destruction would be limited to property only, while the inhabitants would be given the opportunity to flee before the sack began. Most sieges and sacks were quite limited affairs.[37] There were only a few instances in fifteenth-century Italy in which brutal sacks were actually carried out: the famous sacks of Piacenza in 1447 and Volterra in 1472 were such exceptions.

Piacenza had been one of nine client cities of Milan's to declare its liberty in response to the news of Duke Filippo Maria Visconti's death on 14 August 1447.[38] Perhaps at Piacenza resentment against the Milanese was greater than elsewhere, because in that first week after the duke died the Piacenzans razed the Castello di San Antonio to the ground, seized the offices of the governors, and made a bonfire of the tributary tax registers in the piazza below.[39] Indeed, matters developed with lightning speed. On 22 August, the Venetian military advisers Gerardo Dandolo and Iacopo Antonio Marcello arrived there, accompanied by their generals Taddeo d'Este and Guido Rangoni, with a garrison of two thousand cavalry and two thousand infantry. On that day, the Piacenzans formally swore an oath of fealty to Venice.[40]

---

[36] M. Mallett, *Mercenaries* (London, 1974), 168ff.; on public policy and warfare in the territorial states, see also N. Rubinstein, "Italian Reactions to Terraferma Expansion in the Fifteenth Century," in *Renaissance Venice*, ed. J. R. Hale (London, 1973), 197–217. For a different perspective on Renaissance imperialism and its effects, and on patron city–client city relations, see Judith C. Brown's study of Florence's client Pescia, *In the Shadow of Florence: Provincial Society in Renaissance Pescia* (Oxford, 1982).

[37] Mallett, *Mercenaries*, pp. 193–95.

[38] Cognasso, *Storia*, 6.404–5; the other client cities that defected were Pavia, Como, Lodi, Crema, Parma, Asti, Alessandria, and Tortona; Novara alone remained loyal.

[39] Ripalta, *Annales*, p. 893.

[40] Ibid., p. 892.

The response to Piacenza's defection was overwhelming. The roster of famous condottieri who arrived in Milan to take part in the siege of Piacenza in October 1447 was surely unprecedented. Reading like a latter-day *Argonautica*, it included Carlo Gonzaga, Francesco and Alessandro Sforza, Raimondo Boyl, and the brothers Iacopo and Francesco Piccinino.[41] But weeks before the Milanese fleet was due to sail down the Po, some of Sforza's men engaged in acts of terrorism against the Piacenzan people, perhaps to frighten them into surrender.[42] On the night of 23 September, Luigi dal Verme seized stores of grain, salt hams, cheeses, and even furnishings from the house of a Piacenzan merchant, presumably to distribute among Sforza's men. On the night of the twenty-eighth, Giacomo Ricci and his men burned down a great many houses in the city; they roughed up citizens in the streets and stole a cannon. And on the twenty-ninth of the same month, Francesco Piccinino set fire to a castle belonging to Alberti Scotti, the commander-in-chief of the Piacenzan armed forces.

On 1 October, Francesco Sforza, whom the Milanese had hired to bring Piacenza to its knees, set up camp beneath the city walls. And therein began one of the most brutal bombardments in Italian history. The battering of the walls and fortifications went on relentlessly, all day and through the night, until 16 November 1447, when Sforza's troops finally forced their way over the battlements and through the gates of Piacenza. The Brescian chronicler Cristoforo da Soldo, wrote this account of the city's fall:

> On November 16th, Count Francesco mounted an attack on Piacenza, and this was the most grueling battle, and it lasted from morning until 10 in the evening . . . ; they forced their way into Piacenza, which endured every [evil] in the sack [of the city], accompanied by great cruelty in the pillaging; and [the city] was despoiled of about a thousand cavalrymen from the [Venetian] Signory . . . , belonging to the Marquis Taddeo d'Este, who was now [the Count's] prisoner, and about 800 foreign infantrymen from the most distinguished company they had. As for the ravaging of the land that was plundered, it would take a great pile of paper to write down the many cruelties. All the churches were robbed of their relics, crosses, and chalices; everything was rent asunder. As for the shaming of the women, it is monstrous to write; all the women—virgins, married women, widows, and nuns, all of them, were shamed, abused, and wrongly molested. I do not wish to write more, because piety and compassion forbid me to write. The sack lasted more than 50 days. All the citizens were taken prisoner. Each saw his own wife, his own daughters shamed in his presence . . .[43]

[41] Ibid., pp. 893–94.

[42] Ibid., p. 893.

[43] Da Soldo, *Cronaca*, pp. 76–77: ". . . La Conte Francesco dete una battalgia a Piasenza alli 16 Novembrio; la qual fu crudelissima e duro da la maitina per fin a hore 22 . . . , e

Describing the brutality of Sforza's troops in like fashion, the chronicler Antonio di Ripalta, a Piacenzan citizen who was taken prisoner during the sack, wrote that the Sforzeschi took six thousand men captive, raped the townswomen, looted and desecrated the churches, and even exhumed corpses from their graves in their pursuit of booty. He also testified that the occupying army continued to loot the city and abuse the population without restraint for six months after Sforza's troops first penetrated the city's defenses.[44]

Pier Candido Decembrio, the former secretary of the Milanese republic, presented a very different image of Sforza's role in the subjugation of Piacenza. In his history of the period, Decembrio suppressed all reference to the molestation and rapes of the townswomen and the unwarranted destruction of lives and property for which other chroniclers held Sforza responsible.[45] Instead, he insinuated that, at bottom, the stories circulating about the duke's conduct at Piacenza were no more than rumors, started by people who envied him:

> [Francesco] ordered the entire army to lay siege to Piacenza, which was all the more difficult to attack because, supported by fairly large auxiliary garrisons, it fought off enemy forays for a long time. Finally, due to the great toughness of the duke, and the staying-power and courage of his soldiers, the besieged city was taken. The Marquis Taddeo [d'Este], the Venetians' Captain-general in the war, was led [in chains] to Francesco, with all his men. Since booty was there for the taking, the army lived off the city so well for a number of months that it needed no pay. Naturally, since the price of the spoils from the captured booty-money and the arms of the soldiers, all told, easily exceeded the sum of 500,000 gold florins, this victory made people envious of Francesco. The result was that not only the Venetians but even the Milanese themselves were worried by the false rumors and began to be afraid [of Francesco].[46]

---

introrno per forza. La qual Piasenza andò tutta quanta a saccomanno com grande crudelità de robbamento, e fu assaccomanato da circa milli cavalli de la Signoria . . . , li quali cavalli erano de Thadeo Marchese il qual fu anchora lui presone, et da circa otto cento fanti forestieri de la più fiorità compagnia ch'egli havesseno. Del distrassio dela terra saccommanata gli voria uno rismo de paper a scrivere tante crudelità. Fu robbato generalmente tutte le Giesie: Reliquie, Crose e calici; stratiato ogni cosa. Dil vergognar delle donne saria uno stupor a scriverlo: tutte le donzelle, verginelle, maridate, vedue e monege, tutte quante, furno vergognate straciate e mal menate. Non voglio scriver altro perche la pietade e la compassion non mi lassa scrivere. Duro lo saccomanno più de cinquanta giorni. Fu fatto presoni tutti quelli citadini; gli fideva vergognate le sue donne, le sue fiole in sua presentia . . ."

[44] Ripalta, *Annales*, p. 896.

[45] Decembrio, *Vita*, pp. 805–12; on his career, see M. Borsa, "Pier Candido Decembri e l'umanesimo," *ASL* 20 (1893): 5–75 and 358–441.

[46] Decembrio, *Vita*, pp. 805–12: ". . . Exercitum omnem Placentiam obsidere iubet. Que eo difficilius obsidebatur, quo maioribus fulta presidiis, hostiles impetus longe repellebat. Tandem magno ducis robore, militum tolerantia et fortitudine expugnata capitur. Tadeus

The official propagandist of the Sforza regime, Giovanni Simonetta, described the minutiae of the siege—its stages, weaponry, key personalities, and strategies.[47] But he kept his testimony on the sack of the city, particularly on the rapes of the women, to a minimum.

> But Francesco [Simonetta wrote] hurried off to the castello of St. Antonio, where he had heard Taddeo [d'Este] and Gerardo [Dandolo] had fled; there he saw everything in a state of tumult in the city, and saw the majority of the Piacenzans, who had entered with the rest of the crowd and had run weeping toward one another, being dragged off and shouts being mingled with the tumult; and he realized that everything was being pillaged and profaned. Truly, he grieved at the lot of the ancient and noble city and at the wretched disaster of the defection of the innocent, and therefore he quickly dispatched several of his own men (of whose loyalty he was utterly certain) to the various monasteries dedicated to divine worship, and especially to those in the care of the female sex, where, he had heard, a great number of young girls and matrons had fled for security, so that they could be sure to be kept safe from injury and abuse.[48]

Filelfo's "Sack of Piacenza" and the Rhetoric of Imperialism

Gary Ianziti has recently drawn attention to the distinction between Filelfo, who enjoyed relative autonomy as a writer, and other Milanese writers such as Giovanni Simonetta, a chancery bureaucrat and dependent of Sforza's whose works were propagandistic representations of the duke's political and military programs.[49] Filelfo's independence becomes clear only when we compare a book like the *Sforziad*, and its narrative of the sack of Piacenza, for example, with Simonetta's treatment of the same events in the *De rebus gestis commentarii*, his history of Sforza Milan written in the manner of Caesar's *Commentaries*.[50] Filelfo's and Simonetta's narratives of the siege differ in two main areas—apart, of course, from their differences of genre. First, Simonetta gives speech making no place in his narrative, either in his portrayal of the Milanese leaders or the Piacenzan people. Sec-

marchio, Venetorum in bello ductor, cum omnibus suis ad Franciscum perducitur. Urbs prede exposita exercitum per multos menses ita aluit, ut stipendio non egeret. Nempe cum prede precium captivis manubiis armisque militum simul pensitatis quingentorum milium aureorum summam facile excesserit, hec victoria Francisco invidiam attulit, ut non Veneti modo, sed ipsi Mediolanenses falsis rumoribus agitati contremescerent."

[47] Simonetta, *Commentarii*, pp. 201–12.

[48] Ibid., pp. 211 and 212.

[49] Gary Ianziti, "The Production of History in Milan," in *Patronage, Art and Society in Renaissance Italy*, ed. F. W. Kent and P. Simons, pp. 299–311; esp. pp. 306–7.

[50] Ibid., p. 311.

ond, he says little about the suffering of the townsfolk, let alone the rape of the women; instead, his account is taken up with the details of the siege and the siegeworks, with combat or preparations for combat.

Filelfo, on the other hand, who was in Piacenza himself in December 1447 when the pillaging was in full swing, devotes nearly one-half of his narrative in Book 3 to the rhetoric of the generals and to the events surrounding the sack itself.[51] Following the Thucydidean tradition of putting fictional speeches into the mouths of his generals, Filelfo uses the oratory of his two captains, Sforza and the Venetian general Gerardo Dandolo, to develop a key theme in Book 3: the violence of clientage at the city-state level—whether in its implicit form, in the rhetoric of extortion, or in its most explicit expression, in the punishments meted out to the Piacenzans by the troops of the patron city.[52]

At the outset of the book, the reader is given to understand that the entry and occupation of the city is the goal toward which the rest of the book's action is moving: "Come, Polyhymnia, tell how [Sforza] labored," Filelfo asks of his Muse in the prologue, "to turn the captive city into spoils."(7–12)[53] Thus, in the speeches of both Sforza and Dandolo, the repeated threats, and indeed the forecasts, of rape and violation serve as a kind of prurient stimulus that propels the plot forward, to the inevitable seizure of the city—and the quintessential emblem of its property and honor: its women.

Even in the midst of Sforza's first speeches, there is a sense of the futility of eloquence in wartime. Rhetoric is used to authorize the violence of war, and yet war somehow defies the constraints of reason. Regardless of all the goodwill in the world on the part of an army's officers, atrocities will nonetheless be unavoidable:

> At first [Sforza], because he is kind, sets about to attempt everything in a gentle, peaceful manner, showing nothing hostile, nothing tearful in his demeanor. But when he sees time going idly by, and realizes his warnings are of no avail, then he skillfully adds threats. He raises fears, telling about the destruction of the city, the conduct of the crazed soldiery, and the savage insanity. He not only depicts himself as victor amid the sad carnage, but he speaks eloquently of the hardships [of war] and calls their attention to the numerous crimes [that will be perpetrated during the sack], asking them to imagine the killing of their men and the abduction of their wives and daughters. (20–29)[54]

[51] Rosmini, *Vita*, 2.283–84 [=Benadduci, ed., *Atti*, pp. 123–24], contains the only known letter, dated 13 December 1447, that Filelfo sent when he visited Sforza's camp in Piacenza. For obvious reasons the letter makes no reference to local conditions.

[52] See nn. 34 and 35.

[53] All line numbers in the *Sforziad* citations hereafter refer to the text of bk. 3 in Appendix B.

[54] Appendix B.

Sforza's next, and last, warning to the Piacenzans comes at a climactic point in his siege preparations (49–100). And here, descriptions of the duke's offensive operations and the townspeople's defense strategies form a backdrop against which Sforza's speech will be heard. Blocking off all the supply lines into Piacenza via the Po, Sforza has bombarded the small city for forty-four days. And while the townspeople have constructed a mound and dug a new ditch around the walls, Sforza's men have erected two siege towers from which both gunners and archers can shoot at the enemy below (their weapons are referred to as "fulmineae pilulae" and "volucres sagittae" [82]: "fiery bullets" and "winged arrows"). Sforza's speech exemplifies the two contradictory faces of patronage: even as he holds out the benefits of safety, protection, and self-determination to the Piacenzans if only they surrender, he warns them of the vengeance his troops will take if they must penetrate the city's walls forcibly. So far as he is concerned, the Piacenzans have conducted themselves in a provocative manner all along ("vos volentes," 105). The final choice, however, is still theirs to make. They can abide—at their own peril—by the alliance they have already with Venice ("fides," 105), or they can reap the benefits of protection and economic assistance as one of Milan's subject cities ("tuebor," 114; and "commoda," 115). At the same time the duke guarantees the Piacenzans freedom from all interference, even that of the Milanese ("nil quod nolitis ab Insubribus," 115–16). Last come his threats. If the Piacenzans reject his offers of protection, there will be reprisals. Once his troops have entered the city, he warns the townspeople, their men will be slaughtered and their women and daughters will be the victims of criminal assault. And in that event no one—not even he—will be able to restrain his men.

> O wretched citizens, what cruel destiny oppresses you so, while you willingly assent? Or, have you heartlessly conspired against yourselves? Have you not had enough of the Venetians and their pledges—do you not see your own downfall and death? Who will be able to control the insane fury of an armed soldier? . . . Be sane and listen to our warnings. Entrust yourselves to our pledge, and do not test the shifting sands of raging fortune. I will protect your interests; nothing will be done to you wrongfully, or against your will, by the Milanese. (105–9 and 112–16)

When the Piacenzans reject the duke's offers, behind the walls the Venetian general and military advisor, Gerardo Dandolo, delivers a classical *exhortatio* to the townspeople—which, despite its much greater length, is roughly analogous to Sforza's speech to the Piacenzans and is meant to respond to it, in the manner of the paired speeches in Sallust and Livy. In the speeches of the two leaders, Filelfo represents two powerful territorial states vying for the allegiance of a prospective client city.[55] In each speech, the state's aggression is veiled in the venerable euphemisms of patronage: *amicitia*, in the vocabulary of republican and imperial Rome, which, as we have seen in the preceding chapter, would find new sustenance in the fifteenth century.[56] Indeed, protection, economic assistance, and political autonomy (*tuitio, commoda*, and *libertas*) are the commodities Sforza and Dandolo propose to exchange in return for the client city's pledge of loyalty (*fides*). Dandolo's speech to the Piacenzans is remarkably similar to Sforza's. Paternalistic in his tone and manner, the Venetian advisor is careful to show not anger, but pity for the Piacenzans ("miserescimus," 329). The Piacenzans are urged to consider their loyalty ("fides," 317) to the Venetians, who will be both their benefactors and their protectors ("tutatur," 316; and "tueri," 333). If they retain their ties of loyalty with Venice, Dandolo promises, then the Piacenzans will continue, like the Brescians, to enjoy their freedom ("libertate fruitur," 318)—an obvious irony, since the result of Venice's and Milan's combined patronage of Brescia in the 1430s and 1440s was to turn it into a battleground where the two great powers could test their war might, and at a safe distance from home. Dandolo's speech stresses the kinshiplike ties—bonds of mutual obligation—that characterize the *fides* relationship. Venice, he assures the Piacenzans, regards them as allies and brothers, and will continue to treat them not as servants but as *amici* ("socios fratresque putat laetatus amici / nomine non famuli," 322–23). Theoretically, both partners in the *fides* relationship are prepared to perform their duties and services willingly and without coercion. In practice, however, the line between patronage and extortion is a tenuous one. In Dandolo's speech, as in Sforza's, after the bountiful promises of *amicitia* come the threats of sacrilege and rape:

> As long as Brescia protected itself from the arms of the hostile enemy and steadfastly kept its pledge to the Venetian senate, it considered that pledge a benefit to itself . . . For Venice does not force those men to submit to a harsh yoke who align themselves with her cause willingly. These men Venice considers allies and brothers; she rejoices in the name "friend," not "servant" . . . You seek nothing, except not to submit to the cruel and unjust yoke of the Milanese. We pity you and look on you with human compassion; nor are we quick

[55] On the defense strategies of the Quattrocento territorial, see Mallett, *Mercenaries*, pp. 168ff. On Gherardo Dandolo and the top-level military personnel (*provveditori*) that Venice sent to supervise its generals in the field, see Michael Mallett, "Venice and its Condottieri, pp. 1404–54," in *Renaissance Venice*, ed. J. R. Hale (London, 1973), pp. 121–45; esp. p. 137.

[56] On the vocabulary of patronage in antiquity, see P. A. Brunt, " 'Amicitia' in the Late Roman Republic," in R. Seager, ed., *The Crisis of the Roman Republic: Studies in Political and Social History* (Cambridge, 1969), pp. 197–218; on *fides*, see M. Gelzer, *The Roman Nobility* (Oxford, 1969), pp. 62ff.; and Richard P. Saller, *Personal Patronage Under the Early Empire* (Cambridge, 1982).

to treat your own citizens on an equal basis with ours for praise, or for any hope of gain or profit. We are willing to safeguard your lives with our arms, provided that you remain faithful to us in every duty and in all your affairs. But should you be ever so slow to meet the risks involved, or ever so lacking in fervor for hand-to-hand combat, only imagine the thousand humiliations of the enemy, barbarous and panting in the temples of the gods; and think of your daughters, and every evil and disgrace done to your beloved wives . . . (315–18; 320–23; and 328–39)

Thus, on the eve of the annihilation of Piacenza, Sforza and Dandolo, representing Milan and Venice, resort to the euphemisms of patronage. The vocabulary of patronage—*amicitia, tuitio, fides, libertas*—lends itself here not only to ambiguity but to irony. Thus an aspiring patron city's (Milan's) seemingly innocuous offers of friendship, protection, and independence are read by the inhabitants of its would-be client city (Piacenza) as euphemisms for subjection and exploitation.

The ancient Roman term *imperium*, however, had no such fuzziness about it. The territorial states of the fifteenth century were in fact eager not to elicit charges of imperialism against themselves. For as Nicolai Rubinstein has noted, when Sforza wanted to stir up anti-Venetian sentiment in Florence in the late forties, he had only to have his ambassador Nicodemo Tranchedini make allegations that Venice was aspiring to *l'imperio d'Italia*.[57] And since Filelfo and Tranchedini kept in close touch by correspondence during this period, we can be sure that Filelfo was well aware that the speeches he composed for Sforza and Dandolo would be received as the callous rhetoric of imperialism by his audience.[58]

Nor was the theme of imperialism a peculiarly modern one in literature. The seeds, at least, of Filelfo's representation of the rhetoric of expansionism and city clientage in *Sforziad* Book 3 could be found in Livy, Sallust, Velleius, and even in the principal model for his epic—Vergil's *Aeneid*. In Book 8, Aeneas urges Evander, the King of the Arcadians, to join the Trojans in an alliance for their mutual protection. Like Sforza's and Dandolo's speeches to the Piacenzans, Aeneas's speech to the Arcadians, in which he asks for a treaty of friendship (*fides*), turns both on the threat of a hostile takeover and the offer of assistance powerful enough to counter that threat: "Your enemy [Aeneas tells Evander] believes that, once they drive us out, nothing will stop them from completely subjugating all Italy to their rule, and from taking possession of the seas that wash it to the east

---

[57] On Quattrocento perceptions of imperialism, see Rubinstein, "Italian Reactions to Terraferma Expansion in the Fifteenth Century," pp. 197–217.

[58] See Filelfo, *Epistolae*, fol. 93 (21 February 1456); ibid. (19 August 1455), fol. 90, indicates that Tranchedini probably also received an advance copy of the *Sforziad*. On Tranchedini, the closest of Filelfo's friends, see Adam, *F. Filelfo*, pp. 87–89.

and west. Receive our pledge, and give us yours. For our part, we offer hearts and minds that are courageous in battle and a youth tested in warfare."[59] The *Aeneid* also provided Filelfo with a paradigm for the prince who assures his neighbors that he has no territorial designs, and wants only an equitable alliance—despite all evidence to the contrary. Aeneas hears over and over that he is destined to found an empire that will extend its rule not only over the rest of Italy but over lands far beyond its borders.[60] Still in Book 12 he promises the Latins that "I shall never order the Italians to be the subjects of the Trojans, nor do we seek an empire for ourselves. But let both our peoples live as allies forever and under equal laws, neither one being subjugated by the other."[61]

When the Piacenzans resolve to honor their pledges of loyalty to the Venetians and answer the Milanese overtures only with cannon fire, Sforza feels justified in carrying out his threats. But here, as in Livy and Sallust, the ideal *dux* must show his virtue as both *miles* and *rhetor*. Sforza's classical *exhortatio* to his own men demonstrates his ability to manipulate the emotions of his men, to mobilize their frustration and anger, and to cause them to perceive the small city at once as a dangerous enemy and a treasure house of spoils. Reverting again to the rhetoric of patronage, he characterizes the Piacenzans as traitors who bit the hand that fed them ("ingratos," 166). Those ingrates, he tells his troops, should have allied themselves with our side (165–67). The Piacenzans alone, he argues, must bear the full responsibility for the destruction of their city, for "they willingly sought their own doom." (175–77). They have shown, Sforza rationalizes further, that they are unfit to rule themselves, since one can only attribute their conduct to insanity (177 and 193). At the same time, Sforza continues to reiterate even here his pity for the Piacenzans, his sorrow, and his unwillingness to sack their city (173, 178, and 179). Only two new points are added: the standard caveat about the importance of moderation, and the argument from necessity—with winter setting in, it is imperative to capture the city at once.

The points Sforza makes in his last speech to his men before they storm the city walls form a somewhat self-contradictory package. Certainly Sforza's plea for moderation serves more as a stimulus here than as a prohibition. He singles out the churches and the young girls in the community as

[59] *Aeneid* 8.147–49: " 'nos si pellant, nihil afore credunt / quin omnem Hesperiam penitus sua sub iuga mittant, / et mare quod supra teneant quodque adluit infra. / accipe daque fidem. sunt nobis fortia bello / pectora, sunt animi et rebus spectata iuventus.' "

[60] *Aeneid* 4.346–50: "Italiam Lyciae iussere capessere sortes; hic amor, haec patria est . . Nos fas extera quaerere regna"; 6.790ff.: "Augustus Caesar, divi genus, aurea condet / saecula, qui rursus Latio . . / proferet imperium; iacet extra sidera tellus, / extra anni solis vias, etc."

[61] *Aeneid* 12.189–91: " 'non ego nec Teucris Italos parere iubebo / nec mihi regna peto: paribus se legibus ambae / invictae gentes aeterna in foedera mittant.' "

being of especial value: "templis parcite; virgo / salva sit," (204–5). But he has already warned the Piacenzans that their women and daughters will be molested anyway should there be a sack, however much he opposes such conduct (28). Now as he actually goads his men over the walls, only the churches and the young girls need be thought of as forbidden fruit:[62]

> I had believed, friends, that our patience would eventually have some effect on the ungrateful Piacenzans and that this would bring those who were besieged around to our side of their own free will. For this reason I had refrained from using your forces . . . But I was glad to take pity on so devastating a disaster and such cruel plunder as victory brings with it. However, now that these people have given neither ear nor mind to any warnings or peril, and since they willingly seek destruction, let them pay for their madness. I grieve—and may the ruler of the gods be present as my witness—that I plunder unwillingly the city we are about to take. What else could I do in the end? Look, friends, the forty-fifth day is now at hand since we first began to lay siege to this city . . . A grim and difficult winter is coming on quickly . . . Deep snow encrusts the neighboring hills, and inhospitable ice prevents our pack animals from grazing . . . And so, let us go forward at last, and may madness make way for vengeance . . . Meanwhile may the artillery never stop spewing forth their whirling cannon balls, or knocking down the walls with rocks. This will be the day that will heap up all manner of wealth and good things for you. Only it is fitting to be mindful of the deity and justice. I beseech you, spare the churches; let the young girls remain untouched; mingle nothing profane with your booty. (165–68, 173–82, 184–85, 187–89, 192–93, and 200–205).

The Battle around the Walls

After the exhortations of Sforza and Dandolo, the battle at the outer ditch intensifies. Here the suspense mounts before the final push to penetrate the walls of the city, as Filelfo describes each stage of the bombardment. His depiction of the war and its weaponry had added interest for his condottiere audience, not only because of Sforza's fame as a strategist, but also because Milan was renowned as the arms manufacturing center of Europe during these years of rapid technological advance in ballistics.[63] The handgun, for example, in whose mass production the Milanese took particular

---

[62] This is a strange directive and has no precedents in Quattrocento law. See nn. 78, 79, and 80 on the legal codes of the period governing the conduct of invading troops during a siege: rape was generally interdicted with no age specifications.

[63] On the technology of war in the fifteenth century: J. R. Hale, "International Relations in the West: Diplomacy and War," in *The New Cambridge Modern History. The Renaissance: 1493–1520* 1.275–84; Mallett, *Mercenaries*; P. Pieri, "Le milizie sforzesche (1450–1534)," *Storia di Milano* 8.821–863.

pride, played a strategic role in the victories Sforza's armies won at both Piacenza and Caravaggio the following year.[64] Filelfo's scenes of the siege suggest, however, that in fifteenth-century warfare the crossbow remained at least as important a weapon as the handgun.[65]

At some distance from the walls of the city, Sforza positions his cross-bowmen and gunners on the rim of the outer ditch ("quicumque . . . / aut valeant nervo celeris et fune sagittas / tormentisve citis pilulas torquere fre-mentes." 369–72). Next, a company of heavily armed young men stands in front of these marksmen, protecting them with their long shields from the lances of the enemy (373–75). At the rear, behind the marksmen and the shield-bearers, are the cavalrymen with their lances, crying, "Praedam praedamque." ("booty, booty!" 376–77) Meanwhile, under Sforza's steady assault on the walls, of arrows and a stonelike cannonball that "re-sembled lightning and left a trail of smoke under the massive mound," the first wave of foot-soldiers manages to get across the ditch despite its raging current and the rain of pikes and whirling cannonballs coming from the city's defenders on the ramparts ("nec diffusa moratur / vis salientis aquae nec saxa rotata sudesque," 387f.).

Typical in siege warfare of the period were the double artillery towers and the ditches that Filelfo describes both sides as adapting to their own advantage (*geminas turris*, 78 and 81; *fossae*, 65, 76, 81ff., and 132ff.).[66] While the Piacenzans fill the outer ditch to overflowing and are able to control the water level in the ditch by connecting it to a makeshift reservoir (*alveus structus*, 143), Sforza's men, navigating the ditch in a small vessel (*musculus*), set about to fill it in with earth, brush, and stones (132–48).

While Sforza's siege strategy dominates the first half of the book, Filel-fo's scenes of the beleaguered townspeople overshadow its second half. As Piacenza fights for its life, the entire populace—women, children, and the very old—takes part in its defense. And thus, it is the townspeople's nobil-ity, courage, and piety, not that of the Milanese troops, that Filelfo repeat-edly praises here:

> For their part, the besieged people strain to defend their walls with the forti-fications of a ditch and a high mound: nor do they retreat in the face of any calamity. They scorn death because of the sweetness of glory, fear for their sons, sad duty toward their parents, and intense dread for their wives and the city of their birth. The fighting escalates not only in this one place, but war rages in every district, tearing down both city and walls alike. And more and more hard Bellona wears out the brave Piacenzans. (399–407)

[64] On the handgun, see Mallett, *Mercenaries*, p. 157.
[65] On bow vs. gun, see Mallett, *Mercenaries*, p. 154; Hale, "International Relations," *The New Cambridge Modern History*, 1.275ff.
[66] Mallett, *Mercenaries*, pp. 164–70.

At three crucial points in his account of the siege Filelfo breaks off from the narrative to apostrophize to the gods in horror over the brutality of Sforza's men. The first of these apostrophes comes directly on the heels of Sforza's command to his men to abandon all feelings of pity for the Piacenzans (429–30). Filelfo calls on the gods to halt the evil that Sforza and his men are about to perpetrate: "Superi, facinus prohibete nefandum" (432). Filelfo's second apostrophe—in which he questions the reconcilability of war with religious teaching—follows the mortal wounding of Sforza's horse (441–50). What is the good, Filelfo asks, of the doctrine that vengeance is the prerogative of the deities alone, when men have taken it upon themselves to play God? His third apostrophe comes at the end of his narrative of the sack of the city. This time addressing not Jove but Christ, Filelfo implicitly poses the perennial question: if there is a God, why does he do nothing in the face of such evil in the world? "What forebearance, O Christ, has been able to render you so impassive that our impiety moves you not at all? (678–81)

While Sforza's political and rhetorical strategies are at least reminiscent of Vergil's hero, on the battlefield Sforza is very different from Aeneas. Nor should we assume that Filelfo saw buried in the *Aeneid* a subtle critique of Augustus and his policies.[67] Filelfo's famous letter to Ciriaco d'Ancona about the *Aeneid* indicates, on the contrary, that he accepted Servius's and Fulgentius's reading of the *Aeneid* first as a moral allegory, and second as a panegyric of the emperor.[68] Still, Filelfo seems to have been troubled by the insane rage (*ira* and *furor*) that Aeneas evinces in Book 10: while Vergil's hero clearly takes leave of his senses in this part of the poem, first slaughtering a priest of Apollo and moments later stopping to curse and kick at the mutilated corpse of a young warrior he had already decapitated, Filelfo's prince is cut from an altogether different pattern.[69] Dismissing Aristotle's doctrine of just anger, Filelfo believed that the wrath typical of the Homeric hero could never be thought a virtue.[70] Clearly he felt that such emotional abandon was inappropriate in a modern hero.

Filelfo does, however, adopt some aspects of the Homeric hero in his characterization of Sforza. Like Homer's Achilles and Vergil's Aeneas, Sforza during the storming of Piacenza manifests his "aristeia"—a scene de

---

[67] In the mid-1960s a group of influential scholars began to argue that the *Aeneid* might not be an encomium, but a veiled indictment of the emperor and his policies: see Michael C. J. Putnam, *The Poetry of the "Aeneid"* (Cambridge, Mass., 1965); W. Ralph Johnson, *Darkness Visible: A Study of Vergil's "Aeneid"* (Berkeley, 1976); Brooks Otis, *Virgil: A Study in Civilized Poetry* (Oxford, 1963); Adam Parry, "The Two Voices of Virgil's *Aeneid*," in *Arion* 2 (1963): 66–80; Kenneth Quinn, *Virgil's "Aeneid": A Critical Description* (London, 1968).

[68] On the *Aeneid* as panegyric and allegory in the Renaissance, see n. 30.

[69] *Aeneid* 10.537–41 and 10.550–56.

[70] See Filelfo on Aristotle's doctrine on anger in his *De morali disciplina*, pp. 55ff.

rigueur in Homeric epic, in which the hero must demonstrate in the course of a murderous rampage his physical superiority over all other warriors in the vicinity. Filelfo's Sforza, like his epic predecessors, indeed proves to be a competent mass murderer, given the right setting—his entry into Piacenza. The difference is that Sforza never attacks particular enemy soldiers without provocation, but strikes only in self-defense. In this parody of an epic aristeia, three mercenary soldiers, caricatures of Iliadic heroes, whose names are Tharson, Moron, and Aphron (Greek for "Reckless," "Foolish," and "Witless") are slain by Sforza not while they kneel to him in a posture of supplication, as do the victims of Achilles' and Aeneas's murderous wrath, but as they aim a deadly weapon at the general. In this passage Filelfo exaggerates the steamy anger and the cartoonish muscularity of Sforza's opponents to the point of bathos, while Sforza himself appears poised, metallic, and emotionless:

> When this man [Tharson] sees . . . the great-hearted hero [Sforza] inside the walls, gleaming in his armor, he [Tharson] rages, hot with fierce anger. With both hands he raises up a cudgel high in the air so that he can slam down a savage blow on Sforza's helmet—but Sforza swiftly rushes up, his sword whirling with greater force, and hacks off Tharson's hand and stops the blow. Then he, gravely wounded and in great pain called out to his brother Moron, sending heartrending cries to the heavens. Moron now arrived on the scene enraged, sitting astride an enormous horse; and even as he was hurling threats and brandishing a death-dealing scimitar, he received a wound in the middle of his chest, and breathed out his life. After him, Thracian Aphron arrived, the son of an Illyrian mother and a Molossian father. When he picks up a heavy boulder that ten men's bodies could scarcely lift, just as he is about to hurl it at the enemy, he feels his head, neck, and breast being split in two by a sword.[71] (579–600)

The Sack of Piacenza

At the final moment of penetration of the city's defenses, the contrast between the piety of the townspeople and the avarice of the foreign troops, fighting among themselves for spoils, is particularly sharp. As in many of his works, Filelfo seems here to be reacting not only to classical models but to Petrarch's adaptations of those same models. We observed earlier that Filelfo's account of the sack differs markedly from those of his fellow court-

---

[71] Cf. the same idea in *Aeneid* 12.899–900: "Scarcely could twelve choice men endowed with such bodies as the earth produces nowadays, support that boulder on their shoulders." Everything about this passage is parodic, including touches like the epithet "Molossian" (*Molosso*, 592), which is usually used to describe a breed of dog in Horace and Vergil.

iers, Simonetta and Decembrio. Filelfo was a great admirer of Petrarch's works, and was always in some sense under the spell of his Trecento master. Thus it is worth noting that his "Sack of Piacenza" diverges in spirit from Petrarch's epic poem more than from Vergil's. Filelfo's narrative is in fact quite unlike the one siege-and-sack episode in Petrarch's epic poem, the *Africa*—Scipio Africanus's invasion of Cartagena. Petrarch puts the tale of the sack in the mouth of a friend of Scipio's, thus presenting the story in a manner wholly sympathetic to Scipio and the Roman army rather than the besieged townspeople.[72] Filelfo, on the contrary, follows the second book of Vergil's *Aeneid* in describing the sack of the city through the eyes of its victims rather than through those of its victors.

> Their sweet children, their beloved parents, and their dear wives draw the citizens away; booty, valuables, and money draw the foreigners. Still, the very name of slave and enormous love for their dying city bind the hearts of all together. And so, each one tries with unvanquished heart to protect himself in the house of his ancestors. The citizens try to block the streets with planks of wood and heavy chains. And they hope, poor folk, to curb by delay the enemy's rage, when soon on all sides, all the troops burst in, hot with the lust for spoils . . .

> The cornfields vibrate, iron-colored, with the clanging of spears and swords unsheathed. The whole city is despoiled of its booty . . . That man over there hacks away at the doors with an ax, and redoubling his blows he smashes them all to bits . . . Another dares to climb up to windows by ladder or rope, or perhaps with a heavy spear; and when he descends he is overwhelmed by innumerable weapons and a rushing mass of men: thus, bleeding and battered, he readies himself again and again to get possession of what he has so fervently prayed for—booty. (621–30, 635–36, 647–48, and 650–54)[73]

When the frenzy of looting has died down, it is succeeded by nightmarish scenes of the sort predicted by the Milanese and Venetian leaders. The townswomen and the churches now become the quarry of the marauding bands of soldiers:

> The sound of sad weeping rises in the air. Over here a young girl is dragged off; and right over there a pure wife submits, with her husband watching her, to whatever lust and madness dictate. For when sad victory is won, covered

[72] Petrarch, *Africa*, trans. and ann. by T. G. Bergin and A. S. Wilson (New Haven, 1977), 4.352–432, pp. 78–80.

[73] This passage and others at the height of the siege in *Sforziad* 3.433–659 are especially reminiscent of *Aeneid* 2.476–488 and 757–59. The fields glimmering with weapons is an allusion to *Aeneid* 11.601: "ferreus ager, etc." ("the iron-colored field").

with such bloodshed, what leader could restrain the maddened soldiers? All things are torn apart: not even the temples are spared, all are profaned. Not only does the virgin devoted to God unwillingly endure every manner of evil and dark dishonor, groaning tearfully and witnessing to the heavens her shame, but even the eucharist, with which we worship the consecrated body of the ruler of Olympus, lies on the ground as though it were a shameful thing. (664–76)

Filelfo's account of Sforza's attempts to remedy the situation differs curiously here from Simonetta's. Simonetta reports that Sforza ordered all his men to release all the women they had abducted, or face the death penalty if they failed to comply.[74] In the *Sforziad*, when the general learns of the rapes, "the tears roll down his pious cheeks" (688), and this is an image—however anomalous it seems, given the toughness of all Sforza's previous rhetoric—which is altogether in keeping with Filelfo's cartoonlike rendering of Sforza in his mock-Homeric battle with Tharson, Aphron, and Moron. After the general recovers his composure, he offers a reward to any soldier who is willing to confess his part in the rapes.[75] "But who," Filelfo asks skeptically, "would bear witness against himself," particularly for a crime in which the whole army took part (689)? Moreover, Simonetta had testified that Sforza sent special deputies to the convents where the townswomen had already taken refuge before the sack. Filelfo's story is that Sforza, on the contrary, took no action until after the raping and pillaging had been going on for some time. At this point in the narrative, he comments in lines heavy with irony: "Thus, thanks to the bounty and piety of gentle [Francesco Sforza], every woman escaped cruel hands—and that which had already been allowed to happen to her." (695–97)[76]

Notably, the chroniclers and poets of the period were not alone in their censure of rape and other abuses of the civilian population in wartime.[77] Venice had specific laws governing the conduct of its condottieri: there were fifty-six laws on its books concerning, among other things, the pro-

[74] Simonetta, *Commentarii*, 212: "reddendas iussit capitisque poenam, qui non paruerit, constituit."

[75] Sforza's offer is very strange and is nowhere reflected in the legal codes of the period.

[76] "Quod iam sibi posse licebat": as is always the case in reading Filelfo, the irony depends on the reader's point of view. A reader (such as Sforza himself presumably) who was not expecting to find critical innuendos in the poem could read the line "because it was now permitted for her to be able [to escape]." But even so, the other more critical sense remains inherent in the passage—particularly because of the stress in the line on the word *iam* ("now, at long last").

[77] See again chap. 1, pp. 45–47, and Appendix A, for Filelfo's letter to Francesco Sforza (8 October 1438), fol. 16–16v, in which Filelfo censures in no uncertain terms the atrocities he has heard Sforza's troops have committed during the sack of Tolentino.

tection of women and other noncombatants during the siege and sack of a city.[78] Severe fines and punishments were enforced in the case of breaches of these regulations. The Venetians, furthermore, fired their aristocratic condottiere Sigismondo Malatesta, the Signor of Rimini, for his part in the rape of a German noblewoman, which occurred not during the sack of a city but on the road.[79] In Naples, King Alfonso severely punished those of his own soldiers whom he found guilty of the molestation of citizens during a siege; the sentence for rape, on at least one occasion, was public beheading. The king also practiced preventive measures: when he stormed Biccari in 1441, Panormita wrote that he placed all the townswomen under armed guard, prior to the onset of the sack.[80]

In Filelfo's account, Sforza's imprisonment of the townswomen after the rapes had been committed is regarded by the women themselves as a further outrage. From their place of incarceration, they launch into a long song of lamentation (699–763) reminiscent of several choral odes in Euripides. Here, as in Euripides, the perennial subordination of women becomes an emblem for the subjugation and suffering of the captive city in time of war. Filelfo's chorus of Piacenzan women touches upon a number of familiar Euripidean themes: the victimization of women amid the general horror of war (in the *Trojan Women* and the *Hecabe*, from which Filelfo himself had translated selections);[81] the particular sufferings of women, related to their gender—their status as property and their physical vulnerability (*Medea*); their preference for death over slavery (*Andromache*); and the view of their present situation as but the latest in a long history of the enslavement of their sex (*Trojan Women*).[82] Particularly Euripidean is the poignant use of the first-person singular and plural ("I," "we") in the women's song, as in this passage:

Ah woe, nature or God has dealt us a sad fate—our being the female race. No living creature is more submissive, nor more exposed to every evil. We are unwarlike, nor do we have the power to reason, more excellent than any other: our minds are always weak with fear. We have no useful physical strength. Our

[78] Mallett, "Venice and its Condottieri," pp. 132–33.
[79] Luigi Rossi, "Un delitto di Sigismondo Malatesta," in *Rivista di Scienze Storiche* (1910): 362–82.
[80] Alan Ryder, *The Kingdom of Naples under Alfonso the Magnanimous* (Oxford, 1976), pp. 284–85; Antonio Beccadelli (Panormita), *De dictis et factis* (Basel, 1538), 2.20 and 23.
[81] Filelfo's Latin translations of Euripides have been published in Calderini, *Ricerche*, 310–13.
[82] Cf. Appendix B, at lines 710, 716, and 726, the Piacenzan women's charge that first the Carthaginians, then the Goths, the Germans, and the Franks enslaved them and Euripides' *Trojan Women*, 797–850, where a chorus of captive women laments that first Heracles, then Ganymede, and next Eos brought ruin to Troy.

nature has nothing unusual in it which can be displayed in public. And so, we are looked down upon and we bear our slavish yoke deservedly. But of all those on earth, the stars shine with an unfriendly light only on the women of Piacenza. For I remember that when I was a girl, my father told how great a calamity it was when savage Hamilcar lay siege to this city, and when the leader of the Insubrians—may the gods destroy that cruel folk with their light-ning bolts!—turned everything into spoils, burning our houses as he went. What violence, what disgrace has not been committed against us? But why am I recalling the madness? the things that have perished in the long age? the things that time has corrupted?

The Pacification of Piacenza

After the women's song of lamentation Sforza delivers a speech that serves as a kind of epilogue. It is a strange oration in which Filelfo makes a patent liar of his patron. In what was surely an attempt to give his readers a fore-shadowing of Sforza's subsequent strategy of playing both sides against the middle, first defecting to Venice in 1448 (one year after his victory at Pia-cenza) and then returning to the Milanese a little more than a year later, Filelfo has Sforza assign the responsibility for the sack solely to the Piacen-zans—and to God. In this speech neither he, the Venetians, nor his own men share any of the blame for the annihilation of Piacenza. The tiny city, he claims, had more than enough resources to defend itself against any enemy, but its citizens lost the war because "God wished to punish them." The Venetians, he also insists, wanted only peace, had no interest in gain-ing the Piacenzans as clients, and were drawn into the conflict against their own better judgment. For all these reasons the Piacenzans "deserved" to have their city gutted, Sforza concludes:

> O friends, the victory comes not from our right, but from divine might. If it is fitting to speak the truth, we have conquered a city won over neither by reason or arms; and we have placed the captive city under our rule. For it lacked nothing it needed to protect itself and to face dangers from its enemies. But God himself, I believe, wished to punish the guilty because they hastily summoned the Venetians, although there was no war and they feared no losses. They, however, subjected themselves to the Venetians like slaves, though Venice sought no such thing—nor were they forced to play the slave to anyone. The Piacenzans alone are the cause of all the evils because they added flames to dead embers, while the Venetians embraced gentle peace with their entire hearts. Therefore, they have satisfactorily paid the penalty they deserved—by divine retribution. (770–84)

On this note, he calls for the release of all the prisoners of war, and so the book ends with the exodus of throngs of women from their sanctuaries, and the joyous reunion of all the townfolk with their families. Nonetheless, Filelfo's story of Sforza's victory at Piacenza ends in a minor key. Indeed, the bleakness of the final sentence is what sticks in the mind:

> But grievous is the loss of the good.

THREE

HUNGER

MILAN'S WARS with Venice came to an end on 9 April 1454 at Lodi, with the signing of a treaty that would keep peace between the great Italian city-states for the next four decades. All the Peace of Lodi did for Filelfo, however, was dispel his last illusions about his future in Milan. So long as the duke was fighting against Venetian troops or the king of Naples, he could be patient. When he was still having difficulty drawing his university salary in 1455, he began to cast about for other opportunities. Later that same year he wrote his former patron Carlo Gonzaga, "The way things stand with me now, there is nothing I would rather do than move somewhere else."[1] By the following year, in May 1455, he was ready to be more specific in his criticism of Sforza's patronage. In an unpublished letter to Piero de' Medici, he said he had felt deprived at Sforza's court of everything worthwhile in life—honor, utility, and pleasure.[2] Such had, of course, been his complaint about Venice many years before, on the eve of his departure from that city.

Filelfo's trip to Rome and Naples in the summer of 1453 had only increased his dissatisfaction at home. The recognition he had received in those cities, where Pope Niccolò V had conferred on him the title of papal scriptor and King Alfonso crowned him poet laureate, had only made it harder for him to return to Milan. The difference in the patronage styles of the two heads of state, Alfonso and Sforza, was extreme. While Alfonso's brilliant court had, for twenty years, attracted artists and scholars from

[1] Adam, *F. Filelfo*, Appendix 79, p. 435 [an unpublished letter, dated 22 July 1454, in Marc. lat. XIV 262 (4719), fols. 106v–109]: "Ita sum constitutus, ut nihil malim quam mutare caelum." As debts mounted due to Milan's constant wars with Venice during 1450–1454, none of the courtiers were paid; after Lodi, the treasury was still depleted. When Filelfo's daughter married in 1455, he approached both Piero de' Medici and Borso d'Este for dowry money; and in 1457 he complained to Cicco Simonetta of not having the money to buy bread and salad greens (Benadduci, ed., *Atti*, p. 136).

[2] Benadduci, ed., *Atti*, pp. 132–33 [= Rosmini, *Vita*, 2.324], dated 17 May 1455: "Tre cose mi paiono comunemente in questa nostra vita civile et activa desiderarse: onore, utile e piacere . . . E per non tediarve in lungo parlare, a me non pare avere qui ne onor conveniente, ne utilitate necessaria. Il che procede per non esser conosciuto quanto io vaglia, ovver possa valere . . . In sino a ora in nulla mi sono avveduto che questo Signore ne faccia caso ne per utilitate, ne per onore, ne per alcuna dimostrazione. Il perche mi cominciano a cadere le braccia."

all over Italy, Sforza, who had spent most of his life in one military outpost or another, came to the throne with little understanding of what it meant to support the arts. He understood that cultural patronage was essential to his rule, but he lacked the experience necessary to direct such a program. It was precisely there—in drawing scholars and writers of stature to the Sforza court—that Filelfo played such an indispensable role. The duke was aware of Filelfo's importance to him in that area: in the early 1450s alone he brought such men as Theodore Gaza, Porcellio de' Pandoni, Gregorio da Città di Castello, and Demetrius Castrenus to the Milanese court.[3] And yet, the fact remained that Filelfo, and Sforza's other courtiers as well, were only receiving payment on a sporadic basis, and sometimes not at all.[4]

By 1455, he felt he had done everything he should to make himself more attractive to prospective patrons. He had published a fair body of work: his *Satyrae*, four books of an epic poem, several books of his collected letters, two dialogues, and some translations from the Greek were now in circulation. But apart from Florence—and the Greek chair at the Studio had gone to his friend John Argyropoulos that year—he saw nothing in Italy that looked, on balance, much better than his present situation.[5] France, however, offered new possibilities, and he liked what he had heard about the Valois court when King Charles VII's kinsman, René d'Anjou, billeted his troops in Piacenza during the winter of 1453.[6] Charles, according to the fifteenth-century memorialist Thomas Basin, bore a striking resemblance to his cousin, Duke Filippo Maria Visconti, Filelfo's longtime protector.[7] The king, like the late duke of Milan, disliked large cities, preferring to move with his *seraglio* of young women between one or another of his small castles in the country of the Loire valley where the hunting was good.[8]

The year after France's Hundred Years' War with England ended, Filelfo

[3] On Filelfo's patronage of other scholars in the 1450s, see Adam, *F. Filelfo*, pp. 36–37. On Sforza's appreciation of Filelfo's writings, specifically the *Sforziad*, see Rosmini, *Vita*, 2.294–95, F. Sforza to the Regolator and Magistri Intratarum, 23 May 1452: "Noi per niuno modo el vogliamo perdere, la qual cosa seguirebbe quando gli paresse deluso, e non potesse seguitare per manchamento delli dicti 250 fiorini la nobilissima opera per lui in nostra gloria comenzata ne suplire agli altri suoi bisogni."

[4] For the repeated requests by employees of the court for their wages, see ASM, SC, 659–64, September 1452–March 1454.

[5] On Argyropoulos and the situation at the Studio, see Arthur M. Field, *The Beginning of the Philosophical Renaissance in Florence, 1454–1469* (Ph.D. dissertation, University of Michigan, 1980). For Filelfo's letters to Piero de' Medici about Cosimo, see Rosmini, *Vita*, 2.283–84 and 324–26; see also his letters to Tranchedini, fols. 70v–71.

[6] Niccolò Machiavelli, *History of Florence*, ed. F. Gilbert (Reprint. New York, 1966), p. 299.

[7] Thomas Basin, *Histoire de Charles VII*, ed. C. Samuran, 2 vols. (Paris, 1933 and 1944); M.G.A. Vale, *Charles VII* (London, 1974), p. 136; on Visconti's love of hunting and country life, see Pier Candido Decembrio, *Vita di Filippo Maria Visconti*, ed. F. Fossati, in *RIS²*, 20.1.141; and F. Cognasso, *Storia di Milano* (Milan, 1955), 6.394.

[8] Vale, *Charles VII*, pp. 136–37.

mounted an aggressive campaign by mail to obtain either a job offer or an invitation to Charles's court. The men to whom Filelfo turned as brokers between himself and the king were the very powerful chancellor of France, Guillaume Jouvenel des Ursins, and the Greek émigré physician to the king, Thomas Coroneus.[9] During the years 1454–1455, he sent no less than eighteen letters to the two counselors of Charles's, all of them in the published edition of the epistolario.[10] During this period, he also mailed Ursins and Coroneus copies of his *Satyrae*, his translations of Aristotle's *Rhetoric*, Lysias's "Murder of Eratosthenes" and his "Funeral Eulogy," his own *Commentationes de exilio*, and his newest work of all, his lyric *Odae* or *Carmina varia*, as he alternately called his odes.[11] The letters to Ursins and Coroneus are interesting in themselves, since they appear to be modeled on the Giustiniani-Aurispa paradigm of Books 1–3 of the *Epistolae*: in the high-toned Ursins letters, Filelfo demonstrates his mastery of the decorum of clientage, while the more familial-sounding Coroneus letters are full of teasing comments about the doctor's slowness to respond.

According to Filelfo, the king had tendered him an offer of employment of some sort.[12] Indeed, he told both the king's counselors, Ursins and Coroneus, that he counted on being able to cross the Alps into France in mid-June of 1456.[13] When Sforza refused, probably in early June, to grant him permission to leave Milan, assuring him that he would make it worth his while to stay, Filelfo changed the dedicatory prologue to the odes, slipping a new piece addressed to Sforza in front of the old one to Charles.[14] Even so, he had written his passionately antirepublican, promonarchist *Odae* expressly with the French king in mind.[15] An experimental work marking his first attempts at Latin lyric meters, Books 1–3 of the odes comment on the emergence in 1447, after two centuries of monarchy, of a freely elected government, the Ambrosian republic, and of the government's fall just as suddenly in 1450. Book 4 is largely concerned with the plague of 1451,

---

[9] On Ursins, see Vale, *Charles VII*, pp. 83, 98–100, 106, 109–10, 112, 139, 146, 188, 202, and 206; on Coroneus, see Legrand, *Lettres*, pp. 75–76.

[10] See the eighteen letters to Charles's two counselors in Filelfo, *Epistolae*: fols. 85, 89–89v, and 93–96v; see also a Greek letter to Coroneus in Legrand, *Lettres*, pp. 75–76.

[11] On works sent, see *Epistolae*, as in n. 10; on the *Odes*, specifically, see fols. 93v and 94v–96v.

[12] See Appendix C, texts, *Odes* 1.10 and 110–114.

[13] See n. 9; see also Filelfo, *Epistolae*, to Beccadelli (16 July 1456), fol. 95: Filelfo admits he now has the finished work and it contains five books of ten odes in each book (fifty odes altogether).

[14] See ibid., to Tranchedini; and to Mariotto Tertini (1457), fols. 97v–98, for Filelfo's satisfaction with Sforza's treatment of him after his thwarted plans.

[15] Ibid., to Coroneus (25 October 1455), fol. 95v. Filelfo was just beginning to put the work together; he herewith sends only *Odes* 1.1. There will be one hundred poems in the *Carmina*, he promises.

which struck Milan in the wake of the civil war and famine. And, in a series of encomia, Book 5 addresses the potentates whose courts he visited on his three-month tour of central and southern Italy in 1453: Ludovico Gonzaga of Mantua, Pope Niccolò V, Alfonso of Naples, and Charles VII; the encomia also include poems addressed to Charles VII and Basinio Basini, court poet to Duke Federigo da Montefeltro, whose court at Urbino he must also have visited in the summer of 1453.

The Heady Rise and Bloody Fall of the Ambrosian Republic

The story of the meteoric rise and fall of the Ambrosian republic, the chief target of Filelfo's satirical odes, is a little-understood chapter in Milanese history, and one marked by extraordinary violence. It began on 13 August 1447, even while a priest administered the last rites to Duke Filippo Maria Visconti as he lay dying in the Castello di Porta Giovia.[16] On that night a group of nobles and jurists gathered to reconstitute the city of Milan as a republic.[17] Naming the city's new regime after its patron saint, the junta may have sought only to replace the monarchy with an aristocratic oligar-

[16] Cognasso, *Storia*, 6.387–88.

[17] For the history of the Ambrosian republic, the primary sources are Giovanni Simonetta, *Rerum gestarum Francisci Sfortiae commentarii*, ed. G. Soranzo, in *RIS²*, 21.2, the first and most influential account of the rise and fall of the republic; P. C. Decembrio, *Vita Philippi Mariae*; Decembrio, *Vita Francisci Sfortiae quarti Mediolanensium ducis*, eds. G. Carducci, V. Fiorino, P. Fedele, in *RIS²*, 20.1; Cristoforo da Soldo, *La Cronaca*, ed. G. Brizzolara, *RIS²*, 21.3; and Antonio di Ripalta, *Annales Placentini*, in *RIS¹*. Consider also the influence of Filelfo's many letters, odes, and satires about the republican regime, since these works were circulating well before Simonetta and Decembrio published their histories. The early sixteenth-century accounts of the republic: G. P. Cagnola, *Cronache milanesi*, 3 vols. (Milan, 1519; reprint Florence, 1842); B. Corio, *Storia di Milano*, ed. E. de Magri, 3 vols. (Milan, 1503; 2d ed. 1855–1857) all derive from Simonetta. In the nineteenth century, see C. de Rosmini, *Della istoria di Milano*, 4 vols. (Milan, 1820–1821), 2.387–453; P. Verri, *Storia di Milano* (Milan, 1873); and G. Guilini, *Memorie spettanti alla storia* (Reprint. Milan, 1975), 6.421–72; also see M. Borsa, "P. C. Decembrio e l'umanesimo in Lombardia," in *ASL* 20 (1893): 5–75 and 358–422. The nineteenth-century historians were the first to look sympathetically on the republic: A. Bianchi-Giovini, *Le Repubblica di Milano dopo la morte di F. M. Visconti* (Milano, 1848); F. Peluso, *Storia della Repubblica milanese* (Milan, 1871); A. Colombo, "Della vera natura ed importanza dell'aurea repubblica ambrosiana," in *Raccolta di scritti storici in onore del prof. Giulio Romano* (Pavia, 1907); T. Sickel, "Beitrage und Berichtungen zur Geschichte der Erwerbung Mailands durch Fr. Sforza," in *Archiv fur Kunde Osterreichischen Geschichtsquellen* (Vienna, 1855); and F. Butti, *I fallori della Repubblica ambrosiana* (Vercelli, 1891). The most comprehensive modern account of the period is still Cognasso, *Storia di Milano*, 6.387–448; see also E. Resti, "Documenti per storia della Repubblica Ambrosiana," in *ASL* 5 (1954–1955): 192–266; also G. P. Bognetti, "Per la storia dello stato visconteo," in *ASL* 54 (1927): 237–357; and L. Martines, *Power and Imagination: City-States in Renaissance Italy* (New York, 1979), pp. 140–48.

chy. It is not clear whether the Milanese republic was mainly inspired by its leaders' admiration for the more modern bureaucracies of its neighbors, Venice and Florence, as Marina Spinelli has recently argued, or whether it looked more nostalgically to the past, to the corporate communal governments of the late Middle Ages, as Francesco Cognasso and Lauro Martines suggest it did.[18]

Certainly the street theater orchestrated by the republic's Capitani during its first forty days was reminiscent of the workers' uprisings that had occurred in Perugia, Lucca, and Siena in the fourteenth century.[19] On 30 August 1447, the government of the Ambrosian republic ordered the people to dismantle the Visconti family residence, the Castello di Porta Giovia, brick by brick. Two weeks later the Visconti Castello di Porta Romana was also consigned for public demolition.[20] Continuing to stoke popular backing for the new regime, on 22 September 1447, the Capitani staged a public burning of the books and records for all taxes, excises, tolls, indemnities, and public debts.[21] The government also used the regular shouting out of new decrees (*gride*) by criers at specified public places, to the accompaniment of a few trumpet blasts, to build solidarity and support for itself.[22]

When a number of Milan's client cities defected to Venice, the republic hired Francesco Sforza, Visconti's former condottiere, to bring them back to the fold. In the first year of the republic, Sforza led Milanese troops to victory three times against the Venetians, at Casalmaggiore, Piacenza, and Caravaggio. But in October 1448, Sforza defected to Venice himself, and because Sforza's campaigns on behalf of the Milanese had largely been underwritten by Cosimo de' Medici, his defection spelled the beginning of the end for the bankrupt republic.

Whereas prior to 1449 the officers of the republic had primarily been members of the old ruling class of the city, in the January, May, and September elections that year, the popular faction won a majority of the seats

[18] For a revisionist view of the historiography of the period, see Marina Spinelli, "Ricerche per una nuova storia della repubblica Ambrosiana," in *Nuova rivista storica* pte. 1 (1986): 231–52, and ibid. pte. 2 (1987): 27–48. For other recent studies of the social and economic context in which the Ambrosian republic arose, see G. Albini, *Guerra, fame, peste. crisi di mortalita e sistema sanitario nella Lombardia tardo medioevale* (Bologna, 1982); G. Chittolini, *La formazione dello stato regionale e le istituzione del contado. secoli XIV e XV* (Turin, 1979); L. Chiappa Mauri, "I mulini ad acqua," in *Nuova rivista storica* (1984): 231–61; L. Frangioni, "La politica economica del dominio de Milano nei secoli XV–XVI," in *Nuova rivista storica* (1986): 253–68.

[19] Martines, *Power and Imagination*, pp. 132–36.

[20] See Spinelli, pte. 1, p. 247, on the demolition *gride* [= ASM, Reg. Pan., 6, fols. 4; 6; 64, as cited in Spinelli, p. 247]. Simonetta, *Commentarii*, p. 181, expends only a single line on the first demolition order; he does not refer specifically to the second order.

[21] Spinelli, pte. 2, p. 41; the burning of the tax books is not referred to by Simonetta.

[22] Spinelli, pte. 1, p. 241.

in the government, and the three most powerful Capitani were the son of a weaver, a craftsman, and a notary.[23] Summary executions, the incarceration of dissidents, and the confiscation of the estates of the gentry were carried out by the popular faction between the winter and spring of 1449. The most notorious of these executions was the decapitation and public display of the severed head of Giorgio Lampugnano, one of the founding fathers of the Ambrosian republic, in January 1449.[24]

Meanwhile, after his defection, Sforza set in motion a plan to take Milan, not for Venice but for himself. Rather than lay siege to the city, his strategy was to cordon it off from its supply lines, his objective being to starve the Milanese into submission. A year after Sforza's stoppage of the transport of foodstuffs and reinforcements into Milan, in January 1450, both the city records and the chroniclers indicate that the situation in Milan was desperate.[25] The chronicler Cristoforo da Soldo observed that in the last days of the republic, "The people were as badly off as one could possibly say, not to mention the famine because of which they were dying like dogs in the streets and they were eating horses, dogs, cats, and vermin, etc. because there was no bread; still, for the most part, they kept their honor . . ."[26] When the Capitani opened the city gates at intervals to allow the people to scour the countryside for food, Sforza's troops drove the foragers back into the city. But few ventured outside the walls, since street fighting was making it dangerous for people to leave their houses. "I would come to see you every day," Filelfo wrote to a friend in January 1450, "if my fear of the swords I see being brandished in every part of the city did not keep me from doing so."[27] The extremity of the situation, and the sense that the days of the regime were numbered, come through again in a letter Filelfo

---

[23] Giorgio Bizzozero, Giovanni da Ossona, and Giovanni da Appiano, respectively. On the three Capitani, see Simonetta, *Commentarii*, pp. 264 and 267; and Cognasso, *Storia*, 6.430–32. Filelfo lambastes Bizzozero in *Odes* 1.5, an invective directed exclusively against him, and attacks the plebeian Capitani together in *Odes* 3.4.

[24] Simonetta, *Commentarii*, pp. 264–67; Cognasso, *Storia*, 6.431–32: between the January 1449 elections and May of that year, two hundred persons, including members of the oldest Milanese families, were proscribed. Giorgio Lampugnano, the most notable among these, was convicted of treason (Simonetta, *Commentarii*, p. 267).

[25] N. Ferorelli, ed. *Inventari e regesti del regio archivio di stato di Milano. I registri dell'ufficio degli statuti* (Reprint. Milan, 1971), 3.56–87. The vast majority of the hundreds of statutes (*gride*) issued by the Capitani of the republic for the period 1448–1450 pertain to famine control; these statutes attempted to regulate the supply, sale, and allocation of grain within the city walls.

[26] Da Soldo, *Cronaca*, p. 97: ". . . E stando tanto male quanto se potria dir, ne pensare de la fame, per che morevano sulle strate de fame come cani, manzavano, per desasio de pane, cavalli cani gatti e sorzi etc., tamen la mazor parte haveriano fatto suo honore . . ."

[27] Filelfo, *Epistolae*, to Biagio Arretino (1 January 1450), fol. 46: "Venirem ad te quottidie, nisi me id facere prohiberet gladiorum metus, quibus assidue video urbem universam coruscari."

wrote in December 1449 to his old friend Pietro Tommasi, who offered
to help by introducing him to someone high up in government circles,
Leonardo Venerio, the Venetian ambassador. In this letter Filelfo's polite
doubts about Venerio's competence seem to foreshadow both his doom
and that of the republic. For within three months of the letter's dateline,
Venerio would be stabbed to death on the steps of the Palazzo d'Arengo
by a mob of Milanese citizens, while he attempted to defend the offices of
the republic's Capitani.

> I'm delighted and grateful [wrote Filelfo] that you've put my situation entirely
> in the hands of Leonardo Venerio, the Venetian ambassador and a most emi-
> nent man. For he is a powerful presence among the citizens here, and a man
> of the utmost authority and grace, though I do think it will turn out that he
> won't be able to be of much help to me, since everything now is already col-
> lapsing and as good as lost. All over the city and in numbers people are dying
> of hunger. Even if I could scrape up a little money from somewhere, still there
> wouldn't be any place where enough bread could be gotten.[28]

On 25 February 1450, no longer able to hold out, the Milanese overran
the offices of their governors. On the following day, they dispatched en-
voys to surrender to Sforza, thus marking the end of a year of famine and
two of civil war.

The Odes as Antirepublican Propaganda

In Filelfo's *Odes*, a propaganda work meant to attack the Ambrosian republic specifically and to praise monarchy in general, his suppression of
certain major acts of violence perpetrated by the republic is surprising.[29]
There is no mention anywhere in the odes of the public razing of the Vis-

[28] Ibid., to Pietro Tommasi (1 December 1449), fol. 46: "Quod rem meam omnem Venetorum legato, Leonardo Venerio, clarissimo viro: commendaveris, gaudeo tibique ago gratias. Valet enim is apud hosce cives, et auctoritate et gratia plurimum. Quanquam futurum
puto, ut mihi prodesse non admodum possit, ita sunt omnia iam debilitata et perdita. Passim
atque catervatim moriuntur inedia. Mihi vero siquid etiam pecuniolae alicunde abradi posset,
tamen non est unde satis panis parari queat . . ."
[29] For more on Filelfo's ideas on good and bad government, see his *Epistolae*, to Leonello
d'Este, duke of Ferrara (July 1449), fol. 44; Filelfo suggests here that good government depends not on the outward form of the government (tyranny, monarchy, republic), but on the
intrinsic character of its ruler; he distinguishes not between republicanism and monarchy, but
between the self-serving tyrant (*tyrannus*) and the just king (*rex pius*) who believes that his
own welfare cannot be separated from that of the public: "Nec enim ignoramus inter regem
et tyrannum interesse, quod hic omnia refert ad utilitatem suam, contempto divino omni
atque humano iure. At rex secus omnia, qui iustitiam atque pietatem ante oculos semper
ferens, sibi omnia vult cum civitate esse communia, suum atque proprium nihil ducens quod
a publica utilitate dignitateque separetur . . ." (cf. Plato, *Statesman* 301b).

conti residence, the Castello di Porta Giovia, or of the Visconti fortress, the Castello di Porta Romana.[30] Nor are there references in any of Filelfo's writings to the public burning of the tax registers, or to the beheading of Giorgio Lampugnano. As with Filelfo's suppression of the scarring of his face in his published *Epistolae*, here too the salvaging of honor takes precedence over the recording of mere fact. To the extent that the ducal castello was, in a sense, an extension of the body and authority of the signor, certainly the violence done to the monuments of the Visconti would be perceived as a scar upon the family honor. The public burning of the tax books was likewise a species of *damnatio memoriae*—an abnegation, a consigning to oblivion of everything for which the Visconti monarchy had stood. Finally, the mutilation of the body of Giorgio Lampugnano, whose aristocratic republican family had ties with Filelfo's second wife's relations, the Osnaga, was a public affront that may have been a little too close to home.[31]

In spite of such omissions, the *Odes* project is an extremely negative succession of images of the republic, as corrupt, war-mongering, and geared toward pleasing the least educated among the populace. Beginning with the poems about Milan's wars after Visconti's death, and continuing with the fall of the republic and Sforza's succession to the throne in 1450, the dominant themes in Filelfo's *Odes* are hunger and blight—both of the body and the spirit. At base, neither the republican regime nor Sforza's signory could guarantee its subjects access to their most elemental needs: food, shelter, and protection—without which no thought could be given to the fostering of the arts.

So indelible was Filelfo's memory of the city's suffering during the famine of 1449–1450 that, even in *Odes* 3.4, the poem Filelfo wrote to celebrate the triumphal entry of his patron into Milan at the end of the war, the past intruded. The worst of it was, Filelfo commented, that as in the famous disaster at Saguntum when Hannibal lay siege to that town, the famine in Milan was not due to crop failure, but man-made. Though he complained that the Milanese themselves had chosen to starve rather than open their gates to Sforza, it was nonetheless the duke's thirteen-month blockage of the flow of food into the city that had caused the famine. Accordingly, his praises of Sforza are tinged with ambivalence. The duke had indeed brought long-awaited peace to the Milanese. On the other hand, both the war and the grain embargo had been costly:

[30] Filelfo seems to be obliquely alluding to the razing of one or both of the ducal Castelli in *Odes* 2.3.141–44 ("eversam redigas ut arcem," etc.).

[31] Simonetta, a keeper of the ducal registers himself under Sforza, briefly mentions the demolition of the Castello di Porta Giovia (*Commentarii*, p. 181) and the beheading of Lampugnano (*Commentarii*, p. 267), but not the tax record burnings.

He [Filelfo wrote of Sforza] has brought peace and relief to the weary; now true liberty has been established for the people . . . Ah, but what brave man could remember with heart unbroken . . . [the famine]. You would have seen people lying about everywhere, overcome by death, which a second year barren of all grain had brought forth. Why should you remind me in vain of Saguntum or the Jews oppressed by hunger? May there never again be a people said to suffer from a similar Megaera: my stomach turns with rising nausea when I think of our wretched lot. (*Odes* 3.4.9–11, 14–15, and 43–51)[32]

Probably not completed until 1456, the odes portrayed events that had occurred some five to seven years earlier.[33] Nonetheless, the conditions Filelfo inveighed against in the odes had changed very little under Sforza's signory. The severe restrictions of speech and movement into and out of the city, the corruption in the state bureaucracy, the city's crippling war debt, the periodic suspension of the courtiers' salaries, and his own worsening penury—all these continued to be as troubling to him in 1456 as they were in 1449. Indeed, it is the sense of urgency around these issues that gives the odes an immediacy one would not otherwise expect.

In this chapter I have singled out for discussion those odes that best illustrate Filelfo's reactions to the key events and actors of the Ambrosian revolution and its aftermath.[34] The *Odes* were only printed twice, in Brescia in 1497 and in Paris in 1507. Complete texts for 1.10, 2.2, 2.3, 3.4, 4.5, and 4.7 are provided in Appendix C.[35]

[32] For all odes texts cited, see Appendix C.

[33] It is difficult to date the odes with precision. Like Filelfo's other major works the odes appear to have been composed over a period of years, perhaps between 1449 and 1456; and, like his other major works, the *Carmina* was first envisioned as a much bigger work: Filelfo's original plan was to produce one hundred odes in ten books, rather than the fifty odes in five books he actually finished (Filelfo, *Epistolae*, to Des Ursins [15 November 1455], fols. 90v–91). In addition to this letter, Filelfo first mentions his odes in ibid., to Memo da Siena (11 November 1450), fol. 51; he refers to his odes again in ibid., to Guillaume Jouvenel des Ursins (16 June 1456), fol. 96–96v; to Antonio Beccadelli (June 1456), fol. 95; to Thomas Coronaeus (October 1455), fol. 95v; to Pietro Pierleone (June 1456), folio misnumbered; to Giovanni de' Medici (April 1457), fol. 96v; for a Greek letter to Coronaeus on the odes, see Legrand, *Lettres*, p. 73f. Filelfo's virulently antirepublican odes might not have been circulated until after 1450 since severe penalties were imposed for speaking against the government; see the published statutes of the period 1448–1450 in Ferorelli, *Inventari e Regesti*.

[34] On typologies of revolution, see Lawrence Stone, *The Causes of the English Revolution: 1529–1642* (Reprint. London, 1986), on Chalmers Johnson's typology of revolution; the Ambrosian republic would fit the fifth type, the *coup d'état*, the "planned work of a tiny elite fired by an oligarchic, sectarian ideology" (p. 7).

[35] On the fifteenth-century editions and manuscripts of the odes, see Appendix C. Recently several of Filelfo's odes have appeared in print in F. Arnaldi, ed., *Poeti Latini del Quattrocento* (Milan, 1964) (*Odes* 1.2–4; 1.9; 2.4; 3.3; and 4.2); in A. Perosa and J. Sparrow, eds. *Renaissance Latin Verse* (London, 1979) (a brief excerpt from *Odes* 4.5); and with my article, "Humanist Politics or Vergilian Poetics?" in *Rinascimento* 25 (1985): 101–25 (*Odes* 2.2 and

Images of War and Plebeian Rule

In *Odes* 1.10 Filelfo addresses his old friend, the jurist and statesman Niccolò Arcimboldi.[36] The poem is set in republican Milan, during the wars with Venice that followed Visconti's death. Arcimboldi, who like many of his generation and class served first the Visconti and later the republican regime in Milan, has suggested that Filelfo commemorate the republic's recent victories with an epic poem.[37] Filelfo's summary of the latest news about the Ambrosian republic halfway through the ode and his preelection pledge near the poem's end neatly fix the time of Arcimboldi's request immediately before the 1 July 1449 elections, when the Milanese returned the aristocratic faction to power:

> We have driven our own men into exile and increased the enemy's strength; and we have caused a man hostile in battle and formidable in arms to become our enemy. We are awash in the blood of citizens. We are barricaded behind our walls, oppressed by war and famine. Look, anger goads us on. We are at war at home and abroad . . . But if God himself is willing, if the victorious republic will reelect its original leaders, and if the glorious nobility will break the hold of the bumbling rabble, then I'll celebrate the triumphs the Milanese have wrested from the enemy with a grandiose sort of poem—depending on how much strength my Muse can muster. (*Odes* 1.10.50–54 and 103–7)[38]

The "men driven into exile" and the "blood of the citizens" are references to the mass proscriptions and public executions carried out by the republican government when the Milanese returned the radical popular faction to power in the elections of 1 January and 30 May 1449.[39] The "formida-

---

3.4). Nonetheless Filelfo's odes have been even more neglected than the unpublished *Sforziad*; I know of no critical study of the odes other than Gabriella Albanese's fine monograph reassessing all Filelfo's poetic works, "Le raccolte poetiche latine di Francesco Filelfo," in *Filelfo nel V Cent.*, pp. 389–458. W. L. Grant, *Neo-Latin Literature and the Pastoral* (Chapel Hill, 1965), p. 29, cites Filelfo's *Odes* briefly, as one of the earliest collections of personal lyric among the Neo-Latin poets.

[36] Niccolò Arcimboldi, a lawyer and a statesman of legendary erudition, served in the Visconti, republican, and Sforza regimes. See Lauro Martines, *Lawyers and Statecraft in Renaissance Florence* (Princeton, 1968), p. 459.

[37] Among the Augustan poets *gravis* (*Odes* 1.10.1–2: "gravi me voce . . . / canam") is a code word for epic meter (hexameters).

[38] For the text of *Odes* 1.10, see Appendix C.

[39] See E. Resti, "Documenti," pp. 3–6 for a chronology of events under the Ambrosian republic. On the purges, see Cognasso, *Storia*, 6.430–33. On 30 May 1449 the Capitani condemned to death two hundred citizens, among whom were many members of the Milanese nobility: the Visconti, Crivelli, Bossi, Stampa, Caimmi, Lampugnano, Sanseverino, Maino, Borromei, dal Verme, Litta, and Taverna. Cognasso, *Storia*, 6.432, remarks that most histories of the Ambrosian republic, beginning with Simonetta, pin the *general* responsibility for the proscriptions of the nobles and the confiscations of their estates on the plebeian Cap-

ble man" he castigates the Milanese for having alienated is of course Sforza, who by October 1448 had defected to Venice.[40] Now, while Filelfo and Arcimboldi discuss politics, Sforza, who has long since broken with Venice, sits encamped at Vimercate just outside Milan. For months he has kept his troops positioned around the city's walls, blocking the transport of foodstuffs to it from the surrounding countryside. And so, on top of the war there is famine in the city.[41]

At the bottom of the suffering and injustice in the world of Filelfo's odes is war. Thus, Arcimboldi's request that he compose a heroic poem celebrating the republic's victories over France and Venice is for Filelfo a difficult assignment. As a consequence, the poem he offers here turns out to be not so much a victory paean as a debate with himself over the merits of Milan's recent wars, and more generally, all war. What is more, his speech is so filled with ambivalence and wavering, that for every tentative suggestion of praise for the Milanese, there follows a qualification or a contradiction.

Arcimboldi has urged him "justly," he writes, to immortalize Milan's recent military successes (*Odes* 1.10.1–4). But at the same time he warns Arcimboldi that war fever—personified here in the Roman war deity Bellona and her Greek companion Erinys—is already engulfing the world in flames (9–10). While it may be true, he concedes, that true friendship, righteousness, and truth only come to the fore in wartime or other crises (23–26), the destruction of the Lombard plain wrought by the Venetian army is nonetheless irreversible: the Signoria's troops have gutted towns and farmland in the Adda and Po river valleys with the violence of a tornado ("turbinis instar," 15–17). After Visconti's death, the Milanese found themselves the victims of unlawful incursions into their territory by both the French and the Venetians (27–32). Still, they managed to expel the French from their soil, they broke the will of the Piacenzans, and slaughtered the Venetians ("Francos fusos," "Placentini . . . dementia frangitur," "Veneti funesta clade subacti," 32–41). And while it was perhaps praiseworthy for the Milanese to have beaten the Venetians in three important

---

itani Appiano and Ossona, but that neither Simonetta nor subsequent historians have produced evidence to tie them to any specific crimes.

[40] Vat. urb. 701 (identified as an autograph by C. Stornaiolo [*Codices Urbinates Latini*, II, Rome 1912, 219f.]) contains the following gloss: "Fr. Sphortias" in the margin at lines 50–53, written in red ink in the same hand that wrote the rest of the codex. See also Filelfo, *Epistolae*, to Niccolò Ceba (26 February 1450), fols. 46v–47: Filelfo believed Sforza's defection to Venice was prompted by his discovery of a secret plan that the Milanese were developing to remove him from his command, on the basis that after his victory at Carvaggio he had become too powerful. Also cf. the motives for his defection: Simonetta, *Commentarii*, p. 244; Cagnola, *Cronache*, p. 96; Giulini, *Memorie*, 6.444; Rubieri, *Francesco Primo*, 2.110; da Soldo, *Cronaca*, col. 852; and Cipolla, *Storia*, p. 433.

[41] See Albini, *Guerra*, pp. 103–38 on the connection between the war and famine.

campaigns, what was it to destroy Venice, he asks, if not to cast a shadow over the very "sun of Italy" ("ipsum Italiae solem obscurasse," 44–45)? The butt of Filelfo's scorn is not in fact foreign armies, but the Milanese themselves. Because they have been divided by factionalism and are involved in a civil war (52ff.), they are more reprehensible than the Venetians or the Florentines. For they are guilty of the worst sin of all: that they kill one another ("quod se per mutua vulnera caedant," etc., 65–66).

Although Filelfo writes in letter after letter about the danger of airing one's political opinions during this period, still his lack of enthusiasm for the republic and its wars shows up not just in the private context of his *Odes*, but in a public oration he was ordered to deliver in praise of the regime after the November 1448 elections.[42] Instead of lauding the new Capitani of the city Filelfo lapsed, as he stood before the assembled citizens, into a long meditation on "the unhappiness and wretchedness of the human condition, in which there is no solidity, no stability, and no constancy."[43] He enumerated battles Milan had won, but uttered no word of personal praise for the republic's leaders, civilian or military. And this in what was surely a commissioned address, whose express purpose it was to toast the celebrities of the new republic. Likewise in *Odes* 1.10, there is no *speculum principis*. Sforza's resounding victory at Caravaggio, where the Venetians lost ten thousand cavalrymen, is dismissed, with no mention of the condottiere's name, as simply a "sad disaster" ("funesta clade," 41). Filelfo's other patron during this period, Carlo Gonzaga, the commander of the armed forces after Sforza's defection, is only given passing praise as the defender of two of Milan's client cities, Modica and Crema (56–60).

While war is projected in the odes as part of a more distant domain over which one has little or no control, Filelfo invariably returns to the more personal "I" or "you"; to the pain humans inflict upon one another. And the emblem of this pain in the odes is always hunger—or famine, in its collective expression. While he protests in a number of the odes, particu-

[42] On constraints against free speech, see Filelfo, *Epistolae*, to Flavio Biondo (July 1449), fol. 43v; to Giorgio Piatti (July 1449), fol. 43v; to Pietro Tommasi (September 1449), fol. 45v; to Giovanni Aurispa (October 1449), fol. 46; to Catone Sacco (January 1448), fol. 41; to Alberto Zancario (February 1448), fol. 41; and to Niccolò Varo (July 1449), fol. 44.

[43] Ambrosianus F 55 sup., fols. 37–38. *Oratio habita per Philelfum die primo Novembris 1448 in creatione dominorum capitaneorum et defensorum libertatis.* ". . . Vidimus urbem Laudensem, quae tam impudenter atque unique ad hostes defecerat et reliqua Abdua castella atque oppida mirabili cum laude vostra recuperata. Vidimus universum et Bergomensem et Brixiensem agrum actum in deditionem vostram. Audiebatur ad Hadriaticum usque summum tantum nominis vostri terrorem consternatos hostium animos invasisse, ut aliud nihil quam deditionem cogitarent . . . O miseram atque infelicem rerum humanarum conditionem in quibus nulla firmitas, nulla stabilitas, nulla constantia . . . Utpote quae humana haec omnia infirma sunt, fragilia et caduca, itaque omnem spem nostram non in nostris conatibus, sed in dei omnipotentis nutu atque voluntate ponendum esse."

larly those in Books 2 and 3, against the wartime sufferings of the Milanese people, he focuses in *Odes* 1.10 on the connections between physical well-being and artistic creativity, and between patronage and the arts. Arcimboldi has asked him to write a panegyric about the republic, and his response is to point out the inseparability of body and spirit—of tongue and talent. Without physical sustenance, creative inspiration withers. And so, all Filelfo's essays on art and politics come down to economics—to the functioning of the nexus between poet and patron, to the exchange of praise for gifts, and to the proposition that only in an aristocratic society can poetry thrive. But typically Filelfian is the mixture here of the serious and the absurd, of vitriol and jokes about life's incongruities:

> But having performed such a high-toned labor, what could my Muse then hope for? A hungry Muse does not know how to make melodious sounds, as long as she's got the shakes because her throat is dry. After all, the Muse, who prettifies by her praises, does not think praise is such a great thing that she wants to die of hunger and do without a robe by singing much of her day away. The great Vergil had no such obligation. I have no Pollio, no Maecenas. There's no Augustus ready to help me out. I who could sell glory can't buy any for myself. (*Odes* 1.10.72–81)

His most stinging ridicule, however, is reserved for the members of the new ruling class, whom he characterizes as murderers and members of the dregs of society. Contemporary writers, such as Simonetta and da Soldo, and the official *Registri* for the years 1448–1449 make it clear that many nobles were still playing an active role in the republican regime even at the end of its reign.[44] Nonetheless Filelfo depicts the last days of the republic in terms of a class struggle in which an uneducated and criminal plebs stand on one side of the fence and a propertied elite and learned men like himself

[44] Not only does Simonetta not suppress the participation of certain nobles in the republican regime; it is also important to point out that Simonetta's impugning of Appiano and Ossona is coupled with his condemnation of the noblemen Ambrogio Trivulzio and Innocenzo Cotta, "under whose direction and with whose collaboration" (*consilio et opera*) the plebeian Capitani had been acting all along: "Itaque per hunc modum omni reipublicae administratione ad factionem guelfam, deinde ad plebem deducta, Johannes Ossona plebeus infimique mercatorii ordinis, qui magnae per id temporis inter populares existimationis habebatur et Johannes Applanus tabularius, duo sane in civitate homines audaces et temerarii atque omnium confidentissimi, Ambrosii Triultii et Innocentii Cottae, duorum ex nobilitate audacissimorum virorum, consilio atque opera, civiatis totius imperii summam in se transtulerunt; pecuniam frumentumque ad alendos in urbe milites per metum perque vim a Gibellinis dumtaxat civibus omni immanitate extorquendo cogunt." Corio, *Storia*, p. 1270 and Cagnola, *Cronache*, p. 105, repeat the preceding passage almost word for word in their vernacular accounts of the proscriptions; and Verri, *Storia*, p. 35, reiterates the same charges without mentioning the participation of Cotta and Trivulzio. For the rehabilitation of Appiano and Ossona, see Peluso, p. 222; Bianchi-Giovini, pp. 89, 110, and 179; and A. Ghinzoni, "Giovanni Ossona e Giovanni Appiani nella rochetta di Monza," in *ASL* 5 (1878): 205f.

stand on the other.[45] Identifying himself here with an alienated ruling class which has been stripped of its estates and its authority, he sketches a cartoon in which the most marginal elements in society now hold government offices:

> Look, the rabble, girt with their moneybelts, have taken over our noble magistracies. The chicken farmer, the auctioneer, the adulterer, the pimp, the perjuror and his accomplice now put on airs. What should I praise of theirs? The murders they have committed along with their unspeakable plots? The number of citizens they killed so disloyally? Am I supposed to hymn their deeds and remain silent about our citizens? (*Odes* 1.10.93–98)

"I'll have no dealings with the rabble. The foolish crowd can keep their distance; but rather my whole heart turns on thoughts of Charles," Filelfo writes at the end of the poem, in lines that quite self-consciously allude to Horace's tribute to his patron Maecenas's generosity in his *Odes* 3.1.[46] But as we move through Filelfo's polemics, it is worth recalling that whatever virtues he attributed to monarchy as an ideal, in practical terms he saw his position as deteriorating under Sforza's patronage.[47] It was not, after all, under the Ambrosian regime but under Sforza that he spent two years carefully scheming to obtain an appointment at the French court.[48]

Filelfo ends *Odes* 1.10 with a vehement protest against the curtailment of freedom of speech and movement under the republic, a recurrent theme in his correspondence from January 1448 onward.[49] If poets were forbidden to articulate their criticisms of public policy, then what was there left to write about? "What hopes can I have in the end? For rewards or honor? But no, I am permitted neither to leave, nor am I granted the freedom to speak my mind with impunity. Should I speak flatteringly of the place?

[45] In order to assess the role social and economic factors played in the forming of the republic, work still needs to be done on the determinants of political affiliation of the sort that has been done on the Ciompi by Gene A. Brucker, "The Ciompi Revolution," and Raymond de Roover, "Labour Conditions in Florence Around 1400: Theory, Policy and Reality," both in *Florentine Studies: Politics and Society in Renaissance Florence*, ed. N. Rubinstein (London, 1968), pp. 277–356; on the Ciompi, see also Samuel K. Cohn, *The Laboring Classes in Renaissance Florence* (New York, 1980), pp. 130–32.

[46] Cf. Filelfo, *Odes* 1.10.110–11 with Horace, *Odes*, 3.1.1. Horace in *Odes* 3.1.44–48: thanks to Maecenas's gift to Horace of a peaceful place to work, the poet is free to write without constraint.

[47] See nn. 1 and 2 to this chapter.

[48] See n. 10 to this chapter.

[49] For Filelfo's letters on the curbing of free speech in Milan in 1448–1449, see n. 39; for the statutes curbing free speech, see Cognasso, *Storia*, 6.446. For Filelfo's complaints about his inability to get permission to leave Milan, cf. Filelfo, *Epistolae*, to Biagio Aretino (January 1, 1449), fol. 46; to Pietro Tommasi (September 1, 1449), fol. 46; to Niccolò Varo (September 1449), fol. 46; to Giovanni Aurispa (July 1449), fol. 43v; and to Bornio Sala (July 1449), f. 43v.

Flattery has no place in an ingenuous heart. I can't speak lies. Nor am I permitted to tell the truth" (1.10.99–103). As for the freedom of the plebs to redress their own grievances, Filelfo clearly felt in the demands of the uneducated popular classes a threat to his own access to the public lectern. But as we shall see in the story of the riots and the storming of the government palace in the next two odes, Filelfo was glad to see the power of the mob harnessed in the service of what he believed was ultimately right, for both his own cause and that of the city.

Filelfo was not alone among fifteenth-century intellectuals in his scorn for the popular classes (*plebs*, *plebes*, or *ordo plebeus*, in humanist terms). As Marvin Becker has remarked, Quattrocento Florentine historians, Leonardo Bruni among others, were intensely hostile to lower-class participation in government—and in ways Trecento writers were not.[50] Certainly the same bias runs through the work of Milanese writers of the period. The Milanese historian Giovanni Simonetta, for example, wrote the following comment on the election in January 1449 of two plebeian Capitani—a craftsman and a notary:

> Giovanni Ossona, a plebeian and a man of the lowest order of guildsmen, who at this time was greatly esteemed by the people, and the notary Giovanni Appiano—these two being surely the most audacious, heedless, and cocksure of all the men in the city—transferred ultimate jurisdiction over all matters in the state to themselves, with the assistance and counsel of Ambrogio Trivulzio and Innocenza Cotta, the two most arrogant men among the nobles.[51]

Moreover, both Simonetta and Filelfo blamed the plebeian-led republic for the collapse of moral values that they witnessed in the commune in the winter of 1448–1449. And both writers focused on the degradation of women as emblematic of that collapse. "Lust rules the roost," Filelfo wrote, "mourners revel in their spoils. Shame has disappeared . . . The wife who was faithful, even as she cries out and calls upon the gods for help, receives in her bed an adulterer, once her servant; every young girl is raped: all of our laws, sacred and civil, obey the damned."[52] Similarly, Simonetta reported:

[50] Marvin Becker, "Florentine Politics and the Diffusion of Heresy in the Trecento: A Socio-economic Inquiry," in *Speculum* 34 (1959): 75; see also Cohn, *The Laboring Classes*, p. 12.

[51] Simonetta, *Commentarii*, p. 267: "Johannes Ossona plebeus infimique mercatorii ordinis, qui magnae per id temporis inter populares existimationis habebatur et Johannes Applanus tabularius, duo sane in civitate homines audaces et temerarii atque omnium confidentissimi, Ambrosii Triultii et Innocentii Cottae, duorum ex nobilitate audacissimorum virorum, consilio atque opera, civitatis totius imperii summam in se transtulerunt."

[52] See Appendix C, *Odes* 2.2.8–9 and 14–18.

Since women, who were carrying babes at their breasts and leading little children along by the hand, and many young girls, above all, were wandering around in the deserted countryside . . . and since these women and girls had no desire to be taken back to the city, they hid themselves in uncultivated places and woods . . . Among them were many girls, not only married but unmarried, who prostituted their bodies for the pleasure of anyone who came along, just to get what they needed to survive; for these girls had been entirely abandoned by their husbands and, for that matter, by all males over adolescence because of their fear of being put in prison or tortured.[53]

Food Riots and the Storming of the Palazzo d'Arengo

Simonetta and Filelfo both held the radical popular party leaders, who were in power at the end of 1449, responsible for the grain shortages that eventually brought the regime down.[54] Simonetta charged, among other things, that Ossona and Appiano were forcibly confiscating all the grain Milanese landowners produced, to feed the army; nor was the republican regime, as he saw it, taking serious measures to relieve the terrible need of the people.[55] More in the manner of a diarist, Filelfo seemed in the odes to be sketching the street scenes he saw as they unfolded. In *Odes* 2.2, for example, he captured the anger and ferment that was certainly in the air by early February 1450:

> What din of arms is ringing in my ears? Look, rioting has broken out among the people. Again and again they roar, "Bread! Bread!" The noise strikes the very poles of the earth. The wicked be damned. Down with false liberty, crueler than any tyrant, more pitiless than death, more inhuman than the dog that guards Tartarus. (2.2.58–63)[56]

On 25 February 1450, amid the widespread unrest and the food riots that had broken out in most sectors of the city, the Capitani of the republic met in the church of Santa Maria della Scala, "to think up some story to

[53] Simonetta, *Commentarii*, pp. 334–35: "Cum mulieres, quae infantes ad ubera gestabant filiosque parvulos secum trahebant, et adulescentulae insuper multae per deserta vagarentur . . . et in urbem reverti nollent, per rura inculta perque nemora latitabant . . . Inter quas multae fuerunt, non minus nuptae, innuptae, quae vitae sustinendae gratia corpus ad cujusque libidinis usum prostituebant; erant enim a viris maribusque pubertatis annos superantibus, propter captivitatis cruciatusque metum, omnino derelictae."

[54] On the government's attempts to regulate the use and supply of grain, see n. 25. It was not for lack of imposing annonary controls that the regime failed to alleviate the misery of the Milanese.

[55] Simonetta, *Commentarii*, p. 267.

[56] A complete text of *Odes* 2.2 is in Appendix C.

feed the people," as Simonetta put it, until grain shipments could come in from Venice.[57] Meanwhile a mob of citizens outside the church in the piazza began to riot, and somebody went back and started to ring the great bell of Santa Maria della Scala, which had been a signal to the townspeople since medieval times to take up arms. Thus, all those citizens who had not yet decided what course to take now began to arrive in the square in great numbers. Two leaders of the crowd emerged: Pietro Cotta and Gaspar da Vimercate. What happened next is not entirely clear. Simonetta says that after an eloquent speech Vimercate led the mob up the stairs of the Palazzo d'Arengo, and into an interior cortile that led to a dining hall. It was there that the citizens were met by the Venetian ambassador Leonardo Venerio, who, after rebuffing the citizens' demands, was slain on the spot.[58] Cristoforo da Soldo, on the other hand, emphasizes the calming role played by Venerio, who by soothing the frenzied crowd got them to vacate the piazza at least for a few hours in the earlier part of the day.[59] All the contemporary witnesses agree that it was the murder of the Venetian ambassador that evening, followed by the flight of most of the Capitani and by the rebels' occupation of the palace, that signaled the end of the Ambrosian republic. On the next day, 26 February, the Milanese summoned Francesco Sforza from the village of Vimercate, where he was encamped with his troops, and welcomed him as their signor as he crossed the drawbridge into the city at the Porta Nuova.[60]

Odes 2.3 tells the story of Gaspar da Vimercate's leadership of the citizens' siege and occupation of the Palazzo d'Arengo, the murder of Venerio, the Venetian ambassador, the flight of the republican Capitani, the fall of the government, and Sforza's triumphal entrance into Milan. These episodes are framed in what appears at first to be a stock panegyric for Sforza. Indeed, the sugar of the poem's first two stanzas sets the teeth on edge: "You, Sforza, prince—star—gracing all Latium with shimmering light, whereby you cast your rays over all the world, what thanks should I convey to you, who are deserving? O beauty most high which your supreme virtue has brought forth as it moves through all ranks of men, you alone are the protector of me, the city, as long as the gods consent" (2.3.1–8).[61]

[57] Simonetta, *Commentarii*, p. 337: ". . . convenerunt . . . ut aliquid . . . confingerent, quo ignara plebs spe inani pasceretur . . ."

[58] Ibid., p. 339. See also ibid., p. 335: Simonetta shows that resentment had been building up against Venerio among the Milanese for some time.

[59] Da Soldo, *Cronaca*, p. 99.

[60] Simonetta, *Commentarii*, pp. 340–41. According to Simonetta, there was an unpleasant incident at the Porta Nuova when Antonio Trivulzio refused to lower the bridge for Sforza or open the gate without official papers from Sforza; Gaspar da Vimercate remonstrated and Sforza was let in.

[61] See Appendix C for a complete text of *Odes* 2.3.

But the ode is more than a simple encomium of the duke's triumphs. As Gabriella Albanese has pointed out, Filelfo has in fact combined in this ode two topoi that are difficult to reconcile: the classical victory ode and the biblical *lamentatio urbis*.[62] Moreover, he has put the tale of Sforza's taking of Milan in the mouth of the city herself. She, bloodied and trembling, portrays "herself" as a helpless girl, whom Sforza rescues at the end of the war. "You lifted me from the mouths of wolves," she says to him (139–40).[63] And, as she sums up her history, powerful in its imagery—of roving robber bands, foaming streams of blood, the avarice that burns, the god Mars—she seems about to sing the praises of her rescuer: "Shameless gangs of thieves had spattered me, miserable one, with the rivers of blood shed by citizens whom violence, madness, and the fire of greed destroyed. Afterward, first savage Mars laid waste the farmland; then hunger killed all those it afflicted" (2.3.9–14).[64] The ode that follows, however, is full of pessimism. "No hope can bring back the fallen to life. All things hang in the balance," she sings (15–16). Before she can return to her panegyric, she first must go through the story of her delivery from the clutches of the republic—a word Filelfo seldom uses in the odes, preferring to allude to the government instead as "bands of robbers," "false liberty," "the fury Megaera," "the tyrants," and "the wolves" (9; 99; 69; 74; 114; and 139).[65]

The story begins with a rather ambivalent drawing of her deliverer, Sforza, whose chief attribute is that he inspires fear—not a positive quality from Filelfo's point of view, as we know from his advisory letters to Sforza and other heads of state.[66] "Who would dare to go into battle against you," she asks Sforza rhetorically, "before whom all peoples tremble, even kings quake, whom Latium fears, and the world reveres?" (41–44). Continuing in this vein, the city conjures up a cartoonlike picture of Sforza as a lion, who terrorizes the weakest animals of all—the does and the heifers: "Just as a lion separates the fleet-footed does from the slow-moving heifers when he stands in their midst, first terrifying the one group and then the other with a pounce, and just as he makes a sport of them and hems them in, so you show contempt for both our forces and those of the Venetians, and you think them worthless." (2.3.57–62)

At line 85 we come to the real meat of the poem: the city's narrative of

---

[62] Cf. *Lament. Jerem.* 1–4; see Albanese, "Le raccolte," p. 434.

[63] The adjectives describing her, the *urbs*, which in Latin is feminine, are feminine: *miseram*, line 9, *liberam*, line 115, *miseram*, line 139.

[64] For an analogous usage to Filelfo's unusual "habendi ignis," cf. Vergil, *Aeneid*, 8.327: "et belli rabies et amor successit habendi"; cf. also Horace, *Epodes*, 1.7.85.

[65] The standard terms among Quattrocento humanists for republic or republican government are the Latin words *respublica* and *libertas*; Filelfo generally was loathe to dignify the Ambrosian regime with these classical terms.

[66] Filelfo, *Epistolae*, to Cannetuli and to Sforza; Machiavelli, who was a great admirer of Sforza, promotes just the opposite view in *The Prince*.

Gaspar da Vimercate's takeover of the Palazzo d'Arengo and his expulsion of the republican Capitani. Her story of the citizens' coup d'état resembles a liturgical drama more than it does any of the chroniclers' accounts of the coup.[67] In it Vimercate, bathed in light, puts to flight the fury Megaera, her hair a mass of tangled snakes, before he and his posse of citizens chase the evil Capitani down the steps of the Palazzo d'Arengo. Moreover, the coup is represented in such a way that it is reduced to a set of unities: the action takes place against a single backdrop, the Palazzo d'Arengo; on a single day and night, 25 February; and the actors are limited to a single protagonist, Vimercate with his supporting cast of two choruses, the pro-Sforza crowd and its republican opposite number.

In Simonetta's newspaper-style article on the coup, on the contrary, there are numerous characters and a series of fast-changing scenes. Whereas Filelfo's antirepublican propaganda is blatant, Simonetta's commentary is more subtle.[68] He describes a mix of men from both the propertied and the plebeian classes participating in each of the major Milanese factions, the republican Guelphs and the monarchist Ghibellines. Simonetta's villains include the republican nobleman Domenico da Pesaro, whom he portrays as a hangman of innocent citizens, but among his republicans are good men too, like the nobleman Lampugnino Birago, who though he was "not lacking in eloquence" did not succeed in persuading the crowd to disperse in an orderly fashion.[69]

Filelfo, however, represents the coup d'état of 25 February 1450 as a morality play, in which the nobles are allegorical figures for the good and the plebs for evil. The battle at the Palazzo d'Arengo is a clear-cut case of class struggle in Filelfo, with the nobles backing the restoration of the monarchy and the plebs the defense of the republic. In his version of the battle waged in the great halls and corridors of the Palazzo, Filelfo draws the pro- and antigovernment factions in Manichean terms. The antigovernment rebels are called "citizens" and "nobles," while the defenders of the republic are "tyrants," "thieves," "gangs of criminals," and "mobs," who are "plebeian," "vile," "crazed," and "disorderly." ("rabidos tyrannos," "plebei latrones," "latronum turmas," "tumultus," "fures," "sordes," 87–110). The man of the hour is the nobleman Gaspar da Vimercate, who, after

[67] For other versions of Gaspare da Vimercate's leading the citizens' takeover of the Palazzo d'Arengo, see Simonetta, *Commentarii*, pp. 337–41; da Soldo, *Cronaca*, pp. 97–99; and Decembrio, *Vita*, pp. 948–56.

[68] Simonetta, *Commentarii*, pp. 337ff.; cf. Rosmini, *Dell'istoria di Milano*, 2.445–450: Rosmini sees Sforza as the master strategist who plans and orders the occupation of the Palazzo d'Arengo, while da Vimercato acts merely as his agent.

[69] Simonetta, *Commentarii*, pp. 337: "Quae res posteaquam tyrannidis principibus cognita est, mittunt Lampugnunum Biragum collegam suum, virum callidum et non infacundum, ut eos cives, quibus posset verbis deliniret hortareturque ut singuli domum abirent, futurum annuntians, ut rem omnes audirent gratam et salutarem."

delivering a classical *adhortatio* to his men (97–108), leads them up the steps of the Palazzo d'Arengo: "The plebeian criminals rise to arms in powerful numbers . . . The battle is drawn out under the dark night, not with killing alone. The vile rabble fall as they flee. The palace doors are thrown wide open. Gaspar bursts in. A throng of citizens follows, who with the blood of a fallen Venetian, finally set the city free from its savage tyrants" (2.3.89–90 and 109–16).

The mysterious and laconic reference to "the blood of a fallen Venetian" ("Veneti cadentis sanguine") is the only clue Filelfo drops in his narrative of the coup that his "noble citizens" murdered the Venetian ambassador Leonardo Venerio on their way up the palace steps, the blame for which Simonetta ascribes not to Gaspare or the Milanese, but to Venerio's own high-handed manner and his abusive handling of the crowd.[70] This near suppression of the assassination of Venerio by the Milanese is also very much in keeping with Filelfo's sensitivity toward his Venetian patrons, a concern that is reflected in his correspondence with a number of Venetian patricians in the late 1440s and 1450s.[71]

The ode ends the city's description of Sforza's triumphal entrance into the bleak postwar cityscape, as the duke grasps the hands of the people welcoming him and for the first time casts his eyes over "the houses long wretched with weeping" (121–24). A lengthy hortatory section follows, wherein the city warns Sforza to beware of "false friends" and other snares (141–77), and an epilogue in which she wishes Sforza long life and continued renown in war (177–88).

Sforza's Triumphal Entry and the Ritual Theater of Accession

Sforza made two triumphal entries into the city when he took Milan.[72] On 26 February 1450, the day the Milanese surrendered, he and his men entered the town from the Porta Nuova with gifts of bread and wine for the townspeople.[73] A month later, on 20 March, he officially reentered the city through the Ticinese gate, from which point he and his attendants proceeded on horseback to the Duomo, where he was robed in the silken

[70] Simonetta, *Commentarii*, pp. 339: "Qui cum insolentius ingruentes cives appellaret severius accusaret, illico multis confossus vulneribus cecidit exanimus."

[71] Filelfo, *Epistolae*. See esp. bks. 5–10, to Bernardo Giustiniani, Pietro Tommasi, Pietro Perleone, etc.

[72] See A. Colombo, "L'ingresso di Francesco Sforza," in *ASL* 3 (1905): 33–101 and 297–344.

[73] On food distribution after the war, see G. Albini, *Guerra, fame, peste*, pp. 120ff.; and Colombo, "Ingresso," pte. 4, pp. 34ff. Sforza's first tasks after his *Ingresso* were those of alleviating the famine in the city through the importation of grain and other foodstuffs from Milan's client cities and removing tariffs.

gown of *il duce* and given the keys to the city. Filelfo refers to the triumphal entries in two of the *Odes*: in 2.3, but only cursorily as we have just seen; and in 3.4, in which he pays homage to Sforza's second entry in an extended passage.

Before we consider more carefully Filelfo's representation of the *Ingresso*, it will be instructive to look briefly at the very different ways in which three other contemporary observers, Simonetta, da Soldo, and Decembrio, saw and recorded the ceremonial events of 20 March.

Simonetta, in particular, lays stress on the material accoutrements of the duke's investiture—on fabric, style, and the precise details of the ritual theater of empowerment.[74] While Sforza, Simonetta tells us, had arrived at the Ticinian gate on the morning of the procession with his wife and sons, and his cavalry arrayed with the armor, medals, and banners of their service, the Milanese had a more opulent image of their new duke in mind. They had prepared a triumphal carriage with a canopy of white silk interwoven with thread of gold, which he refused on the grounds that he was unaccustomed to such pomp. In the vestibule of the Duomo, however, the priests slid over his shoulders the floor-length white silk vestment that the dukes of Milan had worn for generations on the assumption of the signory. Then, after a solemn oath, the citizens handed over to him the imperial scepter, the sword, the flag, and the seal that the prior dukes of Milan had used, as proof of the transfer of the ducal power itself.

Almost none of this detail is in da Soldo and Decembrio. The Brescian chronicler da Soldo, whose city, despite its status as a protectorate of Venice, was repeatedly invaded by Milan, remarks of the investiture ceremony only that Sforza was robed and given the scepter and hat that the dukes were accustomed to wear. Instead da Soldo emphasizes, quite naturally, given his citizenship, the show of military might that the duke displayed in the procession to and from the Duomo. Accompanying the duke, he wrote, were a thousand *scoppiatori* and a thousand cavalrymen astride their horses holding great lances in their hands.[75] Decembrio, the former secretary of the republic and Sforza's longtime enemy, says nothing about either the duke's apparel or the visual details of the procession and the ceremony of investiture in the cathedral. He concentrates instead on what he observes to be the emotional interaction between Sforza and the Milanese at the ceremonies—on what he perceives as the relief and elation of the citizens, on the one hand, and their shame and guilt on the other:

Who could possibly convey the happiness of that day, the thanksgiving of the nobles, the merrymaking of the people, the peacefulness of the spectators? It

[74] Simonetta, *Commentarii*, pp. 345ff.
[75] The much briefer account of the *ingresso* in da Soldo, *Cronaca*, p. 99, contains almost none of the detail in Simonetta but adds general information not found in Simonetta, such as the preceding details concerning Sforza's military cortege.

would be long to tell. For instead of an enemy they now marveled that a prince, savior, and protector had come . . . They gazed, stricken with awe, and blamed one another for their slowness and suspiciousness, because they had not recognized quickly enough that their own prince was ushering in peace, abundance, and tranquility.[76]

Filelfo's *Odes* 3.4, the only poem in the lyric work that refers at length to the second *Ingresso*, focuses solely on the inaugural ceremonies as the renascence of poetry, song, and the arts in the city.[77] Yet there is more sorrow in this celebratory ode than joy. The first half of the poem depicts Milan as a scene of death and ruin, a city of Vergilian images of metallic gloom, of perverted sexuality, of diseases of the mind and body, and of Boschian birds feeding on the bodies of men:[78]

> Far away from here, Ambrogio, to the remote Triones have savage War and Famine gone at last . . . Dead and gone are the arrogant acts of the cowardly rabble and the horror of their crimes, the rapes, the grim violence, the insanity, and the looting. Ah, what brave man could remember with heart unbroken those rabid beasts, more horrible than any lethal plague, who consumed us with iron jaws and rigid beaks. (3.4.1–5 and 11–18)

At the end of the ode the clouds literally lift, and the skies clear (60–68). Still, central to the second half of the poem is a gory icon: Pegasus's birth from the blood of the severed head of the Medusa. Only through the mutilation and murder of this figure of primordial terror, surely here a double for snaky-haired Megaera, Filelfo's favorite emblem for the republic, can the Muses emerge. With the tap of Pegasus's hoof the waters of Mt. Helicon are set free from their dungeon, and the Muses and poetic inspiration come to life. It is from the demonic, then, that art is born. Thus, Filelfo's painting of the triumph ends with the duke leading the Milanese people in rounds of joyous songs and dancing. Sforza is here represented as Apollo the sun god and healer—the one who "liberated our hearts and our bodies from so foul a pestilence" (3.4.56–58).

> Look, Ambrogio, our Apollo now openly displays his ruddy rays, and now that the clouds have been dispelled from our minds, he looks down on us with shining eyes. He restores the downcast with his sweet light, and refreshes the

---

[76] Decembrio, *Vita*, 958ff.: "Quis diei illius leticiam abunde referre queat? Quis gratulationem nobilium? Quis hilaritatem totius populi? Quis intuentium securitatem? Longum esset enarrare. Hostis enim loco principem, salvatorem, protectorem advenisse mirabantur . . . Stupebant intuentes, ac se tarditatemque et suspicionem accusabant, qui Principem suum, pacem copias securitatem afferentem non celerius cognovissent, etc."

[77] See Appendix C for the complete text of *Odes* 3.4.

[78] Cf. Vergil, *Aeneid*, 6.271–80: "pallentesque habitant Morbi . . . / et mala mentis / Gaudia mortiferumque adverso in limine Bellum / ferreique Eumenidum thalami et Discordia demens," 5.597–98: "rostroque immanis vultur obiunco / immortale iecur tondens," cf. also 6.623–24.

weary. Ambrogio, we perform joyous dances to the accompaniment of melo-
dious song, and not just in a single meter. With our plectrum beating out new
rhythms in concert with wondrous poetry, we call on all that is beautiful to
come to the sacred waters and font of the poets, which the Medusa-born steed
dug up from beneath the lofty mountaintop. Now Mt. Cytheron resounds
with the soaring music of the sisters, which father Paean artfully conducts.
Obeying him, lovely Clio sings for Sforza lyrics well deserved, presenting su-
perb encomia for the leader and father of his victorious people. And lovely
Euterpe, wearing a garland in her hair, rejoices too in his lofty triumphs and
she herself sings wondrous melodies. (*Odes* 3.4.63–83)

The Plague of 1451 and Filelfo's Flight

The year after the war ended, Filelfo's healing Apollo presided over one of
the worst episodes of the pestilence in Milan's history.[79] "That fall and
winter," Simonetta wrote of the years 1450–1451, "the plague began to
snake its way through Milan. It began to grow worse in the spring of the
next year; but by the summer it had reached such a degree of virulence that
often two hundred or even more died in a single day. Nor were any human
measures of any use until the worst season of the year was over and winter
and the dry cold brought an end to the plague. And when [Sforza] asked
for the death toll, he was told that thirty thousand had died in Milan, not
from inclement weather or storms but from the foulness and contagion of
the disease."[80]

Desperate to get out of the city, Filelfo stepped up his correspondence
with friends in Florence, Venice, and Naples in the summer of 1451.[81] He
also let certain of his Milanese friends know that, in his view, it was time
he left the city.[82] It was not as though he would be walking out on a good

---

[79] G. Albini, *Guerra, fame, peste*, p. 126: daily bulletins were issued from Sforza's Officium
Sanitatis announcing the number of plague deaths beginning on 27 September 1451; these
notices are conserved in ASM, SC, 657. For accounts of the plague years 1450–1452 in
Milan, see da Soldo, *Cronaca*, p. 103. Cf. Corio, *Storia*, p. 6; and Guilini, *Memorie*.

[80] Simonetta, *Commentarii*, p. 350: "In autumno vero eius anni atque hyeme, Mediolani
coepit pestis serpere, ineunte vere sequentis anni invalescere; aestate vero tantum incrementi
sumpsit, ut saepe ducenta aut etiam amplius hominum capita singulis diebus obirent; nec ullo
humano auxilio occurri potuit, donec donec circumacto graviore anni tempore hiems et fri-
gorum siccitas finem pestilentiae imposuit et, cum mortuorum numerum perquireret Franciscus, relatum est ei triginta millia hominum capita, non inclementia coeli aut aeris intemperie,
sed pestis iniquitate atque contagione, Mediolani periisse."

[81] See Filelfo, *Epistolae*, to Inigo d'Avalos (13 June 1451), fol. 64v; and to Angelo Reatini
(15 June 1451), fol. 65v.

[82] Filelfo, *Epistolae*, to Benedetto Nursini (15 June 1451), fol. 65v; and to Cicco Simonetta
(15 June 1451), fol. 65v.

job. He had signed his university contract in April 1451, but by July there was still no sign that his salary was forthcoming.[83] So far as conditions in Milan itself went, he wrote Benedetto Nursini, a ducal physician:

> There is no way I can live without enormous mental anguish and anxiety because of this plague which is paralyzing the entire city. Its days and nights are taken up with an unending and numberless train of funerals. I don't know what plans to make. To leave here without my children and my whole family would be an inhuman and shameful thing to do. But to stay here any longer among so many and such inevitable arrow wounds is the mark of a man no less irresponsible than foolish and downright deranged . . .[84]

In September 1451, Filelfo finally got permission to leave the city. *Odes* 4.5, the only long narrative poem in the collection, tells the story of Filelfo's four-day trip, first by wagon train and then by riverboat, to Cremona that month, in the company of his two daughters, his son, a son-in-law, and two serving girls.[85] In the "Voyage to Cremona" ode, Filelfo takes up a key theme from his letters, making it this time the basis for a sustained narrative. As we saw in Chapter 1, Filelfo saw his life as a sea voyage, a metaphor he found developed in Horace's odes in a way that spoke to his own experiences.[86] Life was, in Horace's view, as treacherous and fickle as the ocean. But there was a pattern to be discerned in the changing face of the sea. Whenever the ocean looked its most serene one had to know that swelling seas and stormy weather were not far behind. The irony, then, in

[83] ASM, Autografi 127, 3, Series I, 3; and ASM, Archivio da registri di missive ducali 4, f. 123v. A letter dated 6 April 1451 and signed by Cicco Simonetta assigns a salary of 632 florins per annum to Filelfo for his chair at the university of Pavia, and 200 additional florins over and above that amount is assigned to him from the ducal treasury. See Adam, *F. Filelfo*, Appendix 28, p. 379; see also ibid., pp. 380–81 for two further letters of Cicco's dated 25 June and 2 July 1451, ordering Sforza's treasury officers to pay Filelfo 100 florins of his as-yet unpaid salary.

[84] Filelfo, *Epistolae*, fol. 65v: "Non esse possum sine permagna sollicitudine animi ac molestia ob hunc pestilentiae morbum, quo universa correpta civitas in assiduis innumerabilibusque funeribus et dies consumit et noctis. Neque satis scio quid consilium capiam. Nam sine liberis universaque familia hinc decedere et inhumanum sit et dedecorosum omnino. Diutius vero versari inter tot ac tantos inevitabilium sagittarum ictus est hominis non minus dissoluti quam insipientis planeque insani . . ."

[85] For a complete text of *Odes* 4.5, see Appendix C.

[86] On Filelfo's uses and admiration of Horace, see his *Epistolae*, to Alberto Parisi, fols. 163ff.; on Horace's use of the ship of state–ship of life topos, see esp. Horace, *Odes* 1.14; on the topos in classical literature, see E. Fraenkel, *Horace* (Oxford, 1957), p. 155: cf. Pindar, *Pythian Odes* 1.86; Aeschylus, *Seven against Thebes* 2f.; Cicero, *Letters to Atticus*, 2.7.4. Cf. Horace, *Odes* 1.5, for the same metaphor (the perilousness of the sea) in different setting. For Filelfo's use of ship and sea metaphors, see his *Epistolae*, to Aurispa (15 September 1428), fol. 7; to Giustiniani (9 April 1429), fol. 9; to Lippomano (9 April 1429), fol. 9; to Loschi (19 April 1429), fol. 9; to Bornio Sala (5 May 1433), fol. 13; to Leonardo Bruni (13 April 1436), fol. 13; and to Onofrio Strozzi (9 December 1439), fol. 20–20v.

the letter he inserted in his epistolario under the dateline 9 December 1439 was implicit: "I have taken up residence for the remainder of my life at the court of that most excellent prince, Filippo Maria—a harbor serene and safe, as it were, from those stormy Etruscan floods."[87]

The poem is a strange mixture of autobiography, epic, satire, and invective. Portraying the situation of not only his but many other Milanese families after the war, now faced with both the plague and dangerous shortages of grain in the city, the ode recounts the very real details of Filelfo's harrowing voyage from Piacenza to Cremona on the Po, which culminated in the death from the plague of his serving girl, Antonia. The collapse of Antonia Alipranda, the model for the girl of the same name in the ode, on the wharf below the city walls of Cremona, in fact, was the subject of the only letter in Filelfo's epistolario about his journey to Cremona that September:

> Although we had arrived yesterday evening and were welcomed quite graciously, today we were expelled from the city. The reason was this. I had in our entourage a hired servant, a shy sort of girl from quite a good family, whose name was Antonia Alipranda. We left her at the boat together with your nurse Maria to watch over our luggage, while we went to rent lodgings. In the meantime we were amusing ourselves with Xenophon, your sisters, and your brother-in-law at a decent innkeeper's. Once the matter of our lodgings had been settled, when I went back to the boat to take the women and the luggage to our lodgings today, I found that Antonia had died: struck down by the sudden violence of the plague, she had been placed on the riverbank, and right on that spot a very large crowd had gathered, and there was rioting.[88]

The principal themes of Filelfo's "Voyage to Cremona" ode come from folkloric literature in general and the *Aeneid* in particular: a hero's quest for a promised land for his people; a voyage by water, a storm of floodlike dimensions, prayers offered up to the gods, a stop in a liminal, underworldlike city, the casting out of the hero from the city, his exile in a kind of desert, and finally, the sacrificial death of a woman, which comes at the turning point in the poem, as it does in the *Aeneid*. Yet true to the nature

---

[87] Filelfo, *Epistolae*, to Onofrio Strozzi (9 December 1439), fol. 20–20v: "Ego apud hunc praestantissimum principem, Philippum Mariam, ex illis Ethruscis turbulentissimisque fluctibus tanquam in tranquillum atque securum reliquae vitae portum me recepi."

[88] Filelfo, *Epistolae* to Giammario Filelfo (14 September 1451), fols. 66v–67: "Cum hesterno vesperi Cremonam venissemus essemusque excepti minime inhumaniter, hodie ex urbe eiecti sumus. In causa hoc fuit. Erat mihi serva mercenaria ex familia non ignobili Alipranda, nomine Antonia, et ea quidem puella non inverecunda. Hanc relinqueramus in cymba una cum Maria nutrice tua, ut tantisper res nostras asservarent, dum aedes conduceremus. Nam cum Xenophonte sororibusque tuis ac genero apud honestum cauponem interim diverteramus. Dum post paratas aedes hodie cymbam repeto, quo et res et mulierculas agerem ad aedes, offendo Antoniam subita pestilentiae vi correpta[m] animam efflasse positamque in ripa ibidemque maximum hominum concursum ac tumultum."

of the *Odes* generally, as we have seen, Filelfo's epic themes are cast in a satirical framework. While Filelfo has appropriated a series of motifs from the *Aeneid* in his "Voyage to Cremona," his more immediate model for the ode is Horace's *Satires* 1.5, the famous "Journey to Brundisium." Consequently the tone of *Odes* 4.5 is comedic rather than tragic, despite the gravity of its themes. Filelfo himself plays the role of narrator throughout the ode, as does Horace in *Satires* 1.5. And just as Horace's satire describes the highs and lows of being on the road, so Filelfo's narrative of his journey from Milan to Cremona, first over land and then by river, recounts a similar series of vicissitudes. Horace's satire also serves as a suggestive model not just for Filelfo's travelogue but for all the odes, because of its reference to classical patronage, to the relationship between the poet Horace and his patron Maecenas.[89]

Thus, *Odes* 4.5, the most self-referential and self-consciously intertextual of all the odes, has a complex architectonic structure.[90] First, there is its tripartite metrical plan. The first and third movements, the purely narrative sections of the poem, are in Asclepiadeans, while the middle movement, which is an invective against the Cremonese, is set in elegiacs. Second, there is the palimpsestlike structure of the ode: its layering of facades. On the surface, the poem appears to be a simple travelogue sketched from memory. But beneath that unassuming contemporary skin—like the bleached bones of a first-century Roman temple showing through behind some crumbling Renaissance facade—we glimpse the outlines of a Horatian satire, and then, beneath it, the remnants of a Vergilian epic poem in miniature.

The poem begins—and ends, as we shall see—with fresh memories of hunger. As Filelfo and his family roll out of plague-ridden Milan in their mule-drawn wagon, they cannot help but recall the war and long famine they recently lived through, and as they do so they are prompted, this time again by hunger, to search for shelter and food (4–11). But like Horace in the Brundisium ode, they will suffer in a matter of a few days all the reversals of fortune one usually experiences over a very long span of time. After being almost bodily ejected from the first inn they try in Pavia, they find plentiful stores of bread, wine, and down comforters at the next hostel (12–42).

---

[89] In taking Horace, *Satires*, 1.5 for his exemplar, Filelfo alludes to Horace's accompaniment of Maecenas in 38 B.C. to the conference held near Brindisi, the purpose of which was to bring the civil war to an end.

[90] It is interesting that *Odes* 4.5. is set in the first Asclepiadean mode, the meter Horace uses for his three most self-revelatory odes in terms of what his role as a poet means to him: see *Odes* 1.1, on Horace's choice of occupation; 3.30 on Horace's own claim to everlasting life due to the immortality of his poems; 4.8 on Horace's giving of the greatest gift that can be given—immortality, which is conferred on men by poems praising them.

When the family sets sail on the "rosy colored" Ticino river at the rising of "bow-bearing Titan" the next day at Pavia, and then enters the Po, Filelfo launches his miniature *Aeneid* (44ff.).[91] From here on out, Filelfo drops a series of allusions, each of which evokes associations with death in the *Aeneid*, so as to foreshadow Antonia's tragic end. When the family docks the boat outside Piacenza on the last leg of their journey to Cremona, Filelfo sings of "the anchor that grips the shore with its teeth," recalling the idiosyncratic metaphor that so strikingly marks Aeneas's pause in front of the gates of Hades in *Aeneid* 6.[92] That night a tempest reminiscent of the storms in *Aeneid* 5, with its turbid rains, raging whirlwinds, Jove-sent thunder, and boiling waters, fills the boat's hull and thoroughly soaks the little group as they huddle together for warmth.[93] Only the servant girl Antonia is hot with a fever—though because she behaves "deceitfully," like Dido in *Aeneid* 4, she gives the others no warning of her imminent death.[94] The next day dawns, auspiciously, with Tithonus's wife rising from her saffron couch—an image Vergil employs only twice in the *Aeneid*, once to usher in the day Dido will immolate herself.[95]

On the third day of the voyage, the group docks at Piacenza, only to encounter the toll collector Piccolus, who, like Charon in *Aeneid* 6, tries to

---

[91] *Odes* 4.5.44–45: "roseo surgit ab aequore / Titan arquitenens." Here Filelfo appears to have conflated a number of formulaic conceptions of dawn from Vergil: Titan's unveiling of the earth with his rays (*Aeneid* 4.119 and 5.65, same line in Vergil); Aurora's ascent from the sea or from her golden couch (*Georgics* 1.447 and *Aeneid* 4.129, 585, 9.460, and 11.1); and the rubescence of Aurora and her car (*Aeneid* 6.535 and 12.77; *Georgics* 4.521). The epithet "arquitenens" is the standard one for Apollo in Vergil and Ovid (*Aeneid* 3.75 and *Metamorphoses* 1.441 and 6.265).

[92] Cf. Filelfo, line 52: "quae ripam tenuit dentibus anchora" and Vergil, *Aeneid*, 6.3–4: "tum dente tenaci / ancora fundabat navis."

[93] Cf. Filelfo, lines 53–57 and 69–71: "mox tonat . . . / Iuppiter . . . / Nec pluviae lentius ingruunt / Nimbi praecipiti turbine conciti / irrumpunt rabidis amnibus undique / . . . Penetrant omnia turbidi nimbi. Sic penitus nos quoque vestibus / frigemus madidis . . ." and *Aeneid* 5.694–97: [Here Vergil describes Jupiter's creation of a thunderstorm in response to Aeneas's prayer] "effusis imbribus atra / tempestas sine more furit tonitruque tremescunt / ardua terrarum et campi; ruit aethere tot / turbidus imber aqua densisque nigerrimus Austris / implentur super puppes, semusta madescunt"; cf. also the storm at *Aeneid* 1.88–90. Filelfo's poststorm prayer to Jupiter, "O divum genitor, rector et arbiter / rerum, etc." (58–61) is also reminiscent of Vergil's standard invocation, "divum pater atque hominum rex" (at *Aeneid* 1.65, 2.648, 10.2, and 10.743); but Filelfo's skepticism about divine intervention (61–66) reminds us not of Vergil, but of Horace at the close of *Satires* 1.5.101–4.

[94] Cf. Filelfo, line 74: "Nec fallax referat, etc." and *Aeneid* 4.477: "consilium vultu tegit" [Dido secretly plans her death, while pretending all is well]; 4.675: "me fraude petebas?" [Here Dido's sister accuses her of having behaved deceitfully].

[95] Cf. Filelfo, lines 76–77: "Tithoni croceos [saffron] liquerat excita / uxor iam thalamos [bed]" and *Aeneid* 4.585: "Tithoni croceum [saffron] linquens Aurora cubile [bed]." The line occurs only one other time in Vergil, prior to the grisly deaths of two of Aeneas's companions at *Aeneid* 9.460.

prohibit the family from crossing the river to Cremona, which, as it will turn out, resembles Hades. Piccolus, like Charon, is dirty, unkempt, and swollen with a terrible rage that is assuaged only by the intervention and authority of Sceva Corti, just as Charon's anger must be put down by the Sibyl.[96] At one point, Filelfo tries to use a gilt-embossed letter of safe-conduct from the duke to gain entry to the river, producing it suddenly from beneath his cloak as though it were a talisman and waving it in the tax collector's face, in much the same way that Aeneas handles his magical golden bough.[97] On the fourth day, the Filelfo family lands at Cremona, and when Antonia's dead body is found on the dock, Filelfo's parody of the *Aeneid* ends with the townspeople rushing about in panic, their "cries making the very heavens ring," just as Vergil's Carthaginians do when they hear the news of Dido's death at the close of *Aeneid* 4.[98]

The Cremonese mob forces the Filelfo family to retreat hastily from Cremona (112), and Filelfo follows the story of his expulsion from the city with a strange invective in elegiac couplets (114–62).[99] Since Filelfo had often lectured on Cicero's *Philippics*, it is not surprising that his chief charges against the Cremonese in this fifty-line digression can be grouped under the same general topoi we find in those orations—namely, the charges of bestiality (118, 130–31, 144, and 148–49); of barbarity (116 and 132–43); of criminality (119–20, 125, and 154–57); and of insanity, derangement, or drunkenness (146 and 150–51).[100] More interesting is

[96] Cf. Filelfo, lines 84–85: "quo nil invenias rusticus, nihil / usquam sordidius" and *Aeneid* 6.298–301: ". . . flumina servat/terribili squalore Charon, cui mento / canities inculta iacet, stant lumina flamma, / sordidus . . . dependet amictus"; of the immoderate rage of these two characters, cf. Filelfo, pp. 96–97: [Sceva tells Piccolus to calm himself] "iussit ne stomachum fervere bilicum demens cogeret" and *Aeneid* 6.407: [the Sibyl calms Charon's anger] "tumida ex ira tum corda residunt."

[97] Cf. Filelfo, lines 89–90: "principis . . . me tego litteris" ["I cover myself with my ducal letter."] and *Aeneid* 6.406: "aperit ramum, etc." [Aeneas uses his golden bough to protect himself]. But whereas Charon's *pietas* causes him to yield at the sight of the golden bough, when prompted to do so by the Sibyl, Piccolus is notably lacking in that quality. Cf. *Aeneid* 6.405: "si te nulla movet tantae pietatis imago, etc." [the Sibyl taunts Charon] and Filelfo, p. 92: "nec pietas flectere Piccolum."

[98] Cf. Filelfo, lines 110–11: "Tollitur extemplo cunctis ad sydera clamor: / vesanum passim vulgus ad arma ruit" and *Aeneid* 4.665–69: "it clamor ad alta / atria . . . lamentis gemituque et femineo ululatu / tecta fremunt, resonat magnis plangoribus aether, non aliter quam si immissis ruat hostibus, etc."

[99] Though Filelfo swings into elegiacs in the last part of the narrative, with his arrival in Cremona at line 102, the formal invective does not begin until line 114.

[100] Filelfo refers to Cicero's *Philippics* in Filelfo, *Epistolae*, fols. 61v and 75v. See also Traversari, *Epistolae*, col. 1016, where Filelfo lists in a letter to Traversari the orations of Cicero among the works to be included in his syllabus for the class he is preparing to teach at the Studio in Florence. So popular was the invective in the Quattrocento that it found its way into every possible literary genre: prose oratory, satire, epigrams, epistles, and, in this instance, even lyric poetry.

the fact that Cremona in *Odes* 4.5 is depicted as a repository for all those sins that Filelfo had attributed to the Ambrosian republic and its Capitani. Thus Cremona becomes an analogue not only for Gomorrah but, more importantly, for the Milanese republic, which it resembles in each of its vices.

The poem ends with the family in exile. The voyage is over, the storm winds have died down, and the sea is tranquil. Like Horace recalling the noises and dirt of Appi Foro in his "Journey to Brundisium," Filelfo here portrays a countryside that is no safe haven from the evils of the city. His *contado* boasts a polluted well, croaking frogs, and no place to get a decent meal. Thus, in his quest for Arcadia he has managed to flee neither the famine, nor the pestilence, nor the poverty of the city. Save for the ripe grapes of late September, he and his family can neither gather food from the land nor buy it:

> A small garden greets us—exiles. Here stands a small cottage with a drinking well which chirrupping frogs crowd round . . . No one dares to touch our money, as if the little coins themselves carried the morbid disease too. And so bitter Necessity, which prevents us from eating and from drinking, besets us. Grapes give us back our strength, and if this succulent fruit hadn't soothed our stomachs, hunger and thirst would have overwhelmed us with the pricks of death. (*Odes* 4.5.164–66 and 169–76)

In all the odes there is a sense that Filelfo is a liminal, exilic figure, disaffected and critical toward governments, cities, and patrons. In this, as in all the odes, the city is a bleak, burnt-out shell, inhabited by men who have become feral and birdlike. But life outside the city is no answer, and at the end of the poem Filelfo is back where he started: as he prepares himself for flight again, the gnawing at the pit of his stomach persists. As for the promised land, he has reached the far shore of the river, only to find he will have to move on:

> At Cremona there's no place for the holy Muses, none for Athene or Maia's son. Here only the porno trade does well. Here the profit motive corrupts the whole city. Here great honor goes to pimps, whores, and the learned professors of the dice-box, to tax collectors, gourmands, and poisoners. We must row away from here and go back to the Insubrians. We must sail right now to the next land. Bye-bye Cremona, sacred city of the monstrous shades. (*Odes* 4.7.1–10)[101]

---

[101] For complete text of *Odes* 4.7, see Appendix C.

A portrait of Filelfo attributed to Andrea Mantegna.

An anonymous fifteenth-century portrait of Filelfo in profile.

The Visconti Castello at the Porta Romana in Milan, which the captains of the Ambrosian republic ordered the people to demolish in September 1447. Seventeenth century.

Santa Maria della Scala in Milan, where the citizens assembled at the tolling of the great church bell to take up arms against the republic on 25 February 1450. Seventeenth century.

The Porta Nuova in Milan, where Francesco Sforza and his army entered the city with gifts of bread and wine for the starving citizens on 26 February 1450. Seventeenth century.

FOUR

LEVITY

NOW, DURING the years 1458–1464, the Kingdom of Naples bled from the same wounds of war that Milan and her client cities suffered in the late forties and early fifties in the wake of Filippo Maria Visconti's death. In July 1458 Filelfo's recent host and patron, King Alfonso of Naples died, leaving his vast kingdom to his son Ferrante.[1] Within the year, Duke René d'Anjou's son, Jean, marched into the Campagna with the full support of his kinsman Charles VII of France. There Jean routed the armies of both King Ferrante and the pope in a series of engagements, all the while waiting to take Naples itself. Meanwhile, Ferrante met with the revolt of his barons who moved quickly to support Jean's claim to the throne.

A month after Alfonso's death, Filelfo's former pupil and longtime client, the Sienese Cardinal Enea Silvio Piccolomini, was elected pope. The newly crowned Pope Pius II and Duke Francesco Sforza each pledged their support of Ferrante against Jean d'Anjou. While Pius worried that if Naples fell the papal states would be next to capitulate to France, Sforza reasoned that with both Genoa and Naples under his rule, the Angevin duke's son might strike Milan next. But Pius was far less interested in the wars in Apulia and the Campagna than he was in events a thousand miles away on the eastern front of Christendom, in Greece. Like Calixtus before him, Pius now believed it was his mission as pope to liberate Constantinople from Turkish rule. Thus, with the objective of mounting an expedition against the Turks, the pope summoned the European heads of state to a special assembly in Mantua in the summer of 1459.

But while representatives from Milan, Florence, Venice, and Naples met

---

Chap. 4 is a revised version of my article, "Unknown Greek Poems of Francesco Filelfo," in *Renaissance Quarterly* 37 (1984): 173–206. The title of the chapter alludes to Ambrogio Traversari's influential objections to Filelfo's conduct in 1429: the monk was appalled by, among other things, the young man's "Greek levity" (Traversari, *Epistolae*, to Leonardo Giustiniani, bk. 6, letter 26: for letter text, see chap. 1, n. 89).

[1] On the wars of the succession to the throne in Naples, see Ludwig von Pastor, *History of the Popes*, 4th ed., trans. F. I. Antrobus, 40 vols. (London, 1923), 3.102–23; Ernesto Pontieri, *Per la storia del regno di Ferrante I d'Aragona re di Napoli* (Naples, 1969); and Jerry H. Bentley, *Politics and Culture in Renaissance Naples* (Princeton, 1987), pp. 24–26.

at Mantua to discuss the threat from Islam, Jean d'Anjou led his army to the gates of Naples. In April 1460 Jean marched on Nola, and in July the French routed King Ferrante in a disastrous defeat at Sarno. The next year Jean, who by this time was calling himself the duke of Calabria, took Savelli, Colonna, and Anguillara. It was not until the close of 1461, when the Genoese expelled Jean's father, Duke René, from their city, that a gradual reversal in the course of the war occurred.[2] That year Ferrante and Francesco Sforza's brother Alessandro combined forces to take on Jean's army once again at Troia, this time forcing the French to retreat. With the withdrawal of Jean's troops to France, the majority of the Neapolitan barons renewed their oaths of fealty to Alfonso's son and heir.

In order to meet the mounting costs of shoring up the Aragonese throne in Naples against aggression not only from the French but from Ferrante's own barons, Sforza, according to Filelfo, simply confiscated the pensions of his courtiers in 1458.[3] Indeed, the ducal registers show that Filelfo received no payments from the treasury from 1458 until Sforza's death in 1466.[4]

Filelfo in the 1460s: Fame, Poverty, and Prison

In terms of the recognition accorded his work, Filelfo's career was nearing its apogee in the early sixties. His stock had never been higher, not only in Milan where he was the city's leading poet and critic, but in Italy in general. There was, in short, a marked incongruity between Sforza's demeaning treatment of him and the widespread acclaim that his writings now commanded abroad. Over the last decade he had published five major works: the *Satires*, the *Odes*, the *Jovial and Serious Epigrams*, the *Sforziad*, and portions of his *Collected Letters*. And, most recently, he had completed a substantial collection of poems written in classical Greek. Almost as soon as Pope Pius took office, he established an honorary chair for Filelfo that was to provide him with a sizeable yearly income.[5] Moreover, at the pope's

[2] On the French in Genoa, see Niccolò Machiavelli, *History of Florence and the Affairs of Italy From the Earliest Times to the Death of Lorenzo the Magnificent*, 3d ed., with an intro. by F. Gilbert (New York, 1966), pp. 303–8.

[3] See Adam, *F. Filelfo*, p. 233, n. 33: Filelfo, *Epistolae*, to A. Simonetta (18 May 1460), fol. 116; to Torelli (5 October 1461), fol. 120v; and to Martorelli (15 June 1466), fol. 187v; see also in Benadduci, ed., *Atti*, pp. 154–55, Filelfo to Gonzaga (7 August 1466); also *De iocis et seriis* in Ambros. G 93 inf., fols. 137, 147, 166, 186, and 216.

[4] Adam, *F. Filelfo*, pp. 393–95 reproduces a ducal balance-sheet drawn up in October 1467 of Filelfo's debts, which Adam believes were paid promptly by Galeazzo Maria Sforza's treasurers from the five thousand ducats now owed Filelfo in arrears since 1458.

[5] On the annual pension Pius promised Filelfo in 1458, see Filelfo, *Epistolae*, fols. 102v–103 to Bessarion and Pius II (1 November 1458), fols. 103.

great Congress at Mantua in 1459, Filelfo had accompanied Francesco Sforza as his personal orator and ex officio ambassador. Still, as the months went by, he felt increasingly less certain that he could continue to feed his family.

During the hard years of the civil war under the Ambrosian republic, Filelfo and his family had suffered hunger and privation, but so had everyone else in Milan. In the late fifties, however, conditions in the Lombard city changed visibly. Although the war in the south continued to drain Milan's treasury and Sforza remained the Aragonese king's principal underwriter through the end of the decade and the early sixties, the duke still found funds for certain cultural programs. Indeed, around 1458 Sforza embarked on two substantial new building projects in Milan: the erection of the city's Great Hospital and the restoration of the Visconti's ancestral residence, the Palazzo d'Arengo, under the direction of Filarete, for which frescoes by Foppa, Bembo, and Moretti would later be commissioned.

As for Filelfo's state of mind during this period, two of his letters, one thanking his friend Marco Antonio Torelli for a gift of some bushels of wheat, the other a request for help addressed to the man who was perhaps his oldest friend, Cardinal Bessarion in Rome, give us some idea of the level of distress he was experiencing:

[The gift of] the wheat was as much a delight as a necessity, especially for a man with no farms—no land—who must buy everything for ready cash, and who has precious little of that—in fact none at all because of the war in Apulia over the throne, which is draining the duke's treasury to the dregs. In fact not a cent of my regular salary has been paid me for a whole year now, nor for that matter has anyone else here been paid . . . (7 October 1461)[6]

You can imagine how I feel—I who always showed contempt for money. But it's come to this—I now no longer even have books or clothes left. Everything is in the hands of a moneylender, and is as good as lost, and this poverty is about to finish me off too . . . (9 June 1463)[7]

But Sforza's virtual abandonment of him was not all. It was in the early sixties that Filelfo was surprised by a betrayal particularly hurtful because it came from a man who was not only a fellow poet but a former student

[6] Ibid., fol. 120v: ". . . triticum [esse] . . . rem sane utramque non gratam minus quam necessariam homini praesertim, cui nulli sunt fundi, nulli praedia, et omnia nummis comparanda sunt, et nummi admodum pauci, vel potius nulli propter Appula ista regia bella, quae aerarium nostri principis omne exhauriunt. Nam annum iam mihi integrum e constituta pecunia nihil solvitur, at ne alii quidem cuique . . ."

[7] Ibid., fol. 130v: here Filelfo laments the suspension of his pensions on the parts of both Pius and Sforza, ". . . Quare potes existimare qua ipse conditione sum, qui pecunias contemnere semper consuevi. Quo factum est ut ne iam libri quidem, neque vestimenta ipsa mihi sint reliqua. Omnia sunt apud foeneratorem, quae pereunt et ipse ob inopiam periclitor."

and longtime client of his—a sharer, above all, in his values. When Enea
Silvio Piccolomini, his friend of thirty years' standing, was elected to the
papacy in August 1458, Filelfo saw an honorable way out of his worsening
situation in Milan.[8] Just as he had set his sights on the Valois court in 1455,
so he now mounted a campaign to win an appointment in the newly constituted papal court. Certainly he had good reason this time to believe he
would obtain the post he desired. For three years, 1429–1431, Enea had
been Filelfo's student at the Florentine Studio. And for twenty years after
that, Filelfo had written letters in his behalf, recommending Enea to a
number of his own patrons in Milan—among them Duke Filippo Maria
Visconti, Niccolò Arcimboldi, and Sceva da Curte.[9] The two men neither
saw nor wrote to each other with any frequency in the fifties. When Enea
was crowned Pope Pius II in August 1458, however, he moved at once to
establish a pension of two hundred ducats a year, which was to be paid to
Filelfo in perpetuity without obliging him to perform any official services
for the pope in return.[10] And so in December of that year, buoyed with
hopes of even greater prospects, Filelfo left home for Rome, carrying with
him a deluxe copy of his satires for the pope and undoubtedly a manuscript
of his new poetry in Greek as well.[11]

   Filelfo never received more than the first year's installment of the pension that Pius had allotted him. During the years 1461–1463 he filled the
better part of three volumes of his *Epistolae*, which he was preparing at that
time for publication, with the urgent missives he had sent Pius's cardinals
and other members of the pope's circle, asking them to assist him in secur-
ing his pension.[12] After Pius's death in 1464, however, Filelfo's letters to
clergy, friends, and even to Pius's successor, Pope Paul II, became openly
critical of the late pope for his failure to honor his commitment to him.[13]
At the same time Filelfo began to circulate epigrams that were seen by the
College of Cardinals as slanderous attacks not only on the deceased pope

[8] On Filelfo's long relationship with Piccolomini, see Adam, *F. Filelfo*, pp. 152–60.

[9] Ibid., pp. 153–54.

[10] On the pension, see Filelfo, *Epistolae*, to Bessarion (1 November 1458), fols. 102v–103;
to Pius (1 November 1458), fol. 103; and Germano Gualdo, "Francesco Filelfo e la curia
pontificia: una carriera mancata," in *Archivio della societa romana di storia patria* 102 (1979):
189–236.

[11] On Filelfo's hope of obtaining a post in Rome, see Filelfo, *Epistolae*, to E. S. Piccolomini
(23 August 1458), fol. 102–102v. On his gift for Pius, see *Epist.* to Gaspar da Vimercate (19
January 1459), fol. 105; this manuscript of Filelfo's satires is preserved in Vat. Reg. lat. 1981
as noted by José Solis de los Santos, *Satiras de Filelfo* (Sevilla, 1989), pp. 17–18.

[12] See Filelfo, *Epistolae*, to Cardinal Isadore Ruthenus (12 February 1461), fol. 120; to
Gregorio Lollio (13 April 1461), fol. 121–121v; to Cardinal Ammanati-Piccolomini, fols.
121, 123, 124v, 128, 129–129v, and 130v.

[13] See ibid., to Ludovico Trevisan (23 August 1464), fol. 155–155v; to Bernardo Giustiniani (20 September 1464), fol. 159; and to Paul II (15 September 1464), fols. 156ff.

but on the Church itself.[14] In November 1464 the cardinals dispatched an offical complaint to Francesco Sforza, urging the duke in the strongest possible terms to punish Filelfo. At the cardinals' behest, the duke incarcerated his poet and orator in the Castello for five months.[15]

Thus, for the second time in his life, a powerful constituency demanded that Filelfo be put behind bars for writings allegedly damaging to his patrons. And once again he suppressed in his epistolary autobiography the fact that he had been publicly arrested and sentenced to serve a humiliating prison term. Nor did he refer elsewhere in his published work to the violent restriction placed on his person in the winter of 1464 and the spring of 1465 by his supposed protector, Francesco Sforza. However openly he might suffer in spirit, he took pains in all his writings to make it clear that as long as he was alive he alone would hold dominion over his body. His honor, after all, was at stake.

The *Psychagogia* and the Silver Basin

It was only after Piccolomini's election to the papacy in 1458 that Filelfo had looked to Rome specifically, in drawing up plans for his next major work. His new opus, a collection of forty-four poems in ancient Greek, with its erudite title *Psychagogia*, was designed to draw attention to his unique talents in a way that his earlier publications had not yet succeeded in doing. As early as April 1458 he boasted in writing that he would be the first Italian not merely to try his hand at imitating Homer and Alcaeus, but to publish a substantial collection of poems in classical Greek.[16] The year before, he had already written to the distinguished Greek émigré John Argyropoulus, who was then teaching at the Florentine Studio, to ask for primers on Greek prosody and the Greek dialects, particularly the Aeolic.[17] Six years later, on 1 December 1465, Filelfo wrote Cardinal Bessarion in Rome, then the leading figure among the Greek expatriate scholars, to tell

[14] The epigrams on Pius are printed in Rosmini, *Vita*, 2.320–21.

[15] For the evidence on Filelfo's five-month incarceration in the Castello, see A. Luzio and R. Renier, "I Filelfo e l'umanesimo alla corte dei Gonzaga," in *Giornale storico della letteratura italiana* 16 (1890): 176; see also epigrams of P. C. Decembrio in Rosmini, *Vita*, 3.160–61; and of Antonio Cornazzano in F. Gabotto, "Ricerche intorno allo storiografo quattrocentista Lodrisio Crivelli," in *ASI* 7 (1891), 267–96.

[16] Filelfo, *Epistolae*, to Girolamo Castelli (9 April 1458), fol. 101v: "Nuper enim hoc quoque scribendi genus sum aggressus . . . Latini vero non modo nunc nulli sunt hac tempestate, qui Graecos versus scribant, sed ne ullos quidem de priscis accipimus . . . Nec id una epistola quapiam sum facturus, sed libellis, ut spero compluribus."

[17] See Legrand, *Lettres*, pp. 90–93, for two of Filelfo's letters to Argyropoulus on the Greek poems (5 November 1457 and 13 November 1457); see also p. 91 for his letter to Theodore Gaza (13 November 1457) in which he enclosed an elegy he wrote in honor of Gaza's patron, King Alfonso of Naples.

him that on that day he had put in the mail a finished copy of his three books of Greek poems.[18]

Filelfo's title for his Greek work, *Psychagogia*, cleverly encompassed both the somber funeral elegies and the lighter satirical pieces in his new collection. While *psychagogus* (soul-leader) was the epithet of the god Hermes, the escort of dead souls into Hades, Plato's use of the word *psychagogia* in the *Phaedrus* connoted the playful diversion of men's minds that was the rhetorician's business.[19] The men to whom the poems in the *Psychagogia* were dedicated were largely churchmen, philosophers, and professors—those, in short, who were most likely to be either scholars or readers of ancient Greek by training. His twenty-six addresses included three popes, four cardinals, one bishop, and the Patriarch of Constantinople. Cardinal Bessarion was the dedicatee of four of the poems, and Pope Pius that of three. Accordingly, the collection had a decidedly scholarly flavor, and many of the poems were of a philosophical, questing nature. Ten of Filelfo's addressees were fellow professors, four of them Greek émigré scholars, refugees from Constantinople. Only four of the poems were addressed to secular princes, and there was but a single short piece dedicated to Sforza. As for their themes, twelve of the poems were encomia, fifteen were verse epistles written either to commemorate a particular occasion or to make a specific request, six were funeral eulogies, and eleven were pieces of a lighter, or even satirical nature. Clearly Filelfo, who had visited with a majority of the poems' addressees when he was in Rome in 1458 and Mantua in 1459 for Pius's summit meeting, had composed the Greek work with both the pope's *Congresso* and the papal city in mind.

The collection is a curious mixture of pieces obviously produced to bring in income, those written purely for the sake of amusement or mockery, and those of a graver, more idealistic nature. As we saw in Chapter 1, Filelfo's attempts to advise and counsel such men as Pope Pius and Paul II indicate that the passage he so often cited from Plato's *Republic* continued to inform his own conception of his role as a teacher and writer:

> Unless those whom we now call our kings and rulers pursue the study of philosophy seriously and for enough time, and unless these two spheres of power—the political and the philosophical—are conjoined . . . there can be no end of danger for our states, nor I believe, for the human race. (*Republic* 473d–e)[20]

Filelfo's swings in tone from the sublime to the mocking, typifying his dedicatory poetry in general and the *Psychagogia* in particular, reflect his deeply ambivalent attitude toward money and men of wealth. Although he

[18] Ibid., p. 121–22; Filelfo made the same announcement in *Epistolae*, to Bessarion (July 1465), fol. 173.
[19] *Phaedrus* 261a.
[20] The translation is mine.

clearly needed a fair amount of surplus income to live in the milieu in which he did, he rarely let slip an opportunity to express his disdain for money. Time and time again he would vent his anger at not having been paid for work contracted; and then, in the next breath, he would show his contempt for wealth and the extravagances of the rich. An interesting story Filelfo told about himself concerning his earnings from one of his poems nicely encapsulates his characteristic oscillating between, or his simultaneous embracing of, contradictory attitudes toward wealth and its outward symbols—from appreciation, to need, to scorn—in the *Psychagogia*. In the summer of 1462, he had been given a very large, gold-embossed basin of silver by the Venetian patrician, Jacopo Antonio Marcello, in recompense for a funeral elegy he had written on the death of Marcello's son (poem 3.3). In the midst of a packed assembly in the great hall of the ducal castle in July of that year, Filelfo ceremoniously rose to his feet, approached the podium, and made a formal presentation of the silver basin to Francesco Sforza. He had decided to donate the valuable basin to the duke's treasury, he explained, so that he could demonstrate that he placed his own hopes "not in gold and silver but in God and virtue alone."[21]

Filelfo's carefully planned and staged donation of the silver basin to the duke was a piece of obvious self-promotion. Here, in the most public of arenas and before all the duke's ministers and courtiers, he could assume the persona he had been embellishing for himself all along: he could play the true philosopher to whom the world's wealth meant nothing. Still, one also saw in Filelfo's grandiose gesture other less palatable qualities—a confusing mix of insolence and deference, of humility and hauteur, earnestness and parody, all of which were reminiscent of certain letters Filelfo had written to his patron Giustiniani many years before, on the subject of honor and the need to fulfill one's obligations. In any event, in the context of Sforza's claim during the relatively prosperous late fifties that he was too broke to pay his courtiers because of the war in Naples, the scene with the basin was sheer cabaret on Filelfo's part.

The Form and Content of the Poems

A single autograph codex of Filelfo's Greek poems, perhaps the very one Filelfo sent Bessarion in 1465, survives in the Laurentian Library in Flor-

---

[21] Filelfo, *Epistolae*, to Alberto Zancario (7 July 1462), fol. 127: "Cum praestantissimus princeps noster esset in celebri concessu, ei illam continuo dedi dono, quo ipse quoque simul cum aliis intellegeret me non pluris facere aurum et argentum quam ea omnia quae in nostra potestate non sunt, sed . . . tibi velim persuadeas spes nostras omnis totiusque vitae studium in virtute sola esse deoque collocandum."

ence: Laurentianus 58.15.[22] The codex bears the title *De psychagogia libri III*. It contains three books of forty-four poems alternately arranged in elegiac and Sapphic meters: Book 1 contains sixteen poems, Books 2 and 3 fourteen poems each. On fol. 80v a note appears in Filelfo's own hand cautioning the reader not to copy out any of the poems since he had not yet revised them for publication.[23] In 1892 Emile Legrand published fourteen of the poems contained in Laurentianus 58.15, from transcriptions furnished to him by other scholars, but he was never able to examine the Laurentian codex himself.[24] The remaining thirty poems in the codex have never been published. Moreover, despite the fact that these poems antedate Poliziano's Greek epigrams and must surely be among the first Neo-Greek poems to be written by an Italian humanist, until recently little attention had been paid them.[25]

The language of the poems in both the elegiac and Sapphic meters is Homeric; that is to say, the poems are written in a literary dialect consisting of an admixture of Aeolic, Ionic, and Attic forms.[26] Filelfo skillfully manipulates his Greek verses, both the lyric Sapphic strophes and the more prosaic elegiacs. But he is most successful in the philosophical poems he has set in elegiac couplets, which are especially well suited for the display of a series of learned literary allusions, each germane to the poem's central theme. Although Filelfo's somewhat limited vocabulary, his dearth of orig-

---

[22] A. M. Bandini, ed., *Catalogus codicum manuscriptorum Bibliothecae Mediceae Laurentianae*, 2 vols. (Florence, 1764–1770), 2.450–54. Bandini prints complete texts of two opening poems. The hand in Laur. 58.15 has been identified as Filelfo's own by S. Bernardinello, *Autografi Greci e Greco-Latini in Occidente* (Padova, 1979), p. 55. See also R. Barbour, *Greek Literary Hands* A.D. *400–1600* (Oxford, 1981), who identifies the Greek hand in Vat. Lat. 1790, fols. 155–58 (which contain verses from *Psychagogia* 3.3) as Filelfo's. Laur. 58.15 is the only known complete codex of Filelfo's *Psychagogia*. The Bibliotheca Vallicelliana in Rome has a fifteenth-century codex that contains twenty of the forty-four Greek poems: MS 143, fols. 17–22 and 25, has poems 1.1, 3–7, 10, 12, and 15; and 2.1–4, and 8–14; but the quality of the paper is poor, the hand is sloppy, and in no way does the codex resemble that of the elegant art object that Laur. 58.15 is.

[23] "Hi tres libri neque editi sunt a me Francisco Philelfo, nec emendati. Quare cum multa mutanda sient, ne quis ex hisce quicquam exscribat rogo."

[24] Legrand, *Lettres*, pp. 195–219.

[25] John Edwin Sandys, in *A History of Classical Scholarship*, 3 vols. (Reprint. New York, 1964), 2.56, mentions Filelfo's Greek poems only in passing; J. Hutton, *The Greek Anthology in Italy to the Year 1800* (New York, 1935), pp. 95–96, on Filelfo, makes no mention of his Greek poems; but see Renata Fabbri, "Le consolationes de obitu Valerii Marcelli ed il Filelfo," in *Miscellanea di studi in onore di V. Branca* (Florence, 1983), 3.1.227–50; Gianvito Resta, "Francesco Filelfo tra Bisanzio e Roma," in *Filelfo nel V cent.*, pp. 30–33; see also Enrico V. Maltese, "Osservazioni critiche sul testo dell'epistolario greco di Francesco Filelfo," in *Res Publica Litterarum. Studies in the Classical Tradition* 11 (1988): 207–13; and idem, "Appunti sull'inedita *Psychagogia* di Francesco Filelfo," in ibid. 12 (1989). Currently Maltese is preparing a full commentary and critical edition of the *Psychagogia* for publication.

[26] For a more detailed discussion of Filelfo's Greek, see Maltese, "Osservazioni."

inal images, and his frequent need to resort to stock formulas, particularly in the pentameter of the distich, all mark the poems as undistinguished in terms of their literary quality, the poems are of exceeding importance for the literary history of the period on a number of counts. First, coming from the first great Western European scholar of classical Greek, the poems give a clear indication not only of the breadth of Filelfo's knowledge of classical Greek syntax and prosody, but also of the precise nature of his knowledge of his classical Greek sources. Moreover, addressed as they are to the leading prelates, princes, and pundits of the Quattrocento, the poems furnish an index of the concerns and tastes of the period. It is true that certain encomia in the collection demonstrate little more than the popularity of *speculum principis* literature at the courts. Nevertheless other poems, which contain direct references to the *Republic*, the *Laws*, the *Phaedrus*, and other works that were for all practical purposes unknown in the West until the second quarter of the fifteenth century, furnish evidence of a remarkable level of cultivation and learning at the courts of Pius II, Borso d'Este, Francesco Sforza, and Ferrante of Naples.

Filelfo's philosophical epistles are indeed among the most interesting poems in the *Psychagogia*. A poet and scholar by profession rather than a philosopher, Filelfo nonetheless projects in all his writings his enduring interest in Plato, Aristotle, and the Stoics.[27] During the Milan years he produced a number of works of a philosophical nature that reveal the impact of his study of the Greeks on his thought: the *Convivia Mediolanensia*, the *Commentationes Florentinae*, the *Consolatio ad Marcellum*, and the *De morali disciplina*.[28] Filelfo was the first Italian epitomizer of the Greek philosophers in the Renaissance. Indeed, two of the books he most cherished in his own library were Plutarch's *Moralia* and the *Lives of the Philosophers* of Diogenes Laertius, works themselves rich in epitomes from the philosophers. In the most comprehensive of Filelfo's philosophical works, the *De morali disciplina*, Filelfo characterizes himself as an adherent of no single school of philosophy and no single philosopher. There he asks only to be allowed to "wander through all the precepts of the philosophers" ("per omnia eorum praecepta vagari"), labeling himself ἐκλεκτικός, an epithet borne out in the profusion of obvious topoi, especially from Plato and the Stoics, which we generally find in those poems I have called his philosophical epistles.[29]

[27] Calderini, *Ricerche*, located and cataloged Filelfo's citations of ancient Greek texts in his works; though Calderini did not know Filelfo's *Psychagogia*, I am nonetheless much indebted to his work.
[28] The *Convivia* and *Commentationes* were composed in 1443, the *Consolatio* in ca. 1462, and the *De morali disciplina* in ca. 1475.
[29] *De morali disciplina*, p. 2. Paul Oskar Kristeller, "Marsilio Ficino as a Man of Letters and the Glosses Attributed to Him in the Caetani Codex of Dante," in *Renaissance Quarterly* 36

A synopsis of all the poems in the collection is provided in Appendix D. Texts, translations, and commentaries for two of Filelfo's unpublished Greek poems follow.

Two Philosophical Epistles
Poem 1.3
A Consolation for Palla in Exile

Πάλλαντι τῷ Στρώζᾳ χρυσίῳ ἱππεῖ

Πάλλα ἄνερ, πρώτων ὅν πάντες φασὶν ἐπαίνων
   ἄξιον εἶναι ἄγαν, ἄξιον ὄντα πάνυ.
φίλτατος ὢν ἀτρεκὴς σ'αὐτῷ μάλα πάντα νοῆσαι
   σεῖο πέρι, Στρώζα, σοῦ διὰ βούλομ' ἔπους.
οἶδα σὲ πάντα φέρειν κομψῶς σοφὸν ὄντα βροτοῖσιν   5
   ὅσσαπερ ἄστρα πόρεν, εἴτε πονηρὰ τύχη.
οἶσθα γὰρ ἀνθρώποις ἴδιον μηδὲν ῥα γενέσθαι,
   πλὴν ἀρετῆς, ἥ τὸν ἄνδρα θεὸν τελέει.
σὴν ἀρετὴν πάντες οπουδῆσιν ἐς ἄστρα μεγίοταις
   αἴροντες, σὲ ὅλον φασὶ γενέσθαι ὅλον.   10
οὐδὲ τύχη κατὰ σοῦ οὐδ' ἄλλης φόρτος ἀνάγκης
   ἰσχὺν ἔχει· καὶ γὰρ πάντα σοφὸς δύναται.
οὐ πόλις ἀνδρὶ μόνη πατρίς ἐστιν πάντα νοοῦντι
   εὖ τε φρονοῦντι λίην, αὐτὰρ ὁ κόσμος ἅπας.
κοίρανός ἐοτιν ἀνὴρ ὁ τὰ ἔξω ἐν οὐδενὶ θήσας,   15
   καὶ βασιλεὺς μοῦνος· ταῦτα γὰρ ἀλλότρια.
σοὶ μὲν ἄρ, ὦ Πάλλα, πάοη γῆ πᾶσα θαλάττη
   ἐοτι πατρίς, καὶ πᾶν οὐρανός ὅσσον ἔχει.
καὶ τούτου γε χάριν, πάθος οὐδέν σοι τὰ παρόντα
   πικρὰ φέρει, ὅσσα καὶ φθόνος αὐτὸς ἄγει.   20
σοι δὲ χαρὰν πολλὴν κἀκείνην οἶδα παρεῖναι
   πάντα λογιζομένῳ, οἶσθα σὲ αὐτὸν ὅτι·
σῆς θ' ὅτι καὶ ἀρετῆς γαίας ἐπὶ τέρματα φήμη
   ἦκε σὸν ᾄδουσα τοὔνομα καὶ τὸ κλέος.
οὐδὲ σὲ καὶ πέφυγεν δεῖν πάντως τοὔσχατον ἔργον   25
   ἄνδρα σοφὸν τηρεῖν· τοῦτο γὰρ ἆθλα φέρειν.
καὶ γὰρ ἀεὶ τὸ τέλος γλυκερώτερόν ἐστιν ἀρίστοις
   ἀνδράσιν ἀλλὰ πικρὸν τοῖς γε κακοῖσι πέλει.
πάντων μούν' ἀρετὴ θνητῶν οἴηκα κρατύνει
   μούν' ἀρετὴ δύναται ὄλβιον ἄνδρα φάναι.   30
αὐτὸς ἄρ, ὦ Στρώζα, εὐδαίμων, Πάλλα, ὑπάρχεις.
   ὄλβιος εἶ μοῦνος σὴν διὰ καλλοσύνην.

(1983): 16, points out that around 1457 a number of treatises on the doctrines of these Greek philosophers came out, two of these by Ficino.

ἤδομ' ἐγὼ σὲ λίην τόσον ἤδη τὸν περὶ γαῖαν
πάντῃ ἀλαόμενον ὄλβιον ὅρμον ἔχειν.
ἀνδρὶ σοφῷ πρᾶξις καλὴ σπουδή τε δικαίου   35
ὅρμος ἀεὶ πέλεται, ὃν φθόνος οὐ βέβλαφεν.
τἄλλα μὲν ὁ φθόνος ἐστὶ κακὸν δεινόν τε πικρόν τε·
τοῦτο δὲ καὶ καλὸν καὶ γλυκὺ καὶ ὅσιον.
καὶ γὰρ ἀεὶ δάμασεν σκληρῷ τὸν χτώμενον ἄλγει
ὀφθαλμοὺς τήκων καὶ κραδίην φθονεροῦ.   40

3 σαυτῷ Laurentianus 58.15

[1] All men think you are worthy, wholly worthy, Palla, of the highest praise. Because I am your true and much loved friend, I want to know all about you, Strozzi, from your own words.

[2] I know that you, because you are a wise man, bear graciously everything that the stars and cruel fortune have brought men, For you know that there is nothing a man has of his own except goodness that makes him godlike. All men earnestly exalt your goodness to the heavens, and they believe wholly in your soundness.

[11] Neither fortune nor the freight of any other necessity has power over you, for a wise man is capable in all circumstances. A wise and wholly sensible man calls the whole world his own country, not just a single city. Only the man who puts no trust in externals is lord and king: for these things are irrelevant to him. Every country on every sea is your home then, Palla, and all that the heavens hold. Because of this, the recent bitterness wrought by envy can cause you no pain. But on the contrary, I know you have great joy in your perfect understanding, because you know yourself, and since the report of your goodness has journeyed to the ends of the earth, hymning your glory and fame.

[25] But you are also aware that it is necessary for a sage to take on this highest duty, for this can bring rewards. For the good, the end is always sweeter; for those who are evil, however, it is bitter.

[29] Only goodness strengthens each man's helm, only goodness can reveal the happy man. You then alone, Palla, are fortunate, and you alone have joy because of your beauty. For so long you wandered over all the earth, and now I am glad you have found a safe harbor. Noble action and the quest for justice are always a refuge for the wise man, nor can envy harm him.

[37] Envy is usually an evil, a bitter thing, and a scourge. But in one way it is fair, sweet, and even divine: for it always defeats the man who possesses it with harsh pain, melting down his eyes and his heart.

Poem 1.3 is an epistle in elegiac meter addressed to Filelfo's longtime patron, the Florentine statesman Palla Strozzi (1372–1462).[30] Palla, Flor-

---

[30] Lawrence W. Belle, *A Renaissance Patrician: Palla di Nofri Strozzi, 1372–1462* (Ph.D.

ence's wealthiest citizen according to the Catasto of 1427, was also an eminent scholar of Greek, particularly of Plato and Aristotle. Banished from
Florence from 1434 until his death, Palla moved to Padua, where he remained for the rest of his life. In this epistle Filelfo consoles his friend of
over thirty years on his long period of exile, and he praises Palla's wisdom
and virtue.

The opening four-line prologue is standard for the dedicatory poems in
the collection. In return for an encomium, Filelfo requests a favor from his
patron—in this case, only a letter: "I want to know all about you." (3–4)
Filelfo praises Palla as the Stoic ideal, the man who possesses both wisdom
(σοφία) and moral virtue (ἀρετή, 5–8). The necessary conjunction of these
two qualities in the sage is assumed (5–10): for only through moral virtue—the quality other men recognize and acclaim in the sage (9–10 and
23–24)—can the sage's wisdom be made manifest. Lines 5–6, an adaptation of Plutarch's *Consolatio in Apollonium* 102e, celebrate the patient en-
durance that Palla has shown throughout his years in exile, the quality
most commonly linked with Stoicism: "You a sage bear graciously, etc."
(5) A comparison of Filelfo's verses with *Consolatio* 102e illustrates Filelfo's
imitation of the diction and, to some extent, even the syntax of his model:[31]

εὐλόγιστος δ' ὁ . . . δυνάμενος φέρειν δεξιῶς τά τε προσηνῆ καὶ τὰ
λυπηρὰ τῶν ἐν τῷ βίῳ συμβαινόντων.

The sagacious man is the one who can bear with aplomb both the pleasant and
the painful in life's chance events.

The lines that follow, "nothing except the good makes a god of a man"
(7–8), resemble Plato, *Theaetetus* 176c: "there is nothing more like God
than the man among us who becomes as righteous as possible (δικαιότα-
τος). Filelfo's substitution of ἀρετή for δικαιοσύνη ("righteousness," "justice") as man's most divine possession is Platonic enough given the persistent association of virtue with justice in the *Meno* 73b, *Republic* 335c and
348c, and *Symposium* 209a. Filelfo does not cite the *Theaetetus* by name in
his letters or other works, but certainly he knew the dialogue. Indeed, after
1450 he became increasingly active in his search for Plato codices and in
the study of all Plato's works.[32]

---

dissertation, University of Rochester, 1972); see also Lauro Martines, *The Social World of the
Florentine Humanists: 1390–1460* (Princeton, 1963), p. 317; cf. Vespasiano, *Princes, Popes,
and Prelates*, pp. 235–45.

[31] See Calderini, *Ricerche* for a list of other passages Filelfo mined from Plutarch's *Consolatio*. All Greek texts in this chapter are from the Loeb Classical Library editions unless otherwise noted. The translations are mine.

[32] In addition to the *Laws* and the *Republic*, Filelfo cites by name the *Alcibiades, Cratylus,
Phaedo, Phaedrus, Gorgias, Meno, Parmenides, Symposium*, and *Timaeus* in his letters and other
works; see esp. his *Epistolae*, fols. 131, 150, 150v, 159, 223, 230v, and 264. See also Legrand,
Lettres, on Filelfo's Plato studies.

Having established Palla as ὁ σοφός, Filelfo presents a discourse on the merits of the sage (11–22). The first of those merits, the capacity of the sage to resist fortune (11–12), was a favorite topos among the humanists.[33] Among the ancient Greeks it can be found, for example, in Plutarch, *De fortuna* 97c–98f, the *Consolatio in Apollonium* 102e–f, and in the Stoic philosopher Persaeus of Citium's aphorism, "the wise man cannot be worsted by fortune."[34] This particular citation from Persaeus is preserved in the fourth-century A.D. Byzantine rhetorician Themistius, a manuscript of whose works Filelfo had purchased in Constantinople.[35] The topos of the world citizenship of the sage (13–14 and 17–18) was especially appropriate to Palla, an exile from his native city for almost thirty years at the time of Filelfo's writing of this poem. These lines might have been inspired by two texts in particular, both of which Filelfo knew well: Plutarch, *De exilio*, a work Filelfo had copied out by hand for his own use, and Aristophanes, *Plutus*, a work Filelfo had once cited in a letter to his son:[36]

ὁ δὲ Σωκράτης βέλτιον, οὐκ Ἀθηναῖος οὐδὲ Ἕλλην, αλλα κόσμιος εἶναι . . .

Socrates said a better thing, that he was neither an Athenian nor a Greek, but a citizen of the whole world. (*De exilio* 600f.)

πατρὶς γάρ ἐστι πᾶσ' ἵν'ἂν πράττῃ τις εὖ.

Your own country is wherever you can live decently.

(*Plutus* 1151)

Filelfo's definition of true kingship, as dependent on inner qualities rather than externals (15–16), closely resembles *sententiae* attributed to Philo, Clemens, and Proclus, and fits well in Filelfo's catalog of the sage's merits:

μόνον τὸν σοφὸν βασιλέα.

Only the wise man is king.[37]

σοφὸς μόνος βασιλεὺς καὶ ἄρχων.

---

[33] Cf. Marsilio Ficino's letter to Rucellae on fortune (ca. 1460) in *Ausgewaehlte Schriften*, 2d ed., ed. D. Wuttke, (Baden-Baden, 1980), pp. 149–50.

[34] See Persaeus (a pupil of Zeno) in Ioannes von Arnim, ed., *Stoicorum Veterum Fragmenta*, 3 vols. (Leipzig, 1905–1924), 1.9, hereafter cited as Arnim. For other sources for the topos, see Arnim, 1.53f.

[35] Filelfo, *Epistolae*, to Iacopo Cassiani (8 October 1450), fol. 48v.

[36] A copy of Plutarch's *De exilio* in Filelfo's own hand is preserved in Laur. 80.20, as listed in Bandini, *Catalogus*, 2.210–12. Filelfo quotes lines 676–81 from Aristophanes' *Plutus* in his own Latin translation in a letter to his son Xenophon (see *Epistolae* [28 July 1465], fol. 174).

[37] Philo, *De nominum mutat.*, as cited in Arnim, 3.159. Filelfo listed Philo among the works he brought back to Italy in 1427 in his famous letter to Traversari about his Greek book collection: see Traversari, *Epistolae*, bk. 24, letter 32.

[Only the wise man is king and lord.]³⁸

ὡς γὰρ τέκτονα λέγομεν οὐ τὸν ἔχοντα τὰ ὄργανα τοῦ τέκτονος, ἀλλὰ
τὸν τὴν τέχνην κεκτημένον. οὕτω καὶ ἄρχοντα καὶ βασιλέα . . .

Just as we say that an artisan is not the man who has the artisan's tools but the
one who has his skill, thus it is with a ruler and king.³⁹

Filelfo's consoling remarks to Palla on his insulation from envy (because
he is a sage, etc.) and from τὰ παρόντα πικρά ("the present bitterness"), by
which Filelfo refers certainly to the bitter factionalism in Florence that continued to prevent Palla's repatriation year after year, have an interesting
parallel in *Republic* 500b–c.⁴⁰ Socrates here tells Adimantus that the true
philosopher must stand aloof from the backbiting politicians and rhetoricians who squander their time wrangling with one another, because

οὐδὲ . . . σχολὴ . . . τῷ γε ὡς ἀληθῶς πρὸς τοῖς οὖσι τὴν διάνοιαν
ἔχοντι . . . φθόνου τε καὶ δυσμενείας ἐμπίμπλασθαι . . .

the man who fixes his intellect on what truly is reality has no leisure to glut
himself on envy and bitterness.

Filelfo, however, reserves his highest compliment to Palla for the final topos in his discourse on the sage's merits: οἶσθα σε αὐτόν ("you know yourself," 22), a variation on the famous Delphic inscription γνῶθι σαυτόν
("know yourself").⁴¹ Filelfo was well acquainted with at least two ancient
texts that cite the inscription: Plutarch's *Consolatio in Apollonium* 116d,
which quotes the inscription verbatim, and Plato's *Phaedrus* 230s, which
contains a paraphrase of the inscription.

Lines 25–26 reaffirm the connection already established in the prologue
to the poem, between the philosopher-king and his *vates*, who is by definition a sage. For both the prince and his poet will reap the rewards of
ἀρετή. And here the image ἆθλα ("rewards," 26) seems to trigger a variation on the motif τὸ γλυκὺ καὶ πικρόν ("the sweet and the bitter," 27–28)—
a metaphor for rewards and punishment, or happiness and sorrow, ubiq-

³⁸ Clemens, as cited in Arnim 3.159. Filelfo does not refer to Clemens by name in his
writings.
³⁹ Proclus, *Commentary on Plato's Alcibiades*, as cited in Arnim 3.159. Filelfo specifically lists
Proclus's commentary on Plato in the inventory of 1427 of the books he brought back from
Constantinople; see Traversari, *Epistolae*, bk. 24, letter 32; and Filelfo, *Epistolae*, to Iacopo
Cassiani (8 October 1450), fol. 48v.
⁴⁰ Calderini, *Ricerche*, p. 361, notes that Filelfo cites a neighboring passage, *Republic* 508
in his *Commentationes Florentinae*, bk. 2, fol. 48v and in his *Convivia Mediolanensia*, bk. 1, fol.
10v.
⁴¹ *Liddell-Scott Greek-English Lexicon*, 9th ed., ed. S. Jones (Oxford, 1977) draws a distinction between οἶδα, "to know by reflection" and γιγνώσκω (γνῶναι), "to know by observation."
However, Filelfo's preference for οἶδα throughout the *Psychagogia* in disparate kinds of con-
texts cautions us not to press the distinction.

uitous in Greek literature (cf. Pindar, *Ischmian Odes* 1.7.6; Theognis 301; Aeschylus, *Choephori* 234; *Eumenides*; 152, and Solon 1.5).[42]

Toward the close of the poem (29–30), Filelfo returns again to the theme he introduced in lines 5–12: a man's moral virtue (ἀρετή) is a stronger force than his fortune (τύχη). Filelfo's metaphor, in which virtue is stationed like a helmsman at the rudder (οἴηκα, 29) of life's ship, borrows elements from two Greek epigrams, one of which is contained in a thirteenth-century manuscript Filelfo purchased in Constantinople in 1423:

τὴν δὲ τύχην βιότοιο κυβερνήτειραν ἔχοντες . . . πλέομεν.

We sail, relying on Fortune as our life's helmsman.

(*A. P.*10.65)[43]

ἡ δ' ἀρετὴ σταθερόν τι καὶ ἄτροπον, ἧς ἐπι μούνης κύματα θαρσαλέως ποντοπόρει βιότου.

Moral virtue alone is the steady and unshakable ship on which you can boldly navigate life's stormy seas. (*A. P.*10.74)

Filelfo's use of the standard *sententia* on the necessary coincidence of happiness with moral virtue at line 30 ("only goodness can reveal the happy man") suggests numerous sources, among them Plato's *Laws*, which Filelfo seems to have mined almost as often as he did the *Republic*:

σχεδὸν μὲν γὰρ εὐδαίμονας ἅμα καὶ ἀγαθοὺς ἀνάγκη γίγνεσθαι . . . οὐκ ἂν ἔγωγε αὐτοῖς ποτὲ συγχωροίην τὸν πλούσιον εὐδαίμονα . . . γίγνεσθαι μὴ καὶ ἀγαθὸν ὄντα.

It is almost a necessity that men should be happy and morally good at the same time . . . Nor would I ever agree that a wealthy man could be happy if he was not morally good. (*Laws* 742e and 743a)[44]

Weaving together ideas from lines 19 and 29, Filelfo hammers home in

---

[42] Cf. also Solon's first elegy, which Filelfo might have known from Stobaeus, whose *Florilegio* he seems to have seen or purchased since, in Filelfo, *Epistolae*, to Guilielmo Palaeologi of Monteferrato (September 1472), fol. 253v, he quotes a line from Sophocles preserved only in Stobaeus (as cited in Calderini, p. 393).

[43] *A. P.* (= *Greek Anthology*) 10.65 is contained in a collection of over a hundred Greek epigrams now preserved in Florence, Biblioteca Laurenziana, MS Laur. 32.16, fols. 4–8, which bears the date 1281 (fol. 295); on fol. 9 Filelfo recorded his purchase of this codex from his mother-in-law, John Chrysoloras's wife in Constantinople in 1423. See Bandini, *Catalogus*, 2.369; and Hutton, *The Greek Anthology*, p. 95f. Other epigrams on the mutability of fortune in Laur. 32.16 include *A. P.* 10.62, 64, and 80.

[44] Filelfo cites the *Laws* in his *De morali disciplina*, his *Oratio ad Marcellum*, his *Commentationes*, his *Convivia*, and his *Epistolae*, fols. 179 and 237 (August 1465 and September 1471), as cited in Calderini, p. 362. For the same topos, cf. *Laws* 662b, *Republic* 580b; *Diogenes Laertius* 7.87; Alexander of Aphrodisius, in Arnim, 3.14–16.

lines 33–37 the idea that solely through virtue can happiness and security be attained. Only the sage finds a harbor (ὁρμος) safe from envy.

Taking up the theme of envy from line 36, Filelfo caps the close of the poem with an ingenious expansion of a Greek epigram he had once translated into Latin:

> ὁ φθόνος ὡς κακόν ἐστιν. ἐχει δέ τι καλὸν αὐτῷ.
> τήκει γὰρ φθονερῶν ὄμματα καὶ κραδίην.

How evil envy is. But it has something good in it: for it melts down the eyes and hearts of the ones who are envious. (*A. P.* 11.193)[45]

At the same time Filelfo's reintroduction of the bittersweet motif from lines 27–28 in his paraphrase of *A. P.* 11.193 fittingly evokes the notion of a τέλος (a word the humanists often used to signify the end of a composition), which might be either bitter or sweet.

Poem 1.5
Counsel to the Newlywed Donato on Virtue

Δωνάτῳ τῷ᾽ Ἀκτιόλῳ

Ἀκτίολον τὸν ἐμοὶ Δωνᾶτον φίλτατον ὄντα
  εὔχομαι εὖ πράττειν, Πιερὶς ᾆδε νέον.
ἐν Φλωρεντίνοις Δωνᾶτος γ᾽ ἔξοχα πάντων
  ζητεῖ τὴν ἀρετήν· μοῦνος ἄρ ἐστι μάκαρ.
ἄνδρα γὰρ οὐ τυχερὰ διαπράττοι εὐδαίμονα μοῖρα, 5
  οὐδὲ χροὸς λαμπρὸν ᾧ φίλε εἶδος ὅλου.
ἀνδρὸς ἄρ ἐστ᾽ ἀγαθὸν τὸ ἀεὶ διαμεῖν᾽ ἀδαμάστως.
  τοιοῦτ᾽ ἐστ᾽ ἀρετή. τἄλλα γὰρ ἀλλότρια.
εὐδαίμων δὲ γυνὴ ποιεῖ καὐδαίμονα πάντη
  τὸν πόσιν. ἔστιν ἀνὴρ τοῖος ἄρ ἠδὲ πόσις. 10
᾽ω σὺ δὶς εὐδαίμων Δωνᾶτε πανέξοχε, χρῆσθαι
  σπεῦδε τύχη κἀρετῇ·τοῦτο σοὶ ἀμφότερον.
οὐ γὰρ ἐγὼ Μούσας αἰνῶ εἴκειν᾽ Ἀφροδίτη
  τήνδε γὰρ ἀονίσιν δούλιον εἶν᾽ ἐθέλω·
νυκτὸς ὅσον λίπετο σχολερὸν τόδε Κύπριδος ἔστω. 15
  τἄλλα δὲ τῆς ἀρετῆς ὦ φίλε πάντα πρέπει.
ζῷον ἀνὴρ λογικόν· λόγος οὖν καὶ τέρψις ἀνάγκη
  σώματος ἀντίπαλοι· ἀλλὰ συ εἶκε λόγῳ.
ἔστι μὲν εἰς ἀρετὴν ὁδός, ᾽ω Δωνᾶτε, τραχεῖα·
  τήν δὲ λόγος μοῦνος ἐκμαλακίζει ἄγων. 20
οὗτος ἄνω τε κάτω τε βλέπων ἅμα πάντα νοῆσαι
  μοῦνος ἔχει· μοῦνος οὖν ἀγός ἐστι βίου.

---

[45] See Trivulzianus, fol. 27 (May 1433) and fol. 121v (March 1461), as cited in Calderini, p. 276.

ὥσπερ ἀρ ἡ μήνη φέρεται πρὸς ὑπέρτατ' Ὀλύμπου,
νῦν δὲ παρ' Ἀντίποδας καὶ σφόδρα πάντ' ὁρᾶται·
αὐτὸς ὁ νοῦς οὕτως αἰῶνας πάντ' ἀτελέστου   25
ἠδὲ χρόνου φθαρτοῦ σκέπτεται ἡμέτερος.
τοῖος ἀρ ὢν τὸν νοῦν ἀνὴρ μόνος ἐστὶν ἐπαίνου
ἄξιος. ἀλλὰ τύχης ἐστὶ γελᾶν τὸ ἄγαν.
τοῦτο γὰρ οὐ κρατερόν. μεταβάλλεται ἦμαθ' ἑκάστῳ
σφάλλεται, ὡς δολερόν· ἐλπὶς ἀεὶ κενεά.   30
εὖ δὲ σὺ δρῶν φιλέεις τὰς Μούσας, αἵ σε θεοῖσιν
ποιήσουσι φίλον πρόξενον οὐρανίοις·
αἳ γὰρ ἀείσουσαι τἀγαθὸν θνητῶν τε θεῶν τε
ἀγνοίας τὸ κακὸν ἐκ κραδιῶν ἔβαλον.
ἡ καθαρὰ ψυχὴ ἀκριβεῖ τὸ ἐτήτυμον ὄντος   35
αἰὲν ὁρῶσα λόγῳ αὐτὸ λαβεῖν ποθέει·
τἄλλα μὲν Ἀκτίολον ἡγεῖσθαι πάντα κελεύω
φροῦδα φίλον· μούνη ἐστ' ἀρετὴ τἀγαθόν.
ἡ δ' ἀρετή γε σέβειν καθ' ὑπέρτατα πάντα διδάσκει
τὸν θεὸν οὐράνιον, ὅς μόνος ἐοτ' ἀρετή.   40

[1] Sing to me, Pierian Muse, that young Donato Acciaiuoli, who is very dear to me, fares well, I pray you. Among the Florentines, Donato above all others seeks after virtue. He alone then is blessed.

[5] For neither good fortune nor the shining good looks of a healthy body makes a man happy, my friend: the highest good which belongs to a man eternally and indestructibly then is virtue; for everything else is irrelevant.

[9] A wife who is wholly happy makes her husband happy too—and thus a contented spouse and lover. O remarkable Donato, since you are doubly blessed, try to make the most of both fortune and virtue, for both of these are yours.

[13] Now I don't advise that the Muses should bow down to Aphrodite. I'd rather see that goddess be the Aonian daughters' slave; leave only the idle portion of the night to the Cyprian. The rest of your time, my friend, should be wholly given to virtue.

[17] Man is a rational animal, and so reason and the pleasures of the body must be rivals; but you should yield to reason.

[19] The road to virtue, Donato, is rough; but reason alone softens the road when it leads you. Only reason is capable of viewing all things above and below the earth at the same time. Reason alone then is life's guide. Just as the moon sails now to the Antipodes, and then to the lofty regions of Olympus, gazing on everything intently, so the mind contemplates everything which

exists throughout boundless eternity and corruptible time. Because of his mind, then, man alone is a creature worthy of praise.

[28] But we can laugh at the extremes of fortune, for they have no strength. Fortune changes with each day, and like a trap, it causes us to founder; hope is always fruitless.

[31] You do well to love the Muses, since they will make you a most favored guest of the heavenly gods. For when the Muses extol the goodness of men and gods, they cast from their hearts the evil of ignorance.

[35] Once the pure soul has gazed upon the truth of existence with its perfect reason, it longs to seize it for its own. I urge you, dear Acciaiuoli, to believe that all else vanishes. Virtue alone is the good, and virtue teaches us to revere God in heaven most highly, for God alone is virtue.

Poem 1.5 is a verse epistle in elegiac meter, addressed to Donato Acciaiuoli (1428–1478), the grandson of Palla Strozzi and disciple of John Argyropoulos, the Greek émigré professor of philosophy at the Florentine Studio.[46] The subject of the epistle is the preeminence of virtue as the only reliable source of happiness. Here Filelfo archly advises the newly married Donato, who according to Vespasiano remained celibate until his marriage at the age of thirty-two, not to serve Aphrodite until "the idle hours of the night." In a similar vein, Filelfo wrote Donato in November 1460, warning him not to try to "play the bride's pipe and Muse's at the same time."[47]

The prologue (lines 1–4) follows the format of the encomium to Palla. Filelfo offers Donato the gift of an elegy in exchange for a poem or letter from the young man ("Sing to me . . . Muse . . . that Donato fares well"). But the difference in tone between elegies 1.3 and 1.5 is clear from the first. Filelfo addresses the elder statesman with deference: Palla is the incarnation of the Stoic ideal, the true philosopher. Donato is characterized here as a mere seeker after wisdom, in need perhaps of some instruction.

After the prologue Filelfo introduces the poem's principal theme: the supremacy of virtue (ἀρετή) as the one highest good we ought to seek over all other goods (5–8)—a topos recurrent, as we noted in the commentary to 1.3, in Plato and the Stoics. The emphasis here, however, on the necessary connection between happiness (εὐδαιμονία) and spiritual rather than physical health also reflects Filelfo's lifelong occupation with the texts of Aristotle, of whose *Nicomachean Ethics* he had begun a translation in 1428,

[46] On Acciaiuoli, see Arthur M. Field, *The Beginning of the Philosophical Renaissance in Florence, 1454–69*, 2 vols. (Ph.D. dissertation, University of Michigan, 1980); Eugenio Garin, *Portraits from the Quattrocento*, trans. E. and V. Velen (New York, 1972); and Vespasiano, *Princes, Popes and Prelates*, pp. 276–304.

[47] Filelfo, *Epistolae*, fol. 118v: "utrique arundini et nymphae et Musae simul studere non potes."

and whose *Rhetoric* he translated in 1431.[48] It is instructive, for example, to compare lines 5–8 with the *Ethics* 1.13.1–6:

ἡ εὐδαιμονία ψυχῆς ἐνέργειά τις κατ᾽ ἀρετὴν τελείαν . . . ἀρετὴν δὲ λέγομεν ἀνθρωπίνην οὐ τὴν τοῦ σώματος ἀλλὰ τὴν τῆς ψυχῆς.

Happiness is an activity of the soul in accordance with perfect virtue . . . But what we mean by virtue in men is not the goodness of the body, but of the soul.

Having dismissed the body (and presumably its pleasures) as the locus of human happiness, Filelfo broaches the subject of marriage and sex (9–16). First of all, εὐδαιμονία can be found in marriage with a wife who herself has attained that state of mind. The usage of ἀνήρ and πόσις in line 10, to signify two contrasting aspects of a husband's role, that of lover and legal consort, is rare in classical Greek. Nonetheless, no other interpretation is possible in the context of lines 13–16.[49] Filelfo's source for his mock-serious suggestion that Donato's sexual needs should for the most part be sublimated and his pursuit of virtue advanced through the "service of the Muses" appears to be Plato's *Laws* 783a, the work to which Filelfo repeatedly returns in all his writings.[50]

Filelfo counsels young Donato further that we can only pursue virtue through the proper use of λόγος and νοῦς ("reason" and "mind"), since man is a λογικὸν ζῷον. Filelfo may well have first seen this epithet—a favorite variation among the later Greek philosophers on Aristotle's characterization of man as a "political animal"—in Plutarch, *De Morali Virtute* 450d, a work Filelfo had copied out in its entirety for himself.[51] For the image in line 10 of reason and physical pleasure literally wrestling (ἀντίπαλοι) for supremacy, Filelfo is probably indebted again to the *Nicomachean Ethics* 1.13.15–16, a work to which Filelfo repeatedly turned throughout his life:

φαίνεται . . . ἄλλο τι παρὰ τὸν λόγον, ὃ μάχεται καὶ ἀντιτείνει τῷ λόγῳ.

[48] Ibid., to Niccolò Fava, fol. 6v; in *De morali disciplina*, p. 2, Filelfo states that Aristotle was a principal influence on his thought. On Aristotle's influence on him, see Calderini, *Ricerche*, pp. 271f.

[49] Liddell-Scott, eds. *Greek-English Lexicon*, p. 1453; for a precedent for this usage, see Sophocles, *Trachinae*, p. 550.

[50] See n. 32.

[51] The Plutarch codex that Filelfo copied is preserved in Laur. 80.22 (See Calderini, *Ricerche*, pp. 374ff.). For the epithet λογικὸν ζῷον, attributed to Chrysippus in Plutarch, is also found in Galen, Alexander of Aphrodisias (see Arnim, 3.113 and 2.295), and *Diogenes Laertius* 7.130.

There seems to be another element in opposition to reason, which fights and struggles against reason.[52]

Lines 19–20 provide an interesting example of the way in which Filelfo could dazzle his learned reader by packing a single distich with allusions to Hesiod, Plato, and Plutarch. The "road to virtue" metaphor is first found in Hesiod, *Works and Days*, 287f. (λείη μὲν ὁδός [εἰς κακόν] . . . τῆς δ' ἀρετῆς ἱδρῶτα θεοὶ προπάροιθεν ἔθηκαν; "the road to evil is smooth . . . but on the road to virtue the gods placed sweat"), a work Filelfo knew, since it is also contained in the same codex, bearing his own ex libris, from which Filelfo had drawn the epigram he paraphrased at the close of elegy 1.3 to Palla.[53] Actually, Filelfo appears to have culled the "road" metaphor from *Republic* 364d (cf. *Laws* 718e), the work Filelfo cites more frequently than any other from Plato.[54] Plato, in his quotation of Hesiod's passage, also adds that the road to virtue is "rough" (τραχεῖαν), the same word Filelfo uses in line 19.[55] The sentiment contained in the pentameter, however, appears to be drawn from a passage in Plutarch, *De Fortuna*, 98d–e, praising reason as the one human resource powerful enough to "soften" all men's woes; Plutarch uses here the verb μαλθάσσει, from the same root as Filelfo's ἐκμαλακίζει.[56] The aphorism at line 22, "reason alone is our guide," epitomizing the most common of all topoi in the middle and later Stoic philosophers, proceeds logically from line 17 and nicely concludes this passage on the connection between reason and virtue.[57]

The image of the mind sailing through all eternity like the moon in its nightly course (23–27) points to Filelfo's familiarity with at least two particularly graphic passages from Plato, both of which depict mind (νοῦς) orbiting in space like a heavenly body: *Phaedrus* 247c–d, but still more specifically *Laws* 898a–b:

κινεῖσθαι λέγοντες νοῦν τήν τε ἐν ἑνὶ φερομένην κίνησιν, σφαίρας ἐντόρνου ἀπεικασμένα φοραῖς, οὐκ ἂν ποτε φανεῖμεν φαῦλοι . . .

If we said that both mind and the movement inherent in it resemble the revolutions of a well-turned globe, by no means would we look like fools . . .[58]

[52] On the opposition between reason and appetite, see Plato, *Republic*, 439c–442 and 586d; and *Laws* 689a.

[53] See n. 31.

[54] See Calderini, *Ricerche*, p. 361 for a list of Filelfo's citations of the *Republic*.

[55] The same passage from Hesiod is quoted again in Plato, *Laws*, 718e.

[56] The passage in Plutarch is more complex, breaking down the functions of λόγος and νοῦς into three distinct categories: λογισμός, ἐπιμέλεια, and προνοῖα "reasoning," "concern," and "forethought," respectively.

[57] See Arnim, 2.113 (Galen et al.).

[58] On the influence of the *Phaedrus* in the development of Filelfo's philosopical thought,

Thus because of our rational and moral faculties, fortune (τύχη) poses no threat (28–30). These lines bring to a logical conclusion the discourse on λόγος and νοῦς, while recapitulating the τύχη motif from the opening lines of the poem (5–8). The passage bears an obvious resemblance to two texts Filelfo knew well, Plutarch's *Consolatio in Apollonium* 104a and *A. P.* 10.65, an epigram contained in the thirteenth-century codex he bought in Constantinople in 1423. The resemblance rests on Filelfo's borrowing of a single powerfully evocative word from his models—σφάλλεται (σφάλλοντα in the *Consolatio*, σφαλερός in *A. P.* 10.65, "to cause to founder"):

ὁ δ' ὄλβος οὐ βέβαιος ἀλλ' ἐφήμερος . . . μίκρ' ἄττα τὰ σφάλλοντα, καὶ μί' ἡμέρα τὰ μὲν καθεῖλεν ὑψόθεν τὰ δ' ἦρ' ἄνω.

Happiness is not lasting, but rather ephemeral. Little things cause us to founder. And one day casts down the haughty, whereas the following day raises on high the humble. (Plutarch *De Morali Virtute*, 104a)

πλοῦς σφαλερὸς τὸ ζῆν . . .

Life is a voyage that causes us to founder . . .

(*A. P.* 10.65)

Having disposed of fortune as a source of human happiness and hope, we return in lines 31–34 to Filelfo's earlier exhortation to the young follower of Plato to follow the Muses (13–16), without whom a man cannot control his self-destructive sexual urges (*Laws* 783a) and pure souls cannot receive divine inspiration (*Phaedrus* 245a). Filelfo's allusion to the *Phaedrus* in the previous lines leads next to a pithy condensation of *Phaedrus* 247d. Filelfo has reduced to a single participle and its object (ὁρῶσα πάντα, "viewing everything") Plato's rhapsodic sequence of clauses, each governed by a participle (τρεφομένη . . . , ἰδοῦσα . . . , θεωροῦσα . . . ; "nourished by . . . looking on . . . gazing upon . . .")[59]

ἅ τ' οὖν θεοῦ διάνοια νῷ τε καὶ ἐπιστήμῃ ἀκηράτῳ τρεφομένη καὶ ἁπάσης ψυχῆς, ὅσῃ ἂν μέλλῃ τὸ προσῆκον δέξεσθαι, ἰδοῦσα διὰ χρόνου τὸ ὂν ἀγαπᾷ τε καὶ θεωροῦσα τἀληθῆ τρέφεται καὶ εὐπαθεῖ . . .

The intelligence of God and of every soul too is nourished by both mind and pure knowledge, insofar as intelligence is able to take for itself what is properly

---

see *De morali disciplina*, p. 2; see Calderini, *Ricerche*, pp. 360n and 362n for references to the *Laws* in Filelfo.

[59] For other sources for lines 35–36, see also *Republic* 490b and Plutarch, *Moralia*, 108b–d.

its own; and when it has looked with joy on reality and has gazed on the truth after a period of time, it is nourished and rejoices.

The closing lines (37–40) restate the poem's thesis (5–8), compressing its message into a paraphrase of the standard Stoic dictum, μόνον τὸ καλὸν ἀγαθόν "moral virtue alone is the good."[60] The last line of the poem contains a logical extension of two Platonic ideas: one that God is the source not of everything in the cosmos but specifically of the good (μὴ πάντων αἴτιον τὸν θεὸν ἀλλὰ τῶν ἀγαθῶν. *Republic* 380c), and the other that only through the exercise of virtue can we seek assimilation to God (*Theaetetus* 176b–c and *Timaeus* 90a and d). If nothing, Filelfo reasons, emanates from or proceeds toward God except the good, then must not the good we seek (ἀρετή) be itself transcendent, and hence nothing less than God (θεός)?

[60] Cf. *Diogenes Laertius* 7.88 and 101; see also in Arnim, 3.9–10: Plutarch, *De stoicis repugnandis*; Philo, *De posteritate*; and Alexander of Aphrodisias, *Quaestiones*.

FIVE

BEING

FRANCESCO SFORZA'S death brought an end to whatever security Filelfo once enjoyed at the Milanese court.[1] Though during his sixteen-year rule the duke had not paid him with any regularity, Filelfo felt his presence was valued. Sforza had repeatedly refused him permission to absent himself from court for any length of time—not even, to Filelfo's great regret, when King Charles VII invited him to Paris in the late fifties. But when Sforza's twenty-two year old son, Galeazzo Maria, succeeded his father as the fifth duke of Milan, the aging poet found that his position at court was no longer tenable. In 1467 Galeazzo cut Filelfo's annual stipend to three hundred ducats, half the salary Francesco had allotted him, at least on paper.[2] Still, that year Filelfo had no choice but to mask the sting of dishonor he felt. In the last year and a half or so of Sforza's life, with the accession of Pope Paul II, Filelfo had already begun to press his influential friends in Rome to push his nomination for a curial appointment.[3] Nonetheless, in 1468, the climate in Rome itself seemed to him too uncertain to risk the move there—or so he told Bessarion.[4]

Unlike the conciliatory prelates before him, Pope Paul had proved to be an activist, and so he soon found himself under attack from a variety of quarters.[5] When King Ferrante captured the papal protectorates, Sora and

---

[1] Filelfo, *Epistolae*, to Tranchedini (8 March 1466), fol. 186v.

[2] Adam, *F. Filelfo*, Appendix 46, p. 401, contains a transcript of the letter.

[3] His letters are explicit about matter: see Filelfo, *Epistolae*, to Cardinal Ammanati-Piccolomini (21 August 1464), fol. 155; (15 September 1464), 158v–159; and (6 October 1464), fol. 160; to Cardinal Ludovico Trevisan (23 August 1464), fols. 155–155v; (16 September 1464), fols. 158v–159; (19 September 1464), fol. 159; and (6 October 1464), fol. 160; to Bartholomeo Ravennati (23 August 1464), fol. 155v; and (6 October 1464) fol. 160–160v (6 October 1464). See also Germano Gualdo, "Francesco Filelfo e la curia pontificia. Una carriera mancata," in *Archivio della societa romana di storia patria* 102 (1979): 222–23.

[4] Filelfo, *Epistolae* (28 November 1468), fol. 203v: "Nam ego hinc pedem movere non ausim, cum alias rationes, tum quod istic nescio quid procellarum agitari audio."

[5] On Paul's papacy, see the conflicting testimony and assessments of his contemporary Platina, *Historici libri de vita Christi ac omnium pontificum*, in *RIS*[1], 3.1; of Ludwig von Pastor, *History of the Popes*, 40 vols., trans. F. I. Antrobus (London, 1894), 4.36–194; A. J. Dunston, "Pope Paul II and the Humanists," in *Journal of Religious History* 7 (1973): 287–306; Roberto Weiss, *Un Umanista veneziano: Papa Paolo II* (Florence, 1958); V. Zabughin, *Giulio*

Tolfa, Paul fought to recover those cities as though they were essential to the security of the papal state. After he lost both towns, with Venice as his only ally, he spent the next two years trying to take back Rimini from Roberto Malatesta, though Roberto had the backing not only of his powerful neighbor, Federigo da Montefeltro of Urbino, but of Milan, Florence, and Naples. The Turks' seizure of Negroponte in the spring of 1470, however, sent a wave of fear through the Italian cities, and caused the pope to reconsider his objectives. While the Venetians braced themselves to meet the advancing army of Mohammed, Paul took it upon himself to prevent Galeazzo Maria from attacking Venice's client cities, Bergamo and Brescia.

The city of Rome had become a precarious place for intellectuals under Paul, particularly for those who professed themselves members of the "Academia romana." The Academy was an informal literary society devoted to the cultivation and preservation of Roman antiquity, whose members met at the house of Pomponio Leto, a professor at the Roman Studio. In February 1468 the pope learned that Leto and some of his friends were conspiring to assassinate him. Ordering the arrest of all the Academicians, Paul charged the suspects with sodomy, heresy, paganism, republicanism, and attempted murder. Platina, a friend of Filelfo's and later the curator of the Vatican library, who was among those incarcerated by the pope's select guards, described the first nights and days of the terror in some detail. "They burst into any house they chose indiscriminately, and dragged away to prison anyone whom they suspected of conspiracy," he wrote. "During the night they and their thugs surrounded the house where I was living, they forced their way in, smashing windows and doors in the process, . . . and having taken me prisoner, they dragged me at once to Paul . . . Many were put to torture on that first day and also the next, and of those a great number perished in agony on the instruments of their torment."[6]

Pomponio Leto, 2 vols. (Rome, 1909), pp. 1.38ff.; and G. Calamari, *Il Confidente di Pio*, 2 vols. (Rome, 1932), 1.240–50 and 1.331–46.

[6] Platina, *Historici libri*, 3.1.381–83: "Irrumpunt cuiusvis domum sine discrimine. Trahebant in carcerem quos suspectos coniurationis habuissent . . . Domum ubi habitabam, multis satellitibus noctu circundant; fractis foribus ac fenestris, vi irrumpunt . . . et me in cubiculo hominis captum, ad Paulum confestim trahunt (p. 381). . . . Torquentur prima et sequenti die multi, quorum pars magna prae dolore in ipsis cruciatibus concidit. (p. 383)" On Paul's persecution of Leto and his circle see also Jacopo Ammanati-Piccolomini, *Epistolae et Commentarii* (Milan, 1608); Cardinal Ammanati, confidante to Pius II, also voiced dissatisfaction with Paul's policies: see Ammanati, *Epistolae et commentarii*, fols. 146–159v for his letters to Cardinal Francesco Gonzaga and to Francesco Castiglione, in which he decried Platina's arrest and imprisonment.

The Rome Years: Laura's Death

Paul's death and the election of Pope Sixtus IV in 1471 ushered in an era of well-being for the humanists in Rome.[7] Despite the recent death of his longtime supporter, Cardinal Bessarion, and his own worsening health, Filelfo at seventy-four was more optimistic than he had been in the past about obtaining a papal appointment. The Milanese contingent at Rome had never been more in ascendancy. Leonardo Grifo, the brother of a former student of Filelfo's, was Sixtus's private secretary. Two other old friends, Stefano Nardini and his former pupil Giovanni Arcimboldi, had recently been named cardinals by Sixtus. Nicodemo Tranchedini, who among all Filelfo's friends remained closest to him over the years, now headed the Milanese delegation to the papal court.[8] The numerous letters Filelfo addressed to friends close to Sixtus during the early seventies testify in themselves to his fixation on Rome at this point in his life, and to his determination to secure an appointment in the Curia. The volumes of his *Epistolae* that chronicle the first three years of Sixtus's papacy contain three long hortatory letters addressed to the pope himself, ten lengthy missives to Cardinal Arcimboldi, nine to Tranchedini, and numerous other letters to Leonardo Grifo, Stefano Nardini, Cardinal Francesco Gonzaga and his secretary Giovanni Pietro Arrivabene, the pope's cousin Cardinal Marco Barbo, Cardinal Nicholas of Cusa's secretary Giovanni Andrea Bussi, Cardinal Rodrigo Borgia, and Filelfo's old friend Jacopo Ammanati, Cardinal of Pavia.[9]

Filelfo also harbored hopes during these years of returning to the Florentine Studio. But if he were either to obtain an offer from the pope or to be recalled to Florence after a forty-year absence from that city, he would have to rely on more than patronage and the loyalty of old friends. To those who might argue that the septuagenarian professor was no longer either competent or interesting, Filelfo would have to demonstrate that he was still a writer and thinker to be reckoned with, that far from being out to pasture he was keenly aware of the current issues being debated in phi-

---

[7] See Egmont Lee, *Sixtus IV and Men of Letters* (Rome, 1978); John F. D'Amico, *Renaissance Humanism in Papal Rome: Humanists and Churchmen on the Eve of the Reformation* (Baltimore, 1983); Charles L. Stinger, *The Renaissance in Rome* (Bloomington, 1985).

[8] See Adam, *F. Filelfo*, pp. 87–88: over one hundred of Filelfo's letters are addressed to Tranchedini; it was also Filelfo's custom to write a special letter commemorating their friendship to Tranchedini each year on Filelfo's birthday.

[9] For letters during 1471–1473 to Tranchedini, see Filelfo, *Epistolae*, fols. 232v, 237v, 238v, 243, 246v, 247, 248v, and 252; for those to Arcimboldi, see fols. 244, 247, 248v, 249v–250, 252, 252v–253, 253, and 262–262v; to Sixtus, see fols. 233–233v, 244v–246v, and 248v–249; to Arrivabene, fols. 238v and 265.

losophy and theory, and that he was doing work that clearly spoke not only to university students but to seasoned intellectuals as well.[10]

Although the *Psychagogia* had brought him some commissions, the book failed to elicit the wider acclaim he assumed it would, particularly from the Hellenophilic coteries in Florence and Rome. Thus, sometime after Sixtus's accession, Filelfo decided to undertake a project whose basic lineaments he had begun to formulate back in the fifties when he had revised a number of his shorter philosophical essays for publication as letters in his *Epistolae familiares*.[11] In July 1473 he sent notes to his supporters Grifo and Tranchedini in Rome and Lorenzo de' Medici in Florence to inform them that he was writing a new philosophical work, entitled *On Moral Doctrine* (*De morali disciplina*).[12] As he saw it, this would be his most important book, and the most personally satisfying of his works to date.[13]

It was not just that he looked forward to dealing with topics of current interest among philosophers and theologians; he felt the need now at the end of his life to address questions he had long ignored or set aside, about meaning and knowledge. At last he was addressing an audience to whom it did not seem strange to inquire into the functioning of the soul, the structure of being, the relation between beings and the ultimate source of all being (God), definitions of the good, and Plato's theory of Ideas. Moreover, he hoped, with the publication of this book, to have the last word in the thirty-year-old controversy among theologians over whether the teachings of Aristotle or those of Plato were more compatible with Christian doctrine. This much he suggested to Giorgio Valla, the noted Aristotelian who during the seventies was in residence at the university of Pavia.[14] "If you think the matter over fairly," he wrote Valla, "Aristotle does, in the end, defer in all of his works on ethics to Plato on the Ideas; but he says

[10] Filelfo touches on the theme of the *De morali disciplina*'s appeal to both young and mature scholars in Trivulzianus, to Tranchedini (24 July 1473), fol. 447v and to Francesco d'Arezzo (6 September 1473), fol. 449v.

[11] His philosophical letters were published in his *Epistolae familiares* (Venice, 1473), but were probably widely circulated from the 1450s on. On the fictional dates Filelfo assigned the early letters in his epistolario, see chap. 1.

[12] He announced to a number of friends that his new work, the *De morali disciplina*, was underway: see Filelfo, *Epistolae*, to Giorgio Valla (23 July 1473), fol. 264v; to Alberto Parisi (24 July 1473), fol. 265; see Trivulzianus, to Tranchedini (24 July 1473), fols. 447v–448; to Parisi (27 August 1473), fols. 448v; to the Siennese Francesco d'Arezzo (6 September 1473), fol. 449v; to Francesco Gonzaga (7 March 1474), fols. 458–458v; see also Benadduci, ed., *Atti*, to Lorenzo de' Medici (23 July 1473), p. 198.

[13] *De morali disciplina*, bk. 5, p. 73: "Sed mihi certe non possum non laetari plurimum hoc tempore, qui cum ante scripserim quam plurima de aliis atque aliis rebus et ea quidem tam versu quam soluta oratione non Latine solum, verum etiam Graece, numquam mihi tamen satisfeci magis ulla in materia quam in his praeceptis de moribus."

[14] On Valla, see Margaret King, *Venetian Humanism in an Age of Patrician Dominance*, (Princeton, 1986), pp. 439–40.

that the Ideas have nothing whatever to do with human good. In any case, in a work I've begun writing on moral philosophy I set myself the task of dealing with every issue relating to this one, and in such a way that no doubt will linger in anyone's mind, but everyone will think that Plato was as right as he possibly could have been, and that Aristotle was in no sense contemptible, even though Plato relied on one set of assumptions, and Aristotle on another."[15]

Such advertisements for the new book as these apparently lent weight to the appeals of his friends in the Curia. For in the summer of 1474, the long-awaited call came.[16] He received a firm offer from Sixtus to lecture at the Studio in Rome at an annual salary of six hundred ducats, and a promise of the first secretarial post that fell vacant in the Curia, which would bring him an additional stipend of one hundred ducats yearly.[17]

Meanwhile his new philosophical work, and his move to the Roman curia, did not go unnoticed in Florence. Lorenzo de' Medici had by the early seventies become Filelfo's principal financier and protector. From 1469 onward, in fact, Filelfo's unpublished letters reveal an increasing dependence on Lorenzo's patronage and on the Medici bank.[18] Through the intercession of the Medici bank in Milan, Filelfo was gradually able to recover the precious Greek manuscripts and other valuables he had pawned in the course of two decades of Sforza patronage.[19] Thus, it was to Lorenzo and not Duke Galeazzo that he dedicated his *On Moral Doctrine*.

Filelfo was carrying a presentation copy of the first book of his ethics for Lorenzo when he left Milan for Rome in November 1474 without his family. His thirty-eight-year-old wife Laura had recently been ill with a

[15] Filelfo, *Epistolae*, fol. 264v: ". . . Si recte consyderabis, [Aristoteles] in omnibus suis libris quos de moribus scripsit cedit tandem Platoni de Idea, sed dicit eam ad humanum bonum nihil pertinere. Sed hac item de re in his quae scribere sum aggressus de morali disciplina ita complecti omnia institui, ut nemini dubii quicquam reliquatur, quin omnes sint iudicaturi et Platonem quam rectissime sensisse et Aristotelem non absurde, cum alio Plato et Aristoteles alio utatur fundamento . . ."

[16] See Trivulzianus, to Giovanni Andrea Bussi (18 July, 1464), fol. 469v: having already been approached by the pope himself, Filelfo here commissions Bussi and Leonardo Grifo to speak on his behalf to Sixtus about the details of his salary.

[17] On the papal offer, see Filelfo's letters to Marco Aurelio and Lorenzo de' Medici of 26 October 1474 in Rosmini, *Vita*, 2.372; Benadduci, *Atti*, p. 203; and Adam, *F. Filelfo*, p. 374 (ASF MAP 23, 288). Cf. Gualdo, "Una carriera mancata," pp. 223–24.

[18] For the unpublished letters, see Trivulzianus (8 May 1474), fol. 465v; (8 December 1474), fol. 487v; (30 June 1475), fols. 491–491v. For his Italian letters to Lorenzo, see Benadduci, *Atti*: pp. 181–91, 198–199, and 239. See Adam, *F. Filelfo*, pp. 370–75. See also the published letters in Filelfo, *Epistolae*, to Lorenzo (31 October 1469), fol. 215; (23 November 1469), fol. 215v–216; (11 December 1469), fol. 218v; (22 December 1469), fol. 218v; (20 January 1470), fol. 219; (8 October 1470), fol. 228v; (20 September 1471), fol. 237; (29 May 1473), fols. 259v–262.

[19] See Adam, *F. Filelfo*, p. 373: to Lorenzo (6 February 1474; in ASF MAP 29, 46).

fever and was too weak to endure riding over rough roads for so long a journey. Although Lorenzo was in Pisa when Filelfo arrived in Florence, Donato Acciaiuoli and other leading scholars at the Studio were enthusiastic about the manuscript.[20] Originally he had promised Lorenzo an *oeuvre* of ten or twelve books, but after a month in Rome he wrote his Florentine patron that he would have a more manageable version of the work finished by March, when he planned to return to Laura and their children in Milan.[21]

Filelfo found Laura and their two sons gravely ill when he returned home in June 1475. Within days of his homecoming, the younger of the boys, seven-year-old Cesare Eufrasio, died. Toward the end of July his favorite child, eight-year-old Federico Francesco, succumbed as well.[22] Filelfo stayed on to tend to Laura until the following January, when he set out for Rome once again. But when news of Laura's worsening health reached him in Rome later that spring, he hastily prepared to journey back to Lombardy. By the time he reached Milan on 8 June 1476, he found that Laura had been buried the day before.[23] All day long on 6 June, as Laura lay dying, she had called out to him in vain; it was thus that he imagined her months after she was gone.[24]

Filelfo did not return to Rome after Laura's death. The day after Christmas the year that she died, Duke Galeazzo Maria was attacked by assassins in the church of San Stefano in Milan, while he heard the mass. His assailants slit his throat where he stood, stabbing him afterward in the stomach, the wrist, the left breast, and many times in the back. In 1477 the city fell into turmoil, but Filelfo had long since ceased to work on his book on moral philosophy.[25]

---

[20] See Benadduci, ed., *Atti*, p. 204f. for Filelfo's letter to Lorenzo (8 December 1474): "Arei caro avessi veduta l'opera che fo in vostra gloria, ma Donato Acciajuoli e questi altri vostri docti ne ha veduto uno libro integro, da quali potrete intendere quanto estimare se debba."

[21] See Filelfo's letter to Lorenzo (23 July 1473) in Benadduci, ed., *Atti*, p. 198: "Ora ho rominato una nuova opera, il cui proemio dirigo a voi, e saranno libri X o XII, colla quale trattero tutta questa morale, altrimenti che per molti obtenebrata. Mandovi dunque el proemio sopra el decto volume." See Filelfo's letter to Lorenzo from Rome (14 January 1475) in ibid., p. 206: "Questa Marzo tornerò per Firenze a Milano per condurre la mia famiglia in Roma, e porteròvve finito il nostro libro, *de morali disciplina*."

[22] Rosmini, *Vita*, 2.234.

[23] Ibid., 2.247.

[24] Ibid., 2.430–36, has printed Filelfo's letters about Laura's death addressed to Marco Aurelio, Cardinal Francesco Gonzaga, Leonardo Grifo, Giovanni Francesco Marliani, and Paolo Morosini. In his letter to Marliani (27 June 1476), p. 434, Filelfo broods over his failure to say farewell to Laura.

[25] In the proem to bk. 4 of the *De morali disciplina* (pp. 54–55), Filelfo writes that he is now in his seventy-seventh year (". . . [ego] qui iam agens septimum et septuagesimum aetatis annum."), which would place the composition of that book in the year 1475.

The Plato-Aristotle Controversy

Plotinus and his Neoplatonist followers in late antiquity sought to achieve a synthesis of Aristotelian and Platonic doctrine, though they tended to subordinate Aristotle to Plato.[26] Certainly philosophers throughout the Middle Ages continued to distinguish between the two traditions, and the later Platonists raised serious objections to certain key Aristotelian doctrines, such as the categories. But, as Paul Oskar Kristeller has pointed out, the first systematic attempts to demarcate the teachings of Plato from those of Aristotle would have to wait until the Renaissance.[27] Still, as we shall see in the works of Filelfo and his contemporaries Bessarion, Argyropoulus, Landino, Ficino, and Pico, the tendency to synthesize the thought of the two philosophers prevailed until the end of the fifteenth century.[28]

The fifteenth-century Roman controversy over the compatibility of Plato and Aristotle with Christian doctrine, like so much that was then new in the West, came to Italy from the East. It was at the time of the Council of Florence, in 1439, that Gemistus Pletho, the eminent Byzantine Platonist who had been Bessarion's mentor and teacher, first awakened interest in the question among Italian intellectuals and theologians.[29] According to

[26] I am particularly indebted to Professor John Bussanich for his reading of the section of the chapter that follows, and for his helpful suggestions regarding Plotinus and later Neoplatonism. On the synthesis of the two traditions in post-Plotinean Neoplatonism, see also R. T. Wallis, *Neoplatonism* (London, 1972), pp. 23–25 and 94–137.

[27] Kristeller, *Renaissance Thought: the Classic, Scholastic and Humanist Strains* (New York, 1955), pp. 24–69.

[28] On this tendency in the Quattrocento, see Paul Oskar Kristeller, "The Platonic Academy of Florence," in *Renaissance News* 14 (1961): 147–59; and also his *Eight Philosophers of the Italian Renaissance* (Stanford, 1964), pp. 54–71; Eugenio Garin, *Filosofi italiani del Quattrocento* (Florence, 1942), esp. pp. 1–15; Arnaldo della Torre, *Storia dell' Accademia platonica di Firenze* (Florence, 1902); on Argyropoulos's teaching, see Giuseppe Cammelli, *I dotti bizantini e le origini dell' umanesimo*, 3 vols. (Florence, 1943), p. 2; and Arthur M. Field, *The Beginning of the Philosophical Renaissance in Florence: 1454–1469* (Ph.D. dissertation, University of Michigan, 1980), pp. 101–61; on Bessarion's philosophical orientation see Ludwig Mohler, *Kardinal Bessarion als Theologe, Humanist und Staatsmann*, 3 vols. (Paderborn, 1942; reprint 1967), 1.333–44.

[29] On the Council of Florence, see D. J. Geanakoplos, *The Byzantine East and the Latin West: Two Worlds of Christendom in the Middle Ages and Renaissance* (Oxford, 1966), pp. 84–119. On the Plato-Aristotle controversy, see Mohler, 1.325–70, which contain summaries of the principal texts in the debate and accounts of the circumstances under which these texts were produced: vol. 2 contains the Greek text of Bessarion's *In calumniatorem Platonis* with the original Latin translation that accompanied it; vol. 3 contains other primary texts relevant to the controversy. On Filelfo's role in the controversy, see Concetta Bianca, " 'Auctoritas' e 'veritas': il Filelfo e le dispute tra Platonici e Aristotelici," in *Filelfo nel V Cent.* (Padua, 1984), pp. 207–47. On Pletho and Trebizond, see W. Gass, *Gennadius und Pletho. Aristotelismus und Platonismus in der griechischen Kirche*, 2 vols. (Breslau, 1844); F. Masai, *Plethon et le platonisme de Mistra* (Paris, 1956); and John Monfasani, *George of Trebizond. A Biography and a Study of*

Pletho's own testimony, he had given an informal paper comparing Plato and Aristotle at the request of Cosimo de' Medici and other Florentine followers of his.[30] In this paper, entitled *On the Differences Between Plato and Aristotle*, he attacked Aristotle in a manner that the Florentines apparently found both shocking and appealing.[31] His criticisms of Aristotle centered on major, rather than minor issues. He criticized Aristotle for his failure to conceive of an afterlife for individual souls. He also objected to Aristotle's privileging of the particular over the universal, his rejection of Plato's theory of Ideas, and his concept of God as a mere first mover rather than as Cause and Creator of the world. Moreover, he impugned Aristotle for failing to attribute to God divine foreknowledge, and at the same time he dismissed his definition of the good as too tied to the material world.[32] In short, Pletho, who was known to espouse the divinity of Zeus, Apollo, and Aphrodite with the same fervor he brought to his lectures on Plato, took it upon himself to expose the incompatibility of Aristotle's philosophy with Christian theology.[33]

Filelfo waited for thirty-five years to publish his own formal response to Pletho's *Differences*. Nonetheless his letters, particularly those in the uncut Trivulzian manuscript, indicate that he followed the debate with keen interest from its outset.[34] In 1443 he had published a mock-philosophical

---

His Rhetoric and Logic (Leiden, 1976), pp. 201–29. On Scholarius's role, see M. Jugie, "Georges Scholarios, professeur de philosophie," in *Studi bizantini e neoellenici* 10 (1936): 482–94; and C. J. Turner, "The Career of George-Gennadius Scolarius," in *Byzantion* 39 (1969): 420–55; on Apostolis, see Geanakoplos, *Greek Scholars in Venice: Studies in the Dissemination of Greek Learning from Byzantium to the West* (Cambridge, 1962), pp. 73–109; on Perotti, see John Monfasani, "Il Perotti e la controversia tra platonici e aristotelici," in *Res Publica Litterarum* 4 (1981): 195–231; and G. Mercati, *Per la cronologia della vita e degli scritti di Niccolò Perotti arcivescovo di Siponto* (Rome, 1925), 44–95.

[30] Gass, *Gennadius und Pletho*, 2.113, quotes Pletho's statement that his speech was written to "oblige" his Florentine hosts, who were devotees of Plato (. . . ἐκεῖνα . . . ἐν φλωρεντία . . . τοῖς πλάτωνι προσκειμένοις [ἡμῖν] χαριζομένοις συνεγράφη), and that it had been composed "in the shortest imaginable time" (ἐν βραχυτάτοις οὖν ἐκεῖνά τε συνεγράφη). Ficino claimed, in the introduction to his translation of Plotinus, that Pletho's influence on Cosimo at the time of the Council had prompted him to found the Platonic Academy in 1462 (Kristeller, *The Philosophy of Marsilio Ficino* [New York, 1943], p. 15; Ficino, *Opera omnia* [Basel, 1576], p. 1537).

[31] περὶ ὧν Ἀριστοτέλης πρὸς πλάτωνα διαφέρεται.

[32] Greek text of *De differentiis* with Latin translation in facing columns in Migne, *Patrologia Graeca*, 160.889–932, for Pletho's objections on the previously mentioned topics. Pletho's remark that he only dealt in the *De differentiis* with the "chief" arguments against Aristotle accurately describes his superficial treatment of the *Metaphysics* and the *De anima* here. For a summary of Pletho's arguments, see Mohler, *Kardinal Bessarion*, 1.350–51.

[33] On Pletho's fame as a teacher, see Gass, *Gennadius und Pletho*; Mohler, *Kardinal Bessarion*; and Masai, *Plethon et le platonisme*; according to Gass, *Gennadius und Pletho*, 1.25, Pletho had even been Manuel Chrysoloras's teacher.

[34] Both the Greek and Latin letters in Trivulzianus.

dialogue, entitled *Milanese Symposia*, in which several disputants discussed such subjects as the theory of Ideas and the various schools of philosophy in ancient Greece.[35] Yet the *Symposia* was in no way an attempt to grapple with substantive issues, but skimmed over numerous topics in the manner of Plutarch's *Quaestiones conviviae*.

As early as 1441 Filelfo tried to initiate a correspondence with Pletho.[36] Around the same time he also managed to acquire a manuscript of the *Differences*, which he carefully annotated with his own commentary and queries.[37] Indeed, as Concetta Bianca has recently shown, the extensive number of codices of the Greek philosophers we have with marginalia, glosses, and commentary in Filelfo's own hand, testify to the intensity with which Filelfo occupied himself for most of his working life with the philosophers, above all Plato and Aristotle.[38]

Filelfo's first contacts with Pletho would later prove formative. On entering the debate himself with the publication of his *On Moral Doctrine* in 1474, he was to agree to some extent with Pletho's principal objections to Aristotle. About the same time he was writing to Pletho, he had also begun to correspond with another Byzantine scholar, George Scholarius, about Pletho's anti-Aristotelian tract.[39] Scholarius, whom Filelfo had known

---

[35] On the Ideas, see the *Convivia mediolanensia*, Laur. 53.6, fols. 32–32v; on the schools of philosophy, see ibid., fols. 51ff. The popularity of the *Convivia* in its day is attested to by the issue of several printed editions of the work: Milan, 1477; Milan, 1483; and Cologne, 1537.

[36] See Legrand, *Lettres*, pp. 48–49. Filelfo's letter (dated 1 March 1441) compliments Pletho on his erudition and makes no reference to his stand on either Aristotle or Plato.

[37] See Bianca, " 'Auctoritas' e 'veritas,' " p. 165: Laur. 80.24 contains Pletho's *De differentiis*, annotated in Filelfo's own hand.

[38] See ibid., 148–65, on the following codices (either purchased or borrowed by Filelfo), which contain glosses, marginalia, and commentary in Filelfo's own hand: Laur. 87.26 of Aristotle's *Metaphysics*; Laur. 80.22 of the pseudo-Plutarchean, *De placitis philosophorum*; Vat. gr. 1689 of the *Nichomachean Ethics*; Laur. 85.19 and Marc. gr. Z.262 of Sextus Empiricus; Laur. 81.13 of Aristotle's *Rhetoric* (of which he had published a translation); Laur. 73.1 of Democritus; Laur. 81.13 of Aristotle's *Magna moralia*; Laur. 80.7 of Plato's *Parmenides* and *Republic*; Vat. Palat. lat. 1599 of Plato's *Phaedrus* and *Letters*; Leid. Scal. 26 of Aristotle's *Politics*; and Laur. 28.45 of Theophrastus's *Metaphysics*. Filelfo's translations of Plato's *Letters* and the *Euthyphro* are preserved, respectively, in Ambr. M 4 sup. and Vallic. C87. On Filelfo's references to the Greek philosophers in his letters, see Calderini, *Ricerche*, pp. 204–424; on Filelfo's paraphrases from the Greek philosophers, see chap. 4.

[39] See Filelfo's letter in Legrand, *Lettres*, pp. 31–32 (dated 29 March 1439): here Filelfo first expresses great veneration for Aristotle, but he then goes on to suggest (without ever referring explicitly to Pletho's arguments) that Aristotle was wrong to direct all his abuse at Plato alone, when he was really attacking not one but a number of different theories on the Ideas, since Plato was not the only philosopher in antiquity to espouse the Ideas, as we know from Simplicius and Porphyry, and Plato before them: Δοκεῖ μέν γὰρ τὰ ἐπιχειρήματα πάντα πρὸς Πλάτωνα τείνειν, τῇ δ' ἀληθείᾳ πρὸς διαφόρους περὶ ἰδεῶν δόξας τὴν ἀντιλογίαν πεποίηται ... Ὅτι δὲ πολλαὶ περὶ ἰδεῶν τοῖς παλαιτέροις ἐγένοντο δόξαι, Πορφύριός τε καὶ ὁ Σιμπλίκιος αὐτὸς δείκνυτον, καὶ πρὸ αὐτῶν Πλάτων.

since the twenties, when he was a student in Constantinople, was generally regarded as the leading Aristotelian scholar in Greece.[40] His critical interpretation of Aquinas's *Commentarii* to Aristotle's *Metaphysics* had received wide acclaim, and so when he published two books of his own refuting Pletho's *Differences*, he spoke with authority.

The first attack on Pletho's work to raise the emotional pitch of the debate, though, came from another friend of Filelfo's, George of Trebizond.[41] Trebizond was a Greek émigré who had served as a scriptor under Pope Nicholas V, and who had in the forties been a client of Cardinal Bessarion's. But by the early fifties, when both Bessarion and Theodore Gaza, the most respected of the scholars in the cardinal's immediate entourage, began to complain to the pope that certain of Trebizond's translations of Aristotle contained substantive errors, Trebizond was already estranged from the cardinal and his circle.[42] In 1458 Trebizond published an attack on both Pletho's *Differences* and Plato, in a work he entitled *A Comparison*. The work, which charged Plato with the advocacy of pederasty and tyranny, was generally received among his contempories as an embittered invective.[43] Seven years after the *Comparison* was first issued, Filelfo sent a letter to Trebizond, in which he fondly recalled their fifty-year friendship, and asked his friend for a copy of his essay on Plato and Aristotle.[44]

While Filelfo continued to correspond with the principal disputants in the debate—Scholarius, Gaza, Trebizond, Callistus, and above all Bessarion—throughout the late fifties and the early sixties, he clearly felt that the question of whether Plato or Aristotle was right or wrong was a ridiculous one. "What I'm after regarding the Ideas," he wrote Callistus in 1464, "are neither the arguments for nor against Aristotle. I only want to learn Aris-

[40] On Scholarius, see Turner, "The Career of George-Gennadius Scholarios"; and Jugie, "Georges Scholarios, professeur de philosophie."

[41] On George's differences with various members of the Curia during this period, see Mohler, *Kardinal Bessarion*, 1.327ff.; Monfasani, *George of Trebizond*, pp. 81–83, 104–28, and 212; and Geanakoplos, *Greek Scholars*, pp. 86ff.

[42] See Mohler, *Kardinal Bessarion*, 3.487–89 for Bessarion's letter to Gaza criticizing Trebizond's translations and scholarship.

[43] Ibid., 1.352–58, gives a detailed but highly prejudicial account of the *Comparatio*.

[44] Filelfo, *Epistolae* (30 July 1465), fols. 175–175v: "Pristina illa nostra vetusque amicitia, quae ex illo usque tempore inter nos familiaritate mutua Patavii coepta est, cum tu primum in Italiam navigasti, non difficulter mihi persuadet nullum esse honestum munus quod tu mea causa minus sis subiturus. . . . Praeterea audio te quaedam scripsisse pro Aristotele contra Platonem. Non parvam rem esse puto. Libenter viderem scripta tua. Quae si miseris, et legam libenter et curriculo remittam tibi. Tu si quid ab me desyderas nihil frustra petieras. Vale." In Trivulzianus, to Carlo Barbavara (22 September 1476), fol. 542, Filelfo writes that he had been a law student at the university of Padua at the age of eighteen (i.e., in 1416): "Agebam ego decimum octavum aetatis annum quo quidem tempore Patavii diebus ordinariis studebam legibus et iuri civili . . ." Cf. Rosmini, *Vita*, 1.5–6.

totle's opinion on the subject."[45] Indeed, by the end of the fifties the debate appeared to be driven by personal rather than philosophical aims. When Gaza found fault with a short paper that Bessarion presented in defense of one of Pletho's arguments,[46] Michael Apostolis, an agent of Bessarion's in Crete, circulated a treatise attacking Gaza.[47] No sooner was Apostolis's work out when Gaza's pupil and protégé, Andronicus Callistus, published a defense of his professor's recent paper.[48] But perhaps the most impassioned of all the rebuttals of Trebizond's *Comparison* was an essay entitled *A Refutation of the Delusions of George Trebizond of Crete*, which was the work of Niccolo Perotti, a longtime member of Bessarion's household who frequently served as the cardinal's translator.[49]

Thus, from the fifties onward the debate was principally a Roman affair, stimulated by the ideas and writings of the theologian Cardinal Bessarion and his clients. The primary issue was doctrinal, one of loyalty to the Church. It must also be recalled that in the late sixties Pope Paul, who had been a pupil of Trebizond's, had become preoccupied with matters of loyalty and unity, seeing the purging of possible heretics from the sacred city as his mission. He had, in 1468, ordered the mass arrests and torture of those writers, scholars, and university students who were suspected of certain doctrinal aberrations.[50] Bessarion, to whom many members of the intellectual community turned for protection during the persecutions of the Academicians in 1468, had soon thereafter left Rome for Viterbo. It was there, in a kind of self-imposed exile, that he had in 1469 completed his final version of his refutation of Trebizond's charges against Plato. The work was entitled *Against Plato's Slanderer* (*In calumniatorem Platonis*). Bessarion immediately sent Filelfo a copy of his new work, and at the same time he asked Filelfo to review Trebizond's *Comparison* for him.[51] Filelfo's answer to the cardinal made it appear that he was now ready to enter the debate himself:

---

[45] Legrand, *Lettres*, p. 111, to Andronicus Callistus, also known as Andronicus of Byzantium (29 April 1464): τὸ ζητούμενόν μοι περὶ ἰδέας, ὦ φίλτατε, οὔτε κατ᾽ Ἀριστοτέλους ἐστὶν, οὔθ᾽ ὑπὲρ Ἀριστοτέλους. Ἐβουλόμην γὰρ μόνον μαθεῖν τὸ Ἀριστοτέλει δοκοῦν περὶ ταύτης τῆς ὕλης. On Callistus (a.k.a. Andronicus Bizantinus), a favorite protégé of Filelfo, see G. Cammelli, "Andronico Callisto," in *Rinascita* 5 (1942): 104–21.

[46] On Bessarion's paper entitled "On Pletho's Arguments against Aristotle concerning Primary Being," see Mohler, *Kardinal Bessarion*, 1.393–94.

[47] On Apostolis, see Geanakoplos, *Greek Scholars*, pp. 73–88.

[48] On Callistus (Bizantinus), see Cammelli, "Andronico Callisto."

[49] On Perotti, see Monfasani, "Il Perotti," pp. 195–231; Mercati, *Per la cronologie*, pp. 44–95; and Mohler, *Kardinal Bessarion*, 1.329ff.

[50] On Paul's persecution of the humanists, see nn. 5 and 6.

[51] Cf. Mohler, *Kardinal Bessarion*, 1.386, who claims however that Bessarion never personally sent Filelfo a copy of his *In calumniatorem*. See Mohler, ibid., vol. 3, for the complete text of Bessarion's *In calumniatorem*.

I was quite surprised that George of Crete had succumbed to such madness that he not only disparaged the incomparable learning and wisdom of the most exalted of men, but that he had even convinced himself to pollute with his foul pen [Plato's] completely unblemished life, which has been wonderfully praised by all antiquity. And, to speak frankly with you—I find it difficult to believe that George is so changed that he would speak such brazen lies . . . And so it is that I don't know what to think about the man. But whatever the situation is, it behooves me to read with the utmost care the things George has written against Plato. Once that's done I'll either have learned something or I'll have some teaching to do . . .[52]

Bessarion was of course requesting a testimony of his client's solidarity with him. Certainly the scholarly papers that were later published as part of a collection together with his *Against Plato's Slanderer* were written by the cardinal's clients. But Filelfo's loyalties were conflicted here. His ties with both Bessarion and Trebizond went back half a century. Bessarion had been Filelfo's patron, and Trebizond his colleague and peer. For six months after Bessarion's request for a critique from Filelfo of the *Comparison*, Filelfo continued to express to Bessarion his dismay at Trebizond's paper and his warm support for the cardinal.[53] But he never offered to put in writing a formal repudiation of the *Comparison*.

Filelfo's letter to Giorgio Valla in 1473 makes it clear that he began his own work on the Greek philosophers, the *De morali disciplina*, with a grand design in mind. His work would show conclusively that the teachings of Aristotle and Plato were not inconsistent but could easily be subsumed within a single, unified view of the cosmos, and that Plato in particular was as close to the truth as he could have been *for his time*.[54] The implication was that Filelfo would synthesize the doctrines of the ancient philosophers with those of the Church Fathers. But he completed only three books of the *De morali disciplina*, abandoning the work after 1475.[55]

[52] Filelfo, *Epistolae*, to Bessarion (7 October 1469), fol. 214: "Et sum equidem non mediocriter miratus in id insaniae incidisse Georgium Cretensem, ut non modo incomparabilem summi viri doctrinam atque sapientiam non probarit, sed vitam etiam modestissimam ac pudicam et ab omni vetustate mirifice laudatam impudica arundine polluere se posse animum induxerit. Et, ut tibi ingenue fatear mei animi sententiam, non facile adducor ut credam usqueadeo Georgium istum ab sese alienatum, ut mentiatur tam impudenter. . . . Quo fit ut quid iudicaturus sim de homine non intelligam. Sed utcunque res habet, mihi opera danda est ut quae Georgius in Platonem scripserit quam diligentissime perlegam. Id si fiet, vel discam aliquid vel docebo."
[53] Filelfo, *Epistolae*, to Bessarion (11 December 1469), fol. 217v; and (25 May 1470), fols. 221v–222.
[54] Ibid., to Giorgio Valla; see nn. 12 and 15.
[55] See Filelfo's letter to Lorenzo (6 February 1474), Adam, *F. Filelfo*, p. 373 [ASF MAP 29, 46]: "Io ve harei mandato il proemio dil quarto libro del' opera ve scrivo, ma perchè nulla me havete resposo di tre altri proemii ve ho mandati, sono soperseduto . . ." From this letter,

The work survives in a single printed edition, and has remained, for all practical purposes, unknown since its first publication over four hundred years ago.[56] Rosmini dealt with the work's content only on a superficial level, praising "its erudition" and "the profundity of its arguments."[57] Voigt mistakenly commented that Filelfo completed no more of his *De morali disciplina* than the prologue to Book 1.[58] Neither Burckhardt nor Symonds makes any reference to the work, which is not surprising since the *De morali disciplina* does not fit their categorization of Filelfo as a mere eulogist.[59] Recent studies of the *De morali disciplina*, such as Jill Kraye's valuable work, have focused more profitably on Filelfo's use of his ancient sources.[60]

A Non-Christian Concept of God

The *De morali disciplina* stands out as an anomaly in the Quattrocento because of its decidedly non-Christian outlook. Certainly, in an ethics aimed at a broad range of readers, from students to theologians, it is surprising that Filelfo made no attempt to integrate doctrine that is recognizably Christian into his synthesis of Aristotelian and Platonic thought. It is also

it appears that, before writing the books themselves, Filelfo first completed only the dedicatory proems (which introduce each of the books), which he then sent on to his patron as prospectuses for the larger work.

[56] Published in a volume with two other titles: *Francisci Philelphi De morali disciplina libri quinque. Averrois Paraphrasis in libros de Republica Platonis. Francisci Robortelli in libros politicos Aristotelis disputatio*, ed. Francesco Robortello (Venice, 1552). An anonymous sixteenth-century translation of the work in Italian has been preserved in Laur. 76.69, fol. 1–51v, as noted by Jill Kraye, "Francesco Filelfo's Lost Letter *De ideis*," in *Journal of the Warburg and Courtauld Institutes* 42 (1979): 239n; brief excerpts from bk. 1 have been published in Eugenio Garin, *Filosofi italiani del Quattrocento*, pp. 152–56 with Italian translation; and Kraye, pp. 239–43.

[57] Rosmini, *Vita*, 2.220–25.

[58] Voigt, *Die Wiederbelebung*, 1.365.

[59] For their assessments of Filelfo see chap. 2. See also August Messer, "Franciscus Philelphus 'de morali disciplina,'" in *Archiv für Geschichte der Philosophie* 9.2 (1896): 337–43, whose description of the work appears to be based on Rosmini's.

[60] Jill Kraye in her two articles, "Francesco Filelfo on Emotions, Virtues and Vices: A Reexamination of His Sources," in *Bibliotheque d'Humanisme et Renaissance* 43 (1981): 129–40, and "Francesco Filelfo's Lost Letter," in *Journal of the Warburg and Courtauld Institutes* 42 (1979): 236–49, traces Filelfo's indebtedness to classical, Christian, and contemporary sources. F. Fiorentino, *Il Risorgimento filosofico nel Quattrocento* (Naples, 1885), pp. 216ff., claimed that bk. 2 was chiefly a digest of Cicero's *Tusculan Disputations*; F. Tocco, "Ancora del 'De morali disciplina' di F. Filelfo," in *Archiv für Geschichte der Philosophie* 9 (1896): 486–91, argued that Filelfo was indebted not to Cicero in bk. 2 but to a treatise, written by a fellow humanist, entitled Περὶ παθῶν. Garin, *Filosfi italiani del Quattrocento*, pp. 150ff. printed a brief excerpt from Filelfo's discussion of Plato's Ideas in the *De morali disciplina*, introducing the excerpt by quoting G. Gentile's criticism of Filelfo's treatise as derivative and uninteresting.

interesting that the work Filelfo wrote expressly with Pope Sixtus in mind, and perhaps as the basis of a syllabus for his new courses at the university in Rome, cannot have been exactly what the pope expected of his humanists.

In the *De morali disciplina*, God is conceptualized not as a personal being but as an abstraction. God is pure mind, light, and fire. This being is the light that illumines truth, the fire that kindles the love of virtue ("Deus omnipotens, qui et ignis et lux esse dicitur . . . , intelligentiam ad veritatis cognitionem illuminat. Ignis vero de se calorem emittens sed non amittens, ad virtutis amorem virtutem accendit.")[61] Like the sun, which cannot be seen except by the light it produces, so the deity cannot be seen except by the light of truth itself.[62] The source of all being in the world, moreover, is to be found in eternal, nonmaterial forms that exist solely in the mind of the deity ("ideam esse substantiam a materia separatam quae per sese in ipsius Dei intelligentia imaginationeque existeret").[63] Nor does Filelfo bring into his discourse the figure of Christ, the trinity, divine foreknowledge, divine love, or the relationship between God and humans in his ethics. Ontology, metaphysics, ethics, and the psychological foundations of the will, rather than theology, are the focuses of Filelfo's philosophical investigations.[64]

It should also be noted that while Filelfo's concepts of being, the good, and the will might be Aristotelian enough, his philosophical orientation was far from the civic concerns that were so characteristic, as Margaret King's recent work indicates, of Venetian Aristotelianism.[65] Book 1 treats Filelfo's ontological basis for his ethics and theories of the soul; Book 2, the functioning of reason and the emotions within the soul; and Book 3, the exercise of the will and the cardinal virtues and vices and their duties. Books 4 and 5 survive only as sketches for chapters. Book 4 contains a discussion of the virtues and vices, and closes with a long essay against wrath (*iracundia*). Book 5 continues with an extended discussion of courage and temperance.

Quattrocento Syntheses of Neoplatonism and Scholasticism

Filelfo's *De morali disciplina* has much in common not only with Bessarion's *In calumniatorem Platonis*, but also with Ficino's *Theologia Platonica*,

---

[61] *De morali disciplina*, bk. 2, p. 28.

[62] Ibid.

[63] Ibid., bk. 1, p. 11.

[64] Filelfo's treatment of the will is strictly Aristotelian, dealing with an analysis of the "voluntary" vs. the "involuntary" aspects of will, rather than its freedom in the face of competing forces in the cosmos.

[65] King, *Venetian Humanism in an Age of Patrician Dominance* (Princeton, 1986).

which had no explicit connection with the debate but was written during the same period as Bessarion's and Filelfo's treatises—1469–1473. The treatises of all three men offered, for the first time, a new metaphysics based on both Plato's and Aristotle's works themselves. At the same time, the works of all three authors contain syntheses of the Neoplatonism of late antiquity and the Scholasticism of the high Middle Ages. Plotinus and his Neoplatonist followers had synthesized the thought of Plato and Aristotle in the third and fourth centuries. A millenium later, Aquinas, Scotus, and Ockham reconciled Aristotelian doctrine with Christian theology. But neither Ficino nor Filelfo could have written their treatises before the recovery of the Greek Neoplatonists' commentaries and certain of the lesser-known dialogues of Plato.

Whereas humanist philosophy in the first half of the fifteenth century had primarily been concerned with practical ethics and politics, the Plato-Aristotle controversy and the demand for Greek philosophical texts that accompanied it gave rise to a revival of interest in metaphysics, ontology, and theology. But the new work began with new translations, without which there could be no new interpretations of earlier philosophical traditions. Bessarion completed the first modern translation in Latin of Aristotle's *Metaphysics* in 1455.[66] And by 1464 Ficino had translated ten of Plato's dialogues into Latin.[67] By the nineties Ficino had translated not only the rest of the Platonic corpus, but the Neoplatonist commentaries of Plotinus, Porphyry, Proclus, and Dionysius the Areopagite as well. Bessarion's *In calumniatorem Platonis*, published in 1469 in response to Trebizond's *Comparatio*, was a philosophical landmark in its own right. Drawing heavily on the works of Aquinas and Duns Scotus, as well as the Neoplatonists of late antiquity, Bessarion's work contained comprehensive commentaries to Aristotle's *Metaphysics*, including an extended discussion of the little-known Book 12, on the Divine, the First Causes, and the non-material cosmos. It also included commentaries to Plato's *Laws*, *Republic*, and *Phaedrus*, and to his then scarcely known *Parmenides*. The year Filelfo's *De morali disciplina* came out, Marsilio Ficino published his magnum opus, the *Theologia Platonica*, in which he set out to synthesize all previously known theologies, beginning with Zoroaster and culminating in Aquinas and the Christian theologians of the thirteenth century.

What distinguishes Filelfo's treatise from Bessarion's and Ficino's is that it is not the work of a professional philosopher or theologian, but that of a poet and teacher. Unlike Ficino's *Theologia Platonica*, in which a thoroughly evolved system of thought is elaborated, the *De morali disciplina*

[66] Mohler, *Kardinal Bessarion*, 1.344, dates the completion of the first modern translation in Latin of the *Metaphysics*, that of Cardinal Bessarion, to the pontificate of Nicholas V (1447–1455).

[67] See Kristeller, *The Philosophy of Marsilio Ficino* (New York, 1943).

reveals a quest for a philosophical methodology. In Book 1 an ontological basis for a worldview is sought and posited, but from Book 2 onward the lofty metaphysics of Book 1 are set aside, and no further explicit connection is drawn between the hierarchy of being and Idea of the good, on the one hand, and the functioning of the parts of the soul and the duties of the cardinal virtues, on the other. And yet, like Cicero's *Somnium Scipionis*, Book 1 of the *De morali disciplina* is a serious inquiry into the nature and meaning of the cosmos. Moreover, the book's flowing Demosthenean periods, its sonorities, and its unified structure make it a worthy heir to Cicero's depiction of the harmony of the universe in the *Somnium*.

In this chapter I shall limit my discussion to Book 1 of the *De morali disciplina*, for here Filelfo lays down the metaphysical foundations for his ethics. A complete text of the book is included in Appendix E.

Metaphysical Foundations for an Ethics

For the purposes of analysis, I have subdivided Book 1 of the *De morali disciplina* into six sections. Part 1 (pp. 226–27) contains the prologue with a dedication to Lorenzo de' Medici and description of the intent of the work.[68] The work discourses upon the doctrines of the Greek moral philosophers, whose aim is to teach us to live happily as well as rightly. Parts 2 and 3 are concerned with definitions. Part 2 defines virtue (p. 228) and follows that definition with a discourse on the theories of the soul of Plato, Pythagoras, Epicurus, Democritus, the Stoics, and Aristotle (pp. 228–30). Part 3 contrasts the utilitarian doctrine of the good of the Stoics with the concept of a transcendent ultimate good of Aristotle, Plato, and the Christian theologians (pp. 231–35). The ultimate good for these philosophers is eternal, perfect, and the source of all other good in the cosmos (p. 235). Virtue (*virtus*) is only an intermediate and not the ultimate good. It is the good not for the whole but for part of a man (p. 236). There are two aspects of the good: potentiality (*potentia*) and activity (*operatio*). Both are the constituents necessary to its being (pp. 235–36). The ultimate good is superior to the intermediate good just as the soul is superior to the body (p. 236).

Parts 4 and 5 present an extended discussion of Plato's and Aristotle's doctrines on the good. Part 4 (pp. 237–40) contains an exposition of Plato's theory of Ideas. The Idea, which is the origin of all good in the cosmos, exists in the mind and imagination of God (p. 238). It is eternal, immutable, and separate from matter (p. 239). There is not one Idea but

---

[68] The page numbers (pp. 226–27, etc.) refer to those for the text of the *De morali disciplina* in Appendix E.

many forms for all species and genera of things (p. 239). Only the sage can perceive the Ideas, and only through the contemplation of the Ideas can the soul be liberated from the prison of the body (p. 240). Part 5 sets forth Aristotle's definition of the highest good (*summum bonum*) (pp. 240–43). The highest good is that which pursues its own ultimate end (*finem ultimum*) in accordance with its nature (*secundum naturam*). It is that good which lacks nothing for its own perfection (pp. 240–42).

The good is a function of being (pp. 241–42). The trancendentals—being, the true, and the good—are part of a continuum, in which the highest form of being is the highest good. The two levels of being and the good in Aristotle consist in accidental goods (*ens/bonum accidens*) and intrinsic goods (*ens/bonum per se*) (pp. 242–43).

Part 6 contains Filelfo's final synthesis of doctrines on the good. The one good for all species is based on the concept of analogy (*proportio*) (pp. 243–44). The goodness in each of the diverse genera in the world resembles the One from which all things were originally engendered. Both the Platonic teaching that the Idea is the source of all good in the cosmos and the Aristotelian doctrine of the priority of the *bonum per se* over the *bonum per aliud* are correct (pp. 245–46). Filelfo's ultimate good, then, rests on his equation of the doctrines of *felicitas* with the *bonum per se* (*ens per se*), the Idea, the One, and finally God (p. 246). Virtue, though only an intermediate good, must be nonetheless sought, since for humans it is the necessary means to the final good (*summum bonum*) (p. 246).

Part 2: The Soul as the Conduit for Virtue

"While the emotions surely are the matter with which moral virtue is concerned, reason is its form," Filelfo wrote in his prologue to the *De morali disciplina*, in a paraphrase of Plutarch.[69] The Greek philosophers conceived of reason and the emotions as elements perpetually at war with one another, though they necessarily inhabited the same domicile: the soul. Virtue was attained, the philosophers taught, as much by the correct disposition of one's soul as by correct action. Therefore, no better groundwork could be laid for an inquiry into the nature of virtue than a discourse on the functioning of the soul.

After presenting a detailed exposition of the soul theories of Democritus, Epicurus, the Stoics, Aristotle, and Plato, Filelfo rejects all the philos-

---

[69] Appendix E, p. 230: ". . . Est sane affectio ea materia quam circa moralis versatur virtus, cuius forma ratio est." The passage is a paraphrase of Plutarch, *Moralia*, 440d, a work to which Filelfo was heavily indebted in his Greek poems, as elsewhere. Cf. Calderini, *Ricerche*, p. 337.

ophers' formulations as implausible, except that of Plato's tripartite soul.[70] Plato's soul is a hierarchical structure, consisting in the supremacy of mind (*mens*) over the other two parts of the soul: anger (*ira*) and desire (*cupiditas*). Reason (*ratio*) is the function of mind (*mens*) and hence inseparable from it. Mind thus embraces reason, and cannot be said to be itself without reason.[71] Mind—that is, reason (*mens seu ratio*)—is located in the head because it is farthest from the shameful organs of the body; anger is situated in the heart; and desire below the heart. The mind holds sway over the two inferior parts of the soul, like a queen in her citadel (*regina in arce*). Because of mind, we are empowered to reason, to think, and to curb our unruly passions. Vergil, Filelfo adds, similarly allegorized Plato's tripartite soul in his description of Aeolus's dominion over the winds in the *Aeneid*:[72] "celsa sedet Aeolus arce / sceptra tenens mollitque animos et temperat iras." ["Aeolus sits in his lofty citadel, holding his scepter, and there he tempers passions and soothes souls"] (1.56–57).

Filelfo's reading of the *Aeneid* as a Neoplatonic allegory was still standard in the early Renaissance, as Petrarch, Boccaccio, and Landino's commentaries on Vergil's poem all indicate.[73] Some years before the publication of the *De morali disciplina*, moreover, Filelfo had already discussed Vergil's allegory of the soul in a published letter to Ciriaco d'Ancona, which must have enjoyed wide circulation.[74]

Rejecting Aristotle's matter-bound soul, Filelfo espouses an Avicennian conception of the soul as simple spiritual substance (*simplex substantia spi-*

---

[70] Cf. Filelfo, *Epistolae*, to Ciriaco d'Ancona (31 October 1444), fols. 36–36v; here Filelfo presents a much briefer discussion of the theories of Democritus, Epicurus, Aristotle, Plato, and Thales (but not the Stoics).

[71] Appendix E, p. 230: "Separamus, inquam, animum tripliciter: in mentem qua rationem complectimur."

[72] Cf. *Epist.* to Ciriaco d'Ancona (21 December 1426), fols. 2–3, contains almost the same discussion of Plato's tripartite soul (cf. Cicero, *Tusculan Disputations*, 1.20; Plato, *Timaeus*, 86b and *Republic* 439d) and the same allegory of Aeolus and the winds in *Aeneid* 1.56–57 as parts of the soul.

[73] See Petrarch's *Secretum*, in *Prose*, ed. G. Martelloti and E. Carrara, in *La letteratura italiana, storia e testi*, vol. 7 (Milan and Naples, n.d.), pp. 122–24 (cf. Petrarca, *Sen.* iv.4); and *Il comento di Giovanni Boccaccio sopra la commedia*, ed. Gaetano Milanesi (Florence, 1863), pp. 249–50. For other allegorical interpretations of *Aeneid* 1.56ff. in the Renaissance, see C. Kallendorf, *Early Humanistic Moral Criticism of Virgil's "Aeneid" in Italy and Great Britain* (Ph.D. dissertation, University of North Carolina, 1982), pp. 64–66: Pontano, Patrizi, and Guarino gave the passage a political interpretation; Landino (*Disputationes Camaldulenses*, ed. P. Lohe [Florence, 1980], pp. 160–66) interpreted the Aeolus episode as a struggle between *ratio superior* and *ratio inferior*. See also Kallendorf, "Cristoforo Landino's *Aeneid* and the Humanist Critical Tradition," in *Renaissance Quarterly* 36 (1983): 519–46; and V. R. Giustiniani, "Il Filelfo, L'interpretation allegorica di Virgilio e la tripartizione platonica dell'anima," in *Umanesimo e Rinascimento* (Florence, 1980), pp. 33–44; here Giustiniani discusses Filelfo's use of the allegory in his letter to Ciriaco only.

[74] On Filelfo's letter to Ciriaco (*Epistolae*, fols. 2–3), see chap. 1.

ritualis), distinct from the body but acting upon it.[75] Thus the soul, which encompasses mind and reason, both is self-moving and moves the limbs and organs of the body so long as its nature preserves their fundamental harmony (*elementalis convenientia*).[76] Only through the agency of the soul and that part of the soul known as reason (*ratio*) can humans apprehend true being (*ens*). A passage from Book 2 is particularly worth noting in this connection, because it illuminates what Filelfo means by the term *ratio* in his soul theory. In this passage, *ratio* is endowed with the attributes of the Platonic soul and is the equivalent of Filelfo's *animus*. Likewise, Filelfo uses the term *natura* here the way Augustine uses *idea, forma, species*, and *ratio* in the *Quaestiones*:[77]

> Some men see reason (*ratio*) as that power of the soul that perceives the nature of bodily things, the distinguishing characteristics of their form, and their inherent and accidental properties . . . , since it can abstract those things from bodies which are the fundamental elements in those bodies—not indeed by action, but rather by a species of contemplation. For the nature of a body (*natura corporis*)—the nature, that is, which enables us to say of a body that it is a body—is clearly not body.[78]

While Filelfo believes with Plato in the immortality of certain immutable forms (*Ideae*), which are the underlying causes of the visible phenomena in the world, he asserts the immortality of neither individual souls nor a world soul (*animus*).[79] His focus is rather the ethical functioning of the individual human soul—its service as a conduit for virtue. The right habit and proper tuning (*rectus habitus, recta dispositio*) of the soul lead to virtue; the improper, to vice. The habit of the soul is long-lasting and steadfast: unlike the emotions (*affectiones*) it can be neither altered nor affected with-

[75] N. Kretzmann, A. Kenny, and J. Pinborg, eds., *The Cambridge History of Later Medieval Philosophy From the Rediscovery of Aristotle to the Disintegration of Scholasticism* (Cambridge, 1982), pp. 596ff.

[76] Appendix E, p. 230: "Mea quidem sententia, animus est creata substantia spiritualis simplex rationis atque intelligentiae particeps, quae seipsam movens naturale instrumentaleque corpus tam diu afficit, etc."

[77] *The Cambridge History of Later Medieval Philosophy*, p. 442: see Augustine, *De diversis quaestionibus* 83.42.2.

[78] *De morali disciplina*, bk. 2, pp. 25–66, on the part of the soul Filelfo calls *ratio*: "Alii volunt rationem esse eam vim animi, quae rerum corporearum naturam, formae differentias, propria et accidentia percipit . . . , cum abstrahat a corporibus quae in corporibus sunt fundata, non actione quidem illa, sed speculatione quadam. Natura enim corporis, qua corpus omne dicimus esse corpus, nullum sane corpus est."

[79] A dialogue entitled *Dell'immortalità dell anima* (Cosenza, 1478) is erroneously attributed to Filelfo in Apostolo Zeno, *Dissertazioni vossiane*, 2 vols. (Venice, 1752), 1.305; Rosmini, *Vita*, 2.125–26n, writes that the true author of this dialogue was Jacopo Campora. Cf. Filelfo, *Epistolae*, to Antonio Canobio (7 October 1450), fol. 48, where Filelfo argues that Aristotle conceived of the soul as immortal.

out difficulty. But the realization of this correct tuning of the soul must be rooted firmly in action. Taking Cicero's *De officiis* as his authority, Filelfo insists that *rectus habitus animi* must be accompanied by *recta actio*. The possession of the moral virtues, such as justice, courage, temperance, and the like, is meaningless without the activity (*operatio*) of those virtues:[80]

> And therefore those [philosophers] who say that right action is superior to virtue itself seem in my judgment to have cautioned us quite rightly; of course they did so on the basis that whenever the opinion of the soul is not known one's choice will also be unknown, since choice necessarily proceeds from the disposition [of one's soul] to action.[81]

Thus, although the source of virtue is the simple spiritual substance of the soul (*substantia spiritualis simplex animi*), which is bound neither by the limits of the body nor by time, the activity of virtue can still only be exercised through matter and in time.

Part 3: Definitions of the Good

Arthur Field has recently underscored the dominant place of Aristotle in the curriculum of the Florentine Studio in the middle decades of the fifteenth century.[82] Indeed, Filelfo, in his definition of the good, takes as his starting point Aristotle's *Nicomachean Ethics*. Like Aristotle, Filelfo lists the diverse objects that men have perceived as the good—wealth, power, physical strength, health, pleasure, and the moral virtues.

Filelfo treats with ridicule the Stoics' claim that utility alone is the highest good. The problem with all such notions of the good, he objects, is that they are too narrow: they are not definitions of the good, but teach only its properties. This approach, he complains, is as useless as telling someone who has no idea what a horse is that it is a creature that whinnies. An aspect of the whole clearly cannot define the whole. Likewise, the good of the part is not the same as the good of the whole. The ultimate aim of goods such as health, wealth, pleasure, and virtue is the happiness of the whole man. Thus, Filelfo concludes with Aristotle that while there are numerous

---

[80] Cf. Cicero, *De officiis*, 1.153.

[81] Appendix E, p. 230: "Itaque non absurde ii monuisse videntur mihi qui dicunt rectam operationem esse virtute ipsa praestantiorem, ea scilicet ratione ducti quod ignorata animi sententia ignoratur etiam electio, quae ab habitu [animi] ad actionem proficiscatur necesse est."

[82] Field, *The Beginning of the Philosophical Renaissance*, pp. 101–243; Torre, *Storia dell'Accademia platonica*, pp. 286ff.; and George Holmes, *The Florentine Enlightenment: 1400–50* (London, 1969), pp. 262ff.

intermediate goods (*bona instrumentalia*), happiness alone is the final good (*summum bonum*).[83]

Part 4: Plato and the Theory of Ideas

Aristotle's analytical method, with its relentless definition and redefinition of terms at every step of the discourse, clearly suits Filelfo's preference for a linear, logic-driven form of argumentation over the ambiguities of the dialogue form. On the other hand, Filelfo shares with his Neoplatonist contemporaries a belief in a nonmaterial, immutable, eternal reality that was alien to Aristotelian doctrine—though not wholly so. In the *Metaphysics*, that is, Aristotle posited the existence of an eternal, immutable prime mover, and eternal primary beings.[84]

Certainly in the *De morali disciplina* Filelfo has no difficulty adopting for his own use Aristotle's categorization of the attributes of being as either intrinsic or extrinsic, or as potential or actual. Likewise, he accepts Aristotle's concept of the good as the *primum in aliquo genere*. But he rejects as erroneous Aristotle's criticisms of Plato's theory of Ideas, focusing in particular on his objection to Plato's conception of the Ideas as independent of matter (*separatae a materia*).[85] Filelfo argues that even the most materialistic of all the philosophers, Zeno, who taught that the good was nothing more than utility, and the most cynical of all the Romans, the satirist Juvenal and Cicero's enemy Mark Anthony, believed in the existence of incorporeal, ideal patterns for things.[86]

Drawing not only on Plato but also on Pseudo-Plutarch's *De Placitis philosophorum*, Augustine's *Quaestiones*, and Cicero's *Orator* in his description of Plato's Ideas, Filelfo also introduces paradigms of his own making into the discussion.[87] The Ideas, he suggests, are no different from the conceptualizations of great artists, such as the sculptures of the pair of horses

---

[83] Aristotle, *Nicomachean Ethics*, 1.7.1097b; Appendix E, p. 235: "Quod cum ita sit, haud est obscurum felicitatem ex iis omnibus bonis, quae in hominum actionibus sita sunt, et perfectum esse et optimum et summum bonum."

[84] *Metaphysics* 12.6–7.

[85] Appendix E, p. 237. Cf. Filelfo, *Epistolae*, to Domenico Barbarigo (15 April 1464), fols. 150–151v and the *Convivia Mediolanensia* for Filelfo's prior discussions of the Ideas. Kraye, in "Filelfo's *De Ideis*," studies Filelfo's use of sources in the passage on the Ideas in the *De morali disciplina*.

[86] Kraye, "Filelfo's *De Ideis*," p. 245, notes that Filelfo alludes here to Juvenal, *Satires*, 7.53–57 and Cicero, *Orator ad Brutum*, 18.

[87] Plato, *Phaedo*, 75d–e, *Republic* 6.508 and 7.517f., and *Symposium* 211; Pseudo-Plutarch, *De Placitis*, 1.10.882d; and Augustine, *Quaestiones*, 46, but Augustine's emphasis here, unlike Filelfo's, is all on piety, purity, and divinity; cf. Kraye, "Filelfo's *De Ideis*," pp. 239–46.

and pair of youths by Praxiteles and Phidias on the Capitolium in Rome.[88] So ideal is the molding of these figures that their forms could not have been drawn from life, but must have originated in the minds of the artists who created them. Thus, the source of all things in the phenomenal world transcends mere matter, and all matter derives from one sublime and eternal form—the Idea. The term Idea, Filelfo explains, derives from εἶδος, which signifies form or image. It must also be understood, however, as *ratio* or λόγος. His definition of the Idea as separated from matter and extant solely in the imagination of God, and as the undying and immutable source of all things in the universe (*principalis ratio rerum*), contains echoes again from Cicero's *Orator* and Augustine's *Quaestiones*:[89]

> Just as this image, this form, this principle (the Idea, that is, which at no time had a beginning) will never have an end—for whatever is in God must necessarily be eternal—thus it is shown that all other things which are born, due to their very nature, must perish, flow away, slip from sight, and be dispersed, nor is it evident that these things are able to remain in one and the same condition for very long.[90]

As to whether there are one or many Ideas, Filelfo answers that since the Idea is comparable to divine substance itself, which is said to be one, it must therefore be agreed that the Idea is also one.[91] But in addition to the one preeminent and indivisible Idea (*una simplex Idea*), there exists in the mind of God a vast variety of Ideas, in which all material objects on earth participate, but whose first cause is the one preeminent Idea. The pattern, for example, for the ball, the wheel, the earth, and all the heavenly bodies we observe is one and the same Idea or form.[92] And so, Filelfo reasons, every corporeal body in the cosmos has its own incorporeal, immutable, and divine form (*ratio, species, Idea*), which is its ultimate source.

Only that man can be called a sage who understands the Ideas—and thus the truth behind the phenomenal world. In a rare reference to Scripture, Filelfo remarks that the apostle Paul was this kind of sage, for Paul was able, not with his eyes but rather with the inner and truer part of his mind,

---

[88] The idea for the analogy between the artist and God comes from Cicero, *Orator*, 9; the exempla are Filelfo's.

[89] Cicero, *Orator*, 9–10; and from Augustine, *De diversis quaestionibus*, 46, 2: "Sunt namque ideae, etc."; see Kraye, "Filelfo's *De Ideis*," p. 241.

[90] Appendix E, p. 239: "Quamobrem ut ea species, ea forma, ea ratio (hoc est Idea, quae principium nunquam habuit) finem est nunquam habitura—quicquam enim in Deo est id sit aeternum oportet—ita caetera quae nascuntur ea interire natura omnia, fluere, labi, dissipari, neque diutius esse posse uno atque eodem statu demonstratur."

[91] Ibid., p. 239.

[92] Ibid., p. 239.

to apprehend the divine and ineffable intelligence of God.[93] But echoes from *Phaedrus* 247d, Diotima's speech in the *Symposium*, and from Ficino as well, can also be heard in Filelfo's exhortation to all those who would become true philosophers:

> For it is not permitted for anyone to look at God with human eyes; but one can gaze on him with the eyes of a radiant mind, which has been cleansed and purged of all earthly squalor. Whoever wishes this for himself (for who would not wish it?) must strive with all care, work, zeal, and finally industry and diligence to attain this end and to exert himself, so that his whole mind, once it is free from every crippling and tyrannical disorder of the soul and wholly conscious of itself, may commune with, and never again withdraw away from, the divine intellect, from which it has received all creation, all splendor, and all power to reason and to understand. For whoever does this can surely hope to apprehend . . . the entire force and nature of the Idea.[94]

Part 5: Aristotle's Hierarchy of Being

In his initial definitions of the good, Filelfo concludes with Aristotle that while there are many intermediate goods, happiness alone is the highest good. To pursue this definition further, Filelfo turns to a text less familiar to Quattrocento intellectuals than the *Ethics*—the *Metaphysics* of Aristotle.[95] The problem of the good, as Filelfo sees it, cannot be dealt with apart from ontological questions—namely, what is being, and what, moreover, is the relationship between being and the good?

Filelfo denies that a fundamental distinction between being (*ens*) and the good (*bonum*) can be drawn. He accepts Augustine's dictum, "inasmuch as we exist we are good." (*in quantum sumus, boni sumus*).[96] Like Plotinus,

---

[93] Ibid., p. 240. *Corinthians* 12:2–4. Filelfo refers to the New Testament only once elsewhere in the *De morali disciplina*: bk. 3, pp. 46–47.

[94] Appendix E, p. 240: "Non enim corporeis oculis fas est cuiquam Deum aspicere, sed cunctis terrenis sordibus defecatae atque purgatae ac nitidae mentis luminibus eum licet intueri. Id sibi contingere qui velit (quis enim velle non debet), huic est omni cura, omni opera, omni studio, omni denique industria atque diligentia annitendum ut sese vendicet sibi cogatque, ut prostratis ac domitis cunctis animi perturbationibus mens sua omnis libera ac sui compos cum menta divina, unde creationem atque splendorem vimque omnem accepit et rationcinandi et intelligendi, conveniat ab eaque nusquam discedat. Nam ita qui fecerit, certo sperare potest ut . . . cernat vim omnem naturamque Ideae."

[95] James of Venice and William Moerbeke's translations of the *Metaphysics* (from the Greek, not from the Arabic) had been available since the twelfth and thirteenth centuries respectively. But Mohler, 1.344, points out that Bessarion's translation of the work, completed around 1455, was the first into modern (humanistic) Latin.

[96] Appendix E, p. 242.

Filelfo conceives of being as a continuum in which some good would exist at each stage of its evolution:

> For whatever has simple entity has some good in its very beginning. For there is simple entity in potentiality and in the first stages of being. But if being attains the truth of the perfection of its being through its form, then it has the goodness that belongs to the essence appropriate to its species. But if it has entity through its species, in the form of its species and in those attributes which make its form perfect, then it has perfect goodness.[97]

Filelfo follows Plotinus, Aquinas, and Scotus in viewing being, the true, and the good (*ens, verum, bonum*) as transcendentals in a hierarchy of being, which as such are mutually convertible, one into another.[98] Being, the true, and the good are part of a continuum. They are not distinct from one another in reality, but we draw distinctions between them for the sake of analysis (*secundum rationem*). The doctrines of the hierarchy of being in both the Neoplatonists and the Scholastics, however, are built on Aristotle's conception of being and its perfection (*summum, finis*) in Book 5 of the *Metaphysics*.[99] And the terms Filelfo employs in this connection—the dyad potentiality and activity, or potency and act (*potentia* and *operatio*) are the Latin translations of Aristotle's δύναμις and ἐνέργεια.

> Moreover, being, the true, and the good are indeed converted in conformance with their subjects; they differ, however, in form (*ratio*). For [the philosophers] believe that being is said to be that which in some way has attained the distinguishing characteristic (*differentia*) of its entity (whatever one we may attribute to it). But the true is that which has acquired truth and meaning through the form of its being, which itself is sometimes still imperfect in its power (*virtus*) and activity (*operatio*). But after being and the true, that which has been perfected in its power and activity must also be added. This is the ultimate form of the perfection of the form and moreover its ultimate good

---

[97] Cf. Aristotle, *Metaphysics*, 5.16. For technical terms such as *entitas, simplex, potentia, ens, forma*, and *species*, I have followed the standard translations throughout this chapter from the *Cambridge History of Later Medieval Philosophy*. Appendix E, p. 242: "Nam quod simplicem habet entitatem, id in ipsa inchoatione bonum habet. Entitas enim simplex in potentia est et in primis entis principiis. Quod si entitatis perfectionem veritatem per formae consequitur, habet bonitatem ad essentiam in specie definitam. Sin autem entitatem per speciem habet in speciei forma et iis quae ad formam perfectam consequenter accedunt, tum bonitatem perfectam habet."

[98] Kristeller, *The Philosophy of Marsilio Ficino*, p. 74. On the transcendental concepts in Thomas Aquinas and Duns Scotus, see J. C. Doig, *Aquinas on Metaphysics: A Historico-Doctrinal Study of the "Commentary" on the "Metaphysics"* (The Hague, 1972), pp. 367–69; and J. Weinberg, *A Short History of Medieval Philosophy* (Princeton, 1964), pp. 219ff. On Ficino's similarly Aristotelian ontology, see Kristeller, *The Philosophy of Marsilio Ficino*, pp. 35–91.

[99] See n. 97.

(*summum*); and so it is that the highest good seems quite reasonably to be that which has been perfected by the attainment of its own ultimate end.[100]

Filelfo provides an analogy to make clear the relationship between being, the true, and the good. The good and the true have the same relationship to being as a sexually mature male and a prepubescent male have to the seed from which both were originally engendered. The male seed exists at first only as a potentiality (*potentia*) for procreation; nor is there anything in the form (*forma*) of the seed which can dictate its activity (*operatio*). In this same way the form (*ratio, forma*) of an entity (*ens, entitas*) can predict neither its separateness from (*differentia; transcendentia*), nor its kinship (*communitas*) with its species. We know only that there exists a certain common form for each species of being (*ratio entis*), which contains in it the potentiality for the perfection of its being (*perfectio entis*). Just as when a human being is engendered from a seed and its limbs are still soft and its bodily functions have not yet been perfected, still we call this a true human (*verus homo*). Nonetheless, this human is not yet perfect since it cannot perform the functions that pertain to its completion, such as the procreation of a being like itself. For we call something perfect (*perfectum*), Filelfo explains, when it is capable of creating a being similar to itself. Thus, the true (*verum*), even when it has attained the fundamental form of its being (*ratitudo entis*) and the completeness proper to its substance and species (*perfectio substantialis et specifica*), still may be lacking in that good (*bonum*) which is necessary for the perfection of its form. However, that being which is in perfect conformance with its own form (*secundum propriam rationem*) is "like a man in the prime of life" (*ut homo perfecta aetate*).[101]

Thus, the end toward which each species strives is the fulfillment of the two principal attributes of being: potentiality (*potentia, virtus*) and activity (*operatio*).[102] The ultimate good for each species is attained by the perfect functioning of its constituent parts and by the fulfillment of its potentiality in conformance with its particular species (*forma, ratio*).[103] Moreover, as

[100] Note also that *differentia* has a technical meaning here: "the distinguishing characteristic of a genus" (Cicero, *Topica*, 31). Appendix E, p. 241: "Insuper ens, verum, et bonum secundum subiecta quidem convertuntur, at ratione differunt. Id enim ens dici putant quod (quamcumque demus) differentiam entitatis eam sit quodammodo assequutum. Verum autem id quod per entis formam veritatem ratitudinemque acquiserit, quod ipsum tamen in virtute et operatione nonnunquam est imperfectum. Sed post ens et verum, id quoque addatur oportet, quod virtute et operatione perfectum est. Ultima suae perfectionis forma ac ita continuo fit summum; qua ipsa re fit ut non absurde summum bonum esse videatur quod ultimi finis accessione perfectum est."
[101] Ibid., pp. 241–42; cf. *Metaphysics* 5.16.
[102] Ibid., pp. 235–36; *Metaphysics* 9.3–8.
[103] Ibid., p. 242; *Metaphysics* 5.16.

we have seen in Filelfo's analogy of the seed, every ontological level (from inchoate being to the supreme good) is already immanent *in* being, since every stage marks an evolution *from* being. But the course of this evolution, Filelfo repeatedly emphasizes, depends less on its potentiality (*potentia, forma*) than on its activity (*operatio*).

Having established a hierarchy of being, Filelfo proceeds in a similar manner to set up Aristotelian criteria for a hierarchy of the good *qua* good. There are two principal levels of things which we call the good: to the first level belongs that good which exists by virtue of itself alone (*bonum per se*); and to the second, belongs that good which exists accidentally and by virtue of some other good outside itself (*bonum accidens*). The prior good is that on which the existence of a particular species or thing is predicated. The posterior good is merely accidental to the existence of a particular species or thing.[104] But Filelfo founds his hierachy of goods on two basic ontological premises: first, that there exists a unity of all being in the cosmos; and second, that there exists one supreme good, one First Principle, or Cause, from which all other goods in the cosmos originally proceeded. It is on these grounds, then, that Filelfo can claim that his own philosophy diverges in no important sense from, but rather agrees with, that of Plato, Aristotle, and the Christian theologians:[105]

> For among all goods there must be some one good, from which all other goods proceed, as from a cause. For if this were not so, neither could the entire multitude of them be restored to a unity, nor could their entire multiplicity be restored to a unison, nor could that which is good by accident be again restored to that which is intrinsically good. Indeed, all this would contradict the basic teachings of philosophy. Let it be a given, then, that there is some intrinsic good which, essentially and through no other thing, is good. In addition, who can doubt that there exists in all things that participate in the good a particular nature, so that there will by necessity be that good which a thing has intrinsically (*per se id*), and that which participates in it accidentally (*participans per accidens*)? Just as seeing itself continues to exist in the absence of sight, so the good which the white man has as an accidental, he clearly would not have as an accidental, unless the whiteness in which he participates had some intrinsic good of its own. When a good man therefore possesses an activity of the good, it is necessary to assume that there exists some one intrinsic good (*bonum per sese*) which possesses the same activity; this is the thing we call an intrinsic good. Again, whatever good exists, there exists some other

[104] Ibid., pp. 242–43; *Metaphysics* 5.18 and 30.

[105] Ibid., p. 235: "Hanc nostram bonorum distinctionem si quis recte considerare voluerit, inveniet nos nec a Platone et Aristotele dissentire et cum Christiana philosophia maxime convenire."

former good on account of which we say that the latter good is good. Either a thing is good intrinsically or through some other thing.[106]

Marsilio Ficino employed similar Aristotelian concepts of being and Plotinian notions of the hierarchy of being in his *Theologica platonica*. It is also worth noting that about two decades later, Ficino's intimate friend Pico Della Mirandola published his work *On Being and the One* (*De ente et uno*), which he said he wrote after hearing about the discussions Lorenzo de' Medici and Poliziano were having on Aristotle's and Plato's teachings on being and matter.[107]

Part 6: A Synthesis of God, the One, and the Good

Aristotle's other chief objection to Plato's theory of the One—the Idea, which was to be seen as the source of all good in the cosmos—was that the good varied with each class and genus; a horse's goodness, for example, was different from a lion's, a dog's, or a cow's. If there were, then, no one good applicable to every species, how could there be one preeminent Idea of the good? Filelfo answers Aristotle's objection by adopting the Neoplatonist doctrine of analogy (*proportio*).[108] The concept of *proportio*, which Dionysius the Areopagite introduced into Christian theology, was fundamental to the philosophy of Aquinas. The doctrine of *proportio* was a byproduct of Neoplatonist conceptions of the hierarchy of being, in which the products generated from the One (God) were said to resemble the One. We should be able, Dionysius posited, to construct a mental image

---

[106] Ibid., pp. 242–43: "Enimvero inter omnia bona unum quoddam bonum dandum est, a quo ipso bona omnia tanquam a causa proficiscantur. Nam si secus fiat, neque omnis multitudo [*bonorum*] ad unitatem redigatur, nec etiam omnis multiplicitas ad univocationem, nec id rursus quod est [*bonum*] per accidens ad id redigi queat quod [*bonum*] per se sit. Quae quidem omnia philosophiae praeceptis contraria sunt. Esto igitur quoddam per se bonum, quod et substantialiter et non per aliud bonum sit. Praeterea cui dubium esse debet in omnibus participantibus [*bonum*] eam esse naturam, ut quiddam [*bonum*] necessario sit, quod per sese id habeat [et] quod participans per accidens habet? Sicuti in visus disgregatione est ipsum videre, [id bonum] quod homo albus per accidens habet, neque id sane per accidens haberet, nisi quam participat albedo ipsa haberet [bonum] per sese. Cum bonus igitur vir habeat boni operationem, necesse est ut unum quiddam [bonum] proponatur quod eandem [bonum] per sese operationem habeat; hoc autem illud est quod dicimus per se bonum. Rursus quicquid est bonum, aliud illud [bonum] per quod hoc dicimus bonum esse: aut per se bonum est aut per aliud."

[107] See Giovanni Pico Della Mirandola, *De hominis dignitate, Heptaplus, De ente et uno, e scritti vari*, ed. E. Garin (Florence, 1942); and in English translation *Pico della Mirandola On the Dignity of Man, On Being and the One, Heptaplus*, tr. C. G. Wallis, P.J.W. Miller, and D. Carmichael (Indianapolis, 1965).

[108] See R. T. Wallis, *Neoplatonism*, pp. 60ff. On the importance of the principle of analogy in Ficino, see also Kristeller, *The Philosophy of Marsilio Ficino*, pp. 136ff.

of the One by analogy. Earlier in Book 1 Filelfo established the existence of a hierarchy of the good in which every good was categorized as belonging to one of two species: the prior *bonum per se* or the posterior *bonum per aliud*. He had also demonstrated that at the summit of this hierarchy was one supreme good, from which all other goods were generated, as from a cause. Filelfo now argues that the goodness in all the diverse genera in the world must be analogous to the One (*habere proportionem ad unum*), from which all things were originally engendered, even if the goodness in the different genera is clearly not synonymous (*non aequivoce esse*):[109]

> For the analogy to the One is a similitude of habits with the One, in which things of a different kind nonetheless participate in one and the same analogy—like a pilot's governance over his ship and a king's over his kingdom. For the pilot of a ship does not generally govern his ship following the same principles by which a king governs his realm . . . Nor are the governances of a ship and a kingdom the same in kind, although similarity of habits still exists in each of them. Since we see a single similitude of this sort in all things, with the result that there is one first good, by analogy and comparison to which all other good things are called good, I seem to know with Plato that there is one first good, which is by its substance the good and the efficient cause of the goodness of each individual thing. Indeed, the form of this good is preserved in all things in accordance with their similitude [to the One].[110]

Since Filelfo's first objective in Book 1 is the establishment of a firm ontological foundation for his ethics, it remains for him, at the close of the book, to posit an answer to the question with which the book began: what is the good we ought to seek? He has striven in this work to cast a coherent hypothesis concerning the nature of being in the world, drawing on Aristotle's *Ethics* and *Metaphysics*, Plato's dialogues, Cicero's philosophical works, Augustine's *Quaestiones*, Aquinas's *Summa theologiae*, and the works of the Neoplatonic philosophers. His own ontology will prove to be firmly anchored to Plato's notion of the one sublime and ineffable Idea of the good, which "exists nowhere but in the mind and imagination of God him-

[109] Appendix E, p. 244: "Nam primum quidquid esse in multis dixeris, quod non aequivoce in illis sit, id in uno primo quodam ponas oportet, quod sit aliis omnibus bonitatis causa, etc."

[110] Ibid., p. 244: "Proportio enim ad unum est habitudinum similitudo ad unum, quod diversa in specie et in una proportione participatur, quemadmodum est navis ad gubernatorem et regni ad regem gubernatio. Nam neque eisdem praeceptis navis gubernationem gubernator solet quibus regni gubernationem rex persequitur . . . Nec idem specie est gubernatio navis et regni, cum similitudo tamen habitudinum una sit in utraque. Cum huiusmodi ergo similitudinem in omnibus unam esse videamus, ut unum sit primum bonum, ad cuius proportionem et similitudinem caetera bona dicuntur bona, intelligere mihi videor cum Platone esse unum primum bonum, quod substantialiter bonum est et efficiens causa cuiusque bonitatis. Cuius quidem boni forma secundum proportionem servatur in omnibus."

self" (*in Dei intelligentia imaginationeque*). Moreover, both the Idea of the good and Filelfo's concept of the Deity are inextricably bound up together in his treatise. In a leitmotif that becomes a unifying theme for the whole book, both the Idea of the good and God are repeatedly called the one, eternal, immutable good in the cosmos (pp. 235, 238, 239, 240, 244, 245, and 246). Indeed, at the close of Book 1 he returns again to this theme in his attempt to give weight to both the contemplative and active principles:

> But if anyone should wish to follow and to place before himself the one and first good itself, which is simple, independent, and good of its own nature, which remains measureless, eternal, and is subject neither to mutability, nor motion, nor action, surely he will know that he is good, happy, and blessed—not only with that intermediate good which is situated in the threefold bastion of reason, the intellect, and the moral virtues, but blessed also with that perfect good which is the highest of all goods.[111]

In the closing passage we come to the end of Filelfo's journey in quest of the good. We have traveled full circle to the proposition he put forth in the opening of the book: the ultimate good we all seek is happiness (*felicitas*). While virtue is only a means to the ultimate good, its form is analogous to that of the good. We may not as humans be capable of apprehending the perfect and final end of all being. But if we are to venture on the road toward the good and the true, then we must aspire first to that prior end which is virtue. In order to attain virtue, the possession of its *potentia* is not enough. We must make its *operatio* palpable in the world as well. And this is only a beginning:

> Therefore, if we believe that happiness is in fact the good of the whole man—and that really this happiness is nothing other than God, we ought, on the other hand, to believe that no one can attain happiness, except if he learns beforehand that the way of traveling towards and reaching it is, we say, through the intermediate good of virtue; indeed, every virtue should be practiced and possessed in the best way possible.[112]

[111] Ibid., p. 245: "Quod ipsum unum ac primum et simplex et separatum et sua natura bonum, immensum, sempiternum, nulli mutabilitati, nulli motui, nulli actioni subiectum qui sibi proponere sequique voluerit, non solum bono medio quod in triplici illa virtute intelligentiae et rationis morumque situm est, sed perfecto etiam bono, quod bonorum omnium est summum, se bonum planeque felicem atque beatum intelliget."

[112] Ibid., p. 246: "Quare si totius quidem hominis bonum felicitatem esse volumus—hanc vero aliud nihil esse quam Deum, at felicitatem assequi posse neminem, nisi quod per medium bonum fieri dicimus virtutis, ad eam iter et eundi et perveniendi ante didicerit; virtus certe omnis tenenda est atque exercenda quam optime."

TEXTS AND SYNOPSES

*

APPENDIX A

LETTERS TO HIS FRIENDS

Filelfo to Enea Silvio Piccolomini. The Assassination Attempt. 28 March 1439 (fols. 17–17v)

[1] Et te bene valere te et secundiorem iam tibi aspirare fortunam. Laetor maiorem in modum, quod autem scire cupis quid in causa fuerit, ut relicta patria tua Sena, ubi et pacatissime me agebam et commode inter discordiarum Bononiensium digladiationes me receperim, dicam tibi. Qualis quantosque invidentiae aestus Florentiae paterer, praesens ipse olim coramque vidisti. At ludus erat, quod per id temporis paciebar incommodum ad eas aerumnas, quas quasi Alcides quidam, perferre postea sum coactus.

[2] Nam posteaquam nulla aut iuris aut aequi simulatione perditissimorum hominum rabies nocere mihi potuisset ad arma concursum est. Paratoque sicario aere non parvo, mane cum in publicam illam quam nosti Academiam, docendi gratia pergerem, ex occultis insidiis in me nihil tale neque caventem neque cogitantem impetus factus est. Erat sicarius togatus Florentini mercatoris more, ne posset agnosci, qui educto repente longiore gladio, qui toga tegebatur, cuspidem mihi direxit in pectus. Transfodissetque me omnino, nisi dextera manu facto pugno in eius pectus illico magna vi irruissem. Itaque a proposito loco ictus ille aberrans in sinistrum bracchium me percussit omni illaesum vulnere. Elanguerat enim ictus, quoniam ille a me reiectus pugno paululum esset amotus. Qui rursus sublato gladio, quo me acie feriret in caput, in faciem me percussit.

[3] Qui fuerit sicarius notum est. A quibus autem conductus, etsi nihil habetur certi, infamia tamen in Medices repit et Cosmum, quoniam non solum eius factio mihi semper adversaretur, sed etiam Laurentius frater aperte multa adversus me ageret. Paucis post mensibus ob civilis discordias idem Cosmus in carcerem primo coniectus est, dein relegatus ad Venetos sine alia prorsus ulla civium offensione. Et ita civiles discordiae tantisper quievere, donec in posterum annum iis pecunia corruptis qui summae reipublicae praeerant, Cosmus in urbem revocatur. Tum iura divina omnia humanaque confunduntur. Optimates omnes alii relegantur; alii proscribuntur. Hinc direptiones, latrocinia, caedesque sequuntur.

[4] Quae ipse intuens animadvertens quanto cum periculo in tanto Florentiae naufragio forem, qui antea in summa, ut ita dixerim, malachia naufragus extitissem, subduxi me et ab imminentibus tantorum fluctuum vorticibus in Senensis tuae reipublicae tanquam in portum aliquem maxime opportunum devolavi. Hic autem cum et tranquille et honorifice vitam agerem, neque de re Florentina ulla mihi prorsus cura esset praeter humani

commiserationem ingenii, mense decimo ex quo Florentia decesseram, nulla mea neque culpa neque culpae suspicione, tantum potuit inimicorum coniuratio, ut ipse quoque inter proscriptos civis optimatis proscriberer, id quod ut accepi, universae civitati fuit molestissimum auditu.

Quin in proximum inde annum missus est Senam, ut me interimeret, idem ille sicarius, qui ab eadem ornatus coniuratione in faciem mihi vulnus inflixerat. Hic Philippus est vocatus, patria natus Casale Fluminensi et patre Thoma et avo Bruno, qui etiam ipsi ambo notissimi habiti sunt sicarii. Aberam per id temporis ad Petriolanas balneas, idque non tam ulla mea vel necessitate, vel delectationis quidem gratia quam divino quodam consilio, ut certo puto. Nam eo sum profectus sola visendi causa. Solet enim plaerunque omnipotens deus, quo de perseverantibus in malignitate facinorosisque hominibus aliquando supplicium sumat, certas quasdam easque occultas parare vias ad vindicandum.

Cum eiusmodi ergo tempore sicarius Philippus Senam venisset, neque me usquam videret, adit praeclarum in philosophia virum ac medicum prudentissimum Petrum Iohanetum, qui ex patria Bononia pulcherrimis praemiis accersitus medicinam docebat, ut nunc etiam docet in eius urbis publico studio. Ex eo quaerit et qua in vicinia ipse habitarem et ubi docerem et quot mecum ducerem comites, et quantum valerem gratia apud civis. Ad quae ille, ut est vir calentissimus aeque atque acerrimo strenuissimoque ingenio, inspecto hominis vultu et consyderata verborum temeritate, singulatim ea respondit, quae mihi usui fore arbitraretur. Eodemque die litteris me de ea re omni commonefecit.

Quare Senam ubi continuo revertissem ex illoque liquidius rem omnem coram didicissem; mox adeo praefectum praesidii, quem capitaneum vocant, Honofrium Tifernatem cognomento virilem, hominem subdolum et fallacem. Huic rem ipsam, ut habebat, expono et omnia sicarii signa do, qualia et a Petro Ioanneto didiceram, et ipse quoque dum illum interambulandum obviam habeo, agnosco. Respondit continuo veterator ille et fraudolentus latro: "Grates habeo sempiternas, mi pater observandissime Philelfe, immortali deo, qui mihi causam praestitit, quo tibi aliquo officio meo rem dignam gratificarer. Nam iam pridem cupiebam occasionem offerri mihi morem gerendi tibi. Hominem actutum compraehendam compraehensumque torquebo ita, ut vel concoctum cybum omnem ei eruam e stomacho. Quem si conscium cuiuspiam adversus te perpetrandi facinoris offendero, vita privabo. Sin minus offendero, missum faciam inquiens, aberrasse me in se capiundo, non enim illum esse quem quaerebam."

[5] Fateor equidem, mi Aenea, vel ex iis verbis me illico de homine suspicatum monstri nescio quid. Caeterum quoniam satis mihi de sicario compertum videbatur, egi homini gratias de optima erga me voluntate. Capitur sicarius eodem vesperi. Captus torquetur, et mei interimendi causa se missum confitetur. Idque Honofrius continuo palam facit. Sed ab quo missus foret reticescit. Nec sicarium plectit. Sed differt animadversionem,

modo aliam causam obtendens, modo aliam at verisimilem nullam. Interea temporis increbrescit, non solum apud me sed apud nonnullos gravissimos civis tuos: Honofrium Tifernatem commutasse Philippum sicarium cum praetura Florentina.

Nihil est enim apud Florentinos usque adeo secretum atque arcanum, quod minus quam primum effluat, ita sunt omnes tanquam rimarum pleni. Quod rumoribus fuerat divulgatum, ipsius tandem rei eventus approbat. Nam paulo postea Florentiae praetor declaratus est Honofrius Tifernas.

[6] Sed redeo ad sicarium. Mulctavit hunc Honofrius libris quingentis. Erantque multo antea paratae pecuniae, quibus ille carcere liberatus remitteretur Florentiam. Et quod ridiculosius fuerat in sententia quam impudentissimus latro adversus sicarium tulerat, dicebat illum ad id facinoris perpetrandum fuisse corruptum grandi pecunia et magna remuneratione. Ab quo autem ab quibusve corruptus fuisset, subticuerat. Caeterum longe se sua de sceleratissimo sicario liberando fefellit opinio. Nam ego iniuriarum agens provocatione sum usus ex tuae patriae institutis ad praetorem. Itaque ea omnis causa ab Honofrio latrone devoluta est ad Iacobum Constantium siculum ex Messana qui vir innocentissimus et gravissimus ea tempestate praetorem gerebat Senae.

Hic si potuissem causam ex integro cognoscere, non obscure patuisset, et qui fuisset auctor Florentiae vulnerandi mei, et a quo idem sicarius missus Senam esset ad me interimendum. Nam Florentiae quoque patuit de sicario. Patuit de licitatore conductoreque sicarii. Is enim fuit homo impurissimus ac nequam Hieronymus Brochardus Immolensis. Sed qui fuerint facinoris auctores, qui mercedem quam pepigissent, sicario dissolverit, in obscuro sunt, cum tamen novere plures Laurentium Medicem una cum Nicolao et Carolo frequentare persaepe solitum omnium scelerum officinam infames aedis Hieronymi Brochardi per id temporis, quo sicarius est conductus. Idemque Laurentius Medices Hieronymum coniectum ob id sceleris in vincula carcere liberavit et ab omni poena tutatus est in maxima etiam totius civitatis offensione, quae tota eam inuriam publicam suamque ducebat. Sed vis magnitudoque pecuniae longe plus potuit ac polluit quam leges quam aequitas quam omne iuris piique vel officium vel sanctitas vel decorum.

Sed redeamus ad praetorem. Is inquam Iacobus Constantius cum non posset ex institutis patriae tuae eam de integro agitare causam, quam praefectus cognorat, sed augere poenam duntaxat quod potuit solum, eam Philippo sicario dextram abscidit publico iudicio, quae me Florentiae vulnerarat in faciem, obtruncassetque hominem, quo nece sua reliquis sicariis esset exemplo immanitatis suae, nisi ego id factum iri prohibuissem, utpote qui maluissem vivere illum vitam inutilem atque dedecorosam quam per expeditam mortem liberari animi cruciatu, ut enim magni est animi parvas suasque inurias oblivisci, ita iusti et sapientis de publico humani generis hoste dignam aliquam capere ultionem.

[7] Cum igitur neque pacate, ut audis, nec item commode agerem Senae videremque quanto cum vitae periculo inter gladios venenaque versarer, non enim defuere qui etiam domi ausi fuerunt me veneno perdere. Bononiam eo consilio me recepi ut paucos post menses Mediolanum petam futurus apud unicum nostrae tempestatis solem Philippum Mariam principem sane omnium qui aut sunt aut fuerunt aut futuri sunt munificentissimum et optimum. Apud hunc enim nullae mihi inimicorum artes, nullae insidiae oberunt. Totus ero cum Musis, totus cum amicis, totus mecum. Quod autem me hortaris ne deseram ipse me, ne cedam malignitati fortunae. Hortaris tu quidem et amice et recte. Iampridem animum meum nosti. Non is certe sum qui me nesciam virum esse. Itaque bono sis animo, per me licet. Nunquam me ignaviae accusabis, nec item insolentiae. Quin Horatianum praeceptum illud in universa tuebor vita; omne tulit punctum qui miscuit utile dulci. Tu vero quod ad te attinet, facito me de omni re tua statuque certiorem. Vale.

Filelfo to Francesco Sforza. A Commander's Responsibilities during the Siege and Sack of a City. 8 October 1438 (fols. 16–16v)

Quod ante instituerat consilium magnanime Imperator, festinat hoc tempore necessitas. Nam cum ab humanissimo socero tuo, Philippo Maria, divino Principe, essem nuper ornatissimis litteris, ut ad se irem quam liberalissime invitatus et id me facturum ipse recepissem [1]. Decreveram equidem anteaquam Mediolanum concederem et te visere et patriam, quo benivolum in se alter, altera gratum me esse experiretur [2]. Etenim patriae omnia debeo ab qua genitus, altus educatusque sim. Tibi vero ob praestantem animi tui probitatem inauditamque magnitudinem iampridem incredibili quadam benivolentia observantiaque afficior [3]. Sed mea haec animi sententia turbatur his rumoribus ac nunciis, qui de tua in Tholentinatis meos ira obsidioneque afferuntur; nunciatur enim vulgo te infesto agmine ingentique rerum omnium et formidabili apparatu processisse in Tholentinatem agrum [4]. Eoque igni ferroque vastato obsidere oppidum atque ipsis civibus, non capitivitatem et servitutem modo, sed omnem contumeliam caedemque minitari [5]. Quae quidem ipse audiens sum aeque miratus ac dolui. Qui enim fieri potest, ut tanta et tam eximia virtus tua quicquam audeat vel perpetrare vel moliri, quod non solum ab animo magno elatoque abhorreat, verum etiam iniquum sit et tetrum et immane [6] . . . Es ne oblitus longe magis arte atque beneficentia quam aut minis aut etiam vi et parari et conservari regnum [7]. Quibusnam rebus Cyrus a Medis imperium ad Persas transtulit? Nonne industria et animi magnitudine? Quibus Alexander ad Gangem usque penetravit? Nonne prudentia ac benignitate? Quibus tandem G. Iulius Caesar orbis terrae principatum adeptus est [8] . . . An ultio te delectat, quod aliquid fortassis adversus te (id quod tamen haud concesserim) Tholentinates conati fuerint? At ulcisci foeminarum philosophi, non magnanimi principis, non Francisci Sphortiae esse volunt. Audi quaeso sapientem illum Macedoniae regem, Philippum, Alexandri patrem, qui cum urbes Graeciae, quae malo in eum animo esse viderentur atque novis rebus plaerumque studerent; quidam consulerent praesidiis esse continendas, respondit malle pulchrum se longum tempus quam herum breve appellari. Intelligebat enim rex prudentissimus ea esse tutissima praesidia munitissimasque arces quae in hominum benivolentia caritateque fundatae ac firmatae forent. Nam adversus iustum idemque commune omnium odium nullae vires esse, nulla ingenia satis possunt . . . Capiuntur inquam animi populorum non minus, non minis, non terroribus, non vi, sed cum aliis nonnullis humanitatis officiis; tum blanditiis maxime, quibus cum minus apte Scipio ille posterior Africanus olim uteretur; repulsam habuit consulatus [9]. Itaque siquid praeter voluntatem tuam princeps inclyte Tholentinates ausi fuerint; tuum esse duco non modo non ulcisci, sed et ignoscere potius et eorum tibi animos mansuetudine, facilitate et beneficiis devincire [10] . . . Iustus vero ac beneficus esse nequeat qui aut aliis ultro nocuerit, aut modum rebus suis statuere, vel noluerit vel neglexerit [11]. Quare te Francisce Sphortia, per magnitudinem animi tui praeclarasque virtutes oro atque obtestor ut iram hanc istam omnem, siquam tandem in Tholentinatis meos iram conceptam habes, mitiges ac places. Et omnem denique perturbationem quae consilio prorsus rationique adversatur, prosternas atque abiicias [12]. Nemo scit aliis imperare qui sibi ipse non potest. Nulla victoria maior est, nulla illustrior quam seipsum vincere [13]. Violentum nihil est diuturnum pricipatus ille et firmus sane et perpetuus esse consuevit, quem tum probitatis aegregium aequitatisque exemplum peperit, tum pergrata placabilitas animi munificentiaque munierit [14] . . . Nam neque certe magni est animi admirari divitias, sed summi potius viri est omnia, quae vel corpori vel fortunae subiecta sunt, infra se ducere. Animus enim nobis divinus est, idemque sempiternus, caetera vero mortalia quaeque sunt et ad breve temporis curriculum duratura. Rationi semper, non cupiditati parendum est. Illa enim ostendit in primis quantum nos reliquis animantibus antecellimus [15] . . . Quod siquis a me quaesierit, quid facere oporteat bonum principem, facile constanterque, responderim, non quod temere vulgus solet, et amicis benefacere et malefacere inimicis. Nam id tyrannorum est proprium, sed quod prudentissime Aristo ille Lacedaemonius quod sapientissimus Socrates aliquando consuevit: tum amicis benefacere, tum inimicos reddere amicos [16] . . . Nonne Christus Ihesus humani redemptor generis etiam pro iis oravit, a quibus traditus morti esset? . . . Tu velim quaeque ab me dicta sunt in bonam partem dicta interpraetaris. Non enim me tua minus quam patriae causa, ut haec tam familiter ad te scriberem, hortata est

[17]. Nam et amo te unice et delector mirifice tuis laudibus [18], quas nequaquam—non dicam infamiae—sed ne suspitionis quidem labe pollui patiare, summis precibus abs te peto [19]. Vale princeps florentissime et si quid in me esse animadverteris quod vel usui tibi aliquando, vel voluptati futurum putes, id omne tibi deditum devotumque, intellige [20].

Filelfo to Bartolomeo Francanzani. On Pleasure 1 August 1428 (fol. 6)

Triplicem esse vitam hominibus praecipue expetendam praestantissimi philosophi tradiderunt: contemplationis, actionis, fruitionis. Contemplativa tota est animi, cuius sapientia dux est; activa corpori maxime opitulatur, quam prudentia moderatur et regit. Quae vero in fruendo versatur, eam referunt ad voluptatem, quae ipsa qualis sit, difficile est dictu. Et ne id quidem mirum habet enim magnos oppugnatores. Nam qui ita statuit voluptatem, ut nihil habeat cum ratione coniunctum, is ab enervata pecude nihil differt. Sed quae voluptas est secundum honestatem, hanc non multo ea puto inferiorem, si recte velimus interpretari, quae vera est voluptas et Christiana. Est enim posita et constituta in ea animi securitate tranquillitateque in qua nulli insunt stimuli, nulli tumultuarii motus, nullae perturbationes. Et hanc quidem Graeci *alypian* nominant, quam nos haud absurde appellemus indolentiam. At sunt qui insimulent voluptatem esse solius corporis ac turpem: quasi cum dicimus, "Tuae mihi litterae voluptatem incredibilem attulerunt," non animum laetari dicamus, sed corpus et id turpiter. Excedat e medio istiusmodi omnis calumniosa interpraetatio et ad animum enim et ad corpus refertur voluptas. Nec aliam id verbum significationem apud nos habet, quam *hedone* habeat apud Graecos. *Hedone* enim et animi est et corporis. Potestque et honesta et turpis esse secundum aut rationis aut temeritatis usum. Praeterea aeque inter animi bona voluptatem reponit Aristoteles ac prudentiam et virtutem. Nec sane vero, ut mihi videtur, insimulant Epicurum, quem voluptarium ac lascivum dicunt, cum illum et temperantem virum fuisse constat et eruditum et gravem, cuique praeter crebriora mordacioraque cavilla, quibus in caeteros philosophos utebatur, aliud arbitror obfuisse nihil. Caeterum constat enim virum non de corporis, sed de animi voluptate et sensisse et disseruisse . . . Veritatem vero in iis rebus sitam existimo quae sunt incommutabiles et aeternae. Quid autem aliud sit huiusmodi praeter unum et immortalem deum, haud quaquam intelligo.

Actiones vero ad veritatis intelligentiam ita iudico oportere accomodari, ut sciamus eas omnis ad imperium sapientiae esse referendas. Sapientia enim sola est ea quae, tanquam regina quaedam et imperatrix seque ipsa contenta, quo rerum istarum inferiorum et temporalium cura omni soluta in sempiterni ac supremi illius boni lucem et intendat et figat intutum, caeteris morum virtutibus prudentiam praeficit, quae praebitoris instar per singulas actiones singulis pro suo cuiusque officio faciunda tribuat. Moralis igitur virtutes omnis ad prudentiam referamus, oportet quae rationis est virtus. At prudentiae sapientia dominatur, quae tota est intellectus. Qui autem ita vixerit, qui hunc negat in summa voluptate versari ac plane foelicem et beatum esse, is mihi non stultus modo, sed fatuus et insanus videtur existimandus . . .

Note on the Editions

Filelfo produced, or permitted the production of, three major redactions of his *Epistolae familiares* in his lifetime. The most complete of all the redactions, and the only manuscript containing both his Greek and Latin letters, is Codex Trivulzianus 873, the *Epistolae familiares libri XLVIII*, which survives in a manuscript copy in the Biblioteca Trivulziana, Milan. This manuscript contains forty-eight books of Filelfo's letters. The letters are arranged in chronological order and dated, beginning in the year 1427 and ending in 1477. The watermarks found in this codex identify the paper as a type made in Milan, Cremona, and Pavia in 1480–1487. The codex first appeared in the Biblioteca Capitolare in Milan, to which Filelfo bequeathed his library.[1] A second redaction of his letters is a sixteen-book edition (ending with letters dated to 1461), the *Epistolae familiares libri XVI*. The first edition of the sixteen-book redaction was printed in Venice in 1473 by Wendelin of Speier (Hain, no. 12926). A third redaction of the letters, first printed in Venice in 1502 by Johannes and Gregorius Gregorius, is the *Epistolae familiares libri XXXVII*, which contains thirty-seven books. The Gregorius edition contains all the letters in the Wendelin of Speier edition and, moreover, twenty-one more books of letters dated from the years 1461–1473.[2]

The perhaps posthumously written manuscript Trivulzianus 873 is not only the most complete of the editions of the letterbook; it is also the most carefully edited, emended, and polished of all the editions.[3] Accordingly, it is from this manuscript that any new authoritative edition of the *Epistolae*

---

[1] Caterina Santorno, *I Codici medioevali della Biblioteca Trivulziana. Catalogo* (Milan, 1965), p. 222.

[2] The British Library Catalogue lists thirty-one editions of the *Epistolae* published prior to 1521; the National Union Catalogue lists an additional ten editions. For numerous individual letters and lists of the locations of codices containing letters, see Benadduci, ed., *Atti*, and Paul Oskar Kristeller, *Iter Italicum: A Finding List of Uncatalogued or Incompletely Catalogued Humanistic Manuscripts of the Renaissance in Italian or Other Libraries*, 3 vols. (London and Leiden, 1963, 1967, and 1983).

[3] The following conclusions on the three redactions are based on my collations of the first three books of Trivulzianus 873 with the 1473 *editio princeps* and the 1502 Venice edition, and my spot-checking a number of other early editions of the *Epistolae*.

should be prepared.[4] Trivulzianus 873 and the lost exemplar for the early printed editions of the letters were most certainly descendants of a single, carefully revised and edited manuscript of Filelfo's Epistolario, which contained both his Greek and Latin letters. The first thirty-seven books alone of the Trivulzian manuscript contain many longer versions of letters in the printed editions and, in addition, hundreds of letters not found in the printed editions. The printed editions, however, contain no texts not found in some form in the Trivulzian manuscript.

Filelfo appears in 1473—expressly for the use of Wendelin of Speier and perhaps in conjunction with compositors in the firm—to have put together a radically reduced version of the letterbook he had been assembling for over twenty years.[5] In October 1473 he testified that his "German printers" had recently requisitioned the copying out of thirty-seven books of his letters in preparation for their publication.[6] The much abbreviated thirty-seven-book epistolario that he or his editors prepared at this time for his printers was undoubtedly the exemplar from which the subsequent printed editions of his letters were derived.

Seen as a group, the printed editions constitute one tradition while the Trivulzian manuscript represents another. The printed editions differ markedly from the Trivulzian manuscript, both in format and content. In addition to having fewer books than the Trivulzian manuscript, the printed editions have none of Filelfo's Greek letters, and many of the Latin ones have been either shortened or excised altogether. The book divisions in the printed editions also differ radically from those in the Trivulzian manuscript. In short, while the Trivulzian manuscript must have been a very close copy of the original manuscript of Filelfo's letterbook, the printed editions were another step removed from it. It is also clear that the original manuscript of Filelfo's letterbook must have been a difficult hand to read, and one with many more abbreviations than Trivulzianus 873, since most of the errors in the printed editions are either obvious misreadings of characters (such as *n* for *h*) or misconstrued abbreviations of words.

The letter texts in Appendix A (and elsewhere in the book) have been adapted from the 1502 Venice edition, the most complete and authoritative of all the printed editions of the *Epistolae*. I have retained the orthography of the 1502 edition, altering only the consonant *u* to *v*, expanding its abbreviations, and modernizing its punctuation. Wherever obvious errors in the edition required emendation I have consulted the Trivulzian manuscript for the correct reading.

---

[4] V. S. Giustiniani is preparing a new critical edition of the letters at present.

[5] See Filelfo, *Epistolae*, to Niccolò Ceba (16 February 1451), fol. 62v, in which he announces, for the first time, his decision to publish his collected letters.

[6] Trivulzianus, to Marco Aureli (8 October 1473), fol. 451 [= Rosmini, 2.488]: "Nam Germani isti, librorum impressores quos apellant, libros mearum epistolarum septem ac triginta exscribi curaverunt. Itaque et epistolas caeteras meas et te in illis brevi visurus es."

APPENDIX B

SFORZIAD, BOOK 3

Aurea noctifugus iam Lucifer astra fugabat,
Sphortia cum somni specie vinclisque solutus
parebat soceri monitis pugnamque parabat
impiger; et quidquid nullis hortantibus olim
facturus fuerat, tanto studiosius urget, 5
quod sibi caelicolas certam promittere voti
spem nosset. Praesens age fare Polymnia, quonam
ordine principio veniens obsederit urbem
et quid quoque modo fuerit molitus in omne
Martis opus, captam quo mox victricibus armis 10
invitus multumque dolens mitissimus heros
verterit in praedam superis damnantibus ipsis.
Cum praemissa Padum Ticini pulcherrima classis
praesidiis certoque vigil custode teneret
ac dux bellipotens firmato ponte ligasset 15
navibus innumeris et multo robore flumen,
qua Laudensiaco postquam cessisset ab agro,
arma simul turmasque virum et felicia secum
signa Placentinas properans transvexit in oras.
Omnia qui primum blande mitique benignus 20
aggreditur temptare via nil flaebile prae se,
nil hostile ferens; sed ubi iam tempus inane
ire videt sentitque nihil prodesse monendo,
arte minas addens terretque docetque ruinam
urbis et irati quinam sit militis usus 25
immanisque furor; cum se per tristia cernit
vulnera victorem, tum incommoda quaeque disertus
uxores natasque rapi caedemque virorum
ante oculos ponens millena obprobria monstrat.
At neque blandiciis miseri nulloque moventur 30
hortatu temnuntque minas. Convicia linguae
insuper addentes iaculisque repellere coram
fulmineisque parant pilulis arcere loquentem.
Quare ubi dux ingens temptaverat omnia frustra
et quid fata velint liquido iam novit, in armis 35
castra movet propius pugnamque instructus ad omnem

nixius incumbit terraque Padoque. Tremendus
obsidet infestam validis cum viribus urbem.
Occupat ipse viam Parmensem milite forti;
ad dextramque sui statuit te, Karole, iuxta   40
Eridani ripas, ut cum petat usus, in ipsam
praefectus propere possis conscendere classem.
At Perusina phalanx, natus quam ducit uterque,
Nicoleos dux clare tuus, consederat illic,
qua Ligurum montes adeunt unaque Guidonis   45
arma Faventini. Lodovicus castra tenebat
Vermius ad portam, qua recto limite celsam
Derthonam petimus, via qua sublata vocatur.
Sic alii circum peditesque equitesque locati
obsedere urbem. Nam classis clauserat omne   50
auxilium, quodcunque Padus noctuve dieve
adveheret. Caelum vix tutum restat et aether.
Sic obsessa igitur, sic oppugnata diebus
dura quaterdenis et quattuor inscia somni
urbs et opis pauper—nisi quam sibi quisque parabant   55
obsessi—nulli poterat cessisse labori.
Nam tormenta quidem iam murum funditus omnem
turbarant. Qua Porta vetus Cornelia turrim
ingentem caeloque parem per saecula multa
servarat, turrisque simul prostrata iacebat   60
restabatque agger tantum. Quencunque ruinam
venturam veriti muro turrique caventes
addiderant cives. Agger sublimior omnes
hostilis aditus duplicis munimine fossae
arcebat. Nam fossa vetus distabat ab urbe;   65
quantum lata quidem pauloque superbior ipsum
extera cingebat via per pomoeria murum.
Ast ubi tormentis cives hunc cedere norunt,
mox aliam tali, quae muro fossa subesset,
effodere via, ne, si fortasse priorem   70
transiliant hostes quae multo latior esset
ac facilis captu, muro potiantur et ipso.
Hanc autem tanto rebantur posse tueri
tutius ac melius, quod subterranea, murus
qua patefactus erat, praeberet porta ferentem   75
egressum in fossam, qua de subeuntia taelis
agmina vel tecti cives propellere possent.
Sphortia sed contra geminas deducere turris
imperat, extremo primae quas margine fossae

collocat; e regione quidem qua porta ferebat   80
in fossam constructa novam. De turribus altis
fulmineae volitant pilulae volucresque sagittae:
omne genus taeli quae, quamquam tegmine fossae
altius armatos non quibant laedere, verum
(dum peterent fossam) visos in limine portae   85
vulneribus crebris et saeva caede premebant.
Tunc igitur Venetum ductor Thaddaeus in armis
fortis et ipse quidem sed non callentior usu,
nequid taela queant portam egredientibus ullum
iniecisse metum nec tristis vulnera loeti,   90
aequatas afferre trabes ubi iusserat, altum
occupat his limen portae labrumque profundae
oppositum fossae, quae tanquam ponte ligata
non solum excipiat cives ex urbe profectos,
hostibus at praestet facilem super aggere saltum.   100
Haec ubi vidisset belli doctissimus heros,
sentit adesse diem, qua sit victoria tandem
in manibus iam certa suis. Miseretur acerbae
sortis et obsessos affatu hortatur amico:
"O miseri cives, quae vos tam dura volentis   105
fata premunt? In vos an coniurastis atroces?
Sat Venetis fideique datum, non vestra videtis
excidia et mortes? Rabidas quis temperet iras
militis armati? Murus radicitus omnis
en cecidit turrisque minax. Fore creditis ullo   110
aggere vos tutos? Nam quae fiducia fossae
vana iuvat? Sani monitus admittite nostros.
Dedite vos nostrae fidei nullasque furentis
fortunae temptate vices. Ego vestra tuebor
commoda; nil vobis quod vos nolitis inique   115
fiet ab Insubribus." Quod postquam perculit aures
nomen ab Insubribus populi, quicunque vetustas
sub duce iam Poeno praedas meminisset et ignis
ingentesque alias clades furit, efferus, "Arma!
Arma!" iterum ingeminans ferit altum clamor Olympum.   120
Quin et tergeminae catapultae ex aggeris imis
emissae speculis totidemque per aera saevo
turbine contortae pilulae tibi certa ferebant
vulnera, dux ingens, quas Pallas comminus astans
excipit obiectu clipei reicitque rotatas.   125
Sic ubi se frustra mitem placidissimus heros
tam multumque diuque dedit novitque monendo

iam tandem prodesse nihil, ne longior esset
dedecori mora forte sibi, iubet ocius omnem
aequari fossam, facilis quo transitus esset   130
militibus dura cupientibus urbe potiri.
Musculus armatae plenus fortisque iuventae
ducitur in fossam, quam sic quos intus habebat
funditus aequabant, ut tali tegmine tuti
hostis ab assidua taelorum grandine sensim   135
progrederentur opus facientes. Omnia cives
quae postquam norunt percussi corda trementi
obstupuere metu. Vacuus formidine solus
perstitit Alberthus; cunctos solatur et una
solus opem reperit. Veterem quae circuit arcem   140
nuper humo fusam divi post fata Philippi,
ingens fossa fuit, penitus quaecunque fluenti
exundabat aqua. Structus mox alveus illam
excipit ac fossae mittit, quam musculus aequat.
Sic frustratur opus. Nam nec procedere contra   145
musculus, aequari poterat nec fossa ruenti
vi impedientis aquae; quin et quos ipse tegebat
musculus innumero figunt (exire volentis)
vulnere qui fossae tecti munimine pugnant.
Non illos iaculum, non flamae, scorpio nullus,   150
fulmineaeve trucis poterant offendere plumbi
contortae pilulae, non orbicularia saxa,
aenea quae iacerent tormenta ferentia luctum.
Sic igitur frustra tot postquam Sphortia luces
consumpsisse videt, nullisque laboribus urbem   155
assidui nullo frangi discrimine Martis,
malleque vel praedae positam loetique periclo
Hadriacis servare fidem quam certa salutis
munera complecti, meditans nil longius esse
cunctandum, iubet armatos clangore tubarum   160
acciri socios cunctasque audire cohortes.
Iam radiis Phoebus primis surgebat Eoo,
cum niveo sublimis equo dux clarus in armis
talibus alloquitur stimulans in praelia turmas.
"Credideram, socii, nostra ut patientia tandem   165
flecteret ingratos et nostris adderet ultro
partibus obsessos; hinc vestris viribus uti
distuleram. Nec enim me fugerat inclyta virtus,
qua mira cum laude viros excellitis omnis.
Luce equidem prima vobis vincentibus urbem   170

ipse Placentinam cepissem; nulla nec arma
nec vires hominum nostris obsistere fatis
quivissent. Verum libuit miserescere tantae
cladis et hostilis quam fert victoria praedae.
At postquam nullis monitis nullique periclo   175
dant aures mentemve feri quaeruntque volentes
exitium, capiant quam promeruere furoris
mercedem. Doleo—superum mihi rector adesto
testis—ut invitus populor quam vincimus urbem.
Quid faciam tandem? Iam quadragemimus instat   180
en, socii, quintusque dies, obsedimus ex quo
hanc urbem. Veneti classem viresque pararunt;
auxilio ingentis aderunt ad moenia raptim.
Praeterea en hyemis vis intolerabilis atrae
irruit. Hesterni qui fusi caelitus imbres   185
exauxere Padum nobisque tulere timorem
horroremque simul? Iam nix riget alta propinquis
collibus; armentis glacies vetat horrida nostris
pabula. Consuevi nunquam nisi victor abire,
hostis ubi fixis posui tentoria signis.   190
Quin etiam Insubribus gravis est mora nostra putantque
consulto mihi bella trahi. Quapropter eatur
denique et ultrici cedat dementia poenae.
Karole, praefectus classem conscende propinquam
remulcoque gravem forti cum milite muros   195
mox adigens pugnare para, qua labitur auctus
imbribus hesternis Trebia, qui manat ab alto
atque Pado Fufusta gravi. Sic milite quisque
qua sedet, invadat pugnaque armisque lacessat.
Interea nunquam cessent tormenta rotantis   200
intorquere pilas ac muros vertere saxo.
Hic erit ille dies, qui vos opibusque bonisque
omnibus accumulet. Tantum meminisse decebit
numinis atque aequi: templis, rogo, parcite; virgo
salva sit; in praeda nihil admiscete profanum."   205
Dixerat; atque hilares cunctae assensere cohortes.
Parte alia postquam pugnae videre ferocis
signa Placentini, totam citus excitat urbem
clamor et arma simul cuncti iuvenesque senesque
expediunt. Nec non muliebris turba ministrat   210
omne genus taeli. Metus atque audacia certant.
Unus erat Veneta de nobilitate Gerardus
Dandalus ingenti probitate insignis et idem

maximus eloquio, qui quantum Sphortia cunctis
mortales unus praestaret laudibus omnes   215
iam pridem longe per multa pericula norat;
hic igitur postquam vidisset certa parari
praelia et eventum pugnae clademque timeret,
talibus hortatur cives reliquasque cohortis:
"Magnanimi cives, quorum pietasque fidesque   220
in Venetos perspecta patres erit omne per aevum,
clarior ad nostros omnis ventura nepotes,
en acies hostilis adest, quae vulnus et ignem
ac genus omne probri scelerato pectore verset
huius in excidium summum tam nobilis urbis.   225
Nunc opus est animo. Nunc vires promite vestras.
Si pugnare manu, si vanum corde timorem
pellere pergamus, nobis victoria certa est.
Quid noceant hostes? Prostrarunt ictibus esto
millibus attritum longaevo tempore murum.   230
At superest agger, qui muro tutior omni
stipatur trabibus validis et vimine multo.
Hunc vis nulla queat, non saxa domare superbis
excita tormentis. Sunt et munimina fossae.
Est etiam nobis fortisque et multa iuventus.   235
Sunt arma atque equitum turmae peditumque manipli:
est peregrina phalanx, quae nullos horreat hostes,
quae mortem perferre velit pro munere laudis.
Commodiore loco nobis pugnare licebit,
unde labor nullus subeuntis comminus hostes   240
detorquere manu. Verum licet eminus illos
sistere vulneribus, modo sint tormenta, sagittae
saxaque cum iaculis quavis statione parata.
Quod si quos propius tulerit dementia, calce
ferventique ruamus aqua. Sicisque petamus   245
ensibus hastatis clavisque feraque securi
Non equites valeant muris ipsisve potiri
aggeribus. Pedites vix attollantur inermes.
Hos autem armati non deturbare queamus
et miseris mactare modis? At Karolus, aiunt,   250
qui nihil horrebit, potietur moenibus altis.
Nam mali superant turres, quorum ipse superbus
quisque minas et lata gerit tabulata caruchus.
Quid tandem? Tantamne pedes tot Karolus inter
illustres equitum circum pomoeria turmas   255
intima dispositas descendere temptet in urbem?

Non faciat sane; nam Martis callidus omnes
edidicit numeros Nec se vincendus iniquae
committat pugnae: terrori Sphortia tales
constituit nugas. At vos audentius ite   260
et pugnate feri. Nam si vos fortiter ire
viderit in pugnam nullasque timore pericli
detrectare vices, avertet signa repente
transibitque Padum. Nam non est longius ullam
ut possit differre moram; nanque ostia classis   265
narratur subisse Padi, quae millia secum
tot vehit, ut cuneis vix pluribus agmina terram
Dardaniam petiisse ferant. Metuisse Cremonae
qui debet vel iure quidem rebusque suorum
atque suis, num posse putem ratione furorem   270
Insubrium propria nunc pluris ducere? Non est,
non est Franciscus quem vanus ceperit error.
Prospicit ipse sibi. Festinat ferre Cremonae
auxilium atque suis; illic carissima coniunx
ac dulces nati et rerum tutela suarum.   275
Quid quod cogit hyems invitum castra movere?
Quantus heri terror cunctos invasit, ut imbres,
ut Padus invaluit; vidistis ferre natantis
flumen equos, stabulis quos diripuisset ab altis.
Hinc igitur temptare parat fiducia vestrum   280
quae teneat pectus. Si vos audentius ire
aspiciet contra, retrahet sua signa; nec armis
contendet frustra producere tempus inane.
Sin minus audentes aut armis segnius uti
senserit, incumbet foeta truculentior ursa.   285
Romulidum proles dura, quos prima colonos
deduxit fortuna die, durate; nec aspris
cedite temporibus. Propere fortuna secundis
flatibus aspirans vos rebus dextera laetis
efferet atque bonis cumulabit grata beatis.   290
Brixia quos nuper noctesque diesque labores
pertulit? Et quantis est circumsepta periclis?
Nicoleos ingens, Perusinae gloria gentis,
armorumque decus, pugnandi fulmen et horror
obsidet hanc nostro nudatam milite, nullis   295
viribus adiutam. Muros evertit et altam
ingentemque capit multo cum robore turrim.
Contra autem cives animis audentibus urgent
nec cedunt taelis, non igni: grandinis instar

dum plumbi crepitant pilulae, cum saxeus orbis 300
intonat et late prosternit cuncta ruina.
Acrius incumbunt probitatis praemia vita
ducentes potiora omni quae laude careret.
Scilicet audierant patriam quicunque tuentes
oppeterent mortem non solum linquere nomen 305
immortale suis famaque per omnia dulci
saecula victuros, sed multo grandius ipsos
munus apud superos multoque illustrius aetas
nulla quod interimat laturos, quippe beatos
quos fore nemo negat. Favit deus optimus urbi; 310
mox et enim superatus abit turbatus ab alta
turre ferox hostis civilis robore pugnae.
Odit enim deus ipse viros, quicunque rapina
ducuntur praedaeque inhiant aliena petentes.
At iustisque probisque favet. Dum Brixia sese 315
hostis ab infesti tutatur fortius armis
atque fidem Veneto servat tam firma senatu,
consulit ipsam sibi. Nam libertate quieta
nunc fruitur nulli cedens ingentibus urbi
divitiis. Nec enim Venetus iuga dura subire 320
cogit eos quicunque suis se partibus addunt.
Sed socios fratresque putat laetatus amici
nomine non famuli; nec cuique reddere grates,
sed meruisse cupit. Nunquam vos pressimus armis
terruimusve minis; ultro venistis et urbem 325
egregii cives Veneto nil tale senatu
mente volutanti, dum traditis ore benigno.
Nil aliud petitis, nisi ne subeatis iniquum
Insubrium tetrumque iugum. Miserescimus et vos
humana pietate; citi non laude nec ulla 330
spe lucri aut quaestus nostris ascripsimus aeque
civibus ac proprios cives. Volumusque tueri
arma per et vitam, modo vos estote per omne
officium rebus vestris vobisque fideles.
Ponite ante oculos, ubi segnius ire periclis 335
ac levius pugnare manu studeatis, anhaeli
immanisque hostis ludibria mille deorum
templa per et natas et amatae coniugis omne
dedecus atque probrum. Vestras meminisse cathaenas
ne pigeat qualesque faces iniecerit olim 340
Insubrium vestrae dux urbi saevus Amilcar.
Sin vestris alacres pergetis rebus adesse,

cernite quae rebus accedet gloria vestris,
principe sub Veneto quanta emolumenta laboris."
Dixerat. Et magnam laeta spem fronte gerebat,   345
cum tegeret tristi trepidas sub pectore curas.
At populus quanquam dictis lenitur amicis,
sollicitus tamen ipse gravis terrore pericli
obticet occulto gemitu suspiria ducens.
Haud tamen Alberthus, quanquam ventura timebat
fata sagax, siluisse potest, quin talibus orsus
nos ait: "O Venetum legate vir acer et ingens,   350
fortunae semper soliti contemnere fraudes
atque minas sola probitatis ducimur aura.
An velit incolumnes certae superesse ruinae,
nos deus omnipotens hic solus novit opemque
ferre potest. Non est ut nostris gaudeat hostis   355
moenibus immunis poenae quam reddere dignam
ultrix ira solet. Nam vel vincemus ovantes
vel simul eversa cuncti moriemur in urbe,
tu modo fac, miles ne nos peregrinus in ipso
deserat ancipitis fugiens certamine pugnae."   360
Talia dum Scoptus loquitur iam Sphortia turmas
moverat infestas totisque e partibus urbem
invadebat atrox. Hinnitus clangor et altus
clamor et horrisoni tonitrus quos aenea reddunt
ictibus assiduis tormenta minantia luctum;   365
tellurem pontumque simul caelumque fragore
terrebant. Animis cives ingentibus adsunt
pro muris mortemque pati quam cedere malunt.
Sphortia bellipotens primae sub margine fossae
sistit eos, quicumque manu iacere eminus ictum   370
aut valeant nervo celeris et fune sagittas
tormentisve citis pilulas torquere frementes.
Hos autem cunctos clipeis armata iuventus
texerat, aggeribus ne quae stipata ruebant
laedere taela queant et tristi tradere loeto.   375
Post illos equitatus erat sublimis in hastas
qui "Praedam praedamque!" ferox clamore cieret.
At qua parte Padus Fufustam mittit in amnem,
Karolus urgebat classis discrimine muros.
Sic igitur cunctis qua circum parte sedebant   380
dispositis iussuque ducis clangore tubarum
in trepidam toto properantibus agmine pugnam,
turbine terrifico iaciuntur taela. Sagittae

in muros urbemque volant. Pila saxea praeceps
fulminis instar abit crassoque sub aggere fumat.   385
Hinc pedites alii quibus est data cura ruebant
ac superant fossam, quos nec diffusa moratur
vis salientis aquae nec saxa rotata sudesque.
Iamque propinquabant fossae, quam tecta tenebant
arma virum cuneique graves densique manipli.   390
Hic primum magnis pugnatur viribus; omne
hic animique manusque premunt in praelia robur.
Hic obscura quidem taelorum fervet utrinque
tempestas; hic saxa ruunt; hic ferreus imber
hinc atque inde cadit. Mors ingruit undique saevo   395
vulnere. Certatim pereunt perimuntque vicissim.
Instant Sphortiadae fossam superare patentem
pila per et gladios tollique sub aggere saltu.
Obsessi contra fossae munimine et alto
aggere nituntur defendere moenia nullis   400
cedentes vicibus. Mortem dulcedine laudis,
natorumque metu, misera pietate parentum,
coniugis et patriae nimia formidine temnunt.
Haud hoc pugna loco tantum fervescit; at omni
Mars de parte furit murosque urbemque lacessens.   405
Sed magis atque magis validos Bellona fatigat
dura Placentinos, qua Karolus aestuat armis
Herculea feritate minax. Hic navibus altis
venerat ad muros et tristi percitus ira.
Iam prope sublimem turrim sublimior ipse   410
ceperat, extemplo cum se Cytherea furenti
obtulit; et "Quae te," dixit, "mens excitat ardens,
Karole care mihi? Caedem meditaris et ignes?
Tantum parce nefas manibus patrare cruentis
atque animos cohibere para. Si, Karole, nostris   415
parueris monitis, ingens tibi gratia facti
reddetur. Pulchris nam quam praestare puellis
omnibus Insubrium fatearis nomine Lydam,
dulce per obsequium iungam tibi munere tali."
Dixit et avertens mirum spiravit odorem.   420
Hic stupet atque animos flectit miseratus et urbem
ac promissa deae memori sub pectore servans.
Interea cunctae dum vires undique duro
Marte Placentinos oppugnant nullaque cives
vulnera detrectant, sed contra fortius instant,   425
dumque sagittarum volitant ex aggere nimbi

saxaque cum iaculis feriunt de turribus altis,
"Ite, mei socii," Franciscus clamitat, "Ite.
Expugnate citi. Ne parcite longius urbi
ingratae," quae sic dicens calcaribus armos   430
urgebat spumantis equi fossamque premebat
transiliens. Superi, facinus prohibete nefandum.
Iam pedibus sese quadrupes tollebat in altum,
cum pila fulmineo contorta ex aere ruebat
candentis sub pectus equi, quam struxerat hostis   435
impius, ut tanto privaret lumine terram.
Illa ruit penetrans immani turbine primum
pectus equi longumque uterum partesque repostas.
Eminus inde volans et lata per agmina praeceps
fulminat ac vasta vix tandem caede quiescit.   440
O superi, quae tanta hominum doctrina, quod acre
ingenium terris potuit reperire, quod ipse
Iupiter exorto de nubibus excutit igni.
Num vis tanta hominis pectus tenet, omnia prorsus
ut se posse putet, quaecunque potentior audet   445
(quam sator ipse deum peperit) natura creatrix?
Num salicis carbo sulfurque et quenque madenti
calce tulit paries, sal et aeri subditus ignis
fulmineo tonitru saxum orbiculare furentis
intorquere valent tanta cum mole ruinae?   450
Labitur extemplo sonipes miserandus; at heros
Sphortia, quem praesens deus ad maiora reservat,
non secus immoto se pectore praestitit, alto
quam Leucas pelago firmis radicibus haeret.
Dum rueret quadrupes, stetit hic sublimis et hostes   455
increpat obsessos. Cui mox in tempore Mavors
visus adesse manu laevam capit; altera nanque
tollitur ense minax et talia fatur ad aures:
"Sphortia care deis, te loeto credidit atrox
qui dedit hostis equum. Te Iupiter ipse tuetur.   460
Ast ego, quod valeo, pugnae tibi semper in omnes
casus ductor ero. Quod nunc res ipsa diesque
poscit, equum nostro cape de grege. Duxerat illum,
qui, quasi Bucephalus, tutum discrimine ab omni
te servet fundatque suo terrore catervas,   465
hostili quaecunque manu tibi praelia temptant."
Dixit; et ardentem clipeum concussit et hastam
transliensque celer fossas super aggere saevus
emicuit. "Praedamque fero!" ter subdidit ore.

Obstupuere omnes: et qui sua moenia servant,   470
quique Placentinos cupiunt superare furores.
Spes hos certa tenet; metus illos opprimit acer.
Hoc etiam signo Franciscus alacrius omnes
hortatur socios similique ardore per ipsa
taela volat nullumque timet de moenibus ictum.   475
Nam quis obesse queat cui sit deus ipse saluti?
Aggere tres aderant quos nullus abegerat horror,
taelorumve globi, non certae mortis imago:
Siccus Alexander, Basianus stirpe Gravignus,
Dalmaticaque satus regione Georgius audax   480
centurio fortisque nimis, qui lucidus armis
hastato domat ense viros et mittit ad Horchum,
se propius quicunque ferunt. Hac fervidus illac
dum furit et validis incumbit viribus, ecce
fulgureo micat igne tonans pila saxea pectus   485
quae medium miseri tanta cum mole premebat,
impetuosa ruens, ut totam spargeret urbem
ossibus attritis armisque et carne Georgi.
Proximus huic steterat Basianus fortia iactans
brachia caede natans, quam sica armatus adunca   490
ingentem dederat. Sed et hunc pila saxea summo
vertice dum peteret, non hunc. Nam fugerat ictum
pronus humi lapsus, tabulam sed percutit ille,
tegmine quo tutus centum mactaverat hostes.
Nunc tabulae nimia contusus mole ruentis   495
sternitur extincti similis. Formidine cunctis
aggere submotis et tanta caede fugatis,
solus Alexander gladioque insignis et hasta
restabat, qui nulla timens nec taela nec hostes
nunc stricto ferit ense viros, nunc cuspide terret,   500
nunc ferventis aquae vi multa aut calce feroces
obruit urenti. Nanque haec super aggere vulgus
omnia foemineum media inter taela parabat.
Tantus amor patriae, tantus metus arripit omnes.
Iam magis invicti ducis ira magisque calebat,   505
cum duo Picentum geniti de sanguine fratres,
quae fossae iunxere labrum cum limine portae
illius occultae, trabibus super alta minantes
constiterant saltuque parant super aggere tolli.
Quos ut Alexander vidit, salientis apertum   510
occupat os facibus; rigido premit ense secundum.
Tunc autem Alberthus postquam liquisse videbat

auxilium fossae, quibus est data cura tuendae.
Nam Pilius comitesque omnes ducis arma timentes,
qui super astiterat veluti Iovis ales olores   515
rapturus sub nube volans, mox ocius aura
confugere simul linquentes tegmina fossae.
"O Thaddaee," inquit, "pontem construximus hosti.
Ecce trabes aditum praebent in moenia. Solus
aggere pro capto Siccus iam grandine tectus   520
taelorum lassusque mora pugnaque resistit
hostibus infestis. Miles peregrinus ab omni
Marte vacat. Cives, qua sunt statione locati,
fortiter incumbunt muros patriamque tuentes.
Ni iubeas aliquos de tot quas ipse cohortis   525
hic vacuas astare vides, discrimen inire
et conferre manus hostemque repellere pugna,
en urbs capta perit." Iubet hic succedere Sicco.
Nemo audit. Formido necis iam ceperat omnes.
Dandalus ut tanto cordis torpore Gerardus   530
arma videt peregrina premi; nihil ipse moratus
Alberthusque simul sese super aggere coram
ostendunt. Martemque cient, quos deinde secuti
sunt plures—sed quid frustra contendimus unquam
invitis superis? Hominum delicta nefasque   535
bella per et caedes punit deus. Aggere postquam
Sphortia suspexit validas insistere vires;
ac pugnam instaurare manu iubet inclytus heros
Tristanum se patre satum Bosumque parente
munimenta cito pariter conscendere saltu.   540
Hi parent; rapidique super sese aggere tollunt:
armati cestu Bosus, Tristanus et hasta
enseque fulmineo, quibus invadentibus ictus
occurrunt varii. Verum Tristanus ut hastam
fregit et haerentem loetali in vulnere liquit   545
Euryopos Cyprii (qui se petulantius audax
obtulerat) facit ense viam; cunctisque tremendus
hinc atque inde furit misera cum strage ruentum.
At Bosus triplici loro triplicique rigentem
glande ferox cestum, postquam prius arte rotasset   550
altius attollens, deflexit robore tanto,
ut tris luce viros uno privarerit ictu.
Hic perit in cerebrum penetranti glande per ipsum
quem conum fregisset iens; ruit alter ab alto
vulnere, quod foedum sedisset fronte sub ima.   555

Tertius excussis cum mento dentibus omni
occidit infelix pedibusque cadavera pulsat.
Nec tamen obsessi cedunt, sed morte ruentes
nituntur pensare Lares dulcisque Penates.
Aggere pugnabant validis utrinque lacertis,   560
nec tamen hostiles, qui iam plaerique manipli
illic constiterant, poterant descendere in urbem
ob turmas equitum quas circumstare videbant.
Quid facerent pedites, quos armatura tegebat
aut nulla aut levior tot turmas inter equestris   565
omnibus ornatas armis, seu laedere malint
seu pugnam perferre trucem? Tum maximus heros
ulterius nil esse ratus discrimine tanto
cunctandum convertit equum, qua porta propinquat
tergeminis occlusa seris fortique virorum   570
custodita manu, quo, cum venisset, apertae
sponte ducem valvae—tantus stupor omnia turbat—
accipiunt audetque moras innectere nemo
aut pugnare manu. Quis enim minus horreat unum
cuius caelicolas cunctos curare salutem   575
noverit incolumemque omni servare periclo?
Unus erat Crete quem miserat effera Tharson
mole gigantea cunctis horrendus et audax.
Hic postquam nullo portam custode patentem
magnanimumque heroa videt lucentibus armis   580
moenibus exceptum, furit acri fervidus ira.
Ac geminis manibus sublimis in aera clavam
tollit, ut in galeam faeralem intorqueat ictum.
Sphortia cum propere vaehementius ense rotato
obvius occurrit, vulnusque manusque recidit.   585
Ille dolore gravi confectus in aethera voces
luctificas mittens fratrem Morona vocabat.
Continuo qui se furibundus ut obtulit alto
vectus equo iactansque minas harpenque coruscans
loetiferum medio cepit sub pectore vulnus   590
efflavitque animam. Cui Thrax successerat Aphron
Illyrica genetrice satus sed patre Molosso.
Is grave dum saxum, quod vix bis quina virorum
corpora quivissent, tollit missurus in hostem,
ense caput scindi collumque et pectora sensit.   600
Extimuere omnes; nec iam se comminus ullus
ferre audet, tantus terror ducis occupat omnis.
Sic ubi sublatis certis custodibus omne

praesidium terrore fugit portamque relinquit,
irrumpunt alii subito totamque furentes   605
horrisonis miscent late clamoribus urbem.
At peregrina phalanx postquam intra moenia vidit
signa colubriferi ducis et fulgentibus alis
regalem cognovit avem, perterrita solo
palluit aspectu: veluti qui caerula verrens   610
securus spirante noto videt ostia ponti
Euxinumque audet pelagus superare carina;
quod si trux Aquilo subitis perflare procellis
coeperit et vastos ad caelum tollere fluctus,
pallidus extimuit quaerens ullane tueri   615
se statione queat. Legio peregrina repente
nil cunctata fugae sese omnis tradit et arcem
occupat; ac frustra revocat Thaddaeus et orat.
Tunc etiam cives muros, munimina, turris
deseruere metu celeres sua tecta petentes   620
quilibet. Hos dulces nati, carive parentes,
aut uxor iucunda trahit, sed plurimus illos
thesaurus nummique vocant. Tamen omnibus ingens
stringit pectus amor patriae pereuntis et ipsum
mancipii nomen. Quare se quisque paternis   625
aedibus invicto conantur corde tueri,
transversisque vias trabibus durisque cathaenis
impediunt. Sperantque mora cohibere furorem
hostilem miseri, cum mox e partibus omnes
omnibus irrumpunt flagrantque cupidine praedae.   630
Obsessam quicunque dies tot Marte feroci
pressissent urbem, ruit undique et undique nimbus
militis armati peditesque equitesque tumultu
omnia miscentes findunt clamoribus auras.
Districtisque seges gladiis hastisque coruscat   635
ferrea concussis. Urbs praedae exponitur omnis;
non impunae tamen sublimes nanque fenestrae
omne genus taeli detorquent; arma ministrat
ira fremens trepidusque metus. Ruit imber ab omni
saxorum tecto iaculisque frequentibus horret   640
omne solum. Caedes late premit alta cruorem.
Nec minus interea quos spes vocat improba praedae
et quos ira movet tantis in luctibus audent.
Contempta sed morte ruunt per taela, per ictus
et superant quaecunque modo factura putarat   645
urbs miseranda moram. Nulla impedimenta retardant

hostilem rabiem. Foribus furit ille securi
ingeminans ictus ac vastans cuncta ruina.
Hic postes petit armatos nec vulnera curat
horridus; ille audet scalis aut fune fenestras 650
aut hasta subiisse gravi, labensque dehorsum
obrutus innumeris taelis et mole ruenti;
sic iterumque iterumque parat contusus et altum
saucius ardenti voto praedaque potiri.
Ianua quam multus custos atque arma tuentur, 655
postquam multa diu temptavit praelia frustra,
cogitur infelix tandem concedere. Nanque
valvas flama vorans summa ad fastigia raptim
volvitur exuperans undanti vortice tectum.
Mille vias hominum mens et permotio praeceps 660
invenit. Ingenio nihil est quod cedere musset—
aera compositis tranavit Daedalus alis.
Vincuntur miseri cives iam vulnere lassi
ac vacui taelis. Hululatus in aera maestus
tollitur. Hic virgo rapitur; coniunxque pudica 665
hic spectante viro patitur quodcunque libido
imperet atque furor. Nam quis dux fraena protervis
militibus posuisse queat, perfusa cruore
dum paritur rabidis tristis victoria tanto?
Omnia diripiunt: non templis parcitur ipsis; 670
cuncta profanantur. Non solum virgo dicata
casta deo genus omne probri per dedecus atrum
fert invita gemens ac flaetu sydera testans;
hostia quinetiam qua corpus rite sacratum
regis Olympiaci tanta pietate veremur— 675
ut res turpis—humi iacitur, quo parvulus ipse
thesaurus, quo tecta sedet loculusque nefandis
sit praedae manibus. Quae te patientia, Christe,
tanta deum potuit regemque patremque deorum
reddere tam lentum, nihil ut te nostra moveret 680
impietas? Graviorne olim nos poena moratur?
Quid miremur enim tumulis si condita priscis
(quaeque modo tumulata iacent tot vermibus escae)
eruta rimamur flagrante cadavera cura,
cum sumus in Christum tanta impietate rebelles? 685
Sphortia quae postquam didicisset probra nefasque,
indoluit lachrymasque pio demisit ab ore
quaesivitque diu posita mercede profani
auctorem sceleris. Sed quis sese indicet ullus?

Quod potuit, muliebre genus celer omne coactum   690
raptorum e manibus rapiens in templa reponit;
eque suis fidos custodes praeficit illos
quorum certa fides et longi temporis usus
agnitus impuri cuiusquam criminis omni
suspicione vacet. Sic omnis foemina saevas,   695
ut miseranda, manus evasit munere mitis
et pietate viri—quod iam sibi posse licebat.
Talia cum flaetu lamentabatur amaro:
"Heu miseram sortem, qua nos natura deusve
esse genus muliebre dedit. Servilius usquam   700
est animal nullum, nec probro obiectius omni.
Nos sumus imbelles; nec vis praestantior ulla
in nobis rationis inest animusque pavore
semper hebet. Validae vires in corpore nullae.
Ingenium de se quod possit promere coram   705
nil habet egregii; merito contemnimur ergo
ac patimur servile iugum; ast ex omnibus unas
astra Placentinas inimico lumine lustrant.
Nam memini quandoque patrem narrare puella,
quanta clade ferox hanc urbem pressit Amilcar,   710
cum dux Insubrium (superi quos fulmine perdant
immitis!) flama consumptis aedibus omnem
verterat in praedam. Quae vis, quod dedecus in nos
non est admissum? Sed quid vaesana revolvo
quae longa periere die? Quae perdidit aetas?   715
Praetereo Gotthos Germanorumque furores
antiquasque faces—fortunae vulnera priscae.
Heu miseram sortem, quae semper nostra fatigat
moenia! Quis luctum et tenebras ignorat Othonis
Facinique canis, quas nostrae infuderat urbi?   720
Quae in praedam conversa tulit quaecunque superbus
hostis et invisus voluit, viditque cathaenis
infandis populum per tristia cuncta subactum
urgeri, penitusque vacans se civibus orbam
desertamque suis—saevarum lustra ferarum.   725
Hanc post Francus atrox, post hunc Laudensis avarus,
inde Sigismundus Romani nomen inane
imperii lacerat. Recipit mox ipse Philippus
dux ingens, parvo quam servat tempore tutam
hostis ob insidias sibi quem ducebat amicum;   730
quam postquam rursus dura obsidione recepit.
Finitimas metuens Pandulpho principe vires

civilisque dolos, desertam prorsus et omnis
humani cultus inopem dedit. Inde potitus
hac iterum cives patriae patriamque reductis   735
civibus ascivit, laetamque in pace benignus
(dum vixit) placida studuit servare quietem.
Heu, miseram nimium sortem, quae tempore diro
accidit, heu, miseris nobis. Nunc caelitus omnis
ingruit, infelix fatali sydere pestis   740
perniciesque simul. Nam patria cara, parentes,
et nati et fratres una dulcesque nepotes
et generi et soceri—penitus domus occidit omnis.
Mars alios rapuit. Martis quibus ira pepercit
summa, cathaenatos carcer teterrimus abdit.   745
Nos autem passae quidquid vis dira, libido
effrenata iubet, quidquid victoria demens
suadet et insani mores, sic vivimus, olim
haec sit ut inferior quam vitam vivimus omni
morte quidem. Quis enim mortem moriturus honestam,   750
si sapit, obscurae nolit praeponere vitae?
Oh patriae dulcesque Lares araeque deorum
quas colimus, nobis quae tandem vita futura est,
heu miseris? Num forte velint vaenalis ut hastae
praemia pendamus? Famulari libera nescit.   755
An malint fortasse thorum vice pellicis omne
turpe per obsequium servemus. Adultera qualis
illa fuit, quae se victrix Holophernis acerbos
fudit in amplexus—tali me lege futuram
polliceor moecham! Verum quid pectore verso   760
magnifico, demens? Quid inania vota lacesso?
Cogimur invitae famulari. Cogimur omne
ferre probrum, quodcunque velit qui vicerit hostis."
Talia fundebant lachrymis. Arasque foventes
omnibus in templis simulacra per omnia flaetus   765
votaque mittebant sese patriamque dolentes.
Dux autem cupiens iram Franciscus ovantis
militis horrendam paulum cohibere, feroces
convocat et tali castigat voce cohortes:
"O socii, non est nostri victoria iuris,   770
divinae sed opis. Nam si nos vera fateri
convenit, invictam nulla ratione nec armis
vicimus et captam nobis submisimus urbem.
Nil et enim deerat, quo se minus ipsa tueri
posset et adversis se contra offerre periclis.   775

Sed deus ipse reor voluit punire nocentes,
quod nullo nec Marte citi, nec damna verentes
accierint Venetum, cui se nil tale petenti
subicerent servos—nulli servire coacti.
Sola Placentini cunctorum causa malorum,   780
qui, placidam toto Venetus dum pectore pacem
acciperet, flamas extinctis ignibus addunt.
Quas meruere igitur divino vindice poenas,
en solvere satis. Sit tandem certa malorum
finis et ipsa modum miseris victoria sistat   785
aerumnis, ne forte suas fortuna rebellis
avocet—ingratos si nos adverterit—auras.
Non et enim vitam nostro deducere voto
arbitrioque datur. Nam sunt humana perenni
curae cuncta deo; cuius ne nostra benignam   790
culpa repellat opem, longe caveamus oportet.
Sat nummum rerumque iacet, quas ferre licebit
quo nos cunque vocet belli casusve deusve.
Parcite captivis atque omnis solvite. Missos
si facimus miseros, si libertate nocentis   795
donamus nobis, hominumque deumque favorem
non dubium sperare licet. Quod denique restat:
ite, mei socii, paulum requiescite vosque
tantisper curate, cito dum classica turba
applicet et Venetis opibus vos compleat omnes."   800
Haec ait; et cuncti laeti assensere simulque
iussa ducis faciunt. Mittuntur carcere capti
solvunturque omnes et libertate fruuntur.
Templa recluduntur; mulieres agmine currunt
conquiruntque suos atque oscula mutua iungunt   805
inque vicem sese miserantur, gaudia flaetu
miscentes. Longe libertas reddita cunctos
ipsa iuvat; verum gravis est iactura bonorum.

Note on the Text

No printed edition of the *Sforziad* was ever produced. Eight codices of the work are known, all of them dating from the fifteenth century: Paris, Bibliothecque Nationale, lat. 8126, eight books (written for Filelfo by his friend Fabrizio Elfiteo, here designated *P*); Florence, Biblioteca Laurenziana, Laur. 33.33, four books (autograph, here designated *F*); Milan, Biblioteca Ambrosiana, H 97 sup., eight books (autograph, here designated

A); Milan, Biblioteca Trivulziana, 731 (C 72), eight books (autograph, here designated *T*); Vatican City, Biblioteca Apostolica Vaticana, Vat. lat. 2921, four books; Milan, Biblioteca Ambrosiana R 12 sup., eight books; Rome, Biblioteca Casanatense 415 (C III 9), fragments of Books 1–11 (autograph, no siglum designated since the fragment from Book 3 contains only sixteen lines); Venice, Biblioteca Nazionale Marciana, lat. XIV. 262 (4719), excerpts from Book 4. I have collated the Paris codex (*P*) and the three alleged autograph codices of the *Sforziad* (*A*, *F*, and *T*: each of these appears to be the work of a different hand; nonetheless they bear a family resemblance to one another and should surely be ascribed to Filelfo's circle if not to Filelfo himself). My edition is based then on the four authorized manuscripts *A*, *P*, *T*, and *F*. The two remaining complete codices of Book 3, Ambr. R 12 sup. and Vat. lat. 2921, come from outside Filelfo's circle and contain errors too numerous to list in the apparatus below. I have modernized only the punctuation and capitalization of the text. Otherwise, with the exception of the consonants *j* for *i* and *v* for *u*, I have retained the idiosyncratic orthography of Filelfo and his circle, with its copious employment of diphthongs, its characteristic use of *y* for *i* (as in *sydus, inclytus, digytus*, etc.), and its frequent reduction of consonant doublets to singlets (as in *flama, Iupiter*, etc.). A list of variants in *A*, *F*, *P*, and *T* follows.

Sforziad Book 3: 29 obprobria *FPT*] opprobria *A*; 37 tremendus *AFT*] timendus *P*; 85 limine *AFT*] limne *P*; 129 ocius *APT*] ocyus *F*; 177 superum *APT*] superorum *F*; 219 cohortis *APT*] cohortes *F*; 237 phalanx *APT*] falanx *F*; 240 subeuntis *APT*] subeuntes *F*; 241 eminus *APT*] aeminus *F*; 252 superbus *APT*] tremendus *F*; 281 teneat *AFT*] tenet *P*; 370 eminus *APT*] aeminus *F*; fune *APT*] funae *F*; 410 Cytherea *PT*] Citherea *A* Citharea *F*; 430 calcaribus *AT*] chalcaribus *FP*; 439 eminus *APT*] aeminus *F*; 443 exorto *FPT*] extorto *A*; 479 Basianus *APT*] Bassanus *F*; 489 Basianus *APT*] Bassanus *F*; 516 ocius *APT*; ocyus *F*; cohortis *APT*] cohortes *F*; 531 nihil *APT*] nil *F*; 566 laedere *FPT*] ledere *A*; 578 horrendus *APT*] tremebundus *F*; turris *T*] turres *AF*; 667 imperet *APT*] imperat *F*; 701 obiectius *FPT*] abiectius *A*; 719 ignorat *APT*] ignoret *F*; 720 infuderat *PT*] infuderit *AF*.

SELECTED ODES, BOOKS 1–4

Odes 1.10

Arcimbolde, gravi me voce hortaris ut alta
bella canam, quaecumque modo Mavorte secundo
Insubrium proceres divi post fata Philippi
gesserunt et iure mones. Nam maxima rerum
attulit Italiae populus momenta labanti   5
hic primum nulli cedens pietate nec armis.
Nam dum bella fugit legis servator et aequi,
tranquilla dum pace cupit fovisse quietem,
haud Bellona sinit. Totum perturbat Erinys
effera flagrantem flamis surgentibus orbem.   10
Illinc funereas Aurelia surgit in iras,
elatisque furor Germanus cingitur armis.
Hinc et finitimi cunctas populique ducesque
sollicitant urbes et blandis oppida temptant
pollicitis. Venetum tempestas ingruit inde   15
omnia prosternens ac turbinis instar et ignis
templa domosque una vastansque premensque ruina.
Rebus in adversis animos fortuna recludit,
quos olim fucata fides simularat amicos.
Undique deficiunt socii, fiuntque rebelles,   20
quos decuit servare fidem. Ius omne piumque
una strage perit. Nihil est quod servet honestum.
Celsa quidem probitas firmis radicibus haerens
vim monstrare suam solidumque ostendere robur
tum solet intrepide, cum magnis septa periclis   25
egregios peperit certa pro laude triumphos.
Insubribus postquam pax atque optata negantur
otia, nec possunt ulla vel lege vel aequo
ius apud hostilis animos mentesque feroces
defendisse suum, demum per tristia Martis   30
bella vel inviti dubio discrimine iniquam
vim prohibere parant. Non multo milite Francos
caede sub horribili fusos docuere furentem
in primis nocuisse suis auctoribus iram.
Inde Placentini nimia levitate rebelles   35

edidicere, quibus dementia frangitur armis.
At Venetum classes praedamque necemque minantis
Eridanus sensit flamis ferroque ruentes.
Et ne quaeque loquar quae plurima longius ultro
carmen agant—quali, quam multo milite fraeti   40
iidem etiam Veneti funesta clade subacti,
qua Caravaginos cingebant aggere campos,
humanas res quasque deum curare probarunt.
Ter Venetos vicisse quid est, nisi lumen et ipsum
Italiae solem velut obscurasse micantis?   45
Haec sunt Insubribus bene concordantibus acta,
quae ni stulta hominum mens et discordia praeceps
impediisset, erant iam nobis parta quietis
otia tranquillae rebusque et laude verendis.
Expulimus nostros et vires auximus hosti.   50
Infestumque virum bellisque armisque tremendum
reddidimus nobis. Civili caede natamus.
Moenibus obsessi premimur belloque fameque.
En stimulat rabies. Intus pugnamus et extra.
Nec desunt animi tamen et Mavortia virtus.   55
Te ductore modo defensa Moguntia sensit,
Karole, quam pauci innumeros prostravimus hostes.
Mox etiam Venetum tanta obsidione labantem
tendentemque manus Chremam te Karole rursus
solvimus intrepido belli duce. Promptus et acer   60
est animus nostris cunctisque in rebus agendis
callidus et fortis. Civilis turbat Erinys
omnia, seditio qua ius simul omne piumque
sustulit e medio miscens hominesque deosque.
Haec postrema quidem vitio mihi danda videntur   65
Insubribus, quod se per mutua vulnera caedant.
Laude sed ingenti sunt illa ferenda sub astra,
quis hostes fregere truces, pulchrosque triumphos
advexere suis. Ea nunc si carmine digno
prosequar atque suis bene convenientia rebus   70
munera reddidero, cuncti laudentque probentque.
At mea Musa quidem tam grandi functa labore
praemia quae speret? Nescit ieiuna canoros
expressisse sonos dum siccis faucibus horret.
Non etenim tanti laudes quae laudibus ornat   75
Musa facit, periisse fame quo multa canendo
atque toga caruisse velit. Non tale Maronis
munus erat magni. Nullus mihi Pollio nullus
Mecoenas. Augustus opem mihi ferre paratus

nullus adest. Laudes mihi nullas emero, laudes 80
vaendere cui liceat. Quod si mihi saeva Philippum
servasset fortuna ducem, qui Caesare maior
unus et Augusto fuerat praestantior omni,
non equidem tales successus Martis opimi
interitum Lethes paterer fative subire. 85
Nunc autem quoniam nullis est cura Camoenae,
quin periit virtutis honos, nec lingua nec ipsa
temptet arundo aliquid mea, quod sit Apolline dignum.
Sic ingrata mihi turbat sententia pectus
plebis et istorum, quibus haec respublica serviit 90
(heu miseranda) nimis. Nam quos laudavero? Iustos?
Non licet. Exacti sunt omnes urbe probati
illustresque viri. Gerit en zonaria pulchros
turba magistratus. Fartor licitator adulter
lenoque periurus cum collusore superbit. 95
Horum ego quid laudem? Quas patravere nefandis
insidiis caedes? Tanta impietate necatos
tot cives? Num facta canam civisque tacebo?
Spes mihi quae tandem fuerit? Num fructus honosve?
Quin nec abire licet, nec tuta licentia fandi 100
mi datur. Assenterne loco? Assentatio non est
pectoris ingenui. Nequeo simulata referre.
Nam nec vera licet. Quod si deus ipse favebit,
si proceres victrix repetet respublica primos,
inclyta nobilitas si plebem franget inertem, 105
carmine grandiloquo quantum mea Musa valebit,
prosequar Insubrium partos ex hoste triumphos.
Praemia digna meo ducturus fixa labore,
laude quod extulerim, qui digni laude fuissent.
Nil cum plebe mihi. Procul absit vulgus ineptum 110
quin potius toto mihi pectore Karolus ille,
Francia cui sacro paret fortissima regi,
volvitur, exhortans sibi ne praeponere quenquam
ex hominum numero studeam, quos novit Eous,
novit et occiduus Titan Boreasque Notusque. 115
Plura loqui prohibet Clio, quae prima sororum
ecce canit, citharam digytis dum pulsat Apollo.

Odes 2.2

Omnis tyrannis impium nutrit scelus,
sed nulla detestabilis certe magis

quam plebis impotentis et populi trucis.
En Insubres animi furor quantus rapit.
Immanitas rabidos in omne tristius   5
facinus trahit. Necantur insontes palam
nullo reatus crimine ullius rei.
Libido regnat: praeda funestos iuvat;
abest pudor; nefas per omne publice
dirum nocentes evehuntur altius.   10
Laudi locus nullus: vicissim cum boni
alii exulant, alii relegati probrum
coguntur omne perpeti. Satellitem
pudica coniunx excipit vel lachrymans
testansque caelites adulterum thoro.   15
Stupratur omnis virgo, divina ac item
humana quaeque iura perditis simul
parent. Nec est in improbis ullus modus.
Tutu deorum rector atque hominum parens,
cui servit omne (quidquid et mundus tegit   20
et si quid est inane quod mundum ambiat)
tandem potenti dextera miseris opem
affer. Nec ulterius canes rabidos sine
per efferatos impiam rictus necem
sitire, Iupiter. Velut tigris furit   25
in Indiae vitulos et Aethiops ruens
taurus lupusve Maenali greges petit,
Ossona sic Aplanus et Georgius
Bisulcerus civili haustu sanguinis
alacres feruntur instar acti fulminis   30
et neminem pestis relinquunt horridae
inopem. Perit nullo vir exemplo pius.
Locus nec est ullus refellendi datus.
Obiecta sontes efficit immanitas
trium latronum. Dedecus nostrae ultimum   35
aetatis, omnes posteri quod auribus
stupidis in omnes audiant gentes viri
et horreant longe simul. Nec desinant
nostri execrari temporis foedum scelus.
Exurgat olim, quisquis unus denique   40
gratissimus Iovi fuerit Olympio,
qui nos tenebris eruat teterrimis.
Unus domum ministrat, unus aequore
navim gubernat, imperator bellicis
in rebus unus imperat. Caelum deus   45

ut unus aeterno regit moderamine,
sic unus urbi praesit huic princeps pius,
qui rebus afferat quietem turbidis.
Satis o deus poenae satis sceleri datum,
si quod profanum perpetravimus nefas,   50
qui nobilis modo Philippi funera
neglexius ducis, nec ingentem sumus
honore digno prosecuti principem,
ignosce tandem. Fer benignus flaetibus
opem fatentibus quod admissum est scelus.   55
Audimur? An frustra preces veniam petunt?
Aether ciet tonitrum; micant radiis faces
en caelitus missae. Quis aures Martius
pulsat fragor? Tumultus en populi furit,
"Panem! Panem!" ingeminans. Polos clamor ferit.   60
Pereant scelesti. Ficta libertas ruat
omni tyranno dirior, crudelior nece,
immanior qui Tartarum servat cane.
Bene est: priores vindicat vires sibi
animus receptus, qui modo cecidit malis.   65
Passim latrones dant fugam turpi metu.

Odes 2.3

Sydus illustrans Latium corusca
luce qua totum remicas per orbem,
quas tibi grates referam merenti
Sphortia princeps?

O decus summum, numeros per omnis   5
quod means virtus peperit suprema,
tu mihi solus superis secundis
consulis urbi.

Impii coetus miseram latronum
sparserant fusi fluviis cruoris   10
civium quos vis, furor atque habendi
perdidit ignis.

Hinc ferus Mavors populatur agrum,
hinc fames cunctos perimit subactos.
Nulla spes vitae recreat cadentes   15
cuncta minantur.

Hadriae vires simulant salutem.
Abduam multa rapidum phalange
numine adverso superant et altis
collibus errant.   20

Ipse Franciscus probitate pollens
viribus nullis tremefactus hosti
fortis occurris medioque ponis
castra sub agro.

Nanque mercatus tibi vicus omni   25
nudus et fossa vacuusque vallo
cinctus et nulla lapidum corona
castra recepit.

Octo vix tecum fuerant cohortes
militum, sed quas variis periclis   30
saepe victrices habuisse summo
te duce nosses.

Hinc lacessebas trepidos maniplos
hostis infesti per iniqua Barrhi
montis errantes iuga quosque terror   35
sterneret ingens.

Hinc item nostras celer et tremendus
copias nullo duce se tuentis,
sed quibus demens furor esset auctor
aeminus arces?   40

Nam quis auderet tibi signa contra
ferre, quem cuncti populi tremiscunt
et pavent reges, Latium veretur,
orbis honorat.

Si tibi soli polus est uterque   45
rebus in cunctis pius et benignus,
si deus tecum tua semper unus
signa tuetur,

quae tibi adversae valeant phalanges
arma tam caro superis movere?   50
Quae tibi possint nocuisse vires
hostis iniqui?

Qualis alternas tolerat procellas
Isthmos immotus geminique cunctos
aequoris fluctus reprimit, ned iras   55
curat inanes.

Aut leo qualis medius fugaces
separans cervas vitulasque tardas
has modo saltu modo terret illas
ludit et arcet.   60

Talis et nostras Venetumque vires
inde contemnis nihilique ducis.
Hinc ferox constans, vigil et peritus
fersque premisque.

Quae quidem mecum meditans diuque   65
cogitans dixi, quid amica demens
fata contemno? Superos benignos
odero semper?

Ecce libertas simulata quantam
civibus cladem tulit et ruinam.   70
Publicae nemo studuit saluti
nemo decori?

Hinc dolus manat furor et rapina.
Hinc caput velat rabidis Megaera
anguibus. Cunctos pariter veneno   75
impia fundens.

Phoebus ut solus radiat per orbem.
Ut deus mundum moderatur unus,
sic meas unus gerat et gubernet
ductor habaenas.   80

Qui meus primus bonus atque fortis
audeat civis tenebras fugare
et diem rebus nitidum referre?
Surgat alumnus.

Ecce vir fortis micat inter omnes   85
Gaspar ignavo trepidos timore
excitat cives. Rabidos tyrannos
obsidet aula.

Inde plebeii validis latrones
viribus surgunt. Volitant utrinque   90
taela ceu nimbus celeri citatus
turbine praeceps.

Clarus affatu socios diserto
Gaspar hortatur. Gravibusque vires
Acer incendens animosque dictis   95
pugnat et urget.

"Nobiles," inquit "generosa cives
arma quid tardis manibus moventes
parcitis ferro? Pavidas latronum
fundite turmas."   100

"Hic dies vobis patriam parentes
coniuges natos decus et quietem
reddet. Adversos alacri tumultus
pellite Marte."

"Quisque Franciscum validos videntem   105
Sphortiam secum meditetur ictus
principem nostrum iubar et salutem.
Sternite fures."

Praelium noctem trahitur sub atram
caede non una. Cecidere sordes   110
terga vertentes. Foribus reclusis
panditur aula.

Gaspar irrumpit. Sequitur caterva
civium qui me trucibus tyrannis
liberam tandem Veneti cadentis   115
sanguine reddunt.

Sic dies unus famis atque saevi
Martis optatam tulit ille finem,
nulla quem praeceps abolebit ira
nulla vetustas.   120

Nanque cum primum populi vocantis
accipis dextram veniensque lustras
tecta tam longo miseranda flaetu
urbe receptus,

moenia ingressus pater ipse tecum   125
Liber et laetae Cereris choreae.
Ludus et Comus, Iocus et Voluptas
omnia complent.

Quique tam multas acies agebat
terror hostilis, pavefacta vertit   130
terga, sic cervus trepidus leonem
effugit acrem.

Pace nunc cives hilari fruuntur.
Nunc meus tecum populus triumphat.
Nunc suas hostes timidi ruinas   135
funditus horrent.

Mente quae mecum repetens profunda
gratias summas tibi sic merenti
debeo. Me nam miseram levasti
ore luporum.   140

Restat, eversam redigas ut arcem
ad decus primum monumenta magni
principis nulli procerum secundi
pulchra Philippi.

Inde quod noster populus rogare   145
omnis et tellus latii superbi
pergit, hostiles propera furores
solvere poenas.

Non enim pulsus cupiat quietem.
Maior insurget Venetus. Parabit   150
fortius robur. Socios pericli
undique fundet

quisquis iniusto furias secutus
Marte temtavit tibi sic amico
nuper infestus nocuisse, censes   155
ferre quietem?

Additur saevo metui cupido.
Urit haec pectus, glacie sed ille
urget et nusquam patiens manere
undique vexat.   160

Insuper fidos lateri sodales
iunge fucatos fugiens amicos.
Quos viros monstrat probitas verendos,
utere semper.

Nec tibi quenquam reputes amicum,   165
quem socer duxit sibi non fidelem.
Is necem dudum tibi nil nocenti
fraude tetendit.

Semper ulcisci muliebre censent,
Ast idem nunquam fatui putatur.   170
Qui tenet prudens medium supremis
laudibus ornant.

Si caves vitae insidias serenae,
res geres magnas meliusque natis
consules et me super alta vectus   175
sydera tolles.

Sis diu mecum, superes et annos
Nestoris totos. Mariaeque Blancae
cedat aetati vetus illa vates
Dia Sibylla.   180

Si novam te vix subeunte portam
cessit extemplo ferus ille Mavors
et fames diro sociata luctu
moenia liquit.

Quid putes mi dux fore, si seniles   185
videris annos? Veteres triumphos
Italis reddes super orbe toto
clarus et ingens.

Odes 3.4

Ambrosi, tandem ferus ille Mavors
ac fames, duros etiam Gigantas
quae ferox tetris potuisset umbris
tradere et dirum domitare Ditem,
hinc ad extremos abiit Triones.   5

Nanque Franciscus venerandus heros
Sphortias nobis avibus secundis
caelitus missus rabidos tyrannos
sustulit; pacem requiemque fessis
attulit. Nunc est populo statuta   10
vera libertas. Periere fastus
plebis ignavae scelerumque terror:
stupra vis atrox furor et rapinae.
Heu, quis infracto meminisse fortis
corde vir possit rabidas et omni   15
peste faerali magis extimendas
beluas, quae nos penitus vorabant
ferreo rictu rigidisque rostris.
Vir bonus nemo poterat tueri
nomen invictae probitatis insons,   20
nanque suspecti fuerant et hostes,
quos pios nosset Rabias et ille
rusticus potu cerebrum diurno
laesus et nunquam Cicerus per umbras
sobrius, cui se comitem Decembris   25
Candidus semper misere cinaedis
laevibus septus vitiisque mille
scriba pollutus dederat per omnem
criminis culpam. Bibulis cruorem
civium suadens ferus innocentum   30
latro, qui mulcens malesanus aures
plebis impurae. Nebulo profanis
solus exemplis ea commonebat,
quae nec immanis Phalaris patrasset.
Inde quos saevus gladius vel ignis   35
visque liquisset taciti veneni,
hos fame solus rabida peremit
Candidus, foeno paleaque tritis
posse qui victum solidum parari
diceret, dum se tamen ipse fallax   40
rebus expleret per iniqua partis
cuncta, quae suadet furor et libido.
Videris passim populum iacentem
perditum loeto, Cereris quod expers
annus omnino peperit secundus.   45
Quid mihi frustra memores Saguntum
aut fame pressos referas Hebraeos?
Nulla gens unquam similem Megaeram

passa narretur. Stomachus tumenti
nausea nobis vomitum minatur,   50
mente dum sortem miseram revolvo.
Nam nihil foedi, nihil impudici
liquit afflictus populus quod esse
posset intactum. Meminisse diri
horreo fati merito silendi.   55
Tabe tam tetra generosus heros
nostra Franciscus penitus levavit
corda cum membris docuitque quantus
error humanas penetrare mentes
assolet. Phoebus nebulae decoros   60
dum tegunt crines, nequit intuentes
qua micat semper, facie iuvare.
Ambrosi, nobis radios Apollo
noster en coram rutilos suosque
pandit. Et cunctis animi solutis   65
nubibus nostri, nitidos ocellos
lustrat infusus, recreatque dulci
luce deiectos, reficitque lassos.
Ambrosi, laetos agimus canenti
voce saltatus numeris nec unis.   70
Et novos plectro modulos ciente
versibus miris decus omne vatum
fontis ad sacros latices vocamus,
quem Medusaeus sonipes sub alto
monte defodit. Resonat Citheron   75
ad resurgentis numeros sororum,
quos regit multa pater arte Paean.
Pulchra cui Clio meritas secuta
reddidit voces: referens superbas
Sphortiae laudes ducis et parentis   80
huius invicti populi. Triumphis
cuius Euterpe redimita celsis
gestit, et cantus movet ipsa miros.
Praeferens cunctis merito laborum
Sphortiam nostris simul et vetustis,   85
sola quos virtus dederit verendos.
Si qua te sollers igitur voluptas
captat, ad nostras propera choreas,
quas agit laetam placida per urbem
fronte dux noster populo sequente   90
et simul suavi referente cantu,

quidquid aerumnis gelidis levatus
iusserit cordis renovatus ignis
sorte secunda.

Odes 4.5

Tristes Insubrium denique liquimus
terras, quas rabido syderis ignei
vastant horribiles fulmine caelites.
Plaustro dum vehimur cum Laribus piis
et quidquid reliquum longa protervitas   5
Martis vel Cereris saeva necessitas
fecit, iam penitus fervor Apollinis
omnes corripuit. Nos sitis ac fames
una dum premeret, quae propior fuit
hinc cauponula tendentibus aeminus,   10
qua nos Papia mox excipit obvia.
Illuc numine divertimus horrido
et nummis petimus quod fuit usui.
Turbatus iubet excedere ianua
caupo: "Pestiferae discedite beluae,"   15
inclamitans, "propere linquite, linquite
quos spectant oculis astra benignius!"
Paremus: quid enim pluribus irritum
tempus conterimus? Non asinum lyra
nec vis eloquii leniat inscium.   20
Quod coeptum fuerat prosequimur viae;
et vix assequimur denique blandius
orantes veniam noctis et otii,
qui primas habitat villicus inclyti
horti caupo domos excipit, omnia   25
nobis laeticiae munera porrigens.
Hic primum tenebras luminibus pigras
udis expulimus. Pectora laetior
sensus corripuit: mensa paratior
hic apponitur, hic et Cereris piae,   30
hic primum placidi copia Liberi
fit nobis. Agimus cantibus altius
pulsantes fidibus sydera personis.
Saltatum choreis cymbala mollibus
Miscent. Maeror abest et fugit aeminus   35
omnis cura prior, nam modice quoque

interdum gravitas exhilarascere
nequaquam dubitat. Sic gravior senex
condiri salibus puberis assolet.
Ut Comus tacuit, mox iocus utitur   40
dulci colloquio. Post requiem parat
plumis perlevibus lectus honustior.
Dormitur placide. Nox citius ruit
quam par est. Roseo surgit ab aequore
Titan arquitenens; excitor illico   45
ac me veste parans excito caeteros,
tendens ad Ticinum, quod iacet obvium.
Hinc mox perspicuo flumine—nobilem—
dum namus Ticino, en ingredimur Padum,
quo vecti placidum conterimus diem.   50
Noctu dum requiem praestat et otium
quae ripam tenuit dentibus anchora,
dum somno premimur, mox tonat altius
qui rex omnipotens Iupiter aethera
ducit. Nec pluviae lentius ingruunt.   55
Nimbi praecipiti turbine conciti
irrumpunt rabidis amnibus undique.
"O divum genitor, rector et arbiter
rerum, quas opifex e nihilo creans
(quidquid vis geritur), diluvium," precor,   60
"arce, quo premimur." Nil precibus deus
audit, forsitan auri quod inanitas
nec summis etiam caelitibus placet.
Nam si vera fatentur theoleptici,
non est quod capiatur precibus deus   65
ullis, munera quas nulla praeiverint.
Crebris obruimur caelitus imbribus;
nec prosunt miseris tegmina cymbulae
conductae. Penetrant omnia turbidi
nimbi. Sic penitus nos quoque vestibus   70
frigemus madidis nocte sub horrida.
Dum frigent reliqui sola voracibus
flamis aestuat Antonia vernula.
Nec fallax referat quod patitur malum,
forsan ne reliquis iniiceret metum.   75
Tithoni croceos liquerat excita
uxor iam thalamos. Anchora tollitur
et coeptam sequimur remigio viam.
Vix Aethon rapido subdiderat iugo
collum, nos excipit grata Placentia   80

ac dulci miserans hospitio fovet.
Solus dimminuit munificentiam,
vectigalia qui Piccolus exigit,
quo nil invenias rusticius, nihil
usquam sordidius. Clamitat improbus: 85
"Vectigal volumus. Non opus est libris.
Musarum satis est, si satis est opis
in nummis. Faciunt divitiae deos."
Contra litigo, dum principis optimi,
quas nuper dederat, me tego litteris.   90
Quid verbis opus est? Ius valet efferum
nullum, nec pietas flectere Piccolum.
Solus Scaeva malum deterruit virum,
qui postquam didicit Cortis hic optimus
impuri solitas insidias viri   95
iussit, ne stomachum fervere bilicum
demens cogeret. Expalluit audiens
haec vir nequitia nequior ultima.
Invitusque sinit solvere cymbulam.
Hinc nos Scaeva suis muneribus pius   100
ut pulchris cumulat solvimus impigri.
Quod dum postridie per gaudia pulchra Cremonam
    appulimus pestem iam superasse rati,
dirius in duplicem turbato numine pestem
    syderis incidimus incidimusque soli.   105
Nam vix egressus cymbam, vix urbe receptus
    dum conduco domum, qua residere queam,
vernula, quae rerum custos Antonia navi
    sola relicta fuit, morte cadit subita.
Tollitur extemplo cunctis ad sydera clamor: 110
    vaesanum passim vulgus ad arma ruit,
moenibus extrudor tanquam teterrima pestis
    cum Phoebo et natis mille per obprobria.
Nullane Romulidum plebes vestigia servas
    dira Cremonensis, quam perimant superi?   115
Quae te barbaries cepit saevissima more
    immani, gravibus urbs inimica viris?
Quam bene te divus praedae decrevit habendam
    Augustus, superas quae feritate feras.
Perfida gens sceleri non uni obnoxia, toto   120
    flagitiis pariter orbe notanda tuis.
More peregrinos quo tandem pessima cunctos
    odisti, quibus es omnibus ipsa minor?

Dic mihi: qua tandem polles virtute Cremona?
    Dic mihi: quo vitio dedecorosa cares? 125
Tu sermone mihi tantum blandire doloso,
    raetia dum tendas, dum laqueos iacias.
Quos non inducis fallax? Non fraude suprema
    mittis in insidias omnis inops meriti?
Quid, quod Marmaricus leo te crudelior ullus 130
    non est, immitis vipera nulla magis?
Dic, faex Gallorum, quos nutris pectore fastus?
    Num quia te Gotti constituere nothis?
Nam genus egregium, quod priscis Roma colonis
    ornarat, penitus Attila sustulerat. 135
Quod si quos forsan servavit saeva colonos
    tempestas, si quos nesciit ira probos,
hos tenebris plebs dira suis obscurat et almam
    non sinit in lucem mergere luminibus
nanque quis ignorat quantis se laudibus effert 140
    Melia progenies Bartholomaee tua?
Sola malo gaudes plebes inimica poetis
    nobilibusque gravis stirpe profecta Gethae.
Hinc immanis amor praedae te semper anhaelam
    reddit et infestam, quos alit aura, bonis. 145
Nam quae te rabies agitat, gens impia, doctos
    ut cupias omnis disperiisse viros?
Illustres exosa artes clarumque perosa
    ingenium, somnos atque gulas adamas.
Ebria gens, laeso penitus quae fracta cerebro 150
    insanis, quae te tristis Erinys alit?
Istic nobilitas non est, quae more tueri
    se queat ingenuo laudibus et meritis.
Plebs scelerata furit, quae nullo ducta pudore
    iusque piumque premat, quae malefacta colat 155
O genus horrendum nostrique obprobria saecli,
    non tandem patrii poeniteat sceleris?
Num pestis fortasse faces adveximus ultro?
    Quae nos decepit, ipsa luat facinus.
Num si nota latens aegrotae causa fuisset, 160
    nos tandem longa cymba tulisset aqua?
Humanum crimen, quod culpa insonte carebat,
    humani meruit iudicis officium.
Exactos recipit parvulus hortulus
in quo parva domus cum puteo iacet, 165
quem ranae celebrant cantibus undique.

Hic nos nemo suis colloquiis quasi
dirum prodigium et caelitibus grave
dignatur. Manibus nemo pecuniam
audet tangere nostram, quasi nummuli   170
morbum pestiferum contineant quoque.
Hinc nos obsidet infesta Necessitas,
quae potum prohibet, quae prohibet cibum.
Uvae nos recreant, quae nisi turgidae
fovissent stomachum, nos sitis et fames   175
pressissent pariter mortis aculleis.

Odes 4.7

Musis Cremonae nullus est locus sacris.
Nullus Minervae nec deo Maia sato.
Hic sordidae solum vigent artes palam.
Hic turpis urbem quaestus omnem polluit.
Lenonibus, scortis et aleae vafris   5
doctoribus statutus est ingens honos.
Et publicanis et gulae et veneficis.
Hinc remigandum est ac retro ad Insubribus
terras propinquas navigandum protinus.
Vale Cremona manibus diris sacra   10
infesta cunctis quos alit virtus viris.
Vale, vale inquam tertium et cito cadas
tetris favillis concremata funditus.
Bene est. Preces tetigere Tartareas canes.
Dirae furentis instar adsunt turbinis.   15
Saevum latrontes igneos morsus parant.
Fundunt venenum crinibus iactant faces.
Ardet Cremona nullius nec syderis
flamis nec humano igne. Supplicium facit
immanis ira pectoris, cunctos bonos   20
qua tristis odit. En scelus gentem impiam
cruciat suum, nec sufficit bustis humus.

Note on the Texts

Two printed editions of the *Odae* were produced: the *editio princeps*, *Odae*, issued by Angelus Britannicus (Brescia, 1497); and a second edition printed by Jean Granjon (Paris, 149?). Eight codices of Filelfo's *Odae*

(= *Carminum libri quinque*) are known, all of them dating to the fifteenth century: Paris, Bibl. Naz. lat. 8127 (autograph, here designated *P*); Vat. urb. lat. 701 (autograph, here designated *R*); Laur. 33, 34 (autograph, here designated *F*); Chicago, Newberry Library MS. 103.8; Berlin, Sammlung Hamilton 511; Cesena, Bibl. Malatestiana 23, 5; Florence, Bibl. Naz. Centr. Conv. Soppr. G 2, 866; Vat. lat. 11518. I have collated the three alleged autograph codices of the *Odae*, though each of these codices appears to be the work of a different hand. My edition is based primarily on the Laurentian Library and Paris manuscripts, *F* and *P*. The Vatican manuscript of the *Odae*, *R*, which contains numerous careless errors, is the least reliable of the three so-called autographs. I have modernized only the punctuation and capitalization of the text. Otherwise, with the exception of the consonants *j* for *i* and *v* for *u*, I have retained Filelfo's idiosyncratic orthography with its copious employment of diphthongs, its characteristic use of *y* for *i* (as in *sydus, inclytus, digytus*, etc.), and its frequent reduction of consonant doublets to singlets (as in *flama, Iupiter*, etc.). A list of variants in *F*, *P*, and *R* follows.

Odes 1.10: 6 pietate *FP*] pietatis *R*; 11 iras *FP*] ira *R*; 23 haerens *FP*] haernes *R*; 71 laudentque *FP*] laudemque. *Odes* 2.2: 11 cum boni *R*] *om.* cum *FP*; 64 vindicat *FP*] vendicat *R*; *Odes* 2.3: 21 ipse *FP*] spe *R*; 40 aeminus *FP*] eminus *R*. *Odes* 3.4: 14 infracto *FP*] infacto *R*; 16 faerali *FP*; ferali *R*; 17 beluas *FP*] baeluas *R*; *Odes* 4.5: 10 aeminus *FP*] eminus *R*; 11 qua nos Papia mox excipit obvia *F*] qua nos mox Ticinum suscipit obvium *PR*; 16 inclamitans *FP*] inclamans *R*; 30 opponitur *R*] apponitur *FP*; 94 postquam *FP*] postoquam *R*; 100 hin *R*] hinc *FP*; 113 obprobria *FP*; opprobria *R*; 131 immitis *FP*] invitis *R*; 133 Gotti *FP*] Gothi *R*; 143 Gethae *FP*] Getae *R*; 156 nostrique *FP*] nostrisque *R*; 161 tandem *FP*] eadem *R*; 176; cibum *FP*] cybum *R*.

APPENDIX D

PSYCHAGOGIA: SYNOPSES

Book 1

1 (fols. 1–2v). An encomium of fifty lines in elegiac meter, in praise of King Alfonso of Naples (d. 1458), the strong man Vespasiano praised for his love of the classics.[1] On Filelfo's month-long stay at the Aragonese court in August 1453, Alfonso crowned him with the poet's laurel. Filelfo gratefully addressed this poem to Alfonso, whom he here calls the beloved of the divine Muses and Apollo, and revered by Thetis and Oceanus. "Just as every river flows down to the bright sea," Filelfo wrote to the king, "so do your halls draw and guide all good men." The complete text of the poem is printed in Bandini.[2]

2 (fols. 2v–4v). An encomium of sixty lines in Sapphics addressed to Cardinal Bessarion (d. 1472), the leading Greek scholar at the Vatican and Filelfo's friend for forty years, since the days when he and Bessarion were fellow pupils at Chrysococces' school in Constantinople.[3] Here Filelfo compares Bessarion to Phoebus, Apollo, Heracles, and Christ, but he chiefly praises the Cardinal because he does not "entangle himself in the fruitless opinions and dogmas (ματαίαις δόξαις) of this deceitful world." The complete text of this text is printed in Legrand and also in Bandini.[4]

3 (fols. 4v–6). A philosophical epistle of forty lines in elegiac meter, addressed to Palla Strozzi (see text, translation, and commentary in Chapter 4).

[1] On Alfonso, see Vespasiano, *Renaissance Princes, Popes and Prelates*, trans. W. George and E. Waters (New York, 1963) pp. 59–83; Alan Ryder, *The Kingdom of Naples under Alfonso the Magnanimous: the Making of a Modern State* (Oxford, 1976); Ernesto Pontieri, *Alfonso il Magnanimo re di Napolo (1435–1458)* (Naples, 1975); and Jerry H. Bentley, *Politics and Culture in Renaissance Naples* (Princeton, 1987).

[2] A. M. Bandini, *Catalogus codicum manuscriptorum Bibliotecae Mediceae Laurentinae*, 2 vols. (Florence, 1764–1770), 2.452–53.

[3] On Bessarion, see Ludwig von Mohler, *Kardinal Bessarion als Theologe, Humanist und Staatsmann*, 3 vols. (Paderborn, 1942); on Chrysococces' school, see Filelfo, *Epistolae* (February 1448), fol. 41; see also Legrand, *Lettres*, Filelfo to Bessarion, p. 104.

[4] Bandini, *Catalogus*, 2.453–452; and Legrand, *Lettres*, p. 195.

4 (fols. 6–7v). A paean of fifty-six lines in Sapphics, on the virtues of Borso d'Este (d. 1471), the duke of Ferrara, Modena, and Reggio, who supported a number of humanists at his court, including Guarino da Verona and Giovanni Aurispa.[5] The poem is actually addressed to Borso's personal physician and court poet Girolamo Castelli. Here Filelfo playfully provides Castelli with a lesson on how he should immortalize his patron, Borso, whose lovely locks are like Apollo's, whose eyes resemble Athena's, whose brow and hands rival Heracles', and whose mighty breast is as powerful as Ares'. This unpublished poem can be dated to 1458, when Filelfo wrote Castelli that he had composed a Greek poem in his honor so that "the Greeks themselves would know their friendship was not a common one.[6]

5 (fols. 8–9). A philosophical epistle of forty lines in elegiac meter, addressed to Donato Acciaiuoli (see the text, translation, and commentary in Chapter 4).

6 (fols. 9–10). An unpublished philosophical epistle, consisting of forty lines in Sapphics, addressed to Donato Acciaiuoli's friend and fellow pupil of John Argyopoulos, Andrea Alamanni (b. 1421).[7] As in the epistle to Donato, Filelfo cautions here against the "soft pleasures" of the body, and praises Andrea for his "love philtre of perfect virtue."

7 (fols. 10v–11v). An unpublished encomium, consisting of thirty-eight lines in elegiac meter, addressed to Filelfo's principal patron during this period, the duke of Milan, Francesco Sforza (d. 1466).[8] Addressing his prince here as the "hope of the Latin bards," he calls on Christ to protect and save the duke.

8 (fols. 11v–14v). An unpublished epistle of sixty lines in Sapphics, addressed to Palla Strozzi. Like poem 1.3, this epistle is a tapestry of allusions to Plato, Aristotle, and the Stoic philosophers on the supremacy of reason

[5] On Borso, see Werner L. Gundersheimer, *Ferrara: the Style of a Renaissance Despotism* (Princeton, 1973); Lauro Martines, *Power and Imagination: City-States in Renaissance Italy* (New York, 1979), pp. 222–30; and A. Frizzi, *Memorie per la storia di Ferrara* (Ferrara, 1847–1850), vol. 5, pp. 73f.

[6] Filelfo, *Epistolae*, fol. 101v.

[7] On Alamanni, see Lauro Martines, *The Social World of the Florentine Humanists: 1390–1460* (Princeton, 1963), pp. 345–46; Arnaldo della Torre, *Storia dell'Accademia platonica di Firenze* (Florence, 1902).

[8] On Sforza, see G. Benadduci, *Della Signoria di Francesco Sforza nella Marca* (Tolentino, 1892); C. M. Ady, *A History of Milan under the Sforza* (London, 1907); Carlo de' Rosmini, *Della istoria di Milano*, vols. 1–3 (Milan 1820–1821); and F. Cognasso, *Storia di Milano*, vol. 6 (Milan, 1955), pp. 387–448.

over passion. But it also contains an autobiographical note that gives us an idea of Filelfo's own assessment of some of his creative output: he decries here having "done many things in vain in order to take prizes for sweet praises."

9 (fols. 14v–15). An encomium of fifty-two lines in elegiac meter, addressed to Cardinal Bessarion. Filelfo introduces himself here as a *vates*, the divinely inspired poet-priest of Horace's *Odes* 1.1. Calling himself a seer (μάντις), he prophesies that Bessarion will bring light to the world in a time "when darkness covers the whole earth," a phrase that Filelfo uses here (and again in poems 2.2 and 2.7) to characterize the end of Pope Nicholas's reign with his death in 1455, and the succession of Callixtus III to the papal throne. The complete text of this poem is printed in Legrand.[9]

10 (fols. 15–17). An unpublished encomium, consisting of sixty-four lines in Sapphic strophes, ostensibly addressed to Nicholas d'Este, the young nephew of Duke Borso d'Este. As in poem 1.4, Filelfo again aims his flattering lyrics at the Duke, a man known more for his love of hunting than for his interest in the classics.[10] He urges Nicholas to imitate his uncle, who like Zeus himself "shines on the right for good bards."

11 (fols. 17–18v). A satirical epistle addressed to John Argyropoulos during his tenure at the Florentine Studio (1456–1471), consisting of thirty-eight lines in elegiac meter, on the difficulty of combining wealth with virtue.[11] Filelfo urges the professor by all means "to toil day and night to philosophize and get wealth simultaneously" (φιλοσοφεῖν ἀρ᾽ ὁμοῦ σπεῦ-σον, πλουτεῖν δὲ κατ᾽ ἦμαρ νύκτα τε μοχθίζων), "for otherwise the Florentines will judge you a fool." The complete text of the poem is printed in Legrand.[12]

12 (fols. 18v–20v). An unpublished epistle of sixty lines in Sapphic strophes, gently rebuking Donato Acciaiuoli (the dedicatee of poem 1.5) for his silence and urging him to answer Filelfo's letter.

[9] Legrand, *Lettres*, pp. 197ff.
[10] See n. 5.
[11] On Argyropoulos, see Giuseppe Cammelli, *I dotti bizantini e le origini dell' umanesimo. Giovanni Argiropulo*, 2 (Florence, 1941); della Torre, *Accademia platonica*, pp. 387–99; Arthur Field, *The Beginning of the Philosophical Renaissance*; Garin, *Portraits from the Quattrocento*; Jerrold E. Seigel, "The Teaching of Argyropulos and the Rhetoric of the First Humanists," *Action and Conviction in Early Modern Europe*, ed. T. K. Rabb and J. E. Seigel (Princeton, 1969), pp. 237–60; George Holmes, *The Florentine Enlightenment: 1400–1450* (New York, 1969), pp. 262–65.
[12] Legrand, *Lettres*, pp. 199f.

13 (fols. 20v–21v). An epistle of forty lines in elegiac meter, addressed to the Greek émigré scholar Theodore Gaza (d. 1478), during his tenure from 1455–1458 as resident professor of Greek at King Alfonso's court in Naples. Gaza had fled to Italy in the 1430s after the Turks captured Thessalonica. Like Aurispa, he taught Greek at Ferrara under Este patronage. A longtime client and protégé of Cardinal Bessarion's, in the last years of his life he served Pope Paul II in Rome.[13] In this epistle Filelfo returns to a favorite dilemma: the incompatibility of wealth and virtue, "for every wise man is always poor." But Filelfo tells Alfonso how to unloose the Gordian knot: "Your task, Alfonso, is to shower this man, Gaza, with riches. For you have riches and he songs—and such is fit pay for you both. An elegant poem and fame for posterity are due a shining king; but an honorable man has need of money." The Greek text of the poem is printed in Legrand.[14]

14 (fols. 22–23). A philosophical epistle consisting of sixty lines in Sapphic strophes, addressed to John Argyropoulos. Filelfo proposes here that Argyropoulos write a didactic poem—one both pastoral and metaphysical in its nature. He should "sing of the magnitude of the moon and the whole course of the fiery sun . . . and tell the origin of the human soul, and how souls acquired mind." The complete text of the poem is printed in Legrand.[15]

15 (23v–25). An unpublished epistle, consisting of forty-eight lines in elegiac meter, to Piero de' Medici, Cosimo's son, whom Filelfo affectionately addresses as his son's godfather. Filelfo, whom Cosimo had caused to leave Florence in 1434, seems here to suggest that Piero bring about a reconciliation between himself and his father. "Give me your hand, for I am suffering from fearful shipwreck," he writes Piero, "and bring an end to my harsh fate . . . Time heals every trouble, nor is it right for the wise man to feed his anger."

16 (fols. 25–27). An epistle of seventy-two lines in Sapphics, addressed to Andronicus Callistus, the most renowned of the Greek scholars who

[13] On Gaza, see Deno J. Geanakoplos, "Theodore Gaza, a Byzantine Scholar of the Palaeologan 'Renaissance' in the Italian Renaissance," in *Medievalia et Humanistica* 12 (1984): 61–81; Bentley, *Politics and Culture in Renaissance Naples*; on Gaza's relationship to Bessarion and his circle, see John Monfasani, *George of Trebizond. A Biography and a Study of His Rhetoric and Logic* (Leiden, 1976); and Mohler, *Kardinal Bessarion*.

[14] Legrand, *Lettres*, pp. 200f.

[15] Ibid., pp. 201ff.

came to Italy from Constantinople after Gaza and Argyropoulos.[16] In this verse epistle Filelfo offers friendship and assistance to Callistus, who after the Turks' capture of Constantinople had taken refuge in Palla Strozzi's household in Padua. "If you should desire something of mine," wrote Filelfo, "take it as though it were yours." This poem is printed in Legrand.[17]

Book 2

1 (fols. 27v–29v). An unpublished encomium of fifty-eight lines in elegiac meter, dedicated to Ludovico Gonzaga (d. 1478), Marquis of Mantua and patron of the three principal Italian scholars of Greek other than Filelfo in the first half of the Quattrocento: Giovanni Aurispa, Guarino Veronese, and Vittorino da Feltre.[18] Here Filelfo, now in his sixties, entreats Gonzaga, whom he addresses as the only hope of the Muses, an Ares in war, and a Heracles in body and heart, to assist him. "I have no money," he writes in this poem, "See how winter's frost sets in . . . Time has already taken away my summer. But a poor old man suffers things very much worse than death."

2 (fols. 29v–31v). An unpublished funeral elegy of sixty lines in Sapphics, on the death (in 1455) of Nicholas V (born Tommaso Parentucelli da Sarzana).[19] The first of the great humanist popes, Nicholas founded the Vatican Library and made the papal court an important center for the study of classical texts. Filelfo had been close to Tommaso since 1428, when he taught at the university of Bologna and Tommaso was in the service of Cardinal Albergati in that city. Filelfo here calls on the Muses to "give tears" for the death of his friend of nearly thirty years, now that "darkness has covered over all the earth."

3 (fols. 31v–33). An encomium of fifty-eight lines in elegiac meter, dedicated to Theodore Gaza during his sojourn at King Alfonso's court in

[16] On Callistus, also known as Andronicus of Byzantium see Giuseppe Cammelli, "Andronico Callisto," in *Rinascita* 5 (1942): 104–21; also Legrand, *Lettres*, Filelfo to Callistus (29 April 1464); D. Geanokoplos, *Greek Scholars in Venice: Studies in the Dissemination of Greek Learning from Byzantium to the West* (Cambridge, Mass., 1962), pp. 73–88.

[17] Legrand, *Lettres*, pp. 203ff.

[18] On the Gonzaga, see Alessandro Luzio and Rodolfo Renier, "I Filelfo e l'umanesimo alla corte dei Gonzaga," in *Giornale storico della letteratura italiana* 16 (1890): 119–217; and Jacob Burckhardt, *The Civilization of the Renaissance in Italy* (Reprint. New York, 1958), pp. 60f. and 220f.

[19] On Nicholas, see Vespasiano, *Princes, Popes and Prelates*, pp. 31–58; and Ludwig von Pastor, *The History of the Popes*, 4th ed., 40 vols., trans. F. I. Antrobus (London, 1923), p. 2.

Naples. The poem, which mainly catalogs Alfonso's virtues rather than Gaza's, is in Legrand.[20]

4 (fols. 33v–36). An unpublished encomium of eighty-eight lines in Sapphic strophes, dedicated to Cardinal Prospero Colonna, whom Eugenius IV had defrocked and whom Nicholas V allegedly feared.[21] Filelfo addresses Colonna as the world's greatest spiritual hope since the death of Nicholas.

5 (fols. 36–37v). An epistle of fifty lines in elegiac meter, addressed to Cardinal Bessarion in Rome. Here Filelfo, with tact and a bit of humor, asks the cardinal to return his rare manuscript of Plutarch's *Lives*, which had been temporarily lost. Filelfo reminds the cardinal here that while "nature gives arms to each according to his rank," to Filelfo she has given—books. The complete text of the poem is printed in Legrand.[22]

6 (fols. 38–39). A poem of consolation, consisting of forty-four lines in Sapphics, addressed to Cardinal Isidoro, Patriarch of Constantinople and Cardinal of Ruteno (Russia). The cardinal had escaped from Constantinople disguised as a slave in May 1453.[23] In this poem Filelfo recalls that Manuel Paleologus (the Byzantine emperor whom he had served as a young man in Constantinople), had "vanquished every living king by the luster of his mind." The poet promises, moreover, that the Turkish empire "will fall amid its own deceitful weapons." The complete text of this poem is in Legrand.[24]

7 (fols. 39v–41). A satirical epistle of fifty lines in elegiac meter, addressed to Cardinal Bessarion, on the current state of affairs in Rome. The new pope, Calixtus III (1455–1458), a Borgia and a Spaniard, who showed little interest in art or literature, was deeply resented by the Italian intellectual community.[25] "This pope," Filelfo quipped in this epistle to Bessarion, "works at changing nothing, with this one exception: he yearns to be like a god." Now, he continued, Rome has "no place for the wise, no

[20] 20. Legrand, *Lettres*, pp. 205ff.

[21] On Colonna, see F. Petrucci, in *DBI*, 27.416–18; Mario Emilio Cosenza, *Biographical and Bibliographical Dictionary of the Italian Humanists and of the World of Classical Scholarship in Italy, 1300–1800*, 3 vols. (New York, 1962), 2.1062.

[22] Legrand, *Lettres*, pp. 207ff. See ibid., p. 95 for a similar request for the return of his Plutarch addressed to Bessarion and dated 19 December 1457. See also Filelfo, *Epistolae*, fols. 102v–103: Filelfo had lent his copy of the *Lives* to Nicholas V; he was finally able to retrieve the manuscript on his visit to Pius II in 1458.

[23] Cammelli, *I Dotti*, 1.522ff.

[24] Legrand, *Lettres*, pp. 210ff.

[25] On Calixtus, see Michael Mallett, *The Borgias: the Rise and Fall of a Renaissance Dynasty* (New York, 1969), pp. 59–81.

place for virtue; and standing and authority belong solely to those with wealth." On the other hand, Filelfo here consoles the cardinal with the myth of Heracles, who succeeded in overcoming his Cerberus. The complete text of this poem is in Legrand.[26]

8 (fols. 41–43). An encomium of seventy-two lines in Sapphic strophes, addressed to Murad II (d. 1481), sultan of the Turkish Empire.[27] Murad I had graciously received Filelfo in 1424 when the Byzantine emperor had sent Filelfo, then twenty-six and still a student, to the Turkish emperor as his legate. Moreover, after Murad II took Constantinople, he released Filelfo's mother-in-law and her two daughters from prison in response to a plea for their amnesty from Filelfo. Filelfo concludes this poem, addressed to a man whom most of his contemporaries considered a bloodthirsty savage, wistfully—with a gentle velleity: "If only Christ . . . would give you, Mohammed, the light of his faith (ὄμμα πίστεος)! For then you would indeed be monarch over all the earth, and I would not hesitate to cross so vast an ocean, leaving Italy for lofty Thrace." The complete text of the poem is printed in Legrand.[28]

9 (fols. 44–44v). An epistle of forty lines in elegiac couplets, addressed to another Greek churchman and scholar, Gennadius Scholarius, Patriarch of Constantinople.[29] In this epistle Filelfo renews his acquaintance with Scholarius, a friend from Filelfo's youth in Constantinople, and asks that he write him back soon. The complete text is printed in Legrand.[30]

10 (fols. 44v–46). A companion poem to 2.1, again dedicated to his Mantuan patron Ludovico Gonzaga, but this time his gift to the marquis consists of forty-four lines in Sapphics. In exchange for poems that will purportedly immortalize Gonzaga's glory and magnanimity, Filelfo asks here only for temporary relief: "Your friend, O monarch, shivers from hunger, and suffers other very bitter things because of his lack of money. In providing these things you will banish all my pain."

11 (fols. 46–47v). A companion piece to 1.10 addressed to Niccolò d'Este, this time consisting of fifty lines in elegiac meter. Again, though the poem is addressed to Niccolò, it is an encomium for Borso.

[26] Legrand, *Lettres*, pp. 210f.
[27] See Lucia Gualdo Rosa, "Il Filelfo e i Turchi. Un inedito storico dell' Archivio Vaticano," in *Annali della facolta di lettere e filosofia. Universita di Napoli* 11 (1964–1968), 109–65.
[28] Legrand, *Lettres*, pp. 211f.
[29] On Scholarius see M. Jugie, "Georges Scholarios, professeur de philosophie," in *Studi bizantini e neoellenici* 10 (1936): 482–94; and C. J. Turner, "The Career of George-Gennadius Scholarius," in *Byzantion* 39 (1969): 420–55.
[30] Legrand, *Lettres*, pp. 214ff.

12 (fols. 48–50v). An unpublished funeral elegy of eighty lines in Sapphic strophes, on the death of King Alfonso of Naples. When Alfonso died, Filelfo writes, nature itself grieved: "the earth trembled, the mountains cleaved in two, and turbulent seas grazed the stars in Olympus." Filelfo particularly lauds Alfonso because he "honored orators and was a friend to the best of bards . . . always paying each with full-flowing gifts." At the conclusion of the eulogy we find a typically Filelfian mingling of Olympian and Christian deities: "As long as you lived, Alfonso, you surpassed Zeus and Ares. Apollo, Cronos, and Hermes yielded to you too, and all who have won a place in the stars by dint of their work. Now Christ, whom you worshipped with your entire soul . . . has taken you to the farthest summit of divine Olympus."

13 (fols. 50v–51v). A fourth unpublished paean celebrating the virtues of Borso d'Este, consisting of forty-two lines in elegiac meter, this time addressed to Girolamo Castelli, the duke's physician, as was poem 1.4.

14 (fols. 52–54). An unpublished encomium, consisting of sixty-four lines in Sapphic strophes, addressed to Pope Pius II (Enea Silvio Piccolomini, d. 1464) on his assumption of the papacy following Calixtus's death in 1458. Filelfo here praises his former student in Florence, fellow poet, and friend of thirty years' standing, for his rationality, his piety, his virtue, and his love of God. In the closing twelve lines of Filelfo's encomium he commends above all Pius's plans to mount a military expedition against the infidel (ἀσεβής) Turk.

Book 3

1 (fols. 54–55v). An unpublished panegyric of forty-six lines in elegiac meter, addressed to Borso d'Este. This is the fifth encomium in the collection in praise of Borso's virtue, but the first to be addressed directly to the duke. Filelfo studs his flattering verses with mythological allusions: the Cyprian, Lyaeus, Demeter, Phoebus, and Nestor all come up in turn. But in the last pentameter of the poem Filelfo cannot resist jolting his patron back to earth. If Borso treats the poet well, Filelfo promises in turn to endow him with "undying fame—more beautiful than true."

2 (55v–58v). A consolatory epistle in time of war to Theodore Gaza, consisting of ninety-six lines in Sapphic strophes. Unlike Filelfo's earlier verse epistle to Gaza (2.3), in which Filelfo lavished praise on Gaza's patron, King Alfonso, this poem contains only brief mention of Alfonso's son and successor to the throne, Ferrante.[31] Filelfo assures Gaza that nei-

---

[31] Bentley, *Politics and Culture in Renaissance Naples*, pp. 21–35, traces the negative tradi-

ther God nor Francesco Sforza will abandon the just, and that Ferrante will succeed in repulsing the French pretender to the throne of Naples, Jean d'Anjou—even without the assistance of Pius II, "whose heart the love of gold has withered," Filelfo warns. The complete text of this poem is in Legrand.[32]

3 (fols. 59–62). A funeral elegy of 110 lines, addressed to the Venetian patrician and military leader, Iacopo Antonio Marcello, on the death of his son Valerio.[33]

4 (fols. 62v–63v). An unpublished encomium of forty lines in Sapphic strophes, addressed to Ludovico Gonzaga's son, Francesco, Cardinal of Mantua, whose "tongue," Filelfo writes here, "pours out a stream of honey when he speaks" and whose virtue "flashes like a golden star."

5 (fols. 63v–65). An unpublished epistle of forty lines in elegiac meter to Lazaro Scarampo, Bishop of Como. This encomiastic epistle has two specific objectives other than winning further gifts and support from a patron who has already been generous to Filelfo. First, Filelfo asks the bishop if he knows of a suitable husband for his daughter; and second, Filelfo here submits a letter of recommendation on behalf of Demetrios Castrenus—a Greek émigré scholar "nurtured on the sweet milk of wisdom," whom he hopes the Bishop will support.

6 (fols. 65–66). A funeral elegy addressed to his son Xenophon, on the death of Xenophon's son, consisting of thirty-two lines in Sapphic strophes. This verse epistle has not been published.

7 (fols. 66–67v). An unpublished encomium addressed to Pope Pius II, consisting of thirty-six lines in elegiac meter. This poem appears to have been composed soon after Calixtus's death in 1458, judging from Filelfo's

---

tion about Ferrante's character to the fifteenth-century French historian Philippe de Commynes, *Memoires*, ed. J. Calmette (Paris, 1924–1925); for a reassessment of his rule, see Bentley, and Ernesto Pontieri, *Per la storia del regno di Ferrante I d'Aragona re di Napoli*, 2d ed. (Naples, 1969); and Pontieri, "La Puglia nel quadro della monarchia degli aragonesi di Napoli," in *Atti del congresso internazionale di studi sull'eta aragonese* (Bari, 1972), pp. 19–52.

[32] Legrand, *Lettres*, pp. 215ff.

[33] On Marcello, see Margaret King, *Venetian Humanism in an Age of Patrician Dominance* (Princeton, 1986), pp. 393–96; on the funeral elegies composed by the humanists for Marcello, see Renata Fabbri, "Le *Consolationes de obitu Valerii Marcelli* ed il Filelfo," in *Misc. Branca*, 3.1.227–50; and G. Benadduci, *A Jacopo Antonio Marcello patrizio veneto parte di orazione consolatoria ed elegia di Francesco Filelfo e lettera di Giovanni Mario Filelfo* (Tolentino, 1894); M. King is now preparing a full-length study of Valerio's life and death and the consolatory elegies and orations written for Marcello after his son's death. A codex of Greek poem 3.3 attributed to Filelfo's own hand is also contained in *Vat. Lat. 1790*.

undiluted pleasure at the departure of the Spanish contingent from the papal court. "Because of you," Filelfo writes here, "foreign usage has fled to the crows." Though Pius failed to pay Filelfo the stipend he had promised him early on in his papacy, in this poem he neither hints that Pius had reneged on his commitment nor makes innuendos about the pope's avarice, as he does in poem 3.2.[34]

8 (fols. 67v–68v). A funeral elegy on the death in 1462 in Padua of Palla Strozzi. This poem has not been published.

9 (fols. 68v–71v). A third unpublished epistle in the collection addressed to Pope Pius II, consisting of one hundred lines in elegiac meter. This is a particularly subtle piece, because although Filelfo treats with understanding and delicacy Pius's desire to unite all Italy against the Moslem threat and even to undertake a war against the Turks, at the same time he warns his friend against the perils of such an undertaking. Should the Turkish campaign, Filelfo wonders, be viewed as a test of the pope's sublime virtue? And what if the Venetians were to emerge from the war as the masters of all Italy? But Filelfo's other concern in this epistle is for his own welfare. "Save me," he begs Pius, "for you are my only anchor . . . Do not leave me, father . . . The sea brings me terrible suffering, and I wander shipwrecked into the waves."

10 (fols. 71v–73). An unpublished epistle of sixty lines in Sapphics, addressed to Antonio Beccadelli, who achieved notoriety overnight with the publication of his *Hermaphroditus*, a book of sexually explicit Latin epigrams in 1426. In this epistle Filelfo approaches Beccadelli whom he first met in Bologna in the late 1420s, as "one old man to another."[35] He urges Antonio to write epic poetry celebrating the virtues and military campaigns of his now-deceased patron Alfonso, and if not Alfonso then Ferrante, Alfonso's son and successor to the throne.

11 (fols. 73v–74v). An unpublished epistle in elegiac couplets addressed to Girolamo Castelli at the Este court in Ferrara. This verse epistle, which

[34] For Filelfo's correspondence on the promised pension, see his *Epistolae*, to Bessarion and Pius, fols. 102v–103; for the papal documents concerning the pension and his honorary appointment as a papal scriptor, see Germano Gualdo, "Francesco Filelfo e la curia pontificia: una carriera mancata," in *Archivio della società romana di storia patria* 102 (1979): 189–236.
[35] On Beccadelli, see Michele Natale, *Antonio Beccadelli detto il Panormita* (Caltanisetta, 1902); Vincenzo Laurenza, "Il Panormita a Napoli," in *Atti della Accademia Pontaniana* 42 (1912): 1–92; Alan Ryder, "Antonio Beccadelli: A Humanist in Government," in C. H. Clough, ed., *Cultural Aspects of the Italian Renaissance: Essays in Honour of Paul Oskar Kristeller* (Manchester, 1976), pp. 123–40; Mario Santoro, "Il Panormita 'aragonese,' " in *Esperienze letterarie* 9 (1984): 3–24; Bentley, *Politics and Culture in Renaissance Naples*, pp. 84–100; and Gianvito Resta, *L'epistolario del Panormita* (Messina, 1954); G. Resta, in *DBI*, 7.400–06.

contains the same sort of accolade to Borso's virtues that we see in poems 1.4, 1.10, 2.11, and 2.13, is a letter of recommendation on behalf of a certain young poet, Thebaldo, whom Filelfo asks Castelli to take under his wing.

12 (fols. 74v–75v). A prayer of thanksgiving to God for his bounty. This unpublished piece consists of twenty-eight lines in Sapphics.

13 (fols. 75v–77). The third philosophical epistle addressed to John Argyropoulos in the collection, consisting of fifty lines in elegiac meter. Filelfo asks Argyropoulos, whom he calls here the equal of Calypso, Orpheus, and Demodocus, to write him a poem on serious themes: "tell of the soul's power, of the beginnings and ends of mind and intelligence—if they have an end." Or, should he prefer lighter themes, Filelfo suggests he sing of "shining Phoebus marching across the earth, wearing innumerable flowers in his hair." The complete text of this poem is printed in Legrand.[36]

14 (fols. 78–81). An unpublished poem dedicated to Pope Paul II, the Venetian nobleman Pietro Barbo (d. 1471), consisting of one hundred lines in Sapphics, including several lines of Latin interspersed. Here Filelfo asks for the pope's protection and offers to serve him in either Rome or Milan. He also commends Paul's alliance with King Matthias of Hungary and applauds Paul's plans to use Hungarian infantry to fight the Turks. While Filelfo praises the superior martial qualities of the Italians, such as strength and courage, he regrets only that they seem "always to falter on the battlefield."[37]

[36] Legrand, *Lettres*, pp. 218f.
[37] The text here reads ἀλλὰ διστάζουσιν ἀεὶ συμπολεμοῦντες; *Liddell and Scott's Greek-English Lexicon* suggests "hesitate" or "falter" for διστάζειν.

APPENDIX E

DE MORALI DISCIPLINA, BOOK 1

Part One

D E MORALI DISCIPLINA consultanti mihi diligentius aliquid ad te scribere, Laurenti Medices, quo vel ipse delectareris, si quando a publicis muneribus remittere animum velles, vel tuis liberis, quos tibi opto quam simillimos fore, ad bene beateque vivendum ex hoc iam tempore prospiceres, multa veniebant in mentem quibus non mediocriter commovebar. Nam quanquam non eram nescius officium te hoc meum pro nostra amicitia nequaquam improbaturum, non poteram tamen non subvereri futuros nonnullos qui dicerent frustra esse huiusmodi scribendi munus a me susceptum, cum et Latini viri docti permulti de moribus praecepta tradiderint, et Aristotelis libri ad Nichomachum filium e Graeco in Latinum ab aliis atque aliis interpretibus traducti eloquium nihil intactum aut minus lucubratum excultumque reliquerint, quod in universa morali philolosophia quisquam nosse desideret. Itaque audacis imprudentisque esse hominis me in tanta et tam illustri scribentium multitudine quicquam aggredi, quod reprehendi iure queat. Nam si eadem litterarum monimentis mandata a nobis fuerint quae vel a Platone et Aristotele, vel a M. Tullio Cicerone et M. Terentio Varrone, vel ab Ambrosio et Augustino, ab aliisque quam plurimis eruditissime simul et disertissime sunt tractata, hoc fore tanquam exscribere, non scribere. Sin aliud iter incessero, non deerunt qui stultitiae me accusent, perinde atque unus inventus sim, qui tanquam Leontinus ille Gorgias audeam aliquid supra vires profiteri, quam ob rem ridiculo sim futurus. Accedit ad rei difficultatem quod ne ipsi quidem inter se philosophi de humanae vitae institutione conveniunt, quam singuli pro sua disciplina aliter atque aliter de virtute loquuti sint. Quare si aut hos sequi aut illos voluero, non sunt defuturi qui repugnent ac ultro mecum pertinacius manum conserant; num Stoici quicquam Peripateticis assentiantur, cum hi mediocritatem in affectibus laudent, quos illi omnes tum perturbationes, tum morbos appellent radicitusque extirpandos iubeant, nec ullam in eis mediocritatem inesse posse concedant? Quid enim loquar de Academicis, qui nihil usquam certi afferunt et in omnem partem se acerrimos disserendo praestant? Nam de Epicureis difficile est dictu quanta in caligine eorum versetur opinio culpa fortassis adversariorum, quod secus quam illi senserint quae sunt ab Epicuro scripta vel interpretentur vel falso insimulent plura. Nam et sapientem Epicurum et vitae continentissimae extitisse constat. [end p. 1] Sed hac de re postea.

Nunc eo nostra referat se oratio unde digressa est. Num idcirco quisquam reprehendat hoc meum institutum, quoniam et Graeci et Latini quam plurimi perdocte et copiose huiusmodi materiam sunt complexi? Pythagoras Samius, qui philosophiae Italicae annis centum post Thaletem Milesium principium dedit, omnium primus de virtute disseruit. Et is quidem Zoroastren Persen Ilium sequutus (qui philosophorum omnium antiquissimus fuit) et cum Magorum princeps, tum nullius inops laudatissimae disciplinae—is, inquam, Pythagoras non modo de iustitia gravissime est subtilissimeque loquutus, quam esse numerum diceret aequaliter aequalem, sed virtutes omnes ad numerorum retulit rationem. Nec tamen ulla Pythagorae auctoritas (qua venerabilius nihil erat) impedimento Socrati fuit quo minus omnium primus ex Ionica philosophia praecepta traderet de virtutibus, quas scientias esse affirmabat. Hunc sequutus auditor Plato quam diligenter quamque permulta cum de iustitia, tum de caeteris virtutibus disseruerit, non ii solùm quos decem scripsit de republica, verum etiam libri duodecim de legibus et Menon et Alcibiades et Phaedrus et Phaedon et reliqua eius volumina locupletissimum afferunt testimonium. Aristoteles enim non iis modo qui ante se plaerique de moribus scripserunt, sed ne sibi quidem ipsi pepercit; quin aliis alios eadem de re libros addiderit qui non iidem essent omnino, sed nec admodum diversi. Id autem ita habere tres eius declarant codices: unus ad Eudemum familiarem qui octo constat voluminibus; alter ad Nichomachum filium is quem nostri libris decem habent in manibus; ac item tertius qui duobus voluminibus continetur, quibus Magnis Moralibus nomen est. Enimvero splendida usque ingenia excitantur vel imitatione superiorum scriptorum vel quo etiam ipsa praeclarum aliquid ex sese inveniant, quod caeteris sit aut usui aut voluptati. Et ne id quidem unum inficier me operam daturum effecturumque, ne—si minus caeteri inter se philosophi pro sua singuli disciplina conveniunt—ipse usquam a me dissentiam. Quare nolit se quisquam, obsecro, molestum praebere huic nostro scribendi muneri, quin et legat prius animo pacato atque aequis oculis quae fuerint a nobis excogitata, et deinde consideret ac ita iudicet. Quod si fecerit, non difficulter futurum spero ut hunc quem suscepimus laborem aut laudet aut saltem non improbet. Nam quale de me iudicium sis facturus, Laurenti Medices, satis dilucide mihi videor animadvertere. Sed iam de re verba facere aggrediamur ea tamen ratione, ut intelligas me nulli philosophorum scholae ita addictum quo minus per omnia eorum praecepta vagari liceat et, quae meliora probabiliorave censuero, iis (tum addendo, tum minuendo si opus fuerit tum moderando mutandove) uti pro meis—id quod et Platonem et Aristotelem et caeteros item philosophos, tam Christianos quam Gentiles quos vocamus, persaepe fecisse comperio. [end p. 2]

Part Two

Quoniam moralis disciplina de qua scribere instituimus his virtutibus constat, quibus civilis felicitas comparatur, omnium primum quid sit virtus est definiendum. Ita enim certo quodam ordine ac suo nostra progredietur oratio. Virtus igitur est rectus animi habitus quo et boni sumus et laudamur. Tum enim maxime laudamur, cum ad interiorem virtutis habitum exterior accesserit actio, qua sola virtus recondita prodeat in lucem. At vitium contra est pravus animi habitus quo quis et malus est et vituperatur. Ea vero laudamus quae sunt honesta et vituperamus turpia. Et virtutes quidem morales ab honestate proficiscuntur, ut a turpitudine vitia. Honestum autem id esse dicimus quod sit populari fama gloriosum, ut Aristoteli placet. Nam mea quidem sententia tanta est vis, tanta dignitas honestatis, ut omni laude sit superior. Laudantur etiam ea quae sunt aut virtutis causae aut virtutem sequuntur; aut fiunt a virtute aut eius sunt opera. Nam contraria dantur vitio. Laus vero est oratio quae virtutis magnitudinem demonstrat. Contra vero et quod turpe sit et quod vituperetur est definiendum eadem ratione. Et quoniam virtutem ac vitium ex animi habitu definivimus, animum in suas partes separemus necesse est, ut intelligatur cui potissimum parti sigillatim et virtutes et vitia dari oporteat.

Atque animi quidem partes non eodem modo a philosophis numeratae sunt. Pythagoras enim is, quem paulo ante meminimus, dupliciter animum est partitus tum altius, tum propinquius et clarius. Nam cum primo dixisset duas esse animi partes alteram rationalem et irrationalem alteram; deinde alia quoque est usus secundo loco divisione, inquiens animum distribui in tres partes, quarum altera in se haberet rationem, altera vero quae ea careret duas dividebatur in partes. Quarum una contineret animositatem (hanc enim eo loco θυμός significat, sed animositatem pro ira accipiebat); in altera vero parte cupiditatem ponebat. At Democritus atque Epicurus in partes duas animum separarunt. Nam rationem inhaerentem atque insitam in thorace statuerunt; sed quae pars ratione vacat, eam dispersam esse voluerunt per omnem corporis concretionem. Ad haec ea etiam corpora quae sensu carent Democritus existimavit aliqualis animi participationem habere. Et hi quidem tres ex Italica fuere philosophia. At Stoici, qui auctore Socrate Ionicam philosophiam sequuti sunt, constare hominis animum voluerunt ex octo partibus, in quibus hosce quinque sensus posuerunt: visum, auditum, odoratum, gustum, tactum, et sexto loco partem vocalem, septimo vero eam partem a qua est semen. Partem autem octavam eam esse voluerunt quae principatum obtinens imperat hisce omnibus septem partibus per propria instrumenta. At Plato, qui et Socratem in moralibus audierat et Heracletum in physicis et Pythagoram in divinis atque mathematicis sequutus est, eadem est usus tam primo quam secundo loco partitione animi qua Pythagoram usum didicerat. Nam et in partem quae rationem habet humanum distribuit animum et in partem quae rationis est expers. Rursusque eundem separavit animum in tres partes, ut pote qui mentem ob eam rationem in capite collocarit [end p. 3], quoniam ea corporis pars longius abest a colluvione et sordibus; animositatem vero vigoremque irascibilem qui proprius est ipse (θυμός quem modo memineram) in corde; et cupiditatem quoque subter praecordia. Mens igitur secundum Platonem, ut est prima vis atque potestas animi, in capite tamquam in arce imperat veluti regina primaeque dignitatis estque contemplativa. Nam ea parte et vigemus maxime et ratiocinamur et cogitamus et intelligimus et sapimus. Sed altera vis animi cui Plato secundam tribuit dignitatem, ut est in pectore constituta, praestat ut agamus quae ipsa mens atque ratio imperarit. Vis autem illa quae inferius est posita praestantioribus illis potestatibus paret. Existimavit etiam Plato per omnes artus corpusque universum meare animum atque sigillatim per membra omnia tanquam per instrumenta quaedam vim suam virtutemque ostendere. Praeterea ad eundem animum referri omnia, quaecunque occurrunt sensibus. Quae vero a sensibus referuntur ea esse alia atque alia. Sed Aristoteles, qui annos xx. Platonem audierat ac sectae Peripateticae principium dedit, primis quidem temporibus identidem partitus est animum, ut a Platone didicerat, id quod ex illius scriptis cognosci potest, praecipueque ex eo libro qui de virtutibus inscribitur. Postea vero eum in duas secuit partes: quarum alteram voluit rationem continere, alteram vero carere ratione. Et rursus quae rationem in se haberet, eam quoque in duas dividi partes, quarum altera ita contemplaremur ea quae sunt (sic enim in praesentia dicere malo quam entia), quoad ipsa principia secus habere non possunt, ut parte altera contemplemur ea quae possunt aliter esse, cum ad ea quae alia sunt genere, partes quoque sint aliae genere necesse sit. Alteram vero harum partium Aristoteles scientificam vocat et alteram cogitivam, quandoquidem cogitare aliud nihil est quam consultare. De iis enim quae haberi aliter possunt, consultat nemo. Sedem vero mentis atque rationis in cordis penetralibus esse voluit. Ad quam quidem mentem Aristoteles docet ea referri omnia quae singuli sensus nuntiant; ab eademque de iis fieri iudicium quae sentiuntur; atque examinari cuiusmodi ea sint quae varie occurrunt sensibus. At ea in parte quae sua natura est expers rationis appetitum posuit, qui si a ratione se regi gubernarique patiatur, plurimarum est capax virtutum earumque moralium. Nam, ut Plutarchus ait, mores huius irrationalis partis sunt qualitates, sin ab affectionibus avertatur distrahaturque, sit officina flagitiorum omnium. Mentem, inquam, locatam Aristoteles docet in cordis penetralibus, ubi alias quoque animi species locatas asserit: imaginationem, memoriam, appetitionem. Nam quanquam animi potentiae in uno loco magis apparent quam in alio, ut aliae in cerebro, aliae in iecore, aliae in testibus, aliaeque in aliis membris pro qualitate et convenientia atque aptitudine corporeo-

rum instrumentorum, eorum tamen omnium initia et quasi radices quasdam Aristoteles probat e sede cordis emanare, quando succus concocti cibi
per venas cordis caeterum corpus irrigat et motus corporealis, qui locularis
est, a corde ipso initium sumit. Venarum enim et nervorum initium ac veluti nodus quidam ipsum cor est. Penes cor autem vis intellectiva, agitata
atque ignita pro ratione, eodem se in loco coacervare existimatur [end p.
4] potestate quidem illic habitans, operatione vero effectuque ad corporis
conceptum et viciniam commeans. Sed de Aristotele hactenus multa. Nos
quod instituimus prosequamur.

Quantum ad animi partes attinet, ea mihi distributio probatur maxime
qua Pythagoram secundo loco et Platonem usum legimus. Quae tamen a
prima, quantum ad rem attinet, non abhorret. Separamus, inquam, animum tripliciter: in mentem qua rationem complectimur; et in iram et cupiditatem, ut mens seu ratio in toto sit capite; et ira in corde et cupiditas
subter praecordia. Quam quidem sententiam familiaris noster Maro sequutus est, cum cecinit: "Celsa sedet Aeolus arce sceptra tenens mollitque
animos (hoc est cupiditates) et temperat iras." Quid autem animus sit, mu-
litplex est dissentiensque philosophorum opinio, ut alio loco scripsimus.
Caeterum mea quidem sententia animus est creata substantia spiritualis
simplex rationis atque intelligentiae particeps, quae seipsam movens naturale instrumentaleque corpus tam diu afficit ea vi, quae et vitalis est et sen-
sibilia admittit, quoad eorum natura capax elementalem servat convenien-
tiam.

Hic sane mihi videtur hominis animus, cuius rectus habitus virtus est, ut
vitium pravus. Et rectum quidem habitum rectam vocamus eorum dispos-
itionem, quae neque moveri neque transmutari facile possint. Differre autem ab affectione habitum nemo vel mediocriter doctus ignorat, quum is
quam affectio et permanentior sit et diuturnior. Quales sunt tum scientiae,
tum virtutes quas, ubi tibi vendicaveris, difficulter amittas. Contra vero
affectiones. Nam et faciles sunt et celeriter moventur transmutanturque. Et
est sane affectio ea materia quam circa moralis versatur virtus, cuius forma
ratio est. Haud enim obscurum reor homini docto et erudito virtutem
etiam dari quandam a materia separatam per seque subsistentem ac plane
meram. Sed de habitu nunc virtutis habetur sermo. Per huiusmodi ergo
habitum tametsi boni sumus, non laudamur tamen nisi actio ipsa accesserit.
Parum enim apparet nos animo esse vel temperanti vel forti vel iusto vel
liberali, ni liberalitatis, iustitiae, fortitudinis, temperantiae opera conse-
quantur. Itaque non absurde ii monuisse videntur mihi qui dicunt rectam
operationem esse virtute ipsa praestantiorem, ea scilicet ratione ducti quod
ignorata animi sententia ignoratur etiam electio, quae ab habitu ad actionem proficiscatur necesse est. Nam, ut prudentissime monet Cicero, omnis virtutis laus in actione consistit.

Part Three

At qua bonitate nos deceat bonos esse videtur considerandum. Nam bonum multipliciter dici solet, cum sit bonum quoddam secundum honorem, quoddam secundum laudem, et quoddam secundum potentiam. Atque huic quidem parti et imperium tribuunt et divitias et vires caeteraque huiusmodi, quibus et vir bonus bene et male uti potest. Bono autem laudabili virtutes dantur, ex quarum actionibus laudamur. Bonum vero honorabile vocatur quod et divinum sit et praestantius quoddam bonum. Quod assequutus qui fuerit, eum virum sanctum ac perfectum dicimus iureque honoramus. Praeterea quartum quoddam est bonum quod et servat bonum et facit. Id in exercitatione est positum bonae [end p. 5] valetudinis ac si quid aliud est huiusmodi. Est insuper alia quaedam bonorum partitio, cum alia bona sint et ubique et omnino expetenda, alia vero aspernenda, ut iustitia aliaeque virtutes quae et ubique sunt omninoque expetendae. Vires vero et divitiae et potestas caeteraque huiusmodi neque ubique expetenda dicimus nec item omnino. Praeterea aliter partiuntur, cum dicant bona esse alia fines, alia vero nequaquam fines, ut sanitas finis est, sed quae sanitatis fiunt gratia fines ea non sunt. Et quaecunque hoc modo dixerimus, semper eorum finis melior est. Qua quidem ratione bona valetudo melior est finis quam bonae valetudinis effectiva. Et ne prolixiores simus, finis ultimus iis omnibus praestat qui huius gratia expetuntur. Quare ipsorum finium perfectior finis semper imperfecto est melior. Perfectum vero dicimus finem, quem consequuti nihilo amplius egemus. Nam imperfectus ubi nobis finis contigerit, egemus item aliquo, ut si iusti simus, multis quoque aliis nobis finibus opus est. Sola felicitas ea est, quam adepti, nihil aliud appetentes contenti sumus. Sed de felicitate postea disseremus; haec enim est finis quem quaerimus, optimus ac perfectus et bonorum omnium summum bonum. Et in hac sane bonorum distributione Peripateticos sequuti sumus.

Caeterum puto non incongruum fore nec inutile, si antequam longius nostra progrediatur oratio, breviter complectar qui alii illustres ac summa gravitate philosophi de bono ipso statuerint et quidnam esset et quotuplex. Et omnium primos audiamus Stoicos, qui magnum quiddam ac praeclarum in philosophia profiteri sunt existimati. Hi enim sequentes communes notiones bonum esse utilitatem definierunt aut non aliud ab utilitate. Atque utilitatem quidem ipsam virtutem esse dicunt bonamque actionem. Non aliud ab utilitate esse volunt bonum virum et amicum; virtutem enim (quae imperitantem vim rationis repraesentat) et bonam actionem (quae operatio quaedam sit secundum virtutem) perspicue prodesse; bonum autem virum atque amicum, qui et ipsi e numero sint bonorum, neque utilitatem esse dicere oportere nec ab utilitate alios. Et id quidem ob huiusmodi causam. Nam sectatores Stoicorum partem dicunt nec eandem esse cum toto nec aliam a toto, sicuti manus neque eadem est cum toto homine. Non enim totus homo est manus, neque alia a toto. Nam tota cum manu totus etiam homo intelligitur homo. Ita ergo propterea quod boni viri et amici pars est virtus, pars vero nec eadem esse cum toto possit, nec alia a toto. Dicunt Stoici bonum virum et amicum non esse alium ab utilitate. Itaque omne bonum ea definitione comprehendi putant, sive continuo utilitas sit, seu non sit ab utilitate aliud. Quapropter consequenter bonum tripliciter dicunt appellari. Uno enim modo id bonum dici ex quo aut a quo fit utilitas, quod certe principalissimum existit et virtus. Ab hac enim tanquam a fonte quodam omnis naturaliter manat utilitas. Secundo autem modo id per quod utilitas contingit. Sic enim non solum virtutes dicentur bona, sed etiam quae secundum virtutes actiones proficiscuntur, si quidem per hasce utilitas contingit. Ultimo vero modo bonum dicitur illud quod utilitatem afferre potest. Et haec quidem assignatio complectebatur tum virtutes, tum actiones secundum virtutes, tum amicos, tum bonos viros, tum etiam et Deum et bonos angelos.

Ob [end p. 6] quam quidem causam aliter atque aliter, tum Platonem et Xenocratem, tum apud Stoicos bonum nominatur. Nam illi cum dicunt aliter dici bonum secundum speciem (quae Idea est) et aliter secundum participationem speciei, non quid sit bonum ostendunt, sed boni significata multis modis videntur exponere: et quae invicem plurimum discrepent nec habeant quicquam inter sese commune. Quemadmodum intueri licet in hac voce canis. Ut enim ex hac ipsa voce prolatio quidem significatur, sub quam et animal latrabile cadit et aquatile et astrum et quod unicum est in tesseris punctum (nihil autem huiusmodi prolationis commune invicem habent, neque secunda prolatione prima continetur, neque tertia secunda, nequé quarta prolatione tertia). Eodem etiam modo cum dicitur bonum secundum Ideam et bonum quod est particeps Ideae, expositio quidem eorum bonorum est quae significantur verorum et separatorum, et quibus ne ullum quidem bonum contineri ostendatur. Et hi sane hoc pacto de bono loquuti sunt, de quorum celebri pervagataque sententia quod meum iudicium sit non multo post, ut spero, disseram et ita disseram, ut homini non pertinacius quam par est contendenti nullum omnino dubium relinquatur. Nam neque Stoicis neque ipsi Peripateticorum principi Aristoteli maximo in philosophia gravissimoque viro in iis assentior, quae contra huiusmodi bonum subtiliter magis quam vere disseruit. Caeterum ut redeam ad Stoicos, volunt illi quidem secundum significatum complecti primum, et tertio quoque duo contineri, eademque ratione quarto contineri tria.

Fuerunt autem qui dicerent id esse bonum quod sit propter se expetendum. Alii vero bonum id esse definiunt quod ad felicitatem adiuvat. Et quosdam fuisse legimus qui bonum id esse vellent quod felicitatem compleret. Esse autem felicitatem secundum Zenonis, Cleanthisque et Chrysippi assignationem vitae facilem amoenumque decursum. Veruntamen genus esse huiusmodi voluere quo bonum assignatur. Sed cum bonum tripliciter dicatur, consuevere nonnulli continuo ad definitionem primi significati inquirere secundum quod dicebatur, bonum est id ex quo aut a quo utilitas proficiscitur, ut, si vero bonum est id a quo utilitas fit, solum generalem virtutem dicere oporteat bonum existere; ab hac enim sola utilitas fit. Excidit autem ab ea definitione quaelibet virtus particularis, ut prudentia, ut temperantia caeteraeque virtutes. A nulla enim ipsarum huiusmodi utilitas proficiscitur; sed a sapientia sapere providereve procedit et non quod communius est prodesse. Nam si hoc ipsum prodesse acciderit, non est secundum definitionem prudentia, sed generalis virtus. Et a temperantia, quod de ipsa praedicatur temperantem esse, non quod commune est prodesse. Eodemque modo de caeteris virtutibus dici potest. Contra ii cupientes quam definitionem posuerant sustinere ita respondent: cum a nobis id dicitur esse bonum, a quo utilitas proficiscitur, idem est ac si dicatur bonum id esse, a quo ad aliquid eorum quae in vita sunt proficiscitur utilitas. Hoc enim pacto quaelibet etiam particularis virtus bonum erit quae quidem nequaquam communiter utilitatem afferat, sed eorum aliquid praebeat quibus utilitas fit. Harum enim virtutum alia ut sapiamus provideamusve praestat, sicuti prudentia; alia ut temperantes [end p. 7] simus, sicuti temperantia. At hi quidem Stoici dum volunt huiusmodi responsione primum crimen effugere, in alterum mihi videntur crimen incidere. Si horum enim alterum est quod dicitur bonum id esse a quo utilitas ad eorum aliquid proficiscitur quae in vita sunt, generalis virtus (quae bonum sit) sub definitionem minime cadet. Non enim ab ea ad eorum aliquid utilitas proficiscitur quae in vita sunt, quoniam una e particularibus fiet, sed simpliciter utilitas. Verum quamquam ii alia multo plura in hanc sententiam sunt loquuti non minus supervacanee quam acute excogitata, cum de verbo potius quam de re ipsa disceptare consueverint, nobis tamen sit satis, si ostendimus qui definit bonum id esse quod prodest vel quod per se expetendum est vel quod felicitati est adiumento aut huiusmodi aliam assignationem affert, eum non quod bonum sit docere, sed quod bono accidit declarare. Qui vero quod bono accidit ostendit, haud is mihi bonum videtur ostendere. Continuo igitur et quod quidem conducit bonum et quod expetendum est, secundum quod bonum idcirco hoc appellatur nomine, quod labore sit dignum; πόνος enim unde bonum deductum puto laborem significat, et quod item bonum sit felicitatis effectivum, nemo est qui dissentiat. Quod si rursus quaeratur, quid tandem est hoc prodesse et quod per se sit expetendum felicitatemque efficiat, non modo non consentient, sed dissentient maxime ob eam scilicet rationem, quod de substantia non de accidente quaereretur. Nam alii bonum dicent virtutem, alii indolentiam, alii voluptatem, et eam quidem tum mentis bene compositae rectaeque rationis, tum dissoluti sensus petulantisque appetitus. Alii vero aliud quippiam vel simplex vel coniunctum. Quod si ex superioribus definitionibus patuisset quod esset bonum, haud quaquam dissentirent, perinde ut ignorata natura boni. Non igitur eae definitiones quod sit bonum, sed quod bono accidat omnes docent. Itaque non solum ob hanc causam reiiciendae sunt, verumetiam quia rem quandam impossibilem appetunt. Nam qui aliquid eorum quae sunt ignorat, hic neque illius accidens potest cognoscere, uti si quis ad eum qui equus quid sit ignorat dixerit, equus est animal hinnibile—id quod est equus minime docet. Qui enim equum ignorat, quid etiam sit hinnire (quod equo accidit) ignoret necesse est. Et qui audiat bovem esse animal mugibile nec teneat quid sit bos, huic bos haud monstratur. Neque enim mugire quod bovi accidit is comprehendat, qui bovem ignorarit. Identidem igitur cui quid est bonum obscurum sit, ei frustra et inutiliter dixero bonum id esse quod expetendum est aut quod utilitatem affert. Nam primum quae sit ipsius boni natura discendum est, deinde intelligendum quod et utilitatem affert et quod expentendum est et quod felicitatem efficit. Natura vero ignorata boni, huius quoque definitiones quod quaeritur docere non possunt. Et de his quidem satis ac super. Non enim longiores esse possumus.

Ex his autem quae brevi oratione perstrinximus, quod istiusmodi philosophi malum esse definiant, abunde patere censeo. Malum est enim ea ratione, quod bono contrarium aut detrimentum affert aut non aliud a detrimento. Et detrimentum quidem est quemadmodum vitium atque mala actio. Sed non aliud a detrimento, [end p. 8] quemadmodum malus homo et inimicus. Inter haec autem duo bonum et malum (quae et virtute duntaxat definiuntur et vitio) id esse Stoici volunt quod ἀδιάφορον ipsi nominant; nos recte indifferens appellamus. Id autem est quod neutrum habet. Nam quod indifferens fuerit, id neque in malis est nec in bonis numerandum. Quae enim in triplici illa bonorum partitione animi corporis et fortunae Peripatetici Academicique bona aut mala minima et perexigua esse volunt, corporis et fortunae quae dicuntur, ea Stoici neque in bonis neque in malis aut numerant aut ducunt; sed tum indifferentia, tum commoda vel incommoda, tum praelata aut reiecta vocant; haec enim sunt προηγμένα et ἀποπροηγμένα. Sed quoniam boni substantiam quaerimus potius quam accidens ullum, illud omnium primum intelligamus oportet, quo de bono nobis sermo habendus sit. Nam alia bona sunt quae in hominis actionem non cadunt; alia vero cadere dicimus. Quaedam enim eorum quae sunt, ut nullam habent cum motu communitatem, ita ne cum iis bonis quidem quae cadunt in actionem. Et haec indubitato natura sunt optima, ut pote divina. Quaedam vero habent cum motu communitatem, quare etiam cum actione, sed nequaquam nostra qui mortales sumus, verum cum eorum actione qui mortem pati non possunt. Et ii quidem a Graecis δαίμονες, ut ait Philo Iudaeus, a nostris dicuntur ἄγγελοι et si qui alii sunt caelestes spiritus praeter angelos. Quae autem in humanam cadunt actionem, ea rursus duplicia dicimus; alia enim eiusmodi sunt ut sui ipsorum agamus gratia; alia vero non propter haec ipsa in actionis participationem veniant, ut bonam valitudinem et divitias in eorum genere ponimus quae propter se agantur. At ea quae ad bonam valitudinem pecuniasque pertinent in iis numeramus, quae non propter se, sed horum gratia in actionem veniant. Quod cum ita sit, haud est obscurum felicitatem ex iis omnibus bonis, quae in hominum actionibus sita sunt, et perfectum esse et optimum et summum bonum. Ad quod tamen qui pervenire per media quae dicimus bona instituerit necesse est, ut cum illa sibi etiam proponat bona quae in nostram actionem non cadunt, sed immortalis cuiusdam sunt angelicaeque naturae, tum ad ea omnem mentis aciem intendat quae nulli motui sunt obstricta, sed incommutabilem habent natura stabilitatem suntque sempiterna ac plane optima et ita optima ut nihil nobis sine illis non modo optimum, sed ne minima quidem ex parte bonum esse possit. Hanc nostram bonorum distinctionem si quis recte considerare voluerit, inveniet nos nec a Platone et Aristotele dissentire et cum Christiana philosophia maxime convenire. Ut autem exploratum nobis sit quid bonum esse, definiamus quod quaerimus, ita partimur ut intelligamus illud bonum aliud esse, quod et per sese bonum est et secura sua tranquillitate ineffabilique praestantia gaudet; non modo motionis atque actionis expers, quae aliunde motum accipiens, non sua vi suaque natura et movetur et agit, sed ita omnino bonorum omnium quaeque sunt quaeque dicuntur, et fons est et causa, ut nihil quod eo careat bonum esse possit. Et alterum quoque bonum esse quod aeterniore moderatioreque quam nostra est actione utitur. Nam horum inferiorum nostrorumque bonorum, quis adeo amens sit qui nesciat longe [end p. 9] magis atque magis illud bonum praestare, cuius gratia caetera expetuntur, quam id quod non propter se, se propter aliud expetendum sit?

Sed quoniam paulo ante dixeramus aliud esse bonum perfectum, aliud medium, id quodammodo interesse volumus inter felicitatem et virtutem quod inter hominem et hominis partem, ut hominis bonum sit felicitas, bonum vero hominis partis sit virtus ipsa. Caeterum quo facilius teneamus et dilucidius hominis bonum in eo quo homo est, quid cuiusque rei sit bonum sciamus oportet. Nam ut rem declaremus exemplo, et homo alia quadam perfectione perfectus in eo dicitur secundum quod homo est, et alia leo secundum quod leo est. Atque bonum est cuiusque rei quando in substantia et potentia (quam enim Graeci δύναμιν, nos modo vim, modo potentiam, nonunquam etiam tum potestatem, tum virtutem dicimus)— quando, inquam, in substantia et potentia potest agere quaecunque sunt secundum naturam; id vero in animalibus quibusque intueri licet. Nam potentia (quae instrumentale bonum est) tempore antecedit operationem, at ratione sequitur. Si ad doctrinam enim referatur operatio, et prior est et nobis certior cognitu quam potentia quo ad perfectionem. Alicuius enim rei perfectionem vel potentia dicimus vel operatione; nam huius gratia potentia est. Id autem cuius gratia aliud est, prius hoc esse quis neget quod esse constat propter illud? Et cuiusque rei finis tempore quidem posterior est, at ratione prior. Nam ratione finem proponimus nobis; et ita ad finem quae sunt, quaerimus ac paramus. Omnia igitur primo ex potentia procedunt ad operandum. Verbi causa, ex semine generatur homo, qui tamen neque in quantitate instrumentorum nec in membris quae in ipsis sunt instrumentis continuo perfectus est. Sed ubi membra parvam quandam acceperint quantitatem, et quod humidius est desiccatum fuerit, et qui per membra spiritus defluit perseveranter constiterit, perficitur paulatim in corpore ad corporales operationes. Atque ita de puero vir efficitur. Idem quoque in animi potentiis tam notionis quam motionis, quae naturales sunt animi partes, esse animadvertitur. In ipsa enim hominis generatione ea boni semina sparsim hae virtutes accipiunt, in quibus inchoatio quaedam ad humanum bonum accommodata sita est. Huiusmodi vero semina experimento paulatim et tempore assuetudineque coeunt perficiunturque, et ita quae natura sunt optima possunt agere. Non enim philosophus ille mihi vel habendus vel nominandus videtur, qui ignoret nullam esse potentiam quae ex sese perfecta sit. Necesse est enim ut per habitum perfectionem capiat ad agendum, vel innatum vel comparatum. Nam ut ipsam animi substantiam agilitatemque mentis in aliud commodius tempus reiiciamus, tria in animo inesse, quae operationum actionumque nostrarum principia sint, philosophi omnes consentiunt: potentiam, affectionem, habitum; et potentiam quidem principium esse materiamque affectionis, ut iracundiam, verecundiam; affectionem vero insurgentem quandam potentiae motionem, ut iram, pudorem; at habitum esse partis irrationalis robur atque conatum assuetudine ingeneratum; et eum quidem si recte a ratione instituatur, virtutem fieri, sin autem prave vitium. Quae autem loquimur de activorum potentiis quae perfectione carent nunquam [end p. 10] intelligi nolumus.

Quibus sane rationibus sequi arbitror, ut bonum humanum sit, secundum hominis naturam perfecta posse optimaque perficere. Neque illud quoque ignoremus oportet id esse in partibus etiam accipiendum, quod in toto sit. Nam sicut animus est natura sua corpore perfectior, ita animi partes longe praestant corporis partibus. Sic oculi visio, sic pedis perfectio est ipse incessus. Itaque non ab re apud Aristotelem legimus: si oculus animal foret, eius animus visus foret. Et ita aliud est hominis bonum secundum quod homo est, aliud secundum hominis partes. Atque illud quidem perfectum, hoc tamquam medium et imperfectum; inde fit ut aliud sit cupiditatis bonum, aliud irae, aliud rationis, aliud intellectus et mentis ipsius aliud. Quare cum de hominis bono quaeritur pro ut homo est, ita est id bonum definiendum, pro ut est hominis bonum et pro ut est partium eius. Ut felicitas enim est hominis bonum, ita virtus nequaquam est hominis, sed partis hominis bonum.

Part Four

Sed posteaquam quid esset singularum rerum bonum ostendimus, quidque tum partis, tum etiam totius hominis, reliquum esse puto, ut idem faciamus de bono illo quod bonis omnibus sit commune ac per sese existat et bonorum omnium primum ita dicatur esse, ut ante id bonum aliud nullum reperiatur ac idem in bonis omnibus boni causam esse pateat. Videmus enim secundum Platonem id bonum existimari, quod a prima Idea boni secundum boni formam proficiscitur. Quod ut manifestius reddatur, non erit a nostro instituto alienum, si quam potero brevissime in medium referam et quid Plato (quem unum hac in re iure meritoque sequimur) et quid caeteri philosophi Ideam esse statuerint. Nam quoniam aliter atque aliter de Idea locuti sunt ex ea definitione, qua singulos videmus usos, omnem Ideae rationem intelligemus. Fuerunt enim nonnulli qui Ideam esse dixerunt substantiam incorpoream quae, quanquam ipsa per sese non existit, format tamen informis materias causaque est, ut oculis subiiciantur. At Zenonii Ideas esse voluerunt aliud nihil quam notiones cogitationesque nostras. Peripatetici vero Aristotele auctore ita de Ideis locuti sunt, ut eas a materia separatas esse noluerint. Qua quidem re factum est, ut alterius fundamenti ii ratione usi minus videantur cum Academicis Platoneque sentire. Plato enim Socratis auditor imitatorque Pythagorae Samii arbitratus est Ideam esse substantiam a materia separatam, quae per sese in ipsius Dei intelligentia imaginationeque existeret. Et hae sane de Ideis sententiae sunt, quas antiqui nobis philosophi scriptas reliquere. Nam neque ipsius rei Platonem neque nominis Ideae auctorem extitisse satis superque eo demonstratur libro, quem Pythagorae discipulus Timaeus Locrus multo ante Socratis atque Platonis tempora acutissime scripsit de mundi animo et natura, cuius nos alio loco multam mentionem fecimus—quamquam hunc Cicero non tam Pythagorae auditorem quam Platonis doctorem asserit extitisse. Caeterum ut perspicuum reddatur et quo pacto Socrates ac Plato, et quo pacto caeteri philosophi Ideam accepere, duplicem esse mentem intelligamus necesse est: alteram divinam et humanam alteram. Et humanae quidem mentis Ideam, ut Zenonii et ii omnes qui putaverunt Ideam esse substantiam incorpoream, quae licet ipsa per sese non existeret, informis tamen materias formaret, [end p. 11] et ut eae apparerent exterius esse causae. Voluerint hi sane huiusmodi Ideam aliud nihil esse quam nostram cogitationem atque notionem—eam scilicet quam Graeci ἔννοιαν appellant. Quam quidem sententiam mihi sequutus videtur tum M. Antonius orator, tum Iuvenalis his versibus.

> Sed vatem egregium cui non sit publica vena
> qui nihil expositum soleat deducere, nec qui
> communi feriat carmen triviale moneta.

Hunc qualem nequeo monstrare et sentio tantum
anxietate carens animus facit.

(*Satires* 7.53–57)

Quibus versibus acutissimus poeta Iuvenalis ostendit cogitatione invenire qualem eum esse poetam oporteat, cui ad perfectionem nihil desit, cum talem monstrare neminem queat. Nam M. Antonius in eo libro, quem unum legendum reliquit posteritati, scripsisse fertur se disertos vidisse multos, at eloquentem omnino neminem. Quam enim eloquentiae speciem animo videre videbatur, cum eius effigiem ad aurium iudicium referret, intelligebat frustra quemquam e vivis eloquentiae sibi laudem assumere. Et hi sane duo Zenonem sequuti, Iuvenalis poeta Antoniusque orator cogitaverunt speciem quandam et oratoris et poetae excellentem atque perfectam prorsus, ad cuius imitationem poeticae et eloquentiae dignitatem ac magnificentiam retulerunt. Quod eius rei opifices quoque sequutos arbitramur. Intueri licet vel hac tempestate Romae et equos duos marmoreos et item iuvenes iuxta duos factos e marmore utrosque mirae pulchritudinis magnitudinisque eximiae, quos Praxiteles et Phidias nobili opificio elaborarunt. Non enim aut in equis Cillarum atque Arium aut in iuvenibus fingendis Herculem aliquem et Iasona ante oculos habuerunt ad quorum similitudinem tam praeclara opera posteritati admiranda relinquerent, sed ingenii acrimonia et cogitatione sua pro exemplari sunt usi. Idem existimandum est de Scopa et Polycleto. Idem quoque de nobilissimis illis pectoribus Euphranore, Asclepiodoro, Plisteneto Phidiae fratre, et Apelle, cum pingerent alii deas, alii heroas, alii pugnas, alii victorias. Quanta vero in cogitatione fuisse Niciam putemus, qui servos persaepe inter pingendum interrogaret si lotus esset et pransus? Huiusmodi autem, de qua loqui coeperam, notio atque cogitatio, quamquam persese non existit, ut pote quae oriatur et occidat, materias tamen informis insignit forma effigieque figurat atque efficit, ut videantur exterius. Nec tamen inficier Ideam quoque aliquid esse quod oculis videri possit, ut si quod sibi exemplar artifex proposuerit ad quod respiciens operetur, quidquid tandem operatur. At in divina cognitione non illud esse dicimus ad quod respicit Deus, ut insimulat Aristoteles Platonem voluisse; sed id potius quo respicit. Quare longe omnino secus in Deo sit quam in artifice, ut et Plato sentit et veritas ipsa docet. Est enim Idea quod modo dicebatur substantia a materia separata, quae per sese in ipsius summi Dei intelligentia imaginationeque existit. Et Idea quidem ab εἶδος descendit, quod speciem formamque significat. Idem etiam cum saepe alias, tum in praesentia pro ratione accipitur. Ideam [end p. 12] enim esse intelligimus principalem quandam rationem rerum, quae divina continetur intelligentia, et eam quidem stabilem atque incommutabilem; quae cum formata non sit, sed aeterna eodemque modo habeat semper, quippe quae neque oriatur nec occidat unquam, tamen secundum eam convincit Plato formari omnia quae ortui sint interituique subiecta.

Quamobrem ut ea species, ea forma, ea ratio (hoc est Idea, quae principium nunquam habuit) finem est nunquam habitura—quicquam enim in Deo est, id sit aeternum oportet—ita caetera quae nascuntur ea interire natura omnia, fluere, labi, dissipari, neque diutius esse posse uno atque eodem statu demonstratur. Enimvero quis adeo fuerit aut impius aut fatuus qui negare audeat Deum immortalem pro absolutissima summaque ratione omnia creasse, omnia condidisse? Nec tamen se quisquam debet tantae stultitiae obnoxium facere, ut existimet animalia quae ratione carent—sicuti aquilam, taurum, delphinum caeteraque huiusmodi—eadem esse creata ratione qua hominem quem, cum fecisset Deus ad imaginem et similitudinem suam, ratione certe intelligentiaque munivit. Et ne prolixior in re perspicua iudicer, Idea semper habet eodem modo, sicut etiam substantia ipsa divina, quae ut una est, ita quoque unam esse Ideam est concedendum. Ut autem Ideas atque εἴδη (hoc est species) plurali nominemus numero, aliae atque aliae rerum rationes secundum Ideam productarum sunt in causa. Cui minus cognitum esse debet, exempli gratia, eadem Idea et pilae et vorticuli et alias plures productas esse rotunditates, qua et caelum et terram et universum mundum percipimus? Qui ergo negare queat, quin singula rerum genera propriis producta sint rationibus producanturque quotidie? Huiusmodi autem rationes, si in mente divina non insunt, ubi inesse possint, non intelligo. Errant profecto illi qui Platonis gloriae invidentes se ingratitudinis reos faciunt, cum eius summi philosophi sententiam depravantes Deum insimulent intueri solitum aut hominem quemquam universalem aut aliud quicquam huiusmodi extra se positum, quo tanquam hebes artifex quispiam ad illud exemplar aut hominem aut aliud quod velit producat.

Satis mihi videor ostendisse has Ideas, has species, has formas atque rationes in mente divina per sese existere ab omni materia separatas atque incorporeas, ubi (cum nil inesse possit, nisi incommutabile, nisi stabile, nisi aeternum planeque absolutum atque ex omni parte perfectum) consequens est, ut eas rationes et perfectas esse fateamur et stabiles et omnino aeternas. Quid igitur mirum videri cuiquam debet, si Plato—ut erat ingenio divino potius quam humano—affirmabat tantam vim inesse in iis Ideis, ut nemo sapiens esse possit qui eas minus animo percepisset intellexissetque? Nam eum virum contemplabatur Plato cui nihil deesset ad sapientiam; at sapientiam altius metiebatur quam indocti solent, cum eam referret ad ipsius veri perspicientiam atque cognitionem. Quare ita in rebus coelestibus id positum et constitutum iudicabat, ut nemini contingeret qui divinam substantiam ignoraret. Solum igitur eum sapientem et dicendum arbitrabatur et iudicandum qui Ideam veritatemque calleret. Et cogitanti quidem accuratius mihi videri solet idem Platoni de viro sapienti accidere potuisse, quod et M. Antonio de eloquenti oratore [end p. 13] et Iuvenali de egregio poeta modo memineramus. Nam cum insideret in eius mente absolutissima quaedam et excellentissima sapientiae species, quam etsi optandam potius homini quam sperandam esse censebat, qualem tamen esse oporteret cernebat animo: abunde visus est monere quid desiderandum foret in sapiente.

Non enim ignorabat philosophus acutissimus quicquid esset, de quo ratione et via quaereretur: id redigi oportere ad ultimam quandam formam atque speciem sui generis. Quapropter animo comprehensam perceptamque habebat eam sapientis formam cui nihil deesset ad intelligentiam Idearum, quamvis eam videret in nemine. Non igitur minus sapienter quam sancte Paulus Apostolus cum de hac intelligentia loquitur qua divinam substantiam contemplamur, ad tertium se usque coelum idcirco raptum affirmat, quod interiore mentis sincerioreque acumine divinae illi atque ineffabili intelligentiae cohaeret. Non enim corporeis oculis fas est cuiquam Deum aspicere, sed cunctis terrenis sordibus defecatae atque purgatae ac nitidae mentis luminibus eum licet intueri. Id sibi contingere qui velit (quis enim velle non debet), huic est omni cura, omni opera, omni studio, omni denique industria atque diligentia annitendum ut sese vendicet sibi cogatque, ut prostratis ac domitis cunctis animi perturbationibus mens sua omnis libera ac sui compos cum mente divina, unde creationem atque splendorem vimque omnem accepit et ratiocinandi et intelligendi, conveniat ab eaque nusquam discedat. Nam ita qui fecerit, certo sperare potest ut intelligibili illi circunfusus atque illustratus summae sapientiae lumine cernat vim omnem naturamque Ideae. Atque huius quidem Ideae non Plato, id quod ostendi antea, sed Pythagoras inventor omnium primus fuit, quotquot vel in Ionica vel in Italica philosophia claruissent; sequutus is quidem magis doctores, quibus cum apud Chaldeos congressus est, Zoroastrem philosophorum omnium primum, quem Plutarchus tradit antecessisse bellum Troianum annis quinque milibus. Sed haec de Idea—et quid, quotuplexque sit, et quo pacto secundum Platonem accipienda—nos dixisse sufficiat. Nunc eo redeamus unde digressi sumus.

Part Five

Principio id statuo esse bonum maximum ac summum bonorum omnium cui ultima sui perfectio contigerit. Nam si bonum huiusmodi ab ultimo suae bonitatis fine rationem capit et huiusmodi finis ubi accesserit, nihilo res eget, cum nihil ad id, cuius gratia sigillatim sunt caetera, appetit sibi adiici. Non enim ultimum foret, si qua fieri posset adiectio. Id igitur est summum bonum, quod ultimum sit secundum naturam finem consequutum. Si id praeterea bonum non est cui vitium sit admixtum et cuicunque minus contigeret, huic vitii quippiam inhaeret: quantum autem habet vitii, tanta caret bonitate. Quonam igitur pacto id summum dici convenit bonum, quod ultimam sui ipsius perfectionem consequutum nondum sit? Ad haec nihil cuique rei addi potest praeter huius ipsius rei bonum. At bonitatis quatuor sunt causae: quae efficat, quae materiam praestet, quae formam tradat, quae finem imponat. Quare cum sola ipsius finis causa sit quae ad postremum accedens rem perficiat, quis ambigat solam finalem causam esse illam ad quam accedere nihil queat? Si enim id perfectum est quod nulla re eget, [end p. 14] eo fit ut id nihilo egeat cui, quod ex finis causa fit, nihil addi possit. Quo fit ut id esse oporteat summum bonum, ad quod ultimi finis accesserit perfectio. Rursus si illud statuunt esse summum bonum quod ab omnibus appetitur, hoc ultimum sit oportet. Nam nisi ultimum esset, aliud quiddam appeteretur amplius. Numquam enim quiescit appetitus, quam diu eorum aliquid desit quae addi possunt. Aut igitur nullum est summum bonum aut est hoc necessario, cui ultima contigerit perfectio.

Insuper ens, verum, et bonum secundum subiecta quidem convertuntur, at ratione differunt. Id enim ens dici putant quod (quamcumque demus) differentiam entitatis eam sit quodammodo assequutum. Verum autem id, quod per entis formam veritatem ratitudinemque acquisierit, quod ipsum tamen in virtute et operatione nonnunquam est imperfectum. Sed post ens et verum, id quoque addatur oportet quod virtute et operatione perfectum est. Ultima suae perfectionis forma ac ita continuo fit summum; qua ipsa re fit ut non absurde summum bonum esse videatur quod ultimi finis accessione perfectum est.

Id ut dilucidius pateat, confirmemus exemplo. Eandem habet proportionem bonum et verum ad ens quam homo qui generare iam potest et puer is, cui nondum generandi facultas adsit, habet ad semen ex quo generatur. Ut hominis enim semen primo est in potentia tantum, ut ex eo generetur homo, neque sub forma seminis adhuc est quicquam quod operatione hominis formam habeat; eodem modo entis ratio propter suam transcendentiam communitatemque nihil dicit definite. Dicit autem communem quandam rationem duntaxat, quae ad definita perfectaque entia potentiam habet. Atqui sicut homo simul ac e semine generatus et ortus est mollibus adhuc membris et instrumentis corporeis nondum sua quantitate perfectis, est tamen verus homo. Habet enim quaeque hominis principia interiora, ut animum intelligentiae rationisque capacem, habet corporis secundum naturam instrumenta, neque tamen perfectus est, quippe qui non potest omnia operari quae humanae sunt perfectionis, ut generare similem sui; nam ita quodque perfectum dicimus, ubi tale quicquam possit efficere cuiusmodi ipsum est. Eodem etiam modo id verum est quod iam sit consequutum entis ratitudinem et perfectionem substantialem atque specificam. Quod ipsum tamen quoniam nondum ad virtutem perfectamque ac suam operationem pervenerit, necesse est his bonum addatur. Id enim secundum propriam rationem ita habet, ut homo perfecta aetate, si aut cum eiusmodi puero aut cum semine conferatur. Quare cum omnibus in rebus appareat bonum esse ab ultima perfectione (tum enim quodque bonum est, cum ea optime potest absolvere quae secundum suam sunt naturam), cui sit ambigendum id esse summum bonum quod ita ab ultimo suae naturae fine perfectum sit, ut omnia pro absolutissima suae naturae bonitate perficere possit? Caeterum sunt versuti nonnulli callidique Sophistae qui argumententur bonum ab ultima perfectione differre nihil, inquientes, quicquid est in eo quod sit, bonum esse; cum sint certe permulta quae licet ultimam suae naturae perfectionem consequuta non fuerint, ea tamen esse bona nemo inficietur. Et Aurelius Augustinus summa eruditione ac sapientia vir non ab re ait, "In quantum sumus, boni sumus."

Ad ea facilis [end p. 15] est solutio. Haud enim negaverim unum quodque bonum esse in eo quod est. Nam quod simplicem habet entitatem, id in ipsa inchoatione bonum habet. Entitas enim simplex in potentia est et in primis entis principiis. Quod si entitatis perfectionem veritatem per formae consequitur, habet bonitatem ad essentiam in specie definitam. Sin autem entitatem per speciem habet in speciei forma et iis quae ad formam perfectam consequenter accedunt, tum bonitatem perfectam habet. Quaelibet enim res in forma et in iis, quae deinceps ad formam ipsam accedunt, perfecta et terminata est. Nam quaecunque natura perfecta sunt, modo virtus impedita non sit, secundum proprium et generalem habitum operantur. Quae vero consequuntur ad formam, qualibet in specie sunt et virtus tum naturalis, tum propria et operatio non impedita. Qua quidem re fit, quidquid est in eo quod sit, bonum esse: tantum vero bonitatis habet quantum essentiae. Itaque nihil est ex omni parte bonum, nisi quod ad ultimam sui perfectionem pervenerit.

Et quoniam quid esset per se bonum quaerebatur ante omnia, intelligamus oportet hoc per se, ut vel Aristoteli videtur, dupliciter dici. Est enim per se quod non est per accidens; et est per se quod non est per aliud. Non igitur parum interest, utrum quod dicitur per se bonum, sitne per substantiam et non per accidens, an sit per se ipsum bonum et non per aliud. Enimvero inter omnia bona unum quoddam bonum dandum est, a quo ipso bona omnia tanquam a causa proficiscantur. Nam si secus fiat, neque omnis multitudo ad unitatem redigatur, nec etiam omnis multiplicitas ad univocationem, nec id rursus quod est per accidens ad id redigi queat quod per se sit. Quae quidem omnia philosophiae praeceptis contraria sunt. Esto igitur quoddam per se bonum, quod et substantialiter et non per aliud bonum sit. Praeterea cui dubium esse debet in omnibus participantibus eam esse naturam, ut quiddam necessario sit, quod per sese id habeat, quod participans per accidens habet. Sicuti in visus disgregatione est ipsum videre, quod homo albus per accidens habet, neque id sane per accidens haberet, nisi quam participat albedo ipsa haberet per sese. Cum bonus igitur vir habeat boni operationem, necesse est ut unum quiddam proponatur quod eandem per sese operationem habeat; hoc autem illud est quod dicimus per se bonum. Rursus quicquid est bonum, aliud illud, per quod hoc dicimus bonum esse: aut per se bonum est aut per aliud. Quod si per aliud est bonum, infinita erit progressio.

Sin per se dixerimus esse bonum, tum aliquid est per se bonum, cuius participatione quicquid participat bonum redditur. Unum igitur per se bonum est, per quod omnia bona efficiuntur. Et haec est illa Idea boni; cuius Plato, quod ante ostendimus, non tam inventor fuit quam adamator et confirmator. Quam ego sententiam non solum amplector ac sequor, sed ita facile ac libenter sequor atque veneror, ac si ex aliquo divino veritatis oraculo emanarit. Nec me movent Aristotelis captiones, qui aegre et inique ferens sibi praelatum ad docendum in Academia a caeteris condiscipulis Xenocratem condiscipulum item suum non est veritus, quo illis molestiorem se praestaret, quum alias plaerasque gravissimas optimasque Platonis sententias invertere atque depravare, tum praecipue hanc de Idea, qua nec [end p. 16] acutius quicquam nec sanctius nec melius vel dici potuit vel cogitari. Quid enim affertur contra? Si ponatur (inquit) unum quoddam bonum, quod omnia quae bona sunt participative contineat, hoc sit unum necesse est aut individuo aut specie; sed individuo cum non sit unum, ne specie quidem unum esse potest. Non enim bonorum omnium bonitates specie unum sunt. Nam equi bonitas, ut est bene currere, bene sessorem vehere, et bene hostem expectare eumque terrere, quae omnia Alexandri regis Bucephalum praestare solitum legimus; non eadem quae bovis est bonitas, quae leonis, quae canis, quae cuiusquam huiusmodi animalis quo ad speciem. At ne genere quidem una est. Quotquot enim genera eorum quae sunt argumentatur, tot singillatim reperiuntur bonitates diversae. Quare si neque individuo nec specie nec genere est unum bonum, videtur nullum esse primum bonum. Verum ad istiusmodi Aristotelis Peripateticorumque omnium argumenta perfacilis est vel cum ipso Aristotele responsio. Nam primum ad omnia sequentia relationem habet. Et quo plus aliquid est, eo est relationibus multiplicius. Itaque dupliciter accipi primum potest proportione et natura. Quod autem aut generis aut speciei aut individui natura nihil sit per se bonum a quo bona omnia dicantur, assentiendum puto; sed esse proportione aliquid per se bonum, quod neque per accidens bonum sit nec per aliud (ad quod quidem ipsum si respiciatur, per quandam similitudinem habitudinum bona omnia bona sunt), quis tandem sit qui dissentiat?

Part Six

Et eo bona haec vel meliora dici possunt vel optima, quo sunt illius boni Idealis similiora. Eiusmodi vero bonum est primum bonum, quod substan-

tia perfecta omnia perficit secundum proprias et (ut ita dixerim) connatu-
rales attributiones et id quidem ad propriam operationem, modo impedita
non sit. Ad illius enim proportionem bonum quodlibet tum melius, tum
optimum licet appellari. Nam hoc per se bonum esse dicimus, quod ita per
se bonum sit, nec per accidens est nec per aliud. Quod non sit per aliud
bonum, id intelligi volo: vel tanquam per causam quae eiusmodi bonitatem
efficiat vel tanquam per suae bonitatis formam. Hoc enim utroque modo
primum bonum esse per se bonum et dicimus et volumus, quoniam nec
causam habet quae suam bonitatem efficiat nec etiam speciem ante se quam
participet; cum illud tamen sit, tum omnis boni efficiens causa, tum ad eius
bonitatis rationem (quae et in ipso est et ipsum est) omne bonum proportione sit bonum. Quod ipsum certe primum bonum secundum Ideam ita
primum esse censemus, ut ante id nihil aliud boni sit. Et cum aeque in aliis
omnibus bonum esse constet, tum bonitatis causa in bonis omnibus. Nam
primum quidquid esse in multis dixeris (quod non aequivoce in illis sit), id
in uno primo quodam ponas oportet quod sit aliis omnibus bonitatis
causa. Non enim aequivoce est in multis quod secundum proportionem ad
unum sit in omnibus. Nam ad unum aequivocatio proportionem non habet. Proportio enim ad unum est habitudinum similitudo ad unum, quod
diversa in specie et in una proportione participatur, quemadmodum est
navis ad gubernatorem et regni ad regem gubernatio. Nam neque eisdem
praeceptis navis gubernationem gubernator solet quibus regni gubernationem rex persequitur, ni forsitan eadem Typhis, quae Iason praeciperet
[end p. 17] et quae Aeneas, Palinurus. Nec idem specie est gubernatio navis et regni, cum similitudo tamen habitudinum una sit in utraque. Cum
huiusmodi ergo similitudinem in omnibus unam esse videamus, ut unum
sit primum bonum, ad cuius proportionem et similitudinem caetera bona
dicuntur bona, intelligere mihi videor cum Platone esse unum primum
bonum, quod substantialiter bonum est et efficiens causa cuiusque bonitatis. Cuius quidem boni forma secundum proportionem servatur in omnibus.

Ad haec si omnis multiplicitas, ut arithmetici docent, ad unum redigitur,
quod primum est totius multiplicationis principium, cumque magnam
adeo bonorum multiplicitatem cognosci liceat, ut fere ad infinitatem tendat
(id quod in omni et arte et scientia est vitandum), huiusmodi scilicet infi-
nitas contrahatur oportet. Qui autem contrahi quicquam possit, nisi ab
uno proficiscatur redigaturque ad unum? Quod est enim a pluribus, non
contrahitur, sed diffunditur potius. Quamobrem primum quoddam
bonum detur est opus, a quo similitudo ipsa substantialis boni in bona
omnia diffundatur; insuper, omnis resolutio in uno est posita, sive poster-
ius resolvatur in prius, sive compositum in simplex, sive effectus in causam
efficientem. Sed cum multa bona esse videamus quae neque priora sunt nec
simplicia, sed composita, nec etiam causae efficentes, sed effecta, ea neces-

sario sunt in unum resolvenda secundum omne resolutionis genus. Esto igitur resolutio in uno primo, quod indubitato bonorum omnium primum est; at postremum quod est in quovis ordine vel primum est vel a primo. Quo fit ut in eorum ordine quae bona sunt aut quodque bonum primum esse aut a primo concedendum sit. Et quum eorum quodque bonum primum esse aut a primo concedendum sit, et cum eorum quodque primum esse non possit, necessario est a primo. Igitur unum quoddam primum statuendum est quod sit aliorum omnium causa. Et id certe secundum Ideam esse si quis ignorat, is rationem omnem ignorare bonitatis mihi videtur.

Nec me sane fugit quod a Peripateticis dici solet argutius. Primum, quod est consequentium causa, ita esse in consequentibus, ut de eorundem esse ratione putandum sit. Nihil autem unum est quod de ratione bonorum omnium quae numero, specie ac genere differunt putari oporteat. Nam eorum quae genere differunt nullo modo una ratio esse potest. Quod si ita est (sicuti certe est), fit ut aliquid bonum esse non possit quod aliorum omnium causa sit et ratio. Caeterum ad ea Stoici, qui nihilo sunt quam Peripatetici obtusiores, ut solent omnia et acute et diligenter, primum dupliciter partiuntur: tum principii, tum generis ratione. Sed quod esse dixerint secundum generis rationem, id quidem et de consequentium omnium ratione et eorum esse causam dicant necesse est; nam inde suae essentiae principium capiunt. At primum, quod est secundum principii rationem, nulla fit necessitate ut de eius vel essentia vel substantia quicquam sit. Ut punctum enim est lineae principium, neque tamen quicquam est nec de essentia nec de substantia lineae quo substantia scilicet est subiectum, sed eiusmodi principium esse constat, in quo ponatur lineae inchoatio, quamvis huiusmodi inchoatio neque ad essentiam lineae nec ad subiectum terminata sit. Eodem etiam modo in alia quaque natura usu venit, ut principium [end p. 18] id sit quod est de illius generis essentia; hoc autem vocamus genus. Ac rursus principium sit quod simplex est formae inchoatio et ea quidem neque ad essentiam nec ad subiectum terminata; hoc vero principium dicimus, non genus. Quare hoc modo qui posuerit unum principium esse bonorum haud errarit. Et id quidem genus neque in genus nec in speciem cum bonorum aliquo queat incidere.

Atque sub hoc huiusmodi bono caetera bona omnia continentur communitate principii, non generis. Quod ipsum unum ac primum et simplex et separatum et sua natura bonum, immensum, sempiternum, nulli mutabilitati, nulli motui, nulli actioni subiectum qui sibi proponere sequique voluerit, non solum bono medio quod in triplici illa virtute intelligentiae et rationis morumque situm est, sed perfecto etiam bono, quod bonorum omnium est summum, se bonum planeque felicem atque beatum intelliget. Neque dubitabit quid sibi sit potius expetendum, honestumne an utile vel nunquid magis voluptatis ratio id efficiat. Nam praestantissimo illo ineffabilique secundum Ideam bono tum haec omnia absolutissime continentur, tum quaecunque alia vel dici possint vel excogitari. Id autem nusquam est, si in mente divina minus esse concesserimus. Est id (inquam) in divina mente divinaque sapientia et in ea quidem sapientia quae non multiplicitate, sed unitate dicenda sapientia est, cum ipsa tamen infinitos bonorum thesauros complectatur.

Aliud autem bonum esse quod alio bono dicatur bonum; aliud vero quod seipso bonum sit, puto esse iam perspicuum omnibus. Et hoc profecto bonum solum est simplex, incommutabile, proptereaque et aeternum et immortale et ita summum ac perfectum, ut eo superius nihil esse possit, nihil perfectius. Caetera enim bona omnia sunt a Deo, sed de Deo certe non sunt. Nam si de Deo ea esse dixerimus, necessario fateamur idem esse quod Deum. Non enim quod a Deo factum est idem esse quod Deum, par est dicere. Itaque si solus Deus et imcommutabile et simplex est bonum, quaecunque ab illo bona sunt facta, quoniam ex nihilo facta esse constat (hoc est ex eo quod ante non esset—sive chaos id, seu sit alio appellandum nomine), mutabilia certe sunt et non simplicia. Facta enim sunt, non genita. Nam quod de simplici bono genitum foret, id etiam foret simplex idemque omnino, quod illud est de quo sit genitum. Quare si totius quidem hominis bonum felicitatem esse volumus—hanc vero aliud nihil esse quam Deum, at felicitatem assequi posse neminem, nisi quod per medium bonum fieri dicimus virtutis, ad eam iter et eundi et perveniendi ante didicerit; virtus certe omnis tenenda est atque exercenda quam optime. [end of Book 1]

Note on the Edition

Filelfo's *De morali disciplina* was printed only twice: in a volume edited by Francesco Robortello that includes two other titles, *Francisci Philelphi De morali disciplina libri quinque. Averrois paraphrasis in libros de Republica Platonis. Francisci Robortelli in libros politicos Aristotelis disputatio* (Venice, 1552); and in a reprinting of this edition in *De republica recte administranda atque aliis ad moralem disciplinam pertinentibus rebus* (Venice, 1578). No manuscripts of the work are known. My text in Appendix E is an adaptation of the Venice 1552 text; the page numbers in brackets indicate the pagination of the 1552 edition of the text. I have altered the original only by using the consonant *v* for *u*, expanding the abbreviations, and modernizing the punctuation. Otherwise Robortello's orthography has been retained throughout. In addition, I have made the following emendations: p. 17 *Robort.* Cleanthe] Cleanthis; p. 24 *Robort.* antecidit] antecedit; p. 29 *Robort.* essent] esse; p. 33 *Robort.* negari] negare; p. 40 *Robort.* perfectionis veritatem per formam] perfectionem veritatem per formae; p. 40 *Robort.* oportet] oportet hoc.

CHRONOLOGY

1374   Death of Petrarch.

1398   Birth of Filelfo in Tolentino, 25 July.

1401   Birth of Francesco Sforza in San Miniato, 23 July.

1414   Filelfo begins study of law at Padua; pupil of Gasparino Barzizza.

1416   Begins career as professor of rhetoric at Padua.

1417   Professor of rhetoric and moral philosophy at Vincenza.

1420   Secretary of Venetian delegation to Emperor John Paleologus in Constantinople; studies with John Chrysoloras and Bessarion's teacher Chrysococces.

1423–1424   Acts as Emperor John Paleologus's envoy to Murad I, Poland, and Hungary.

1425   Marriage to Teodora Chrysoloras, daughter of teacher John Chrysoloras and kinswoman of Emperor.

1426   Birth of first son Gian Mario in Constantinople, 24 July.

1427   Departs from Constantinople on 27 August for Venice at request of patron Leonardo Giustiniani; waits out plague without work in Venice until February 1428.

1428   Begins teaching at Bologna as professor of rhetoric and moral philosophy in February; civil war breaks out in August.

1429   Begins teaching at Studio in Florence as professor of Greek; his sponsors were Cosimo de' Medici, Ambrogio Traversari, Palla Strozzi, Niccolò Niccoli, and Leonardo Bruni.

1429   Florence's four years of war with Lucca begin.

1431   Order for Filelfo's arrest, deportation from Florence, and incarceration in Rome issued 10 March; rescinded 12 March. Governors of Studio remove him from teaching post in October; restore him to post in December. Future patron King Charles VII of France sanctions execution of Joan of Arc in Rouen, in May.

1432   Filelfo translates Lysias's funeral oration and *Murder of Eratosthenes*, Xenophon's *Agesilaus* and the *Constitution of Sparta*, Aristotle's *Rhetoric*, and Plutarch's lives of Lycurgus and Numa.

1433   Birth of son Xenophon in Florence, on 25 March. Alleged attempt on Filelfo's life on 18 May by Medici hireling. Albizzi party seizes power in Florence in October; Cosimo de' Medici expelled from city.

1434   Cosimo de' Medici restored to power in October. Rinaldo degli Albizzi, Palla Strozzi, and other members of Albizzi party including Filelfo expelled from Florence.

1435   Begins teaching in Siena. Second assassination attempt in Siena by alleged Medici hireling.

1436   Begins *Satyrae*.

1437   Begins dialogue *Commentationes de exilio*.

1438   Francesco Sforza besieges Tolentino.

1439   Death of Ambrogio Traversari. Filelfo begins teaching at Bologna in February; departs for Milan in June; Duke Filippo Maria Visconti names him professor of rhetoric at Pavia. Council of Florence meets: Gemistos Pletho delivers paper on Plato and Aristotle.

1441   Death of first wife, Teodora (3 May), who bore him two daughters and two sons. Marriage of Francesco Sforza to Bianca Maria Visconti, daughter of Duke F. M. Visconti, in Cremona.

ca. 1442   Filelfo marries Milanese noblewoman Orsina Osnaga (exact year uncertain).

1443   Completes dialogue *Convivia Mediolanensia*.

1444   Death of Leonardo Bruni, chancellor of Florence.

1446   Death of Leonardo Giustiniani.

1447   Death of Duke F. M. Visconti; founding of Ambrosian Republic in Milan on 14 August. Public burning of tax books; dismantling of Visconti residences. Defection of Milan's client cities; civil war and wars with Venice and France begin. Francesco Sforza leads Milanese army to gates of Piacenza on 1 October; sack of city begins on 16 November. Niccolò V becomes pope.

1448   Sforza leads Milanese to victory against Venice at Cassalmaggiore on 17 July and at Caravaggio on 15 September. Sforza defects from Milan to Venice on 18 October; one year later he defects from Venice.

1449   Capitani of Ambrosian Republic confiscate lands of gentry and execute hundreds of nobility in January and May; Filelfo's pupil Giorgio Lampugnano's severed head displayed at January bloodbath. Aristocratic faction of Republic returns to power after 1 July elections.

1450   Fall of Ambrosian Republic on 20 February. Investiture of Francesco Sforza as duke of Milan on 26 March. Death (exact year uncertain) of Filelfo's second wife Orsina Osnaga, who bore him one son and three daughters.

1451   Filelfo begins *Epistolae*. Sforza appoints him professor of rhetoric at Pavia in April. Flight from plague-ridden Milan with family in September; return to Milan in December.

1453   Led by Murad II, Turks take Constantinople. Hundred Years' War ends in France: King Charles VII and Henry VI of England withdraw troops. Filelfo begins *Sforziad*. King Alfonso crowns him poet-laureate in Naples. Filelfo's marriage to third wife Laura Maggiolini (exact year uncertain).

1454   Peace of Lodi signed by Milan, Venice, and Florence on 9 April, ending decades of war. Filelfo translates Plutarch's *Apophthegmata* and two more of his *Lives*.

1455   Calixtus III becomes pope.

1456   Filelfo completes *Odae* (= *Carmina varia*). Trip to France at invitation of King Charles VII forbidden by Sforza, probably in June.

1458   Pius II becomes pope. Death of King Alfonso of Naples in July; Alfonso's son Ferrante comes to throne; Neapolitan barons defect to Jean d'Anjou, son of Angevin Duke René. Pius and Sforza aid Ferrante. Filelfo tours Mantua, Ferrara, Bologna, Cesena, Perugia, and Rome.

1459   Filelfo attends Pope Pius's Congress of Mantua as Sforza's orator. Begins Greek opus *Psychagogia*. Sicilian friend Giovanni Aurispa dies.

1462   Death of Palla Strozzi. *Consolatio* for Venetian Iacopo Antonio Marcello's son Valerio, for which he receives silver basin.

1464   Paul II becomes pope. Cosimo de' Medici dies.

1465   Sforza imprisons Filelfo and son Gian Mario for slandering deceased Pope Pius II. Filelfo begins *De Iocis et seriis*.

1466   Death of Francesco Sforza on 8 March. Filelfo delivers eulogy in Duomo.

1467   Investiture of Sforza's son Galeazzo Maria as Duke.

1470   Death of Filelfo's son Xenophon.

1471   Sixtus IV becomes pope. Deaths of Antonio Beccadelli (Panormita), Duke Borso d'Este of Ferrara, and King Ferrante of Naples.

1472   Death of Cardinal Bessarion.

1473   Filelfo begins *De morali disciplina*.

1474   Appointed professor of moral philosophy in Rome by Sixtus IV; promised first vacant scriptorship in Curia; departs for Rome in November.

1475   Returns to Milan in June. Deaths of infant son Giannantonio Celestino, and seven- and eight-year-old sons Cesare Eufrasio and Federico Francesco in July. Departs in October, stopping at Modena, Bologna, Florence and Siena before arriving in Rome in January.

1476   Assassination of the fifth duke of Milan, Galeazzo Maria Sforza, on 26 December at mass at S. Stefano. Death of Filelfo's third wife, Laura Maggiolini, on 6 June. Return to Milan on 8 June from Rome. Seven of Filelfo's twenty-four children survive: two sons, Gian Mario and another not named; five daughters: Tarsia and Prudenza, married; Augusta and Pandora, in convents; and five-year-old Giulia, still at home.

1477   His correspondence ends.

1478   Deaths of Lodovico Gonzaga and Theodore Gaza.

1479   Investiture of Lodovico (il Moro) Sforza as sixth duke of Milan.

1480   Death of Filelfo's son Gian Mario on 1 June.

1481   Filelfo leaves Milan to occupy Chair of Greek at Florentine Studio in July. Dies in Florence on 31 July.

1484   Death of Sixtus IV.

1492   Death of Lorenzo de' Medici, grandson of Cosimo.

BIBLIOGRAPHY

The bibliography is organized under three headings: Manuscripts, Published Primary Sources, and Secondary Works. It includes all works cited, with the exception of unpublished materials from archival collections and classical texts, which are from the Loeb Classical Library editions unless otherwise noted. Full information on the archival materials cited is contained in the footnotes. Under Manuscripts, only those codices referred to in this study are listed.

MANUSCRIPTS

Berlin, Sammlung Hamilton
  MS 511: Filelfo's odes
Cesena, Biblioteca Malatestiana
  MS 23, 5: Filelfo's odes
Chicago, Newberry Library
  MS 108.8: Filelfo's odes
Florence, Biblioteca Medicea Laurenziana
  Laur. 28.45: Theophrastus, Filelfo's marginalia
  Laur. 32.16: selections from the *Greek Anthology*, owned by Filelfo
  Laur. 33.33: Filelfo's *Sforziad*
  Laur. 33.34: Filelfo's odes
  Laur. 53.6: Filelfo's *Convivia mediolanensia*
  Laur. 73.1: Democritus, Filelfo's marginalia
  Laur. 76.69: an anonymous translation of Filelfo's *De morali disciplina*
  Laur. 80.20: Plutarch's *Moralia*, Filelfo's hand
  Laur. 80.22: Plutarch's *De morali virtute*, Filelfo's hand
  Laur. 80.24: Pletho's *De differentiis*, Filelfo's marginalia
  Laur. 81.13: Aristotle's *Rhetoric, Magna moralia*, Filelfo's marginalia
  Laur. 85.19: Sextus Empiricus, Filelfo's marginalia
  Laur. 87.26: Aristotle's *Metaphysics*, Filelfo's marginalia
Florence, Biblioteca Nazionale
  Conv. Soppr. G 2.866: Filelfo's odes
Milan, Biblioteca Trivulziana
  Triv. 731 (C 72): Filelfo's *Sforziad*
  Triv. 873: Filelfo's Greek and Latin epistles
Milan, Biblioteca Ambrosiana
  Ambr. F 55 sup.: Filelfo's orations
  Ambr. G 93 inf.: Filelfo's *De iocis et seriis*
  Ambr. H 97 sup.: Filelfo's *Sforziad*
  Ambr. M 4 sup.: Filelfo's translations of Plato
  Ambr. R 12 sup.: Filelfo's *Sforziad*

Paris, Bibliotheque Nationale
  MS lat. 8126: Filelfo's *Sforziad*
  MS lat. 8127: Filelfo's odes
Rome, Biblioteca Casanatense
  MS 415, C III.9: Filelfo's *Sforziad*
Rome, Biblioteca Vallicelliana
  MS C 87: Filelfo's translations of Plato
  MS 143: Filelfo's *Psychagogia*
Vatican City, Biblioteca Apostolica Vaticana (BAV)
  Vat. Reg. lat. 1981: Filelfo's satires
  Vat. Urb. lat. 701: Filelfo's odes
  Vat. Urb. lat. 1022: Filelfo's life of Federigo d'Urbino
  Vat. gr. 1689: Aristotle's *Nicomachean Ethics*, Filelfo's marginalia
  Vat. lat. 1790: Filelfo's funeral elegy for J. A. Marcello
  Vat. lat. 2921: Filelfo's *Sforziad*
  Vat. lat. 11518: Filelfo's odes
  Vat. Pal. lat. 1599: Plato's dialogues and letters, Filelfo's marginalia
Venice, Biblioteca Nazionale Marciana
  Marc. gr. Z. 262: Sextus Empiricus, Filelfo's marginalia
  Marc. lat. XIV. 262: Filelfo's *Sforziad*, excerpts

PUBLISHED PRIMARY SOURCES

Ammanati-Piccolomini, Cardinal Iacopo. *Epistolae et commentarii*. Milan, 1608.
von Arnim, Ioannes, ed. *Stoicorum Veterum Fragmenta*. 3 vols. Leipzig, 1905–1924.
Basin, Thomas. *Histoire de Charles VII*, ed. C. Samuran. 2 vols. Paris, 1933 and 1944.
Beccadelli, Antonio. *De dictis et factis Alphonsi regis*. Basel, 1538.
Benadduci, Giovanni, ed. "Prose e poesie volgari di Francesco Filelfo." In G. Benadduci, ed., *Atti*, xli–262.
da Bisticci, Vespasiano. *Renaissance Princes, Popes, and Prelates. The Vespasiano Memoirs: Lives of Illustrious Men of the XVth Century*, trans. W. George and E. Waters, with an intro. by Myron Gilmore. New York, 1963.
Bruni, Leonardo. *Epistolarum libri VIII*, ed. L. Mehus. Florence, 1741.
Castellani, Giorgio. "Documenti veneziani inediti relativi a Francesco e Mario Filelfo," in *ASI* 17 (1896): 364–70.
de Commynes, Philippe. *Memoires*, ed. J. Calmette. Paris, 1924–1925.
Decembrio, Pier Candido. *Vita di Filippo Maria Visconti*. In F. Fossati, ed., *RIS²*, 34 vols., 20.1.141. Bologna, 1900–1958.
———. *Vita Francisci Sfortiae quarti Mediolanensium ducis*. In G. Carducci, V. Fiorino, and P. Fedele, eds., *RIS²*, 20.1. Bologna, 1919.
Ferorelli, N. *Inventari e regesti del regio archivio di stato di Milano. I registri dell'ufficio degli statuti*. Milan, 1926. Reprint 1971.
Ficino, Marsilio. *Opera omnia*. Basel, 1576.
Filelfo, Francesco. *Commentationes Florentinae de exilio*. In Eugenio Garin, ed., *Prosatori latini del Quattrocento*, pp. 494–517. Milan, 1952.

————. *De morali disciplina libri quinque. Averrois Paraphrasis in libros de Republica Platonis. Francisci Robortelli in libros politicos Aristotelis disputatio*, ed. Francesco Robortello. Venice, 1552. Reprinted in *De republica recte administranda atque aliis ad moralem disciplinam pertinentibus rebus*. Venice, 1578.

————. *Epistolarum familiarium libri XXXVII*. Venice, 1502.

————. *Epistolarum familiarium libri XVI*. Venice 1473.

————. *Odae*. Brescia, 1497.

————. *Odae, Satyrae*. In Francesco Arnaldi, Lucia Gualdo Rosa, and Liliana Monti Sabia, eds. *Poeti latini del quattrocento*. Milan, 1964.

————. "Vita di Federico d'Urbino," ed. G. Zannoni. In G. Benadduci, ed., *Atti*, 265–393.

Frassica, Pietro, ed. *"Chroniche de la citta di Anchona" di Gian Mario Filelfo*. Ph.D. dissertation, Boston College, 1977.

Giustiniani, Leonardo. *Orationes et epistolae*. With Bernardo Giustiniani. N.p., n.d.

Kohl, Benjamin G. and Ronald Witt, eds. *The Earthly Republic: Italian Humanists on Government and Society*. Philadelphia, 1978.

Machiavelli, Niccolò. *History of Florence and of the Affairs of Italy*. Intro. by F. Gilbert. Reprint. New York, 1960.

Legrand, Emile, ed. *Cent-dix lettres grecques de Francois Philelphe*, Paris, 1892.

Mullner, Karl. *Reden und Briefe italienischer Humanisten: Ein Beitrag zur Geschichte der Padagogik des humanismus*. Vienna, 1899.

Migne, Jacques Paul, ed. *Patrologia Graeca*. 161 vols. Paris, n.d.

Perosa, Alessandro and John Sparrow, eds. *Renaissance Latin Verse*. London, 1979.

Petrarca, Francesco. *Africa*, trans. T. G. Bergin and A. S. Wilson. New Haven, 1977.

————. *Letters on Familiar Matters. Rerum familiarium libri IX–XVI*, ed. and trans. Aldo Bernardo. Baltimore, 1982.

————. *Rerum familiarium libri I–VIII*, ed. and trans. Aldo Bernardo. Albany, 1975.

————. *Secretum*. In G. Martelloti and E. Carrara, eds., *Prose*, in *La letteratura italiana, storia e testi* 7 (Milan and Naples, n.d.): 122–24.

Pico della Mirandola, Giovanni. *De hominis dignitate. Heptaplus, De ente et uno, e scritti vari*, ed. E. Garin. Florence, 1942. English trans., *Pico della Mirandola. On the Dignity of Man, On Being and the One, Heptaplus*, by C. G. Wallis, P.J.W. Miller, and D. Carmichael. Indianapolis, 1965.

Platina. *Historici libri de vita Christi ac omnium pontificum*. In L. A. Muratori, ed., *RIS¹*, 3.1.

Poliziano, Angelo. *Opera omnia*, ed. I. Maier. 3 vols. Turin, 1971.

————. *Opera*. Basil, 1553.

di Ripalta, Antonio. *Annales Placentini*. In A. Muratori, ed., *RIS¹*, 25 vols., 20. Milan, 1723–1751.

Sabbadini, Remigio, ed. *Carteggio di Giovanni Aurispa*. Rome, 1931.

————. *Epistolario di Guarino Veronese*. Venice, 1915–1919.

Salutati, Coluccio. *Epistolario*, ed. F. Novato. 4 vols. Rome, 1891–1911.

Simonetta, Giovanni. *Rerum gestarum Francisci Sfortiae commentarii*. In G. Soranzo, ed., *RIS²*, 34 vols., 21.2. Bologna, 1900–1935.

da Soldo, Cristoforo. *La Cronaca*. In G. Brizzolara, ed., *RIS²*, 34 vols., 21.3. Bologna, 1900–1935.

Trebizond, George. *Comparatio*. Venice, 1523.

Traversari, Ambrogio. *Aliorumque ad ipsum, et ad alios de eodem Ambrosio latinae epistolae*, ed. L. Mehus. 2 vols. Florence, 1759.

Valla, Lorenzo. *De voluptate*. Basel, 1519.

Walser, Ernst. *Poggio Florentinus. Leben und Werke*. Leipzig, 1914.

SECONDARY WORKS

Adam, Rudolf Georg. "Francesco Filelfo at the Court of Milan: A Contribution to the Study of Humanism in Northern Italy (1439–1481)." Ph.D. dissertation, Oxford University, 1974.

Ady, C. M. *A History of Milan under the Sforza*. London, 1907.

Agostini, Giovanni degli. *Notizie istorico-critiche intorno la vita e opere degli scrittori vinziniani*. 2 vols. Venice, 1752–1754.

Albanese, Gabriella. "Le raccolte poetiche latine di Francesco Filelfo." In *Filelfo nel V Cent.*, pp. 389–458.

Albini, Guiliana. *Guerra, fame, peste. crisi di mortalita e sistema sanitario nella Lombardia tardo medioevale*. Bologna, 1982.

Allen, D. C. *Mysteriously Meant: The Rediscovery of Pagan Symbolism and Allegorical Interpretation in the Renaissance*. Baltimore, 1970.

d'Amico, John. *Renaissance Humanism in Papal Rome: Humanists and Churchmen on the Eve of the Reformation*. Baltimore, 1983.

Bailey, F. G., ed. *Gifts and Poison: the Politics of Reputation*. Oxford, 1971.

Bandini, A. M., ed. *Catalogus codicum manuscriptorum Bibliothecae Mediceae Laurentianae*. 2 vols. Florence, 1764–1770.

Barbour, Ruth. *Greek Literary Hands* A.D. *400–1600*. Oxford, 1981.

Bayley, C. C. *War and Society in Renaissance Florence: the "De militia" of Leonardo Bruni*. Toronto, 1961.

Becker, Marvin. "Florentine Politics and the Diffusion of Heresy in the Trecento: A Socio-economic Inquiry." in *Speculum* 34 (1959).

Belle, Lawrence William. *A Renaissance Patrician: Palla di Nofri Strozzi, 1372–1462*. Ph.D. dissertation, University of Rochester, 1972.

Benadduci, Giovanni. "Contributo alla bibliografia di Francesco Filelfo." In G. Benadduci, ed., *Atti*, pp. 459–535.

———. *Della Signoria di Francesco Sforza nella Marca*. Tolentino, 1892.

———, ed. "Prose e Poesie volgari di Fr. Filelfo." In G. Benadduci, ed., *Atti*, pp. xli–262.

Bentley, Jerry H. *Politics and Culture in Renaissance Naples*. Princeton, 1987.

Bergin, T. G. *Petrarch*. New York, 1970.

Bernardinello, Silvio. *Autografi greci e Greco-Latini in Occidente*. Padua, 1979.

Bernardo, Aldo. *Artistic Procedures Followed by Petrarch in Making the Collection of the "Familiares"*. Ph.D. dissertation, Harvard University, 1949. Reprinted in part in *Speculum* 33 (1958).

Bianca, Concetta. " 'Auctoritas' e 'veritas': il Filelfo e le dispute tra Platonici e Aristotelici." In *Filelfo nel V Cent.*, pp. 207–47.

Bianchi-Giovini, A. *Le Reppublica di Milano dopo la morte di F. M. Visconti*. Milano, 1848.

Billanovich, Giuseppe. "Petrarch letterato, 1. Lo scrittoio del Petrarca." In *Storia e letteratura* 16 (1947): 3–55.

Black, Robert. *Benedetto Accolti and the Florentine Renaissance*. Cambridge, 1985.

Bognetti, G. P. "Per la storia dello stato visconteo." In *ASL* 54 (1927): 237–357.

Borsa, M. "Pier Candido Decembri e l'umanesimo." In *ASL* 20 (1893): 5–75 and 358–441.

Bottari, Guglielmo. "La 'Sphortias.' " In *Filelfo nel V Cent.*, pp. 459–93.

Brown, Judith C. *In the Shadow of Florence: Provincial Society in Renaissance Pescia*. Oxford, 1982.

Brucker, Gene A. "The Ciompi Revolution." In N. Rubinstein, ed., *Florentine Studies: Politics and Society in Renaissance Florence*. London, 1968.

———. "The Structure of Patrician Society in Renaissance Florence." In *Colloquium* 1 (1964): 8–11.

Brunt, P. A. " 'Amicitia' in the Late Roman Republic." In R. Seager, ed., *The Crisis of the Roman Republic: Studies in Political and Social History*, pp. 197–218. Cambridge, 1969.

Burckhardt, Jacob. *The Civilization of the Renaissance in Italy*. 2 vols. Intro. by B. Nelson and C. Trinkhaus. Reprint. New York, 1958.

Burke, Peter. *Culture and Society in Reniassance Italy*. New York, 1972.

Butti, F. *I fallori della Reppublica ambrosiana*. Vercelli, 1891.

The Cambridge History of Later Medieval Philosophy from the Rediscovery of Aristotle to the Disintegration of Scholasticism, ed. N. Kretzmann, A. Kenny, and J. Pinborg. Cambridge, 1982.

Cagnola, G. P. *Cronache milanesi*. 3 vols. Milan, 1519; reprint Florence, 1842.

Calamari, G. *Il Confidente di Pio*. 2 vols. Rome, 1932.

Calderini, Aristide. "I codici milanesi delle opere di Francesco Filelfo." in *ASL* 42 (1915): 335–411.

———. "Ricerche intorno alla biblioteca e cultura greca di Francesco Filelfo." In *Studi italiani di Filologia Classica* 20 (1913): 204–424.

Cammelli, Giuseppe. "Andronico Callisto." In *Renascita* 5 (1942): 104–21.

———. *I dotti bizantini e le origini dell' umanesimo* 3 vols. Florence, 1941–1943.

Chiappa Mauri, L. "I mulini ad acqua." In *Nuova rivista storica* (1984): 231–61.

Chittolini, G. *La formazione dello stato regionale e le istituzione del contado. secoli XIV e XV*. Turin, 1979.

Cipolla, C. *Storia delle signorie italiane dal 1313 al 1530*. Milan, 1881.

Cognasso, Francesco. *Storia di Milano*. 6.387–448. 16 vols. Milan, 1955.

Cohn, Samuel K. *The Laboring Classes in Renaissance Florence*. New York, 1980.

Colombo, A. "Della vera natura ed importanza dell'aurea repubblica ambrosiana." In *Raccolta di scritti storici in onore del prof. Giulio Romano*. Pavia, 1907.

———. "L'ingresso di Francesco Sforza." in *ASL* 3 (1905): 33–101 and 297–344.

Corio, B. *Storia di Milano*, ed. E. de Magri. 3 vols. Milan, 1503; 2d ed. 1855–1857.

Cosenza, Mario Emilio. *Biographical and Bibliographical Dictionary of the Italian*

Humanists and of the World of Classical Scholarship in Italy, 1300–1800. 3 vols. New York, 1962.

Cusin, F. "L'impero e la successione degli Sforza ai Visconti." In *ASL*, n.s., 1 (1936): 4–116.

De Man, Paul. "Autobiography as De-facement." In *Modern Language Notes* 94 (1979): 919–30.

Dizionario biografico degli italiani. Rome, 1960–.

Doig, J. C. *Aquinas on Metaphysics: A Historico-Doctrinal Study of the "Commentary" on the "Metaphysics"*. The Hague, 1972.

Dunston, A. J. "Pope Paul II and the Humanists." In *Journal of Religious History* 7 (1973): 287–306.

Eakin, Paul John. *Fictions in Autobiography: Studies in the Art of Self-Invention*. Princeton, 1985.

Eisenstadt, S. N. and L. Roniger. *Patrons, Clients, and Friends: Interpersonal Relations and the Structure of Trust in Society*. Cambridge, 1984.

————. "Patron-Client Relations as a Model of Structuring Social Exchange." In *Comparative Studies in Society and History* 22 (1980): 43–48.

Fabbri, Renata. "Le consolationes de obitu Valerii Marcelli ed il Filelfo." In *Miscellanea di studi in onore de V. Branca*, 3.1.227–50. Florence, 1983.

Fabroni, Angelo. *Magni Cosmi Medicei vita*. 2 vols. Pisa, 1789.

Fenigstein, Berthold. *Leonardo Giustiniani (1383?–1446): Venetianischer Staatsmann, Humanist und Vulgardichter*. Halle, 1909.

Feo Corso, L. "Il Filelfo in Siena." *Bollettino di storia patria* 47 (1940): 181–209 and 292–316.

Field, Arthur M. *The Beginning of the Philosophical Renaissance in Florence, 1454–1469*. Ph.D. dissertation, University of Michigan, 1980.

Fiorentino, F. *Il Risorgimento filosofico nel Quattrocento*. Naples, 1885.

Foucault, Michel. *Discipline and Punish*, trans. A. Sheridan. New York, 1979.

————. *The History of Sexuality*, trans. R. Hurley. New York, 1980.

————. "Preface." In G. Deleuze and F. Guattari, *Anti-Oedipus*, trans. R. Hurley, M. Seem, and H. R. Lane, xii–xiii. Minneapolis, 1988.

Frangioni, L. "La politica economica del dominio de Milano nei secoli XV–XVI." In *Nuova rivista storica* (1986): 253–68.

Frizzi, A. *Memorie per la storia di Ferrara*. Ferrara, 1847–1850.

Gabotto, Ferdinando. "Ricerche intorno allo storiografo quattrocentista Lodrisio Crivelli." In *ASI*, 7 (1891): 267–98.

Garin, Eugenio. "La cultura milanese nella prima meta del XV secolo." In *Storia di Milano*, 16 vols., 6.545–608. Milan, 1953–1966.

————. "L'eta Sforzesca dal 1450 al 1500." In *Storia di Milano*, 16 vols., 7.539–97. Milan, 1953–1966.

————. *Filosofi italiani del Quattrocento*. Florence, 1942.

————. *Italian Humanism, Philosophy and Civic Life in the Renaissance*, trans. P. Munz. New York, 1947.

————. *Portraits from the Quattrocento*, trans. E. and V. Velen. New York, 1972.

————, ed. *Prosatori latini del Quattrocento*. Milan, 1952.

Gass, W. *Gennadius und Pletho. Aristotelismus und Platonismus in der griechischen Kirche*. 2 vols. Breslau, 1844.

Geanakoplos, Deno J. *The Byzantine East and the Latin West: Two Worlds of Christendom in the Middle Ages and Renaissance*. Oxford, 1966.

―――. "Theodore Gaza, a Byzantine Scholar of the Palaeologan 'Renaissance' in the Italian Renaissance." In *Medievalia et Humanistica* 12 (1984): 61–81.

―――. *Greek Scholars in Venice: Studies in the Dissemination of Greek Learning from Byzantium to the West*. Cambridge, Mass., 1962.

Gellner, Ernest and J. Waterbury. *Patrons and Clients in Mediterranean Societies*. London, 1977.

Gelzer, M. *The Roman Nobility*. Oxford, 1969.

Genovese, Eugene. *Roll, Jordan, Roll: The World the Slaves Made*. New York, 1947; reprint 1976.

Ghinzoni, A. "Giovanni Ossona e Giovanni Appiani nella rochetta di Monza." In *ASL* 5 (1878): 205–9.

Giri, G. "Il codice autografo della Sforziade di Francesco Filelfo." In G. Benadduci, ed., *Atti*, pp. 420–57.

Giulini, Giorgio. *Memorie spettanti alla storia, al governo ed alla descrizione della citta e campagna di Milano ne' secoli bassi*. Milan, 1857; reprint Milan, 1975.

Giustiniani, Vito R.. "Il Filelfo, L'interpretation allegorica di Virgilio e la tripartizione platonica dell'anima." In *Umanesimo e Rinascimento. Studi offerti a P. O. Kristeller*, pp. 33–44. Florence, 1980.

Grafton, Anthony and Lisa Jardine. *From Humanism to the Humanities: Education and the Liberal Arts in Fifteenth- and Sixteenth-Century Europe*. London, 1986.

Grant, W. L. *Neo-Latin Literature and the Pastoral*. Chapel Hill, 1965.

Gualdo, Germano. "Francesco Filelfo e la curia pontificia: una carriera mancata." In *Archivio della societa romana di storia patria* 102 (1979): 189–236.

Gualdo Rosa, Lucia. "Il Filelfo e i Turchi." In *Annali della Facolta di lettere e filosofia. Universita di Napoli* 11 (1964–1968): 109–65.

Gundersheimer, Werner L. "Patronage in the Renaissance: an Exploratory Approach." In G. F. Lytle and S. Orgel, eds., *Patronage in the Renaissance*, pp. 3–23. Princeton, 1981.

Hale, J. R. "International Relations in the West: Diplomacy and War." In *The New Cambridge Modern History. The Renaissance: 1493–1520*. 14 vols. 1.259–91. Cambridge, 1957.

Holmes, George. *The Florentine Enlightenment: 1400–1450*. New York, 1969.

Hutton, J. *The Greek Anthology in Italy to the Year 1800. Cornell Studies in English XXIII*. New York, 1935.

Ianziti, Gary. "The Production of History in Milan." In F. W. Kent and P. Simons, eds., *Patronage, Art and Society in Renaissance Italy*, pp. 299–311. Oxford, 1987.

Johnson, W. Ralph. *Darkness Visible: A Study of Vergil's "Aeneid."* Berkeley, 1976.

Jordan, E. "Florence et la succession lombarde (1447–1450)." In *Ecole Francaise de Rome. Melanges d'archeologie et d'histoire* 9 (1889): 93–119.

Jugie, M. "Georges Scholarios, professeur de philosophie." In *Studi bizantini e neoellenici* 10 (1936): 482–94.

Kallendorf, Craig. *Early Humanistic Moral Criticism of Vergil's "Aeneid" in Italy and Great Britain*. Ph.D. dissertation, University of North Carolina, 1982.

———. "Cristofori Landino's *Aeneid* and the Humanist Critical Tradition." In *Renaissance Quarterly* 36 (1983): 519–46.

Kent, Dale V. *The Rise of the Medici: Faction in Florence. 1426–1434*. Oxford, 1978.

Kent, Francis William. *Household and Lineage in Renaissance Florence: the Family Life of the Capponi, Ginori, and Rucellai*. Princeton, 1977.

Kent, Dale V. and Francis William Kent. "Two Vignettes of Florentine Society in the Fifteenth Century." In *Rinascimento* 23 (1983): 237–60.

Kent, Francis William and Patricia Simons, eds. *Patronage, Art and Society in Renaissance Italy*. Oxford, 1987.

Kettering, Sharon. *Patrons, Brokers, and Clients in Seventeenth-Century France*. Oxford, 1986.

King, Margaret. *Venetian Humanism in an Age of Patrician Dominance*. Princeton, 1986.

Kraye, Jill. "Francesco Filelfo's Lost Letter *De ideis*." In *Journal of the Warburg and Courtauld Institutes* 42 (1979): 236–49.

———. "Francesco Filelfo on Emotions, Virtues and Vices: A Re-examinatiion of His Sources." In *Bibliotheque d'Humanisme et Renaissance* 43 (1981): 129–40.

Kristeller, Paul Oskar. *Eight Philosophers of the Italian Renaissance*. Stanford, 1964.

———. *Iter Italicum: A Finding List of Uncatalogued or Incompletely Catalogued Humanistic Manuscripts of the Renaissance in Italian or Other Libraries*. 3 vols. London and Leiden, 1963, 1967, and 1983.

———. "Marsilio Ficino as a Man of Letters and the Glosses Attributed to Him in the Caetani Codex of Dante." In *Renaissance Quarterly* 36 (1983).

———. *The Philosophy of Marsilio Ficino*. New York, 1943.

———. "The Platonic Academy of Florence." In *Renaissance News* 14 (1961): 147–59.

———. *Renaissance Thought: the Classic, Scholastic and Humanist Strains*. New York, 1955.

Labalme, Patricia H. *Bernardo Giustiniani: A Venetian of the Quattrocento*. Rome, 1969.

Labowsky, Lotte. *Bessarion's Library and the Biblioteca Marciana: Six Early Inventories*. Rome, 1979.

Laurenza, Vincenzo. "Il Panormita a Napoli." In *Atti della Accademia Pontaniana* 42 (1912): 1–92.

Leclerq, Jean. "Le genre epistolaire au moyen age." In *Revue du moyen age latin* 2 (1946): 63–70.

Lee, Egmont. *Sixtus IV and Men of Letters*. Rome, 1978.

Luzio, Alessandro and Rodolfo Renier. "I Filelfo e l'umanesimo alle corte dei Gonzaga." In *Giornale storico della letteratura italiana* 16 (1890): 119–217.

Mallett, Michael. *The Borgias: the Rise and Fall of a Renaissance Dynasty*. New York, 1969.

———. *Mercenaries and Their Masters: Warfare in Renaissance Italy*. London, 1974.

———. "Venice and its Condottieri, 1404–54," In J. R. Hale, ed., *Renaissance Venice*, pp. 121–45. London, 1973.

Maltese, Enrico V. "Osservazioni critiche sul testo dell'epistolario greco di Francesco Filelfo." In *Res Publica Litterarum. Studies in the Classical Tradition* 11 (1988): 207–13.

———. "Appunti sull'inedita *Psychagogia* di Francesco Filelfo." In *Res Publica Litterarum. Studies in the Classical Tradition* 12 (1989).

Martines, Lauro. *Lawyers and Statecraft in Renaissance Florence*. Princeton, 1968.

———. *Power and Imagination: City-States in Renaissance Italy*. New York, 1979.

———. *The Social World of the Florentine Humanists: 1390–1460*. Princeton, 1963.

Masai, F. *Plethon et le platonisme de Mistra*. Paris, 1956.

Mercati, G. *Per la cronologia della vita e degli scritti di Niccolò Perotti arcivescovo di Siponto*. Rome, 1925.

Messer, August. "Franciscus Philelphus 'de morali disciplina.' " In *Archiv fur Geschichte der Philosophie* 9.2 (1896): 337–43.

Mohler, Ludwig. *Kardinal Bessarion als Theologe, Humanist und Staatsmann*. 3 vols. Paderborn, 1942. Reprint 1967.

Molho, Anthony. "Cosimo de' Medici: *Pater Patriae* or *Padrino*?" In *Stanford Italian Review* 1 (1979): 5–33.

Monfasani, John. *George of Trebizond. A Biography and a Study of His Rhetoric and Logic*. Leiden, 1976.

———. "Il Perotti e la controversia tra platonici e aristotelici." In *Res Publica Litterarum* 4 (1981): 195–231.

Murrin, Michael. *The Allegorical Epic: Essays in Its Rise and Decline*. Chicago, 1969.

Natale, Michele. *Antonio Beccadelli detto il Panormita*. Caltanisetta, 1902.

Novara, A. "Un poema latino del quattrocento: *La Sforziade* di Francesco Filelfo." In *Rivista ligure di scienze, lettere, ad arti* 28 (1906): 3–27.

Oliver, Revilo P. "The Satires of Filelfo." In *Italica* 26 (1945): 23–46.

Olney, James. *Metaphors of Self: The Meaning of Autobiography*. Princeton, 1972.

O'Malley, John W. *Praise and Blame in Renaissance Rome: Rhetoric, Doctrine, and Reform in the Sacred Orators of the Papal Court, c. 1450–1521*. Durham, 1979.

Otis, Brooks. *Virgil: A Study in Civilized Poetry*. Oxford, 1963.

Parry, Adam. "The Two Voices of Virgil's *Aeneid*." In *Arion* 2 (1963): 66–80.

von Pastor, Ludwig. *History of the Popes*, 4th ed., trans. F. I. Antrobus. 40 vols. London, 1923.

Pieri, P. "Le milizie sforzesche (1450–1534)." In *Storia di Milano*, 16 vols., 8.821–63. Milan, 1955.

Pellegrini, A. "Tre anni di guerra le reppubliche di Firenze e di Lucca (1430–1433)." In *Studi e documenti di storia e diritto* 19 (1898), pt. 1.

Peluso, F. *Storia della Repubblica milanese*. Milan, 1871.

Peristiany, J. G., ed. *Honour and Shame: the Values of Mediterranean Society*. Chicago, 1966.

Pitt-Rivers, J. *The People of the Sierra*. London, 1954.

Pontieri, Ernesto. *Per la storia del regno di Ferrante I d'Aragona re di Napoli*. 2d ed. Naples, 1969.

———. "La Puglia nel quadro della monarchia degli aragonesi di Napoli." In *Atti del congresso internazionale di studi sull'eta aragonese*, pp. 19–52. Bari, 1972.

Putnam, Michael C. J. *The Poetry of the "Aeneid"*. Cambridge, Mass., 1965.

Quinn, Kenneth. *Virgil's "Aeneid": A Critical Description*. London, 1968.

Resta, Gianvito. *L'epistolario del Panormita*. Messina, 1954.

———. "Francesco Filelfo tra Bisanzio e Roma." In *Filelfo nel V cent.*, pp. 1–60.

Resti, E. "Documenti per storia della Reppublica Ambrosiana." In *ASL* 5 (1954–1955): 192–266.

Robin, Diana. "Humanist Politics or Vergilian Poetics?" *Rinascimento* 25 (1985): 101–25.

———. "Reassessment of the Character of Francesco Filelfo." In *Renaissance Quarterly* 36 (1983): 202–24.

———. "Unknown Greek Poems of Francesco Filelfo." In *Renaissance Quarterly* 37 (1984): 173–206.

Romanin, S. *Storia documenta di Venezia*. 10 vols. Venice, 1853–1861. Reprint 1912–1925.

de Roover, Raymond. "Labour Conditions in Florence Around 1400: Theory, Policy and Reality." In N. Rubinstein, ed., *Florentine Studies: Politics and Society in Renaissance Florence*. London, 1968.

de' Rosmini, Carlo. *Della istoria di Milano*. 4 vols. Milan, 1820–1821.

———. *Vita di Francesco Filelfo da Tolentino*. 3 vols. Milan, 1808.

Rossi, Luigi. "Un delitto di Sigismondo Malatesta." In *Rivista di Scienze Storiche* (1910): 362–82.

Rubieri, E. *Francesco Primo Sforza*. 2 vols. Florence, 1879.

Rubinstein, Nicolai. "Italian Reactions to Terraferma Expansion in the Fifteenth Century." In J. R. Hale, ed., *Renaissance Venice*. London, 1973.

Ryder, Alan. "Antonio Beccadelli: A Humanist in Government." In C. H. Clough, ed. *Cultural Aspects of the Italian Renaissance: Essays in Honour of Paul Oskar Kristeller*, pp. 123–40. Manchester, 1976.

———. *The Kingdom of Naples under Alfonso the Magnanimous: the Making of a Modern State*. Oxford, 1976.

Sabbadini, Remigio. *Le Scoperte dei codici latini e grechi ne' secoli xiv e xv*. Florence, 1905.

———. *Vita di Guarino Veronese*. Turin, 1964.

Sacchi, F. "Cosimo de' Medici e Firenze nell' acquisto di Milano allo Sforza." In *Rivista di scienze atoriche* 2 (1905): 340–46.

Saller, Richard P. *Personal Patronage Under the Early Empire*. Cambridge, 1982.

Sandys, John Edwin. *A History of Classical Scholarship*. 3 vols. Cambridge, 1903–1908; reprint New York, 1964.

Santorno, Caterina. *I Codici medioevali della Biblioteca Trivulziana. Catalogo*. Milan, 1965.

Santoro, Mario. "Il Panormita 'aragonese.'" In *Esperienze letterarie* 9 (1984): 3–24.

Schmitt, Charles B. *A Critical Survey and Bibliography of Studies on Renaissance Aristotelianism, 1958–1969*. Padua, 1971.

Seigel, Jerrold E. "The Teaching of Argyropulos and the Rhetoric of the First Humanists." In T. K. Rabb and J. E. Seigel, eds., *Action and Conviction in Early Modern Europe*, pp. 237–60. Princeton, 1969.

Sickel, T. "Beitrage und Berichtungen zur Geschichte der Erwerbung Mailands durch Fr. Sforza." In *Archiv fur Kunde Osterreichischen Geschichtsquellen*. Vienna, 1855.

Solis de los Santos, José. *Satiras de Filelfo*. Sevilla, 1989.

Spinelli, Marina. "Ricerche per una nuova storia della reppublica Ambrosiana." In *Nuova rivista storica* pte. 1 (1986): 231–52 and pte. 2 (1987): 27–48.

Stinger, Charles L. *Humanism and the Church Fathers: Ambrosio Traversari (1386–1439) and Christian Antiquity in the Italian Renaissance*. Albany, 1977.

———. *The Renaissance in Rome*. Bloomington, 1985.

Stone, Lawrence. *The Causes of the English Revolution: 1529–1642*. Reprint. London, 1986.

Stornaiolo, C. *Codices Urbinates Latini*, vol. 2. Rome, 1912.

Symonds, John Addington. *The Revival of Learning: The Renaissance in Italy*. 3 vols. London, 1877; 2d ed. New York, 1888.

Thompson, E. P. "Eighteenth-century English Society: Class Struggle without Class?" In *Social History* 3 (1978): 133–66.

Tiraboschi, G. *Storia della lettera italiana*. 4 vols. Milan, 1772.

Tocco, F. "Ancora del 'De morali disciplina' di F. Filelfo." In *Archiv fur Geschichte der Philosophie* 9 (1896): 486–91.

della Torre, Arnaldo. *Storia dell' Accademia platonica di Firenze*. Florence, 1902.

Trinkhaus, Charles. *In Our Image and Likeness: Humanity and Divinity in Italian Humanist Thought*. 2 vols. Chicago, 1970.

Turner, C. J. "The Career of George-Gennadius Scholarius." In *Byzantion* 39 (1969): 420–55.

Vale, M.G.A. *Charles VII*. London, 1974.

Verri, P. *Storia di Milano*. Milan, 1873.

Voigt, Georg. *Die Wiederbelebung des classischen Althertums*. 2 vols. Berlin, 1888–1897.

Wallis, R. T. *Neoplatonism*. London, 1972.

Weiss, Roberto. *Un Umanista veneziano: Papa Paolo II*. Florence, 1958.

Weissman, Ronald. *Ritual Brotherhood in Renaissance Florence*. New York, 1982.

———. "Taking Patronage Seriously: Mediterranean Values and Renaissance Society," in F. W. Kent and P. Simons, eds., *Patronage, Art and Society in Renaissance Italy*, pp. 25–45. Oxford, 1987.

Wilkins, Ernest H. *Life of Petrarch*. Chicago, 1961.

Witt, Ronald. "Medieval 'Ars Dictaminis' and the Beginnings of Humanism: A New Construction of the Problem." In *Renaissance Quarterly* 35 (1982): 1–35.

Weinberg, J. *A Short History of Medieval Philosophy*. Princeton, 1964.

Woodward, W. H. *Vittorino da Feltre and Other Humanist Educators*. Cambridge, 1897; reprint Cambridge, 1905.

Zabughin, V. *Giulini Pomponio Leto*. 2 vols. Rome, 1909.

Zeno, Apostolo. *Dissertazioni vossiane*. 2 vols. Venice, 1752.

Zippel, Giuseppe. *Il Filelfo a Firenze (1429–34)*. Rome, 1899. Reprinted in *Storia e cultura del Rinascimento italiano*, ed. G. Zippel, pp. 215–53. Padua, 1979.

INDEX

Acciaiuoli, Donato, 131–37, 143, 216, 217
Adam, R. G., 18
Aeneid. See Vergil's *Aeneid*
Alamanni, Andrea, 216
Alamanni, Ludovico, Cardinal, 31, 32
Albanese, Gabriella, 99
Alberti, Leon Battista, 4
Albizzi party, 28, 43, 44
Alexander the Great, 46
Alfonso I, king of Naples (Alfonso V of Aragon), 42, 57, 59, 60, 79, 85, 116, 215, 218, 222; literary patronage of, 82–83
Alipranda, Antonia, 106–9, 210–11
Ambrosian republic of Milan (1447–1450), 7–8; citizens' overthrow of, 88, 97–98, 100–101; civil war during, 87, 91; curtailment of speech under, 90, 90n, 95, 95n, 96; defection of client cities under, 86; executions of gentry and property confiscation under, 87, 91; famine under, 8, 87, 87n, 88, 89–90, 92–93, 94; food riots under, 97–98; historiography of and Simonetta, 85n, 86n, 91n, 94n; odes concerning, 84, 197–209; public burning of tax registers under, 86; public demolition of Visconti palaces under, 86; regulation of grain sale by, 87n, 97n; as revolution, 90, 90n, 95n; rise and fall of, 85–88
Ammannati, Cardinal Jacopo, 139n, 140
anger (*ira*), humanist opinion on, 46, 75, 75n
antirepublican fervor. *See* Filelfo, Francesco
antiwar sentiment, among humanists, 58n, 75, 89, 91–93
Apostolis, Michael, 148
Appiano, Giovanni da, 96–97
Aquinas, Thomas, 147, 152, 165
Arcimboldi, Niccolò, 29, 91, 119
Argyropoulos, John, 83, 120, 133, 216, 217, 218, 219, 225
Aristophanes, *Plutus*, 128
Aristotle, 9, 48, 49; on being, 160–65; and Christian doctrine, 48; dominant place in humanist curriculum of, 157; on good(s), 158; *Magna Moralia*, 51; matter-bound

soul of, 155; *Metaphysics*, 147, 158, 160–63, 164, 165; *Nicomachean Ethics*, 50–51, 133, 134, 157, 165; and Plato's theory of Ideas, 141. *See also* being, hierarchy of; good(s)
Arrivabene, Giovanni Pietro, 140
Augustine, St., *Quaestiones*, 156, 158; on being and good, 160, 165; on Ideas, 159
Augustus, emperor of Rome, 53, 75, 75n. *See also* Sforza in *Sforziad*
Aurispa, Giovanni, 30–34, 61, 216, 218; books of, 31, 33. *See also* books; humanists
Averroes, 51
Avicenna, 51, 155–56

Barbaro, Francesco, 23, 29, 36
Barbo, Cardinal Marco, 140
Barzizza, Gasparino, 4, 22
Basin, Thomas, 83
Basinio, Basini, 85
Beccadelli, Antonio (Panormita), 4, 11, 29, 59, 79, 224
Becker, Marvin, 96
being (*ens*), 52; *differentia* in, 161, 162; evolution of, from *entitas* to *perfectio entis*, 162; the good as a function of, 154, 160–64; hierarchy of, 160–64; potentiality and act (*potentia, operatio*) in, 162. *See also* Aristotle; Ideas; Plato
Bernardus of Sylvester, 52
Bessarion, Cardinal, 9, 118, 120–21, 138, 140, 144, 147–49, 218; *In calumniatorem Platonis*, 148–49, 151–52; commentaries on Plato by, 152; death of, 140; Filelfo's Greek poems for, 215, 217, 220–21; synthesis of Neoplatonism and Scholasticism in, 152; translation of Aristotle's *Metaphysics* by, 152. *See also* Plato-Aristotle controversy
Bianca, Concetta, 146
Birago, Lampugnino, 100
Bizzocchi, Tommaso de, 18–21
Boccaccio, 155
Bologna: university of, 52; Filelfo in, 27–28, 31–32